"Who doesn't want to protect ki
But our current sex offender laws are turning
into pariahs when they don't—can't—understand our social cues and
taboos. The result is harsh punishments that don't make children any
safer, even as they decimate lives that were already heartbreakingly
difficult. Kudos to Dubin and Horowitz for bringing light to one of
the saddest and most infuriating issues facing our country."

—*Lenore Skenazy, founder of the book, blog
and movement* Free-Range Kids

"Although this book's focus is on the lack of justice in the criminal
justice system for those with disabilities such as autism, it's much
more—a well-documented demonstration of the continuation of
legislation and policies driven not by evidence and efficacy, but by
fear, anger, revenge panic and politics."

—*William C. Buhl, retired Circuit Judge and former
District Judge and Prosecuting Attorney*

"An intimate look at the social and sexual challenges of people
with Autism Spectrum Disorders to an informed critique of child
pornography prosecutions and the hyper-punishment of sex offenses.
The resultant proposals are rational, just, and humane, not only for
people with development disabilities but for all criminal defendants."

—*Judith Levine, author of* Harmful to Minors: The
Perils of Protecting Children from Sex

of related interest

The Autism Spectrum, Sexuality and the Law
What every parent and professional needs to know
Tony Attwood, Isabelle Hénault and Nick Dubin
ISBN 978 1 84905 919 0
eISBN 978 0 85700 679 0

CAUGHT in the WEB of the CRIMINAL JUSTICE SYSTEM

Autism, Developmental Disabilities, and Sex Offenses

Edited by LAWRENCE A. DUBIN, J.D. and EMILY HOROWITZ, PH.D.

Foreword by ALAN GERSHEL, J.D.
Introduction by MARK MAHONEY, J.D.
Afterword by TONY ATTWOOD

Jessica Kingsley *Publishers*
London and Philadelphia

First published in 2017
by Jessica Kingsley Publishers
73 Collier Street
London N1 9BE, UK
and
400 Market Street, Suite 400
Philadelphia, PA 19106, USA

www.jkp.com

Library of Congress Cataloging in Publication Data
Names: Dubin, Lawrence, 1943- editor. | Horowitz, Emily, editor.
Title: Caught in the web of the criminal justice system : autism,
    developmental disabilities and sex offenses / edited by Lawrence A. Dubin
    and Emily Horowitz ; foreword by Alan Gershel.
Description: London ; Philadelphia : Jessica Kingsley Publishers, 2017. |
    Includes bibliographical references and index.
Identifiers: LCCN 2016058447 | ISBN 9781785927133 (alk. paper)
Subjects: LCSH: Autistic people--Legal status, laws, etc.--United States. |
    Offenders with mental disabilities--Legal status, laws, etc.--United
    States. | Sex offenders--Legal status, laws, etc.--United States. | Autism
    spectrum disorders--Law and legislation--United States. | Sex
    crimes--United States.
Classification: LCC KF480.5.A94 C38 2017 | DDC 345.73/02530875--dc23 LC record
available at https://lccn.loc.gov/2016058447

British Library Cataloguing in Publication Data
A CIP catalogue record for this book is available from the British Library

ISBN 978 1 78592 713 3
eISBN 978 1 78450 298 0

Printed and bound in the United States

Contents

Foreword

Alan Gershel, Former Acting U.S. Attorney
for the Eastern District in Michigan

I am a former assistant United States Attorney for the Eastern District of Michigan. I served in that office for 35 years while acting at times as chief of the criminal division as well as the interim United States Attorney.

In 2009, I retired from public service and accepted a position on the law faculty of Thomas Cooley Law School. Thereafter, I have been frequently contacted to represent people charged with crimes, including by my former office. It is not uncommon for a former prosecutor to use his knowledge of the criminal justice system in thereafter accepting representation of people accused of crimes. There is no moral or ethical barrier that would prevent a former prosecutor from doing so.

When I left my position as a U.S. Attorney, I decided that I would refuse to represent people charged with crimes. I did so because I believed that, after my years as a prosecutor, I had developed a certain mindset that would limit my ability to properly undertake the ethical responsibilities of a defense lawyer. Therefore, on the many occasions when I was offered employment as a defense lawyer, I routinely said, "No, thank you."

Then in December 2010, I received a telephone call from attorney Ken Mogill who told me he was representing a client, Nick Dubin, on the autism spectrum who was charged with possession of child pornography on his computer. I had great respect for Ken and knew that the information that he gave me about this case would not be inflated or inaccurate. Ken explained how this young man's neurological disability from birth created a serious social and sexual delay in his development. He further explained that Mr. Dubin had also been examined by leading experts in the field of autism who opined that he was not a threat to anyone and there was a legitimate issue as to the nature and quality of his ability to be held accountable for his criminal responsibility for the charged acts. These experts strongly believed that diversion from the criminal justice system was the best way to resolve this case.

I told Ken I was sympathetic about a person on the autism spectrum being charged with a serious federal crime, but that in general I don't accept defense cases and didn't have sympathy for people who view child pornography. Ken convinced me to at least meet this young man and he would accept whatever my decision was as to joining him in the representation.

I met Nick Dubin at his home a few weeks later. I was very blunt with him regarding my feelings about people who commit the crime with which he was charged. I asked him many very personal questions. I'm sure it was an unpleasant experience for him to have to be confronted by specific questions about his sexual thoughts. When we were finished, I told Ken and his client that I would need some time to think about my decision. I undertook some reading about autism spectrum disorders and learned information of which I was not previously aware.

After much reflection in the passing days, I concluded that Mr. Dubin should not be prosecuted and convicted for the crime he was charged with and thereby stigmatized as a lifelong federal felon and a registered sex offender. Although I had great respect for the lawyers in my former office who were prosecuting this case, I believed that they needed to better understand how Nick's autism was a special circumstance that needed to be considered in the exercise of prosecutorial discretion.

I became co-counsel with Ken in representing Nick. We presented a strong and compelling case for Nick to receive diversion from the criminal justice system. Since my role as Nick's defense attorney is the only case that I will ever have as a defense attorney, I feel it is my ethical obligation to state that I believe my former office did not do the right thing in requiring Nick to enter a plea of guilty for the crime of possession of child pornography. All the experts who examined Nick, including two appointed from the government (one being a neuropsychologist for the FBI), expressed clear reasons for why Nick should not be so convicted. Unfortunately, Nick had no real option to go to trial and face the possibility of incarceration, and therefore Ken and I had to recommend that he accept this imperfect plea agreement.

I hope this book opens the eyes and minds of prosecutors and judges and compels defense lawyers to better understand the nature of autism. Getting a conviction in and of itself is not justice when the accused is not a danger to anyone and the crime is understandable due to a neurological disability from birth. Real justice in this case would have permitted Mr. Dubin to have lived his life only with his disability from birth and not the additional disability created by having a felony conviction and having to register as a sex offender.

Introduction

Mark Mahoney, Noted Criminal Defense Attorney Who Has Expertise in Defending ASD Individuals Charged with Criminal Offenses

There are too many heartbreaking stories. Stories about families whose child with Asperger's Syndrome, was arrested, convicted, imprisoned and labeled as a "sex offender" for having accessed child pornography, or engaged in other inappropriately sexual communications, "online." Parents were told, even by very experienced defense attorneys, that their son's autism was not a "defense" and would "not make a difference." These lawyers typically knew very little about autism, but knew a lot about how impervious prosecutors typically are to "excuses" or pleas for "sympathy" in these cases. Judges, without any in-depth understanding of the autism condition of the accused, or how it relates to the conduct, or to the likelihood of future offending, tended to follow their usual sentencing patterns—if not worse, out of fear of the "odd" defendant—imposing prison terms of more than ten years on some and rarely less than five on the rest. This was followed by mandatory sex offender treatment programs ill suited and traumatic to those with this developmental disability. Life for the individual with Autism Spectrum Disorder in prison, on supervision, and labeled as a "sex offender" is torturous, what I call "civil death."

How often this pattern has repeated itself we do not know. Slowly, however, there is change. There is hope. And this book is a reflection of, and an instrument of that change.

Nick Dubin did not go to prison, as he surely would have without extraordinarily informed advocacy and clinical consensus proving that he was no threat to children, despite engaging in what is considered deviant behavior. So this at least sets a hopeful example. But, as any objective reader can tell, it was not necessary to prosecute Nick at all.

It was not necessary to label him as a "sex offender." And he probably only got probation because his defense team had proven this to be so.

Nick's case was especially challenging because it is so terribly difficult for those investigating and prosecuting violations of child exploitation offenses to understand, or accept, how someone as bright and accomplished as he could not appreciate the social or legal opprobrium directed at this behavior, or why it was considered so wrong, or how he could have an interest in viewing child pornography without having any interest in abusing any child. But in other cases where prosecutors and judges were meaningfully informed of the nature of the defendant's autism, and its relation to the behaviour resulting in the charges, and how it can provide assurance that he will follow the "rules" once he understands them, we have seen many sentences of probation, or prosecutors agreeing to reduce charges to offenses not requiring sex offender registration, or even complete diversion of the case from criminal prosecution. This, of course is what Nick's defense team sought, which is so important, because and having that objective was surely critical to the result achieved, even though it was harsher than what Nick deserved.

The collective wisdom in this book points the way to diversion of these cases from criminal prosecution, and enables prosecutors and judges to achieve this with complete confidence, and with no compromise of their concerns for the protection of children. But this will not come about easily, because it requires bridging a gap in understanding between two very different worlds.

The world in which our child pornography laws evolved was a world of fear and panic, fostered by no small amount of mythology and ideology. The public and legislatures were flooded with wild and fantastic accounts of thousands of children being abducted each year, in the United States alone, to create child pornography. With no factual basis, claims were made in popular magazines like the Ladies Home Journal and in newspapers, and by Congress members that there was a child pornography industry in the United States with annual revenues as high as $46 billion, and using as many as 2.4 million children to do it.[1] In fact, no evidence of such a domestic industry, or

---

1   Rooney, Innocence for Sale: A Special Report on Child Pornography, Ladies' Home J., April 1 983, at 79. 128-30; Kermani, 'Kid Porn: A Billion-Dollar Scandal. Albanv Times Union, Apr. 25, 1982; 134 Cong. Rec. S645-46 (daily ed. Feb. 4, 1988) (statement of Sen. DeConcini)

such abductions—to any degree—ever existed. But this became an irresistible breeding ground for legislation. Of course there can be no quarrel with harsh punishment for those who create and seek to profit from this exploitation of children. I have had to view thousands of these images in my work, and it never ceases to shock me and sadden me, and I have complete sympathy for the outrage and devotion of investigators and prosecutors who want to be a part of stopping it. But this is easy when talking about those who create and profit from this business.

But what about those who merely possess or look at child pornography which is now widely available for free on the internet? The Supreme Court had long before determined that the private possession of obscene "adult" material could not be criminal, notwithstanding unempirical arguments that pornography led to rape. But for those who possess child pornography, there is the legitimate fear that some of these individuals, based on their interests in such material, present an actual danger of "hands on" offenses against children – an entirely different problem than child pornography. Still, this was a concern fueled by the same irrational fear of rampant abduction of children by strangers for purposes of sexual exploitation, but also the well founded fear that pedophiles will abuse children to whom they are not strangers, such as relatives, and children in their care.

The legal problem is that fear that a person will commit a crime is not enough to imprison a person. Fundamental principles of lawmaking do not permit criminalizing mere thoughts, where those thoughts do not result in plans or actions to harm others. It cannot be criminal to be a racist, greedy, sociopathic—or a pedophile. So, how to uphold the laws prohibiting mere personal possession of child pornography? Congress and the courts relied primarily on two principles, one of which has significantly evaporated, and another that is purely ideological. First, before the internet, attaining child erotica of all sorts required personal participation in an "underground" sometimes entered through coded personal ads in "swinger's" club magazine or "naturist" publications. The ultimate attaining of material was in an exchange, for money or other erotic images of children. There was in fact a kind of marketplace. So, this was the background for the holding of the Supreme Court, in *New York v. Ferber*, 458 U.S. 757 (1982), that the possession of child pornography contributed to the "market" for child pornography.

With the onset of the Web, this changed fundamentally. Downloading of an image does not decrease the "supply" or therefore increase the "demand." Rather, the producers and their emulators flood the internet with child images, establishing a "supply that creates its own demand," in the same way—but far less expensively—that the tobacco companies used to hire pretty young women to pass out free cigarettes on city streets in the early 1970s. Whereas a person interested child porn previously had to be persistent to obtain this material, now a browser search for erotic images on the Web can yield links to child pornography for those not even looking for it, or paying for it.

The other rationale that has been relied on to validate the punishment of mere possession of child pornography is that viewing an image of child pornography constitutes a "re-victimization" of the abused child. This is an ideological precept, not something with any empirical basis, but it is used to rationalize the criminalization of possession of child pornography, and the enhancement of sentences based on the number of images possessed, and frequent orders of financial "restitution" to victims to compensate for this harm to them. These ideas of "contributing to the market" and "revictimizing" are such articles of faith that even empirical researchers in the area of online offending and therapists feel obliged to incorporate them, however uncritically in describing the situation.

The point of this discussion is that, though driven by fear of potential harm to children, the laws criminalizing the possession of child pornography, and prosecutions, do not necessarily hinge on actual harm. Moreover, the manner of enforcement against mere possessors casts a very wide net which necessarily includes people who prosecutors and investigators will concede do not present any danger. Nor is ther any requirement in the federal law, or most state laws, that the accused have any awareness that their actions are "wrong" in any sense. Only the exercise of prosecutorial discretion can limit the scope of enforcement to those who present a real danger, or know that what they were doing was "wrong."

There are two major problems with expecting prosecutors to use discretion to narrow the application of these laws. First, prosecutors have their "marching orders," whether from superiors in the Department of Justice, or what they perceive as a public that is averse to any show of mercy to one viewing child pornography. Second, prosecutors do not feel equipped to differentiate between the wide range of "excuses" and "disabilities" that are often raised in mitigation in these cases. They are institutionally, and usually personally, less concerned about the risk of visiting a conviction upon persons posing no real danger, or do not know that what they did was wrong, than they are concerned about the risk that a particular accused person, with ASD or otherwise, will nonetheless act out against a child if not imprisoned, at least for that period of imprisonment and kept track of with sex offender registration. So, this is a world driven by fear, and buoyed, as this whole book tells us, by a tragic unawareness of the reality that is familiar to those in a different world: the parents, teachers, clinicians and researchers whose daily lives revolve around persons affected by this pervasive developmental disorder.

So, let us look at this other world, which this book opens for the reader. One of the most gratifying things about defending individuals with this highly consequential social learning difference, is contact with the researchers, the parents, the teachers, the diagnosticians and the organizations who devote their lives to helping these children. These people are as dedicated to children affected by autism as any law enforcement officers are to the children who are exploited, and at risk of being exploited. They have a firm understanding of the capabilities and deficits presented in individuals with "high functioning" autism who are most exposed to the risk of being prosecuted under these laws. This is the knowledge and experience that can form the bridge between these two "worlds."

The primary thing is that this is not about sympathy for those with differences in development. This is about science. And it is about the moral foundation of the criminal law, which hinges criminal liability on blameworthiness. At a minimum this means awareness of wrongdoing. There are very few instances where we tolerate criminal prosecution and punishment for those who are not aware that what they have done is "wrong," in the sense understood by those who made the conduct a crime.

But this is the problem with those with autism. From birth, a combination of neurological differences in the brain of one with autism conspire to blind the individual to learning from social interactions about the feelings and intentions of others, and the social mores that become second nature to typically developed individuals. As Ami Klin and his teams of researchers have shown, repeatedly, the individual with Asperger's simply *does not see* those countless cues in expression, intonation, and "body language" that give meaning to social interactions and understanding to communications.

The difficulty in processing social encounters not only correlates with extreme isolation, but also with a severe deficit in the social learning ability needed to understand what is acceptable in public and private behavior. When, in their isolation, young men with ASD go looking on the internet to learn about sex and romance, they, like their peers, will look at pornography. But, when they come across child pornography, no "red flag" goes up, no filters are in place to tell them that, though depicting sex also, these are inappropriate to view—whether because of the origins of the material, or our collective sense of what is "normal" when it comes to sexual interests.

I want to make clear that the issue is not that these individuals do not know that their behavior is *illegal*—which they do not. Rather, it is that they do not know that looking at underage images is any more "wrong" than looking at any other kind of pornography, behaviour which they would typically find embarrassing to discuss with their parents or others, but do not know is wrong in any greater sense.

Tests of adaptive functioning (social communication) and sexual interest repeatedly confirm that these are individuals who are not deviant, but simply unaware of the social opprobrium attached to the sexualization of children, and who are also unable to intuit the abusive and cruel natter of the circumstances under which these images are created. They present what is best described as "counterfeit deviance"—they engage in behavior we consider deviant, without the mental understanding or blameworthiness we assume on the part of people engaging in the behavior.

Equally important, those experienced in dealing with persons with autism will describe how their rigidity and "rule bound" nature make them generally assiduous in following the "rules," once they learn them. Research is now showing greater compliance with conditions of supervision by persons with ASD. I view it as an understandable, yet serious, mistake to think that viewing child pornography is too entrenched a behavior, that it equates to the "circumscribed interest" which may be diagnostically significant. Though obsessive collecting represents a strong trait of autism, we know that viewing child pornography is not itself a "circumscribed interest," because none of these individuals perseverate about the topic or think about it all the time as they might locomotives, roller coasters, or astronomy.

The tragedy is this: parents and those providing autism services have long been concerned about these individuals being victims of crime and deception, largely because of their extreme naivete. But they had not thought about this problem of online viewing of child pornography. There are no programs in place to warn them or protect them from this exposure and becoming a victim of those purveying these materials. It never fails: mention the idea to any parent or any clinician or care giver and they will immediately recognize that any one of the young men they deal with could end up in this dire situation. Not because of deviance, but because of extreme social immaturity.

What we have in this book is the collective wisdom needed to form a bridge of understanding, and overcome the legitimate, but often unwarranted fears of law enforcement and prosecutors and judges. I have seen this happen. In 2013 Dr. Donald Hoppe, in Baton Rouge, La., was consulted in a case of a young man with ASD charged with viewing child pornography. He went beyond merely diagnosing and measuring his autism condition: he advocated, saying in his report: "_____is not a child predator or sex offender in need of rehabilitation. He is an under-socialized young man who needs to be 'habilitated' in order to understand and survive in the world." He personally persuaded the prosecutor on this and charges were dropped. There were similar occurrences in Cincinnati and Columbus Ohio. As of this writing, federal prosecutors in Utah, Missouri, New York, and California, in five different cases involving defendants with ASD, have agreed to the entry of guilty pleas to offenses which do not require registration as sex offenders, and probation sentences were imposed requiring therapy suited to their autism, and not the typical "sex offender" therapy. State prosecutors in New York and Virginia have agreed to the same thing.

Each of these cases required hard work, and the accomplishments are wonderful and against the odds. But, truly, diversion from prosecution should be the presumptive result. With this book we see what needs to be presented, what needs to be done. Certainly lawyers need to prepare to inform prosecutors and judges. Clinicians need to understand the viewpoint of prosecutors and prepare to explain the relationship between the autism condition and the behavior in question. They need to address the therapies available for socially educating an individual with ASD and advocate for diversion. Many of the most skilled autism clinicians are reluctant to do "forensic" work, with the risk that they might have to appear in court. They need shed that fear, realizing that the greatest threat to the well-being of their patient is not their autism condition, but a criminal justice system which does not understand it.

Researchers have established that there is a substantial segment among those who view child pornography online who have no interest in sexual offending. But they need to team up with autism experts to explore that data to determine the extent to which those with developmental disabilities are concentrated in that least risky population.

Authors in this volume cite to the "Principles for Prosecutors" policy statement, since its promulgation in 2008 no new organizations have signed on to this protocol, which is not yet subscribed to by what are regarded the leading autism organizations in the United States. They need to be part of this effort. Autism organization at all levels have failed to get involved in direct advocacy of any sort in these cases, no doubt out of fear that their official presence could be misinterpreted as a suggestion that individuals with ASD were prone to sexual offending. In reality, if they do not step up and help stem the tide of these prosecutions, the resulting convictions, though unwarranted, will indeed lend this "deviant" stigma to the ASD male population. They could make a real difference in prosecutorial attitudes.

The Department of Justice needs to recognize, on an official policy basis, the need for pretrial diversion of first offenders who have autism and similar social learning deficits. They should agree to meet with qualified representatives of those with autism, the autism advocates researchers, and clinicians to develop such a policy. If they do this, state and local prosecutors will surely follow.

There is yet another dimension to this difficult problem which has yet to be acknowledged by prosecutors, or adjudicated by courts: there is a human rights dimension to this issue, beyond the question of faithful and responsible enforcement of a particular criminal law. We have a national policy to protect and accommodate those with developmental disabilities, reflected in the Americans with Disabilities Act, and the correlative Rehabilitation Act. This sets a national policy that applies to those in law enforcement and must circumscribe their exercise of discretion. In "Examples and Resources to Support Criminal Justice Entities in Compliance with Title II of the Americans with

Disabilities Act." USDOJ, Civil Rights Division, Technical Assistance Publication, January 11, 2017, p.2:[2]

> Nondiscrimination requirements, such as providing reasonable modifications to policies, practices, and procedures and taking appropriate steps to communicate effectively with people with disabilities, also support the goals of ensuring public safety, promoting public welfare, and *avoiding unnecessary criminal justice involvement for people with disabilities.* (*Emphasis added*).

This is express acknowledgment of the problem of "counterfeit deviance," and in the "unnecessary criminal justice involvement for people with disabilities" arising from their involvement in behaviour which is only apparently deviant, but lacks the culpable mental state or blameworthiness which would normally attend such actions by persons who are typically developed.

This guidance expressly notes the importance of "assessing individuals for diversion programs" on the basis of DD. *Id.* It later gives as an example of compliance with the ADA the setting of "eligibility criteria for diversion programs such as community services, specialty courts, or probation programs" *Id.* and "[r]equir[ing] court staff to explore reasonable modifications to allow qualified individuals with these disabilities to participate in diversion and probation programs and specialty courts." *Id.* at 3. This falls under the category of "reasonable modifications in policies, practices, or procedures when necessary to avoid disability discrimination."

But these American policies reflect inernational consensus and law. The UN Convention on the Rights of Persons with Disabilities was adopted in 2006. The pertinence of this to criminal law enforcement was at the United Nations Autism Awareness Day Conference on March 31, 2017, where the keynote address was delivered by Professor Simon Baron-Cohen, Director of the Autism Research Centre at Cambridge University, and one of the leading researchers on the problem of law enforcement and persons with autism. Prof. Baron-Cohen ended his address focusing on this problem and the rights of persons with developmental disabilities to "protection of the law" guaranteed by this Convention. Though there are "person[s] with autism [who] became tangled up with because of their social naivete… a product of their disability, and yet the courts often ignore autism."

---

2   https://www.ada.gov/cjta.html

Thus we have a problem of law enforcement with tragic dimensions, defendants truly innocent in any moral sense, victims, and important principles of human rights and dignity for the developmentally disabled at stake. There is hope, reflected in the dedication and insight of these authors, and the in the fact that many experienced prosecutors and judges have allowed themselves to remain open to what this book teaches, putting that knowledge and understanding to the fore, and the usual fears behind.

Introduction

Caught in the Web of the Criminal
Justice System: Autism, Developmental
Disabilities, and Sex Offenses

Lawrence A. Dubin and Emily Horowitz

This book explores a range of topics that emanate from the draconian laws that have emerged from years of myths, misinformation, moral panic, and public hysteria about child sexual abuse. These laws have not only created state and federal sex registration requirements that raise many questionable constitutional issues, but they are characterized by a "one size fits all" approach to sex offenses, on the basis that all those labeled "sex offender" are predatory, uncontrollable, and incurable, and thus need public branding and banishment in addition to harsh punishment. This book explores one group that has been caught in the web of these ineffective and dangerous laws: non-violent people who have been born with developmental disabilities. More specifically, the crime of possession of child pornography from the computer of a person with autism (formally referred to as Asperger's or high-functioning autism) is subject to felony convictions, prison sentences, and registration as sex offenders against a group of disabled people who generally pose no danger to children.

The case of Larry's son, Nick Dubin, will serve as the main case study that can help prosecutors, defense lawyers, and judges who operate our criminal justice system to better understand the relationship between the neurological deficits of autism as a developmental disability and the vulnerability of this population committing this crime. The bigger issue, of course, is the unjust nature of sex offender laws in general, and we believe the example of those on the autism spectrum, individuals with disabilities and particular vulnerabilities, who are prosecuted without regard for their disability, highlights the draconian nature of these laws.

The information about a person being on the autism spectrum that can be gleaned from Nick's case study could be relevant in cases involving other types of non-violent sex crimes such as stalking, indecent exposure, and improper touching. These cases often require expert testimony regarding the nature of an autism spectrum disorder (ASD) and its bearing on certain legal issues such as diminished or lack of criminal responsibility, competency, determination of sentence under existing guidelines, ineffective assistance of counsel, Miranda compliance, and risk assessment.

The main purpose of the book is to educate and sensitize lawyers, judges, psychologists, social workers, teachers, parents, and people on the autism spectrum about the relationship between this developmental disorder and non-violent sexually related crimes. The potentially harsh criminal sentences and the difficulties of living life under the label of being a registered sex offender for this population need to be carefully examined and better understood. The lack of this discussion will certainly cause defense lawyers to be less competent, prosecutors to not use discretion in seeking justice, and judges to not apply the necessary independence to the application from the sentencing guidelines.

WHY THIS BOOK IS NEEDED: EXAMPLE OF JOHN

A typical example of a person on the autism spectrum charged with possession of child pornography on his computer is John (pseudonym). As a result of his neurological disorder, he had experienced throughout his life many social deficits including his inability to have normal social experiences with peers. He was convicted of possession of child pornography in both the State of Florida and federal court. John's forensic psychologist opined that he had no interest to ever harm a child, yet he was sentenced to 30 months at a federal prison in Butner, North Carolina, and then supervised release for an additional three years. In the following statement, John, in his own words, briefly describes the events that led to his arrest, conviction, confinement, and requirement to be a registered sex offender. His life history as a person on the autism spectrum is typical for those ensnared by the criminal justice system for conduct that occurs in the privacy of one's dwelling for viewing (without making any payment) prohibited images on a computer without any physical contact.

My name is John. I am 32 years old with Asperger's syndrome. I have had problems my entire life with social interactions and understanding other people. This has caused me to lose out on many things such as job opportunities and friendships. More than anything, I have always wanted friends and to be accepted by my peers. Throughout my school years, I was constantly bullied and was a social outcast. This is because I would give off inappropriate social signals, try too hard to make friends, and not know when to stop talking or acting in a strange way in the eyes of others. It's not like I intentionally act in these ways. Rather, I have had to pretend to appear normal, even though I know that I am different from most people.

Between the ages of 15 and 18, I was a *Star Trek* fan and tried to make friends by working at *Star Trek* conventions, but even in that setting, I was still treated as an outcast. I would work the convention and then go home and try to talk online, but would get kicked out of the chat rooms due to my slow typing and childish responses.

I knew I was different from other children since kindergarten, but none of the psychologists I saw throughout my life did anything constructive to help me other than to misdiagnose me. I truly wish I had received appropriate support while I was growing up.

A guy I knew introduced me to the world of chat rooms as a way to make friends. But even in chat rooms I was not able to make friends. This same guy also introduced me to pornography both online and offline. We would go to an adult magazine store and buy pornographic materials. Throughout my life I did not understand pornography. I always viewed pornography as not being real, just like a Hollywood movie that was scripted.

Later, my friend introduced me to child pornography. Again, the child pornography never seemed real to me. I wasn't able to put two and two together. Through viewing child pornography, I found people online who were willing to talk to me. People sent me messages and I would respond back via instant message. I had conversations with others if I traded pictures with them. If I had understood that I was doing something wrong, and in fact illegal, I never would have done it. All that mattered to me was that for the first time, I was being accepted by people who I viewed as friends.

I soon learned how my sense of reality was completely mistaken. I was in a chat room on America Online talking and exchanging pictures with people who I thought were my friends. One of these people turned out to be an FBI agent who sent me an encrypted file that corrupted my computer. I sent him a photo which I had gotten and saved on my desktop to try and keep the conversation going. Next thing I knew, my computer stopped working.

I didn't know anything about computers so I took my computer to a repair shop having no sense of any impropriety about the pornographic images I had been trading. However, when the people at the repair shop viewed these images, they called the Broward County, Florida Sheriff's Office who then obtained a warrant for my arrest. They showed up at my parents' house where I was residing and interrogated me. I was so naïve I asked them if I could still go to Australia the following Sunday as I had planned to do. I found out that the answer was "no" when I was thereafter arrested.

A few months later I was arrested again by the FBI for the photo I had sent to the FBI agent a few months earlier. When it was time to plead guilty in federal court to possession of child pornography on my computer, the judge seemed very understanding of the circumstances that brought me before him. I was sentenced to 30 months in the federal prison in Butner, North Carolina, and three years on probation for doing something that I had no clue was wrong. I certainly came to that understanding thereafter.

Since being released from prison, it has been extremely hard to reintegrate into a society where I had always been viewed as an outcast but now, in addition, I am a convicted felon and a publicly labeled and registered sex offender. If I had killed someone, sold drugs, or robbed a bank, life after prison would have been better because there is no similar registration required for any of those serious crimes. Thus, without a job (finding one with the stigma of being a registered sex offender and with my disability makes it nearly impossible), my family had to pay my rent and living expenses. I don't know what I would have done without their help. (Letter sent to Larry Dubin)

At John's sentencing in federal court on the charge of possession of child pornography, federal judge Daniel Hurley acknowledged how the worst perpetrators who harm children are not the people likely to be charged with crimes.

In this whole area of child pornography, what we are trying to do is protect children; and recognizing that we don't have the ability by and large to get at these people who are creating these pornographic images, people who are either molesting their own children, or children they are able to come into contact with, we do the next best thing and, that is, we make it a crime to possess it…

In assessing John as a person, the judge stated, "I have before me an older gentleman who had a serious physical disability who...I think you could say with absolute certainty that there was simply no likelihood that he was ever going to...pose a danger to anybody else." The judge further asserted that he was "well satisfied" that the diagnosis of Asperger's syndrome was correctly applied to John, and that this condition "played a significant role" in explaining the criminal charges brought against him. The judge further recognized that John had no previous criminal record and that he has "lived a life where he has some very significant accomplishments given the limitations that he is dealing with." John is a typical example of the increasing number of defendants charged with possession of child pornography and other non-violent sex crimes who are on the autism spectrum. Many of these defendants, through no fault of their own and due in part to neurological deficits from birth, have certain characteristics that make them vulnerable to committing these types of crimes. In general, they pose no threat to harm anyone and can learn not to be repeat offenders through proper therapeutic intervention. As Judge Hurley stated about John, he posed no danger to anyone, he had no criminal record, and his criminal acts were related to his disability. It is our fervent hope that the reader can keep an open mind while reading through the pages of this book. After all, the goal of prosecutors in the criminal justice system is not simply to convict, but also to act as "Ministers of Justice." It seems irrational to condemn a person like John to being labeled a felon for the rest of his life after he served a 30-month prison term and upon his release from incarceration require him to become a registered sex offender. The injustice bestowed upon John reflects the larger portrait of an overreaction to sex offenders in general who must contend with laws that unduly discriminate against them without any rational basis for doing so. An understanding of this thesis is also an important objective of this book that may seem counterintuitive because it is natural to want to have laws that clearly protect children. But when laws are designed to protect children but fail in meeting that objective and have the unintended consequence of unnecessarily ruining the lives of people without any public benefit (people with developmental disabilities also need the protection of the law), greater examination of this reality is necessary.

BOOK OUTLINE: CHAPTERS AND CONTRIBUTORS

The following authors have each written a chapter in this book. Each author has acquired expertise that provides a necessary perspective in understanding why defendants on the autism spectrum commit non-violent sex offenses and why this example helps illuminate the irrationality of our overall approach to those charged with these crimes.

Alan Gershel wrote the foreword to this book. Mr. Gershel was chief of the criminal division of the U.S. Attorney's office in the Eastern District of Michigan and served as acting United States Attorney for that district as well. Thereafter he was a Professor of Law at Cooley Law School. He currently serves as Grievance Administrator for the Michigan Attorney Grievance Commission as an appointee of the Michigan Supreme Court.

Mark Mahoney, wrote the first Introduction based upon a wealth of research and experience he has accumulated in representing many men on the autism spectrum throughout the United States charged with sex related crimes. With over 40 years of experience as a criminal defense lawyer, he has also taught law students and lawyers about the skills and knowledge necessary in being an effective criminal defense lawyer.

In "Child and Juvenile Pornography and Autism Spectrum Disorder" (Chapter 2), Dr. Gary Mesibov and Dr. Melissa Sreckovic describe how

> [u]nfortunately, child pornography presents the "perfect storm" for individuals with ASD (Mahoney, 2009); specific characteristics inherent in ASD make computers especially attractive and engaging to them and vulnerable to invitations to access child pornography without understanding that their actions are potentially illegal and harmful to young children. With their lack of social skills and extreme social naivety, individuals with ASD are easy targets to be manipulated and, once engaged in the criminal justice system, struggle immensely to advocate for themselves and navigate the criminal justice system.

Dr. Gary Mesibov is a licensed Psychologist, Professor Emeritus at the University of North Carolina, editor, and author. He was Director of TEACCH, founded by the University of North Carolina as a pioneering program for assisting with ASD education, research, and service delivery for children and adults. He is an internationally recognized leader in autism research and practice. Dr. Mesibov provides concrete information about the characteristics of autism spectrum disorders, the neurological and psychological deficits that are caused by this disorder, and its relationship to the commission of certain sex crimes, including the consequences of imposing imprisonment and/or registration as a sex offender on such individuals.

Dr. Melissa Sreckovic is an assistant professor of special education at the University of Michigan-Flint. Dr. Sreckovic has worked with children and young adults on the autism spectrum in a variety of settings including schools and homes, and in clinic-based settings. Her research focuses on evidence-based practices for addressing the behavioral and social needs of students with ASD, best practices for inclusive classroom instruction, and school-based bullying prevention and intervention. Prior to this, she was an elementary school inclusion teacher. As an advocate for individuals with ASD, Dr. Sreckovic is interested in partnering with her local community on the social and behavioral characteristics of individuals on the autism spectrum to promote inclusive practices.

Ken Mogill, as an experienced criminal defense lawyer who has argued cases before the United States Supreme Court, had never represented a defendant who was on the autism spectrum until retained to represent Nick Dubin. Therefore, the case study that he presents in Chapter 3, "Representing an Autism Spectrum Disorder Individual Charged with Possession of Internet Child Pornography," reflects the situation that most lawyers face when first confronted with a client on the autism spectrum. Fortunately, Mr. Mogill immediately recognized his need in providing competent representation to become well versed in understanding that Nick had an autism spectrum disorder with significant neurological deficits as well as intellectual strengths. It then becomes the lawyer's responsibility not only to get the necessary experts to be able to evaluate an ASD client, but to help explain the large gap between the client's average or even above-average intelligence with significant below-average psycho-sexual development. This gap is the key to understanding that someone like Nick can have college degrees yet be very young and inexperienced socially and sexually without ever having any intent to harm anyone. The information that these experts can provide is invaluable to prosecutors and judges in assessing alternative dispositions to cases that would otherwise likely lead to a prison sentence.

Dr. Dennis Sugrue is a licensed psychologist who specializes in human sexual development. He has been an expert witness in criminal cases involving people on the autism spectrum. He has a private practice, is an author of books on human sexuality, and is also a professor in the Department of Psychiatry at the University of Michigan. In Chapter 4, "Forensic Assessment of Individuals on the Autism Spectrum Charged with Child Pornography Violations," Dr. Sugrue makes a compelling case for why a judge, prosecutor, and defense lawyer will greatly benefit from a forensic evaluation by an expert in human sexuality when the accused is on the autism spectrum and charged with possession of child pornography or a non-violent sex-related crime. In these cases, relevant issues may include competency and criminal responsibility with additional questions arising with respect to the most appropriate disposition of a case based upon the following considerations: prognosis, risk assessment, mitigating factors, and treatment options and recommendations.

Mark H. Allenbaugh is a former staff attorney with the U.S. Sentencing Commission. He currently is co-founder and Chief Research Officer for Sentencing Stats, LLC (www.sentencingstats.com).

Dr. Richard Wollert is a clinical psychologist. He has provided psychological services as a solo private practitioner specializing in the assessment and treatment of sex offenders. He also evaluates respondents who are the subjects of sexually violent predator proceedings and often consult or testify as to their status on the criteria that define this construct. Dr. Wollert has been retained in over 200 such cases in seven states (Washington, California, Iowa, Illinois, Massachusetts, New Jersey and Wisconsin); he has also provided mental health services to offenders convicted of federal sex offenses and to defendants accused of federal sex offenses who are awaiting adjudication by the federal courts. Dr. Wollert alsos devote a substantial amount of time conducting research on the sexually violent predator construct, and he has published widely on these subjects.

Alexander Skelton a registered clinical psychologist who, prior to his retirement in 2016, worked for over 35 years as a clinician and policy advisor for the Office of the Chief Psychologist, Department of Corrections, New Zealand. Alexander has combined an enduring interest in population-level statistics with the development of actuarial approaches to the measurement of risk. He was primarily responsible for the Automated Sexual Recidivism Scale (ASRS), the Departments' core static risk measure for predicting sexual offender recidivism risk.

Dr. Fred Berlin, M.D., Ph.D. is the founder of the The Johns Hopkins Sexual Disorders Clinic and serves as director of the Sexual

Behaviors Consultation Unit. He has been an Attending Physician at the The Johns Hopkins School of Medicine since 1978 and has been a professor since that time. He has both his Ph.D. in Psychology and his M.D. degree and is a board certified Psychiatrist. In 1992 he founded the National Institute for the Study, Prevention and Treatment of Sexual Trauma. He has written multiple academic papers on pedophilia. He has also testified in court as an expert psychiatric witness.

Dr. Erin Comartin presents the consequences for family members of those on the sex offender registry in Chapter 9, "Collateral Damage of Sex Offender Management Policies for Individuals with Asperger's Syndrome and Their Family Members." Dr. Comartin joined the WSU School of Social Work faculty in 2016, after leaving a four-year faculty position at Oakland University in Rochester, MI. She received her Ph.D. and MSW degrees from Wayne State University. Her research focuses on social welfare policies and interventions for vulnerable populations in the criminal justice system. Her work predominantly focuses on individuals convicted of sex crime perpetration and the laws that manage their re-entry into the community. Additionally, she has also evaluated interventions designed to divert individuals with severe mental illness from the criminal justice system. Her work has been published in *Deviant Behavior, Psychiatric Services, Journal of Policy Practice,* and *The Journal of Social Work Values and Ethics.*

Prior to her research career, Dr. Comartin worked in residential facilities for runaway and homeless youth and survivors of domestic violence and sexual assault. She has worked as a crisis-line worker, an intervention specialist, a case manager, and a director within these programs. She has conducted program evaluations for various social interventions, mostly related to afterschool and early childhood education programs, as well as in substance abuse and mental health.

In "An Alternative Universe: The Perspective of an Autistic Registrant," Chapter 10 in this volume, **Nick Dubin** outlines the difficulties he faces as someone on the autism spectrum dealing with being publicly labeled a "sex offender." He also discusses his profound guilt and shame, and gives insight into what it is like to be publicly labeled a monster. Nick was diagnosed with Asperger's syndrome in 2004. He holds a Bachelor's Degree in Communications from Oakland University, a Master's Degree in Learning Disabilities from the University of Detroit Mercy, and a Specialist Degree in Psychology and Psy.D. from the Michigan School of Professional Psychology. He has authored many books on autism spectrum disorders, including *Asperger Syndrome and Anxiety*, also published by Jessica Kingsley Publishers. Nick lives in a suburb of Detroit, Michigan.

Professor Catherine Carpenter is the Honorable Arleigh M. Woods and William T. Woods Professor of Law at Southwestern Law School, Los Angeles, California. Professor Carpenter is the author of Chapter 11, "Navigating Judicial Responses for Those Caught in the Web." In this chapter, Professor Carpenter explores the potential options for judges adjudicating child pornography cases, and highlights the context of fear and myth, rather than reason, that dominates judicial decision-making as well as sex offender laws in a general sense.

Professor Carpenter is a recognized national expert in sex crimes and sex offender registration laws, and she was elected to the American Law Institute (ALI) in 2012 where she serves on the Advisory Committee examining the Model Penal Code's laws on sexual assault. Her scholarship has been cited by courts and has helped guide attorneys advocating for their clients. For example, her 2012 law review article entitled "The Evolution of Unconstitutionality in Sex Offender Registration Laws," published by *Hastings Law Journal*, and her 2010 *Buffalo Law Review* article, "Legislative Epidemics: A Cautionary Tale of Criminal Laws that Have Swept the Country," were both cited in *Doe v. Department of Public Safety and Correctional Services*, which overturned Maryland's sex offender registration laws on *ex post facto* grounds.

Professor Carpenter's recent scholarship has highlighted the injustice of juvenile sex offender registration laws. "Against Juvenile Sex Offender Registration," published at the University of Cincinnati in 2014, and "Throwaway Children: The Tragic Consequences of a False Narrative," published in the *Southwestern Law Review* in 2016, argue that juvenile sex offender registration violates fundamental tenets of the juvenile justice system and is based on the false presumption of high recidivism rates. It is a message that has resonated in the public arena. "Throwaway Children" was cited by mainstream media including reason.com and newsweek.com. In addition to her criminal scholarship which has been beneficial to courts and attorneys alike, Professor Carpenter has worked extensively with the American Bar Association's Section of Legal Education and with other accrediting bodies. Her efforts within the legal academic community earned her the designation by *National Jurist Magazine* in 2013, 2014, and 2015 as "One of the Most Influential People in Legal Education."

In the final chapter in this book, "Asperger's Syndrome and Downloading Child Pornography: Why Criminal Punishment is Unjust and Ineffective," Dr. John Douard and Pamela Schultz apply their work on the moral panic underlying sex offender laws to the case of those with autism charged with child pornography possession. This chapter is the most political in this volume; in no uncertain terms, Douard and Schultz argue that the hysteria surrounding sex offender policy is responsible for unjust punishment that is also ineffective—and punishing autistic defendants without looking at the mitigating circumstances is yet another example of the panic and irrationality surrounding this issue.

Dr. John Douard has a doctorate in philosophy, with a special focus on philosophy of cognitive science, from the University of Illinois at Chicago. He is currently an adjunct professor in the Department of Philosophy at Rutgers, The State University of New Jersey. He received his Juris Doctor at Rutgers/Newark School of Law and works as a full-time criminal defense appellate attorney in New Jersey. For three years, Dr. Douard represented men who were civilly committed under New Jersey's Sexually Violent Predator Act. He has published articles in philosophy journals and law reviews, and a book, co-authored with Pamela Schultz, called *Monstrous Crimes and the Failure of Forensic Psychiatry* (Springer, 2013).

Pamela Schultz is Professor of Communication Studies at Alfred University. She is the author of two books focusing on the narratives surrounding child sexual abuse and sexual abusers, *A Critical Analysis of the Rhetoric of Child Sexual Abuse* (Edwin Mellen Press, 2001) and *Not Monsters: Analyzing the Stories of Child Molesters* (Rowman & Littlefield, 2005); *Not Monsters* was translated into Japanese and Korean. She co-authored with John Douard the book *Monstrous Crimes and the Failure of Forensic Psychiatry* (Springer, 2013). Other articles include: "Revelations and Cardinals' Sins: Moral Panic over 'Pedophile Priests' in the United States" (2013); "Scapegoating the Sex Offender—The Monstrous Other" (2011) (with John Douard); and "Naming, Blaming, and Framing: Moral Panic over Child Molesters and its Implications for Public Policy" (2008).

Tony Attwood, Ph.D is a psychologist who is well known for his books and lectures throughout the world on various aspects of

Autism Spectrum Disorders. He also maintains a clinical practice for people on the autism spectrum in Brisbane, Australia.

FROM THE EDITORS

We both have contributed chapters to this volume. In Chapter 1, Larry reflects on his experience as both a father and lawyer in trying to understand what brought his only child Nick to be charged with a serious federal crime that created the frightening possibility of a lengthy prison sentence for him, a socially fragile individual who had never been in any trouble in his entire life. Nick was born with autism and has struggled in many ways throughout his life. He is a kind and gentle person who has and would never hurt anyone. Understanding how someone like Nick, with his life history, could find himself as an accused criminal became his task. Also, as a father, his desire to protect Nick from the harsh potential repercussions of the criminal justice system became the primary objective in his life.

Larry was faced with some major questions. Why wasn't he aware of the information that existed among world-renowned experts in autism who already knew that people like Nick were vulnerable to viewing child pornography? Why weren't prosecutors and judges knowledgeable about autism spectrum disorders where people on the spectrum view child pornography on their computer free of charge and present no danger to children and often lack criminal responsibility? Furthermore, why aren't prosecutors aware of the detrimental harm and unnecessary consequences of resolving these cases with prison terms and registration as sex offenders when diversion would be a more just outcome?

Larry's hope is that this book properly educates defense lawyers, prosecutors, judges, mental health professionals, parents, and teachers to better understand the ASD population. People on the autism spectrum deserve compassion and understanding for the many difficulties that are often linked to their lack of criminal intent when being charged with non-violent sex crimes such as possession of child pornography. Prosecutors need to take off their blinders that erroneously provide too narrow a view and understanding of the situation. They need to distinguish rationally a true criminal act from one committed by a person on the autism spectrum that is based upon his social and sexual innocence related to the deficits of the disability. In making this distinction, the criminal justice system will be better able to achieve justice for this disabled population in resolving criminal cases involving ASD defendants.

Emily's chapter reflects a tension in this book. In Chapter 5, she explores the context of the harsh and draconian sex offender laws that have been growing in scope since the early 1990s. When Emily met Nick Dubin, after publishing her book *Protecting Our Kids? How Sex Offender Laws Are Failing Us* (Praeger, 2015), she was horrified that an individual on the autism spectrum was not viewed in that context by the judicial system. Having spent nearly a decade studying hysteria surrounding crimes against children and sex offender laws, she wasn't shocked that a diagnosis of autism had little meaning for the courts. In his first public lecture about Nick's experience in the criminal justice system, Larry explained how the prosecution's expert concurred with the autism diagnosis and how they presented evidence that the diagnosis was related to his downloading child pornography, and that Nick was not at risk for reoffending or for engaging in a contact offense, but that didn't save him from having to register as a sex offender. Emily had heard many similar stories of people at low risk for reoffending involved in child pornography offenses, and this was yet another angle to view the injustice and irrationality inherent in sex offender laws. This book thus reflects the same tension: each chapter addresses the general failure and unjustness of sex offender laws, while also focusing on a few case studies of how autistic defendants facing charges of child pornography possession are "caught in the web" of draconian sentencing. While Larry emphasizes the special unfairness of not using diversion programs for first-time child pornography possession involving autistic defendants (see the Appendix for an outline of how diversion can be used in these cases), Emily argues that the sex offender registry and related laws must be viewed in a political context, and the politics explain why all those charged with sex offenses are subject to irrational treatment. This tension aside, we, and the authors in this volume, all share the same aim: to use the example of the egregious treatment of those on the autism spectrum to help shed light on the destructive and useless realities of our current sex offender policies. Until we bring reason and rationality to the treatment of all those charged with sex offenses, we must defend the most vulnerable among us—including those on the autism spectrum and with other disabilities who have no criminal history.

CHAPTER 1

A Father's Journey to Protect His Son

A Legal Perspective[1]

Lawrence A. Dubin

INTRODUCTION

> A story is more powerful than a statistical analysis. If Nick Dubin could end up as a convicted felon and sex offender, it could happen to anyone on the autism spectrum.
>
> Julia Press, Austin, TX

On October 6, 2010, the morning started out in a typically routine manner only to become the worst day of my life. I left my home in suburban Detroit to drive downtown to work. It was a beautiful, sunny fall day. Life seemed good. I was on my way to the University of Detroit Mercy School of Law where I have been a law professor for the past 35 years and taught classes in legal ethics, evidence, trial practice, and advanced seminars. I loved teaching law students how they can use their skills to make a positive contribution to society. I was an ardent believer in the legal system and very proud to be a lawyer.

My positive attitude about being a lawyer came from having practiced law for almost a decade, following my graduation from the University of Michigan Law School, before starting my academic career in 1975. During my years practicing law, I litigated many kinds of cases representing all kinds of clients, from wealthy corporate executives to indigent clients. I have had numerous articles and several

---

1   Some content of this chapter has been published previously in Attwood, Hénault and Dubin (2014).

books published about legal ethics, rules of evidence, and effective techniques for trial lawyers. For eight years, I served as a member of the Michigan Attorney Grievance Commission (appointed by the Michigan Supreme Court), which has the responsibility to investigate and prosecute lawyers who commit acts of misconduct. I have also received multiple awards from the State Bar of Michigan for public television documentaries that I have produced to help people better understand and appreciate the workings of our legal system. In my programs, I strove to illustrate how injustices could be rectified by the legal system. As a documentarian, I had the honor of interviewing Rosa Parks, her famous civil rights attorney Fred Gray, the late United States congresswoman Barbara Jordan, and others whom I greatly admire for being fighters for justice.

On my way to the law school that fateful morning, I received a call on my cell phone. An unfamiliar voice identified himself as an FBI agent. I immediately assumed the call had something to do with a former student who needed a recommendation for a job in government. I had frequently received calls from the FBI for that purpose. However, this call was different and turned out to be a life-changing moment. The male voice told me FBI agents were in the process of executing a search warrant at my son Nick's apartment concerning his personal computer. I learned later that child pornography was found on his computer. The agent thought that it would be wise for me to come there immediately due to Nick's emotional and physical condition. When I arrived at Nick's apartment, there were close to a dozen FBI agents milling around both inside and outside of his small quarters. Nick was on his couch in a fetal position with half his face tucked under a pillow. I went over to him, and in front of the agents who were present, put my arm around him and whispered in his ear, "I love you."

STATEMENT OF FULL DISCLOSURE

As a lawyer and Nick's father, I recognize that some readers may discount my statements as being biased. Although I admit that I love Nick with all my heart, I would never rationalize or not take seriously any criminal act that would knowingly and directly harm a child. My intention in this chapter is to share my personal experience in helping Nick cope with the criminal justice system as well as to impart the research I've gathered during this process. I do not believe that those on the autism spectrum are more likely to be criminals or child predators. In fact, I believe just the opposite. People on the autism spectrum tend to be honest, law-abiding individuals who inherently like to follow rules. I also want to be clear that, as a lawyer, I understand the importance of stating the facts of a case in an honest manner. In Nick's case, the facts were never really in dispute. What was in dispute was the appropriate way to resolve his case.

As difficult and challenging as life has been for Nick to live with a developmental disability, I have always marveled at his resiliency. Throughout his life, he has had to cope with many barriers and obstacles as well as his neurological limitations. As a result of these difficulties, he has suffered from chronic depression and anxiety and has been severely bullied by his peers. Nevertheless, Nick has always had the courage to confront these challenges and to maximize his potential while trying to help others avoid or successfully cope with some of the same hardships that he experienced.

SEXUAL EXPLORATION VS. SEX OFFENDER

Nick is the last person anyone would have imagined becoming involved in the criminal justice system. He has never acted in an aggressive way towards anyone and prefers solitude to socializing. Others might perceive him as quirky or different, but no one ever has a bad word to say about him. He is simply a kind and gentle soul, or, as one expert stated, just "a good person."

Throughout Nick's life, my wife and I have tried to provide him with the necessary emotional support he needed because of his lack of social interaction with peers. When he was bullied at school or had academic problems, we would do whatever we could to try to alleviate the problem. We frequently met with his teachers, who didn't seem to understand his academic needs and often wrote him off as not trying hard enough, which was not the case. Every week or so another problem would pop up that required our intervention and support.

Children on the autism spectrum tend to be very dependent on their parents and have many needs that can be extremely challenging for parents to meet. This point is well stated in Andrew Solomon's (2012) acclaimed book, *Far from the Tree*. In referencing the disability of autism, he states: "If you have a child with a disability, you are forever the parent of a disabled child; it is one of the primary facts about you, fundamental to the way other people perceive you" (p.6). In other words, you are never free from feeling a sense of responsibility for the wellbeing of your child even as he or she ages through adulthood.

Nick has written honestly about the difficulties he had socializing during his middle and high school years when he wasn't able to engage in the normal friendships or experiences of adolescence, like attending football games, school dances, or parties. Without normal social maturation, Nick experienced sexual identity issues that were beyond my understanding and required professional assistance. Like most parents, I wanted my child to be well liked and accepted by his peers. I wanted him to have friends who would always be welcome at our home. It was deeply painful for me to see Nick suffering as he realized that he didn't fit in with others, and that he felt inferior to his peers, who seemed to enjoy being with each other. With the passing of every year, I hoped that Nick would mature a little more and become able to develop friendships with others. Yet, in reality, as he became older, it only became more difficult and painful for him to develop friendships with his peers. The gap between his intellectual growth and his social immobilization kept widening as time went on. By middle school and then into high school, he became very depressed and isolated. Being the victim of severe bullying and sexual taunting further intensified his dark moods and, as I subsequently learned, contributed to his sexual confusion. I was not aware at the time that he was being sexually harassed. What made matters even worse was that we had no idea what was causing his social adjustment problems as he had not been diagnosed at this time.

During his adolescence, it was difficult for me to think of Nick as a sexual person. He didn't socialize and never expressed any sexual interest in other people. It was obvious that he was lonely and in pain. More than anything, I just wanted him to be happy. To that end, I would take him on trips to simply be away from home. We would attend national tennis tournaments, visit and explore different cities, and go on adventures like whitewater rafting or hiking. My real intent on these ventures was to try to lift his spirits by giving him some breathing room through a change of environment. On these occasions, I would try to engage him in more open conversation about his feelings and inject some words of encouragement.

What I have come to realize is that Nick was and is a sexual person. Although that statement may seem obvious, many people on the autism spectrum are often viewed as asexual when, in reality, they simply have no sexual outlets. Raising a special needs child requires parents to address so many other problems that dealing with the issue of sexuality can easily take a back seat to the more pressing concerns that often arise on a daily basis.

Even under the best of circumstances, sex is never an easy subject for parents to discuss with their children. Through no fault of their own, children on the autism spectrum often lack the social skills to have the experiences necessary during the adolescent years to develop into healthy sexual beings. This lag in Nick's development was a major factor in bringing him into contact with the criminal justice system. Sadly, prosecutors often lack sufficient knowledge about people on the autism spectrum and misinterpret behavior that reflects sexual immaturity rather than the knowing commission of a serious criminal act. I would never want to imply that people on the autism spectrum would likely commit a criminal act involving inappropriate sexual conduct. That would be like saying everyone with autism is a gifted pianist, a brilliant mathematician, or a talented painter, even though those talents might be causally related to being on the autism spectrum. I want to be clear that I am not making any generalizations about people on the autism spectrum. Rather, I hope that sharing Nick's story as well as the research I've uncovered will in some way resonate and be helpful to others.

The truth is, Nick's viewing of adult and child pornography had nothing to do with ever wanting to hurt anyone, but rather reflected his delayed social and sexual development. What was an inappropriate and ill-advised way for Nick to gain more knowledge about sex through the use of his computer in the privacy of his apartment unwittingly resulted in the commission of one of the most serious federal crimes.

Best-selling author John Elder Robison discusses developmental delays in his 2013 article "Autism and porn: A problem no one talks about" in *Psychology Today*. Robison explains:

> Many people with autism experience significant developmental delays, and those delays are often imbalanced and even offset by exceptionalities in other areas. For example, when I was twelve, I had the language skills of a college professor with the social intelligence of a five-year-old... Harmless as that was, it shows the disparity between emotional and logical development that can exist in a person with autism.

The challenge I faced after Nick's arrest was to help Nick's lawyers find the most knowledgeable experts to offer their honest opinions to the prosecutors as to what the most appropriate and reasonable disposition should be for the charges brought against him. I knew I had to do my own research to better understand how to proceed.

Since his diagnosis in 2004, I had put a lot of effort into educating myself on autism spectrum disorders. I attended many autism meetings and had even been a speaker at a national conference. During that time, I had never heard or read any information about autism and sexual development issues. However, after Nick's arrest, what I learned from my research shocked and compelled me to make this information available to those on the autism spectrum, their parents, mental health professionals, and those lawyers who operate our legal system.

AUTISM, SEXUALITY, AND THE LAW: A HIDDEN ISSUE

The first piece of information I came across in my research took my breath away. It was a detailed letter written on August 4, 2008, two years before Nick's arrest, by Ami Klin, Ph.D., who, at the time, was the Harris Professor of Child Psychology and Psychiatry at the Yale Child Study Center and is presently Professor and Division Chief of Autism and Related Disorders at Emory University School of Medicine. Dr. Klin's letter had been sent to a federal judge as well as to the prosecuting attorney and defense lawyer in a case where a defendant with Asperger's was to be sentenced for the crime of possession of child pornography. As one of the nation's leading experts on autism spectrum disorders, Dr. Klin wrote that he had consulted with several individuals with Asperger's who faced the same charge, which "convinced me I was seeing the tip of the iceberg and, indeed, I have since learned that similar cases are beginning to arise in courtrooms around the country" (Klin, 2008a). Dr. Klin expressed his fear that because those in the criminal justice system are unfamiliar with people on the autism spectrum, their behavior is "easy to misinterpret with devastating consequences" (Klin, 2008a). He emphatically stated: "This is an issue of national concern, which I and my colleagues feel compelled to begin to address through a systemic effort to educate stakeholders in the criminal justice system" (Klin, 2008a).

I was stunned that one of the leading experts about autism spectrum disorders in the country was expressing this level of concern and yet I had never heard about the correlation of Asperger's creating a vulnerability to the commission of this crime. I read Dr. Klin's letter shortly after Nick's arrest and was afraid that those in the criminal justice system would not understand someone with Asperger's like Nick. Dr. Klin's letter was extremely illuminating in explaining why those with autism are especially vulnerable to viewing child pornography; I will be referring to this key letter throughout my chapter.

Another document that proved to be of great significance was a report entitled "Joint Study Committee on Autism Spectrum Disorder and Public Safety," that was presented to the North Carolina General Assembly (Parker, 2008). The legislature authorized the University of North Carolina School of Government, in consultation with the Autism Society of North Carolina and other organizations, to study and provide training to those in the legal system who deal with persons with autism. Part of this study generated a document entitled "Autism Principles for Prosecutors." This document, drafted by Michael D. Parker, a North Carolina District Attorney, stated: "Prosecutors should take the nature and effects of autism spectrum disorder (ASD) into account in determining both whether to prosecute and how to resolve a criminal case involving a defendant affected by ASD" (Parker, 2008). The study encouraged prosecutors to seek out ASD experts to help them in "evaluating appropriateness of such cases for prosecution" (Parker, 2008). As for the specific crime of possession of child pornography, the recommendation was:

> Prosecutors should encourage therapeutic intervention…and seriously consider probationary periods and deferred prosecutions to monitor compliance before actual prosecutions in such cases… Prosecutors should pay particular attention to whether the offender has ASD, and whether there is any prior history of directly offending against children. (Parker, 2008)

A separate and independently drafted document entitled "Principles for Prosecutors Considering Child Pornography Charges against Persons with Asperger's Syndrome" (Carley et al., 2008) was sponsored by Dr. Fred Volkmar, Director of the Child Study Center at Yale University and Professor of Pediatrics, of Psychiatry, and of Psychology and Chief of Child Psychiatry at Yale-New Haven Children's Hospital, along with major autism organizations, including the Organization for Autism Research, Asperger Education Network, Connecticut Autism Spectrum

Resource Center, the Global and Regional Asperger Syndrome Partnership, MAAPP Services for Autism and Asperger Syndrome, Asperger's Association of New England, and Asperger Syndrome and High Functioning Autism Association. This document stated that it was generated because "enough cases have arisen to demonstrate the need for prosecutors to inform themselves of the condition and adopt a policy of restraint in the investigation and prosecution of such cases." The "Principles for Prosecutors" puts forth the very same concerns previously stated by Dr. Ami Klin as well as the North Carolina Study:

> Given the lack of social adaption on the part of AS patients, interest in pornography as a means to explore ideas of sexuality…is expected. At these times AS is directly involved in the individual's obliviousness to the social and legal taboos surrounding child pornography and the inability to intuit that the visual depictions are the product of any kind of abusive relationships. This behavior is not predictive of future involvement with child pornography or offenses against children. There is nothing inherent in Autism Spectrum Disorders to make individuals inclined to sexual deviance of any kind… Persons with AS are far less likely to be predators than victims, because of their naiveté and ineptness in interpreting or deflecting the advances of others and their inability to initiate social contact with others or effectively direct or manipulate any social contact. (Carley et al., 2008, pp.1–2)

The document goes on to discuss the need for not pursuing criminal prosecution in these cases:

> Asperger's Syndrome is a lifelong disability which on its own creates substantial hurdles for the patient. Criminal prosecution, conviction and the typical sanctions imposed in such cases are not necessary to protect the public in the case of an AS patient, but they are imponderably harsh, cruel and debilitating to persons with AS and their families on whom they are dependent. Generally these individuals are not a threat to society: it's the other way around. AS patients are frequently the target of abuses… (p.2)

Additionally, I read an important and illuminating recent study that found that adolescents with autism spectrum disorders are clearly vulnerable to being criminally charged as sex offenders (Fenclau et al., 2012). This study examined 37 male juveniles who had been charged with some type of sexual offense and were thoroughly evaluated to determine whether any of them were on the autism spectrum. The findings showed that 22 of the 37 defendants (60%) were diagnosed to be on the autism spectrum. The authors concluded: "Given the current findings showing the presence of individuals with ASD in the sex offender population, it is clear that the acquisition of sexual knowledge and development of individuals with ASD should be further examined" (p.8).

My research also included a detailed article by Natalie Gougeon (2010) that explored the sexual development and conduct of autistic people. Gougeon recognized that ASD individuals are sexual beings who have difficulties in their sexual development due to their social disability. She states: "While individuals with autism do present with development delays in many areas (referring in part to sexual development), their physical development is not equally delayed" (p.354). This finding certainly applied to Nick. As he got older, his physical development matured like others his age, yet his social and sexual development did not.

Besides the gap between physical and social/sexual development, there is also a divide between intellectual and social/sexual development. This was also true of Nick. He could easily write and deliver a brilliant two-hour presentation at a national conference, but was too uncomfortable to socialize with the organizers afterwards. In high school, he was captain of his tennis team but never fraternized with any of his teammates. Dr. Klin (2008a) comments on this gap:

> Asperger Syndrome is a disability of social cognition, social learning and communication... Adults, even those with high measured intelligence, may in a practical sense function like much younger children both emotionally and in their adaptive (life skills) behavior. Expectations for their understanding, skills and abilities are misplaced if development is based on IQ and chronological age.

Some other information I learned came not from research but from others going through similar circumstances. Over the past three years, I have received numerous calls from distraught parents referred to me by the Child Study Center, Yale University, the Asperger's Association of New England, and others. These parents contacted me because their adult sons had Asperger's and had been arrested for possession of child pornography. Although each case may have had some differences, there were striking similarities. These young men, who were all intelligent, in college or college graduates, in their 20s and 30s, had been socially isolated their entire lives and had no sexual experience. In none of these cases, as was true for Nick, was there concern that any of these individuals had inappropriate sexual contact with children. These parents told me their sons were not aware of the legal consequences of viewing child pornography or that they had even committed a crime. Talking to all these desperate parents made me extremely sad, but also increased my awareness that Nick's case was not an isolated one. In addition, I did some legal research and found many reported cases in both federal and state courts involving males on the autism spectrum charged with possession of child pornography. In these cases, I read forensic psychological reports that were similar to the ones written about Nick.

Some of the parents with whom I spoke had sons who were currently serving time in prison and unable to cope with incarceration. I received one call from a woman whose nephew had been sent to federal prison for possession of child pornography. He could not deal with the harsh complexities of prison and eventually had to be put in solitary confinement, where his life became unbearable. In his 2008 letter, Dr. Klin wrote: "It is, frankly, horrifying to contemplate what would happen to someone with this disability in a penal institution" (Klin, 2008a).

Former Judge Kimberly Taylor, Gary Mesibov, Ph.D., and Dennis Debbaudt in their 2009 article, "Asperger Syndrome in the Criminal Justice System," reinforced my sense that many of those on the spectrum charged with sex offenses were unaware that they were even committing a crime. Taylor, Mesibov, and Debbault write:

> People with AS often get into trouble without even realizing they have committed an offense. Offenses such as…child pornography and stalking…would certainly strike most of society as offenses that demand some sort of punishment. This assumption…may not take into account the particular issues that challenge an ASD individual.

John Elder Robison also states in the previously quoted article that autistic defendants who are charged in sex crime cases "needed much more help than punishment. Ignoring that reality is like ignoring the teachers who locked autistic people in basements at school when I was a kid" (2013).

In light of all the new information I was acquiring, I wasn't surprised to learn of the serious concern Asperger's/autism organizations and leading experts in autism spectrum disorders had about autistic defendants within the criminal justice system. These organizations and professionals are rightly worried about the harsh and unnecessary prosecutions and lengthy prison terms people on the autism spectrum frequently receive who are convicted of possession of child pornography.

To be completely clear, I am an ardent proponent of the legal system ensuring and protecting the safety and the best interests of children. I strongly believe that those convicted of sex offenses deserve appropriate punishment. When children or adults are sexually victimized, those who perpetrate these acts should be prosecuted through the criminal justice system. At the same time, I also believe that our draconian approach to sex offenses often leads to an unjust and "one size fits all" approach to punishment. Just as our children need to be protected by our laws, so do our developmentally disabled who don't intend to cause harm to anyone. That protection is not being afforded to those on the autism spectrum. My research revealed that those with AS were unnecessarily prosecuted for behavior that is clearly related to their disability and who do not pose any threat or danger to others. In these cases, compassion coupled with an appropriate treatment plan to rehabilitate and educate the person with ASD should be considered as a preferable alternative to a felony conviction with the possibility of prison and registration as a sex offender.

From the moment Nick was charged with this crime, I wanted to protect him from the severe consequences of the criminal justice system. I was aware that the charges brought against him could result in a prison sentence as long as ten years. That realization was surreal and frightening beyond words. The only thing that I could do was to hire an attorney who understood autism and was determined to educate the prosecutors about its significant relationship to the criminal charges Nick faced. The power of the federal government is massive and overwhelming. The fact that I could not protect Nick from the ongoing terror he was experiencing was a source of great sorrow and frustration for me.

Nick was fortunate to have lawyers who recognized the importance of him being evaluated by the most credible experts who would be able to educate the prosecutors about how his deficits may have contributed to the acts that brought him into the criminal justice system. For Nick, looking at adult and child pornography was a safe and solitary way to learn about his own sexuality. Because of his social disability, he was unable to acquire that experience through direct social contact with other people. Nick's use of his computer was the way he customarily acquired information about the outside world. The computer was like his auxiliary brain. Dr. Klin (2008a) elaborates on this notion:

> The Internet can be explored from the apparent security and privacy of one's own room. Most individuals with Asperger Syndrome are very socially isolated. Curious about sex, it is not surprising that a person with Asperger Syndrome would explore the abundant supply of erotic material freely available on the Internet. The problem arises, of course, because the material that is available on the Internet— and which is designed to attract attention and encourage interest— includes unlawful depictions of underage children.

Perhaps one could argue that it makes sense that prosecutors would have difficulty understanding how someone like Nick, a college graduate with advanced degrees, could also be so naïve. It could be confusing that someone could have such intellectual strengths while at the same time having such serious social impairments. Without a clear explanation of asynchronous (uneven) development, prosecutors and judges might have difficulty understanding those on the autism spectrum.

After the FBI searched Nick's unit, it took 26 months for the prosecution to formally charge him with one count of possession of child pornography. The reason for this long delay was that the prosecutors saw Nick as presenting a special case. Rather than immediately putting Nick's case on the trial docket, they were willing to review relevant expert evaluations about Nick in deciding whether to prosecute him. This type of review, termed prosecutorial discretion, reflects the fact that not every person charged with a crime needs to or should be prosecuted. Nick's lawyers strongly believed that, using this discretion, the prosecutors' only way to achieve justice was to place Nick in a diversion program. This option would have permitted Nick to meet the terms of a probationary period and receive helpful counseling, and at the end of that period he would not have any criminal record.

As a recognized expert in legal ethics, having taught and researched the subject for decades, I understood that prosecutors are considered "Ministers of Justice." This designation is at the heart of their job, requiring them to use their prosecutorial discretion to seek a just result. That understanding of the role of a prosecutor gave me hope.

Five different experts, two of them selected by the prosecution, evaluated Nick. Each of these experts intensively questioned him about his most private sexual thoughts. I would like to share some of their most important findings and opinions, since this was the information that was made available to the prosecutors to make their final determination as to Nick's fate.

THE EXPERTS
The Defense Experts

The first expert the defense lawyers consulted was the psychologist Nick had been seeing regularly for almost nine years. Dr. Green (not his real name) is a highly regarded clinical psychologist who specializes in human sexuality. He stated in the conclusion of his report:

> Having worked closely with this young man over the last nine years, I can say in complete honesty that he is not only a very decent human being, but in light of his considerable impairment, a true innocent. I hope the prosecution can exercise not only the compassion but also the courage to spare this young man not only incarceration but the further inordinate burdens that would go along with a felony conviction.

Nick was also examined and tested by Dr. Andrew Maltz, a highly respected forensic psychologist who specializes in autism spectrum disorders. In his report to the prosecutors, he stated:

> Mr. Dubin has never been aggressive towards others. He has never, prior to the aforementioned complaint, been in trouble with the law. He has been vulnerable to others because of his inability to appreciate intent, and, to that end, he was exploited by his peer group as either an object of aggression or entertainment.

Dr. Maltz also commented on the results of his extensive psychological testing of Nick:

> He does not have a personality profile, in any way that is consistent for individuals who are antisocial or psychopathic. His profile is not characteristic for individuals who will manipulate others, take advantage of others or lack a conscience regarding their behaviors… Mr. Dubin does not think of children as sexual objects in a manner consistent for [adults] with sexual drives who have, for unfortunate

reasons, attached their interests to young children. It is highly unlikely for him to intentionally or purposefully plan or engage in bringing harm to anyone.

The third expert to examine Nick was Dr. Fred Volkmar of Yale University. Nick met with Dr. Volkmar who, after taking an extensive history and reading all relevant prior records, opined that a criminal conviction would be inappropriate. Dr. Volkmar determined that Nick, even with above-average intellectual skills, has, because of his neurological disability, severely delayed socially. He stated in his report: "Individuals with Asperger's disorder and autism have problems with social understanding, social learning and communication." He did not believe that Nick belonged in the criminal justice system, but would do well with properly administered therapy. He explains why Nick should receive appropriate psychological treatment as opposed to criminal prosecution:

> Most individuals with these conditions are victims rather than victimizers. The experience of bullying and social isolation is frequent. The sometimes rigid pursuit of collecting things often appears to mask or attempt to cope with chronic anxiety... Fortunately, individuals with these conditions can respond to clear limit setting and a neuropsychologically informed psychotherapy where explicit guidance is provided. Nicolas appears both highly suited to such an approach and motivated to engage in it.

The extensive reports from these three highly qualified experts and the FBI's analysis of the content on Nick's computer were submitted to the prosecutors. Based upon this information, prosecutors offered Nick an agreement to plead guilty to one count of possession of child pornography and probation. However, this agreement would cause Nick to have a lifelong felony conviction and register as a sex offender. Nick's lawyers strongly advocated that this plea offer was not appropriate, and in conflict with the recommendations from the experts that he be placed on diversion, receive therapy, and have no criminal record.

When that offer was refused, the prosecutors then informed Nick's lawyers that they didn't really understand how Asperger's differed from a mental illness. Nick's lawyers agreed to provide additional information to help the prosecutors understand that difference. Drs. Green and Maltz wrote supplementary reports that explained in very clear terms how Asperger's, unlike a mental illness, is a pervasive neurological and developmental disorder that begins at birth and causes a widening gap over time between a person's intellectual capacity and his emotional, social, and sexual development. They also detailed how being on the autism spectrum impacted Nick's social and sexual development. When these supplemental reports were presented to the prosecutors, their contents and conclusions were never disputed. However, the prosecutors still refused to change their plea offer to Nick, requiring him to be a felon and a registered sex offender.

The Prosecution Experts

Nick's lawyers were very confident in the integrity and credibility of the experts who had examined Nick and their resulting opinions and recommendations. Yet when Nick's lawyers asked the prosecutors whether any of their experts had reviewed the reports, the prosecutors admitted that these reports had not been so examined. Nick's lawyers encouraged the prosecutors therefore to select their own expert to review the previously submitted reports. A month later, the prosecutors contacted Nick's lawyers and requested that Nick travel to the J. Edgar Hoover FBI Building in Washington D.C. to be examined by an FBI neuropsychologist who specialized in autism spectrum disorders. This FBI neuropsychologist worked for the FBI as Clinical Program Manager for the Office for Victim Assistance. In other words, he supervised the programs that offered assistance to children who were the victims of child pornography. The prosecutors informed Nick's lawyer at that time that this examination would provide the last information they would need to make a decision on the disposition of Nick's case.

Nick's lawyers believed that this offer was a positive sign that the prosecutors were trying to understand the special circumstances of this case. Consequently, a month later, Nick and I flew to Washington D.C. where he submitted to an intensive six-hour examination with the FBI neuropsychologist who had clearly reviewed all the previously submitted evaluations about Nick. At the end of this exhausting day for Nick, the FBI neuropsychologist indicated to us that, upon the request of the prosecutor, he would write a report about his examination to assist the prosecution and the presiding judge. Nick and I gave our consent for him to do so.

After waiting with great anxiety every day for the next four months for a response from the prosecutors, Nick's lawyers finally initiated a phone call to them. The prosecutors told Nick's lawyers that the FBI neuropsychologist had basically agreed with the defense experts' opinions, test results, and recommendation that Nick not be prosecuted as a criminal but rather be placed on diversion. Yet, despite what initially appeared to be good news, the prosecutors were still not willing to drop their prosecution. Our family was shocked. Not only were the prosecutors disregarding their own expert's assessment, but they were also unwilling even to request a written report from him. I was starting to wonder why they had even sent Nick to Washington D.C. in the first place.

Nick's lawyers were sufficiently concerned that they decided to go above the assistant prosecutors who were handling the case and appeal directly to their superior, the U.S. Attorney. A meeting was scheduled with the U.S. Attorney, the chief of the criminal division, and the assistant prosecutors who had been handling Nick's case. At this meeting, Nick's lawyers argued that all the experts, including the government's, had agreed that diversion was an appropriate adjudication for Nick. The U.S. Attorney consented to further consider this matter. Nick's lawyers were encouraged. The prosecutors then called Nick's lawyers later that same day saying that the U.S. Attorney now wanted Nick to be examined by yet another psychologist.

It seemed unfair that Nick was going to have to endure another intense examination, especially so soon after the FBI neuropsychologist's evaluation. At first, the prosecutors told Nick's lawyers that this next examiner should have sufficient expertise in autism spectrum disorders to conduct a fair evaluation. That statement reassured our lawyers that the prosecutors were acting in good faith. However, shortly thereafter, the prosecutors reversed course and told Nick's lawyers they were insisting on a particular forensic psychologist, who was not an expert in autism spectrum disorders, to conduct the examination. This forensic psychologist was well known and often testified in high-profile cases on behalf of the prosecution. After another agonizing four-month wait, the prosecutors finally scheduled an appointment for Nick to see him.

The examination lasted over six hours and included additional psychological testing. A month later, a copy of the forensic psychologist's report was sent directly to Nick's lawyers. The report stated that after the personality tests he performed on Nick.

neither test profile points to the likelihood of antisocial attitudes or behaviors, any tendency to act in defiance of social norms and the rights of others, or any propensity to lose impulse control generally... Mr. Dubin's developmental problems, and the limitations they have imposed, may well have a bearing on the behavior in question, namely accessing child pornography.

The forensic psychologist concluded his report with important words of advice to the prosecutors:

In fact, there does not appear to be any basis for concluding that he [Nick] is at any particular risk of sex offending... What Mr. Dubin is accused of doing... is not sexual offending in any case... Mr. Dubin faces substantial challenges in making his way in the world, achieving a greater level of social connectedness and independence, and finding ways to cope with the depression and anxiety that his developmental disorder has produced. He had not proceeded without misstep and error, but he does appear to be strongly motivated to do better and to make use of the support and opportunities for advancement he has been given. It is worthwhile, from all points of view, for him to continue without the imposition of new impediments, particularly ones that would limit his access to social support and opportunities for social learning. His path is hard enough as it is.

His recommendation to the prosecutors who had hired him was not to impose any "new impediments" on Nick. The prosecutors rejected that advice, along with the conclusions of all the other experts. They again insisted that Nick enter a plea that would require him to be a convicted felon and register as a sex offender. It seems clear that the government's own forensic psychologist did not want this result having recognized that Nick was not a sex offender.

In the end, the prosecutors had Nick submit to two comprehensive examinations by experts they selected and then did not accept the recommendations of these experts. With a plea agreement offered for no prison but a felony conviction and registration as a sex offender, the only option left was for Nick to go to trial. However, after two and a half years of unrelenting stress and anxiety as well as his physical health being negatively impacted, Nick was worn down. He lacked the emotional stability and physical stamina to endure the rigors of a trial. At this point, even Nick's lawyers had to recommend that he take the plea. Like the vast majority of those facing prosecution for alleged sex offenses, he took a plea and his fate was sealed. He was to become a convicted felon and registered sex offender.

THE GOVERNMENT'S SENTENCING MEMORANDUM

Before a defendant is sentenced in federal court, prosecutors prepare a memorandum providing the judge with pertinent information about the case. In that memorandum, prosecutors in Nick's case acknowledged the following:

> [His] history is replete with difficult and unfortunate hardships directly related to Asperger's Syndrome…that he has…continually suffered from anxiety and depression; symptoms commonly associated with Asperger's Syndrome…and that he has had limited intimate relationships as he suffered with severe social deficits that are at the foundation of the disorder of Autism. (Sentencing Memorandum filed by the United States Attorneys in the case of *United States v. Nicolas Dubin*, Eastern District of Michigan, 2013)

The memorandum also recognized the gap between Nick's intellectual and social development: "Despite impressive academic and professional accomplishments, Defendant has remained dependent on his parents and…use of his computer was a way for someone like Nick to learn about sexuality…without suffering the laborious and uncomfortable contact with real people."

In addition, the prosecutors credited Nick for his diligence in seeking the therapeutic help he needed:

> Due to his Asperger's Syndrome, Defendant has regularly participated in therapy and appears to continue to successfully address his particular needs. Defendant has no criminal record and no history of aggression or violence… Defendant has taken steps to help himself beyond what was required of him by Pre-Trial Services. The government is satisfied that Defendant's post-arrest conduct has demonstrated his respect for the law.

The prosecutors' statements about Nick reflect their acceptance of the findings of the experts who examined him: above-average intellect, below-average adaptive functions, respect for the law, no criminal record, no prior acts of aggression, not a sexual predator, and the progress he made toward rehabilitation. Although the prosecutors acknowledged the findings on which the experts based their recommendation not to convict Nick for possession of child pornography, I was deeply saddened that they came to such a different conclusion.

The federal judge before whom Nick appeared at sentencing stated on the record that he was convinced that Nick would not be a repeat offender. He also acknowledged his previous work record history was "impressive."

THE IMPACT ON OUR LIVES

Nick's conviction and registration as a sex offender has shattered our family. Since the day the FBI searched Nick's apartment and throughout the subsequent criminal proceedings, Nick was severely traumatized and our lives have been turned upside down. I have spent hours with him trying to confront his depression head on, discussing his bleak thoughts, and trying to find hope in a very dark future landscape. It has been a very lonely and scary period that defies most other human experiences.

The federal prosecutors, who have enormous power over people's lives, had the opportunity to see that justice was served in a way that would have both protected the public and prevented imposing an unnecessary and almost insurmountable obstacle on Nick's already challenged life. Their decision has caused great personal suffering and psychological damage to our family.

MY CONCLUSIONS

What I have come to realize is that the laws relating to possession of child pornography and sex offender registration are not only grossly unfair to people with autism and other developmental disabilities, but to all people. Prior to 1980, there was no federal legislation that prohibited possession of child pornography. With these images easily accessed on a computer, the laws have dramatically increased over the years so that within a very short time it became one of the most serious and fastest-growing federal crimes resulting in federal incarceration.

As for sex registration laws, they have developed based upon a few high-profile murders of children and have now been shown to be ineffective and unnecessarily punitive to those registrants. As in Nick's case, the prosecutors acknowledged that he posed no danger to others, but required him to be publicly listed as a sexual predator, further limiting where he could work or live.

I will let the other contributing writers in this book establish the truthfulness of my above conclusions and will present other sources as references at the end of this chapter to provide additional information for the disbelievers.

ADVICE TO PARENTS, MENTAL HEALTH PROFESSIONALS, CRIMINAL DEFENSE LAWYERS, PROSECUTORS, JUDGES, AND CONGRESS AND STATE LEGISLATURES

I am aware that others throughout this book will be offering advice to various groups of people. Without wanting to be redundant, but rather for emphasis, the advice I have to offer is from the perspective of being a lawyer and Nick's father, so I ask that you please keep my unique perspective in mind when reading the following.

To Parents

I know the love and dedication that is required of parents raising a child on the autism spectrum. There are so many issues that are extremely difficult to navigate. I have great admiration for parents who work hard to find and pay for necessary services while helping their children deal with the many social, sensory, speech and language, and other issues that can arise. With my deepest respect for these special and dedicated parents, let me offer this advice in light of our family's heart-breaking experience:

- Recognize that your child is a sexual being. Although it may be difficult to deal with your child's sexual issues, don't ignore them. Seek professional help if necessary. Current research indicates that a variety of problems can arise with respect to sexual development for those on the autism spectrum.

- Make clear to your child that certain behaviors could lead to an encounter with the criminal justice system and even to imprisonment. These behaviors include viewing child pornography on the internet, stalking, unwanted touching, having meltdowns in public, and indecent exposure. Your child must understand the severe legal consequences that can occur when these types of charges are brought against people on the autism spectrum who may not understand that they were even committing a criminal act. It may be appropriate to place restraints on your child's computer to ensure only lawful use.

- Nick's case was processed under the federal law of the United States. Although most countries criminalize possession of child pornography, the elements of the crime, the possible defenses, and the potential prison sentences are not uniformly followed. Parents should become familiar with the laws pertaining to child pornography in the country in which they reside.

- Be sure your child knows that if he or she is ever confronted by the police, with respect to having committed a crime, he or she should be polite and ask for a lawyer to be present without making any further statements. The trusting and naïve nature of people on the autism spectrum, who typically want to please authority, make them easy candidates to be taken advantage of by trained police officers who can question them without the protection of a lawyer. The law allows police officers to make certain false statements in order to get a confession that can and will be used against the person. There is also the danger that false confessions can occur. It is always best to have a lawyer present to represent the interests of a person on the autism spectrum before making any statements to law enforcement personnel.

To Mental Health Professionals

Those on the autism spectrum have certain unique needs that even the most experienced therapists may not understand or be familiar with. It is extremely important for therapists who are treating these clients to undertake the responsibility of educating themselves about people with ASD, their sexual and social development, and the proper ways to provide treatment. Dr. Klin (2008a) states:

Individuals with Asperger Syndrome benefit from behavioral intervention that provides them with clear instruction, explicit rules, and an understanding of the reasons for those rules… This intervention can be done by an experienced mental health professional, and there are specific curricula for such interventions in the area of sexuality… The individual's conduct should be monitored for compliance and positive feedback should be provided in response to his understanding of the situation.

It is essential for therapists to check in regularly with their ASD clients about sexual issues and to repeatedly reinforce the reasons for not viewing child pornography, including the harm done to the children during the production of this material. Dr. Klin explains:

Because of their disability, individuals with Asperger Syndrome would be likely to miss the connection between consuming child pornography and supporting the exploitation of children. Because of their difficulty reading emotion and understanding non-verbal communication, the person with AS would have difficulty recognizing or would entirely miss the emotions of fear, anxiety and discomfort on the faces of children in the pictures… Non-verbal communication that most people recognize and respond to intuitively is unseen by those with autism spectrum disorders. (2008a)

High-functioning autism can cause a disconnect between intelligence and social understanding. Dr. Tony Attwood explained how this gap is a developmental issue for a person on the autism spectrum like Nick Dubin in the book he co-authored with Dr. Isabelle Henault and Nick Dubin, *The Autism Spectrum, Sexuality and the Law* (Attwood *et al.*, 2014, p.135):

Two further significant characteristics of Asperger's Syndrome would have had a direct impact on Nick's viewing of child pornography. Psychologists use the term "impaired Theory of Mind" to describe a difficulty in understanding and appreciating the perspective, thoughts and experiences of another person. Nick would have had greater difficulty than a typical adult appreciating the perspective, thoughts and experiences of another person. Nick would have had greater difficulty than a typical adult appreciating the perspective and experiences of the child in the photograph or movie. There would have been a sense of emotional detachment while he was viewing those images on his computer.

Dr. Attwood further explained that the additional characteristic of impaired executive functioning would have caused Nick "difficulty appreciating the broader perspective of his actions and consequences to himself" (p.135).

These characteristics described by Dr. Attwood reinforce why mental health professionals need to be knowledgeable about the unique ways in which people on the autism spectrum will understand the grave dangers of learning about sex by viewing illegal images. Dr. Klin in his August 4, 2008 letter to a federal judge stated that the type of mental health intervention needed for an AS person requires "clear instruction, explicit rules, and an understanding of the reasons for those rules" (Klin, 2008a).

Academic psychologists also need to establish and support a joint program in higher education that combines expertise and knowledge in autism spectrum disorders with human sexuality. It is difficult to find an expert in one of these fields who also has expertise in the other field. Yet for the proper therapeutic treatment of people on the autism spectrum, the treating professional needs to be knowledgeable in both disciplines.

To Criminal Defense Lawyers

It is imperative that those in the criminal justice system be aware of the current statistic from the Centers for Disease Control and Prevention that one out of every 40 males is currently diagnosed on the autism spectrum. Based on the information presented in this chapter, a high likelihood exists that there will be a much greater interface between the criminal justice system and those on the autism spectrum. There are a whole host of issues that criminal defense lawyers will need to understand in defending autistic clients. Nick was fortunate to have criminal defense lawyers who undertook a comprehensive study of autism and how that condition and resulting life history were related to the criminal charges in question, in addition to the resources needed to pay for attorneys and evaluations. The absence of an attorney willing to understand the relationship of autism to the criminal charges would have significantly increased the likelihood that Nick would have been sent to prison. I am eternally grateful that he was not incarcerated. Knowing my son and his disability as I do, I feel strongly that Nick would not have been able to survive that experience. There are many legal questions that are currently being raised throughout the country about how autism can impact criminal responsibility. It is critical to understand this cutting-edge issue and to not handle cases in a one-size-fits-all fashion.

Defense lawyers also need to be aware that those on the autism spectrum who are charged with a crime will be highly anxious, depressed, and in need of compassionate counsel. Lawyers need to take into account the emotional needs of the autistic client who finds dealing with uncertainty, especially of this magnitude, unbearable.

To Prosecutors

Having been a lawyer for over five decades, I have seen how being a long-time prosecutor can cause one to see all people charged with crimes as dangerous criminals who need to be convicted and shown no mercy. This attitude can deprive a prosecutor of appropriate compassion when it comes to exercising prosecutorial discretion. Law without compassion can be cruel. Compassion without law can be dangerous. I urge prosecutors to keep in check the tremendous power they possess and use discretion wisely when dealing with people on the autism spectrum charged with crimes. Compassion can often help in making good decisions and achieving justice with the finest degree of discernment. When appropriate, prosecutors can help people on the autism spectrum rehabilitate their lives, rather than labeling them as criminals. Justice doesn't always mean getting a felony conviction. As Dr. Ami Klin (2008b) stated:

> While the criminal justice system judges conduct assuming that adults possess reasonable common sense and an understanding of what is right and what is wrong, the ability of the individual with Asperger Syndrome to make those judgments is severely disrupted. It is not that persons with Asperger Syndrome lack values. Rather, their developmental disorder impacts their appreciation of these things without explicit instruction or clear rules.

I strongly recommend that prosecutors read the following from the letter Dr. Klin wrote to his colleagues at the Yale Child Studies Center to address a "public policy crisis" faced by individuals with AS and their families. The letter offers a clear perspective and sound advice to attorneys prosecuting AS defendants in child pornography cases:

> The prosecution of child pornography cases is a high priority for both the Department of Justice and state prosecutors. The state and federal laws originally targeted those who produced and distributed child pornography, which in turn is based on the raw sexual exploitation

of children. The laws are also directed at those who purchase child pornography, on the reasoning that purchasers provide the economic incentive to produce child pornography. However, in recent years many prosecutions are directed at those who have obtained such material for free over the Internet, or simply viewed them on the Internet. (Klin, 2008b)

The basis for spreading the net so far is the belief that those who have an interest in such materials are pedophiles and present a risk to children. Indeed, this presumption of dangerousness is so strong that there is no process in child pornography prosecutions for distinguishing between those who are truly predatory pedophiles and those who are not pedophiles, with no interest in inappropriate contact with children. It is no defense to a charge of possessing child pornography that the accused is not a danger to children.

As a result of all this, the experience in most cases we are aware of is that it is very difficult to get prosecutors to forego prosecution in these cases. Prosecutors are focused on the possibility, however remote, that an accused might be a danger to children. There is tremendous political pressure to be harsh on "child pornographers" and there is virtually no voice for restraint.

Like most people, prosecutors judge behavior from a perspective which assumes common sense and an understanding of what is acceptable and what is not. When it comes to defendants with disabilities, and there are many, prosecutors often view this as something that may evoke sympathy for the plight of the accused, but which does not affect culpability. Prosecutors find the features of Asperger's syndrome especially hard to accept in child pornography cases because they run counter to the presumption of dangerousness. They find it hard to grasp that the suspect who appears high-functioning is so socially immature and unable to pick up on the social taboos and legal rules which these laws enforce.

Having demonized those possessing child pornography as child predators, it is hard to accept the idea that the accused Asperger's patient is, in such significant ways (such as in their severe limitations in understanding implicit mores and regulations that are common sense in our culture—and from the standpoint of social judgment), just a child himself whose interest in the sexual images of children does not fit the stereotype. They find it hard to accept what is typically true, that all such an individual needed was to have been told very concretely, very literally, and very firmly that this behavior is unacceptable.

The outcomes of cases involving Asperger's sufferers are deeply tragic. These individuals would be required to register as a sex offender after completion of their sentences. In most states, they would be unable to reside near any school, playground, or day care center, which gets very problematic if they need to live with family, as many Asperger's patients do, and their residence falls within a prohibited area.

All these consequences would be difficult enough for a "neurotypical" person. For the individual with Asperger's syndrome, these impediments will be piled on top of disabilities that, on their own, will be already difficult to manage throughout their lives.

Federal and state prosecutors have the authority to "defer prosecution." That is, before or after arrest they can reach an agreement with a person that he will comply with certain conditions, over a period of usually up to 18 months, whereupon the charges would be dismissed. This would allow a prosecutor time to ensure that the individual is getting treatment, and does not present a risk to children, before writing off the charges. We need the Department of Justice and state prosecutors to adopt a policy of deferring prosecution in appropriate cases.

To Judges

Judges also need to use their discretion wisely. They have a tremendous amount of power over the lives of the people who come before them. There are people on the autism spectrum who pose no danger whatsoever and are still incarcerated for long periods of time and are required to register as sex offenders upon release. Sending harmless people on the spectrum to prison illustrates that prosecutors and judges lack an understanding of the lifelong and devastating impact this punishment will have on them and their families.

When the federal judge sentenced Nick, he said he had learned something new from reading the pre-sentence report, which was that Asperger's was neurological in origin and not a mental illness. This judge showed that he had a willingness to learn about autism spectrum disorders. I wish all judges would adopt this same attitude.

To Congress and State Legislatures

Recognize that you have passed laws pertaining to possession of child pornography and sex offender registration that are irrational when viewed in the light of the low recidivism rates for sex offenders and the lack of dangerousness of most people convicted of child pornography possession. The laws unnecessarily ruin the lives of many harmless people who are not likely to reoffend.

A PLEA FOR CHANGE IN THE LEGAL SYSTEM

Mark Mahoney, an attorney in Buffalo, New York, who has defended several AS defendants in child pornography cases, wrote an extensive document entitled *Asperger's Syndrome and the Criminal Law: The Special Case of Child Pornography* (2009), which is available on the internet. Here is the conclusion to Mahoney's well-researched document:

> There is no tragedy without hope. Individuals with AS and their families hope for a "normal" life, but they have great difficulties in achieving that dream. In part this is due not to the inherent nature of the disability, but the misunderstanding of the individual by those who cannot understand how a person with apparently normal intelligence could not appreciate the oddness, or the apparently deviant appearance of their behavior. There cannot be a more tragic example of this than the AS individual who, because of his greater skill and comfort and trust in the world of his computer and the internet, and because of his obliviousness to legally-created taboos, wanders into child pornography. He is a victim of a marketing scheme to which his disability makes him the most susceptible and he is at the same time most easily caught because of his naiveté as to how his computer has been opened to the world. At that point he is exposed to criminal conviction and the harshest civil disabilities devised which can literally ruin his entire life. (pp.68–69)

While prosecutors and judges "have heard it all before" when it comes to people "excusing" misbehavior, including the possession of child pornography, the unique features predominant in AS, together with the backdrop of hysteria, sentiment, and fervor concerning child pornography, create a "perfect storm" in which AS individuals and their families are engulfed. This unique diagnosis calls upon prosecutors and courts to draw distinctions between dangerous and non-dangerous offenders and between those who may access offending depictions because they need to, as opposed to those who simply do not know better. Generally, AS individuals should not be charged at all. It is totally unnecessary. If they are charged, every effort should be expended to avoid civil disabilities of incarceration, and to ensure treatment suitable to the AS diagnosis.

In order to avoid such "perfect storms," the "experts" and advocates in the field, trying to bring hope to these individuals, need to help inform the legislators, prosecutors, and judges, so that they can make informed decisions in this area so ripe for tragedy.

THE ROAD AHEAD

Standing beside Nick at his sentencing hearing in federal court was an excruciatingly painful moment for me. My heart stopped beating when the court clerk called out, "United States v. Nicolas Dubin." I thought to myself: I will not accept, and, in fact, I explicitly reject, the United States Government publicly labeling Nick as a felon and a sex offender.

As with every other instance in his life where someone has misunderstood him, I am encouraging Nick not to let others define him as a person. I hope all parents of children on the autism spectrum will reinforce this important message to their children: Do not let other people define you. Nick has been given a label that doesn't fit him. My goals for now, and in the long road ahead, are to help Nick believe in himself again, to increase awareness of this important subject, and to advocate for change in the legal system.

FINAL THOUGHTS

As Emily Horowitz outlines in Chapter 5, the public does not benefit from having an onerous sex registration system, and the Federal Sixth Circuit Court of Appeals in 2016 agreed with her stated empirical research. In the case of Doe v. Snyder (15-1536/2346/2486), decided on August 25, 2016, the prominent and highly respected Judge Batchelder found the Michigan Sex Registration system to be punitive and subject to the *ex post facto* of the United States Constitution. The opinion also states that the court record established "significant doubt" about a high recidivism from sex offenders. Even more striking, the court described:

[a] regulatory regime that severely restricts where people can live, work and "loiter," that categorizes them into tiers ostensibly corresponding to present dangerousness without any individualized assessment thereof, and that requires time-consuming and cumbersome in-person reporting, all supported by—at best—scant evidence that such restrictions serve the professed purpose of keeping Michigan communities safe…

I can only hope that people who have been unnecessarily punished by the criminal justice system, who have paid and will suffer by being convicted of a crime, do not need to be denied the right of rehabilitation and entry back into society without any real public benefit. Furthermore, even more outrageous is to saddle the disability that *Doe v. Snyder* acknowledges is imposed by being a sex registrant on a person who has a developmental disability that is related to the conduct that was deemed criminal.

REFERENCES

Attwood, T. Hénault, I., and Dubin, N. (2014) *The Autism Spectrum, Sexuality and the Law*. London: Jessica Kinglsey Publishers.

Carley, M.J., Gerhardt, P., Jekel, D., Klin, A., *et al.* (2008) *Principles for Prosecutors Considering Child Pornography Charges against Persons with Asperger's Syndrome*. Available at www.harringtonmahoney. com/content/Publications/Principles%20for%20Prosecutors%20-%209-14-08.pdf (accessed January 12, 2017).

Fenclau, E., Huang, A., Hughes, T., Lehman, C., *et al.* (2013) "Identifying individuals with autism in a state facility for adolescents adjudicated as sexual offenders: A pilot study." *Focus on Autism and Other Developmental Disabilities 28*, 3, 1–9.

Gougeon, N. (2010) "Sexuality and autism: A critical review of small selected literature using a social-relational model of disability." *American Journal of Sexuality Education 5*, 4, 328–361.

Klin, A. (2008a) Letter dated August 4, 2008 to United States District Judge Richard Bennett for a sentencing hearing of defendant who was on the autism spectrum and convicted of possession of child pornography.

Klin, A. (2008b) Letter dated August 22, 2008 to his colleagues at the Child Study Center, Yale University.

Mahoney, M. (2009) *Asperger's Syndrome and the Criminal Law: The Special Case of Child Pornography*. Available at www.harringtonmahoney.com/content/Publications/Aspergers%20Syndrome%20 and%20the%20Criminal%20Law%20v26.pdf (accessed January 12, 2017).

Parker, M. (2008) University of North Carolina School of Government, "Joint Study Committee on Autism Spectrum Disorder and Public Safety." *North Carolina General Assembly*, 1–3.

Robison, J.E. (2013) "Autism and porn: A problem no one talks about." *Psychology Today*, August 6, 2013.

Solomon, A. (2012) *Far from the Tree: Parents, Children and the Search for Identity*. New York, NY: Scribner.

Taylor, K., Mesibov, G., and Debbaudt, D. (2009) "Asperger Syndrome in the criminal justice system." Available at www.aane.org/asperger-syndrome-criminal-justice-system (accessed January 12, 2017).

SUPPLEMENTAL READING

Ackerman, A.R. and Burns, M. (2016) "Bad data: How government agencies distort statistics on sex-crime recidivism." *Justice Policy Journal 13*, 1, 1–23.

Aviv, R. (2014) "The science of sex abuse." *The New Yorker*, January 14, 2013.

Calleja, N. (2016) "Deconstructing a puzzling relationship: Sex offender legislation, the crimes that inspired it, and sustained moral panic." *Justice Policy Journal 13*, 1, 1–17.

Douard, J. (2008–2009) "Sex offender as scapegoat: The monstrous other within." *New York Law School Law Review 53*, 31.

Ellman, I.M. (2015) "Frightening and high": The Supreme Court's crucial mistake about sex crime statistics." *Constitutional Commentary 30*, 495–508.

Ewing, C.P. (2011) *Justice Perverted: Sex Offense Law, Psychology and Public Policy.* New York, NY: Oxford University Press.

Families Against Mandatory Minimums (2013) *An Introduction to Child Pornography Sentencing.* Washington, DC: FAMM. Available at http://famm.org/wp-content/uploads/2013/09/FS-Intro-to-Child-Porn-8.22.13-fixed.pdf (accessed January 12, 2017).

Gottschalk, M. (2015) "The New Untouchables: The War on Sex Offenders." In *Caught: The Prison State and the Lockdown of American Politics.* Princeton, NJ: Princeton University Press.

Hamilton, M. (2012) "The child pornography crusade and its net-widening effect." *Cardozo Law Review 33*, 1.

Haralson, J.B. and Cordeiro, J.R. (2012) *Unprecedented: How Sex Offender Laws Are Impacting Our Nation.* PCG Legacy.

Horowitz, E. (2015) *Protecting Our Kids? How Sex Offender Laws Are Failing Us.* Santa Barbara, CA: Praeger.

Long, S. (2014) "The case for extending pretrial diversion to include possession of child pornography." *University of Massachusetts Law Review 9*, 2, 4.

Marcus, A.J. (2016) "Challenge to SORNA retroactivity reaches Pennsylvania Supreme Court." Collateral Consequences Resource Center, May 16, 2016. Available at http://ccresourcecenter.org/2016/05/16/challenge-to-sorna-retroctivity-reaches-pennsylvania-supreme-court (accessed January 12, 2017).

McLeod, A. (2014) "Regulating sexual harm: Strangers, intimates, and social institutional reform." *California Law Review 102*, 6, 6.

Pask, L., Hughes, T.L., and Sutton, L.R. (2016) "Sexual knowledge acquisition and retention for individuals with autism." *International Journal of School & Educational Psychology 4*, 2, 86–94.

Stabenow, T. (2011) "A method for careful study: A proposal for reforming the child pornography guidelines." *Federal Sentencing Reporter 24*, 2, 108–136.

The New York Times (2015) "The Pointless Banishment of Sex Offenders," Editorial, *The New York Times*, September 8, 2015. Available at www.nytimes.com/2015/09/08/opinion/the-pointless-banishment-of-sex-offenders.html?_r=0 (accessed January 11, 2017).

Wollert, R., Waggoner, J., and Smith, J. (2012) "Federal Internet Child Pornography Offenders—Limited Offense Histories and Low Recidivism Rates." In B. Schwartz (ed.) *The Sex Offender: Current Trends in Policy and Treatment Practice.* Kingston, NJ: Civic Research Institute.

Wright, R. (2014) *Sex Offender Laws: Failed Policies, New Directions.* New York, NY: Springer Publishing Company.

CHAPTER 2

Child and Juvenile Pornography and Autism Spectrum Disorder

Gary Mesibov and Melissa Sreckovic

Behaviors and concepts related to sexuality are sometimes confusing and difficult to interpret for those observing adolescents and adults with autism spectrum disorder (ASD). While individuals with ASD usually develop biologically and physically close to the same speed as adolescents without ASD, they are typically delayed by at least five years in their sexual and social-emotional maturity. Their significant delay in sexual and social-emotional maturity coupled with very limited social and sexual experiences and friendships drives these individuals to use the computer as a vehicle to learn about sexuality in the privacy of their own homes. Lack of information and sexual education programs also increases the risk of using pornography as a reference. Unfortunately, child pornography presents the "perfect storm" for individuals with ASD (Mahoney, 2009); specific characteristics inherent in ASD make computers especially attractive and engaging to them and vulnerable to invitations to access child pornography without understanding that their actions are potentially illegal and harmful to young children. With their lack of social skills and extreme social naivety, individuals with ASD are easy targets to be manipulated and, once engaged in the criminal justice system, struggle immensely to advocate for themselves and navigate the criminal justice system. It is very unlikely for an individual with ASD to be a pedophile; however, it is imperative the ASD community understand why these individuals are vulnerable to accessing child pornography without understanding it is a crime. This chapter will discuss the characteristics of this neurological disorder and how it relates to the vulnerability of accessing child pornography and lack of criminal understanding.

AUTISM SPECTRUM DISORDER:
A NEUROLOGICAL DISORDER

Autism spectrum disorder is a lifelong, neurodevelopmental disorder characterized by challenges with social communication and interaction, and the presence of narrow or restricted behaviors, concepts, interests, and activities (American Psychiatric Association [APA], 2013). The cognitive, social, and communication impairments associated with ASD greatly affect an individual's ability to function independently and the overall quality of life. Although all individuals with ASD demonstrate some level of difficulty within each of these areas, the degree to which their problem-solving and learning, independence, and relationships are affected varies from person to person.

Autism is a neurological disorder, meaning that the brain of an individual with ASD organizes, processes, and uses information differently to that of an individual without ASD. Many individuals with ASD have problems with central cohesion, which means they focus on specific details and lose sight of "big picture" concepts. They often have difficulty applying skills and information to novel situations or using previously learned information to problem-solve; these are examples of an ability called fluid reasoning. Working memory, or the ability to hold and manipulate multiple pieces of information in conscious thought at one time, also is often impaired. Certain components of executive functions (EF) such as directing and sustaining attention, planning, organizing, and inhibiting behavioral responses are also challenges for many individuals with ASD. Fluid reasoning, working memory, and EF abilities rely on communication between several regions of the brain.

Recent neuroimaging studies provide evidence that there is a disruption in brain connectivity—the communication—between different regions of the brain in individuals with ASD. Just *et al.* (2004) proposed the underconnectivity theory of autism and argue that the behavioral characteristics of ASD are caused by a disruption in communication between the frontal and posterior brain regions. For example, individuals with ASD have difficulty with theory of mind (ToM), which is the ability to understand the perspectives and intentions of others. During one neuroimaging study, when participants with ASD completed a task requiring them to make inferences about the intentions of animated geometric figures, the functional connectivity between frontal and posterior ToM areas was lower compared with individuals without ASD (Kana *et al.*, 2009). Limited communication between brain regions may be explained by abnormalities in white matter in individuals with ASD (Schipul, Keller, and Just, 2011). White matter is responsible for the communication between different brain regions. Compared with children without ASD, children with ASD experience a rapid growth in white matter between the ages of two and four, followed by a decreased rate of white matter growth between the ages of 3 and 12 (Courchesne *et al.*, 2001). Due to this abnormal growth rate, it is speculated that the white matter does not develop properly. Indeed, several studies have documented that children and adolescents with ASD have lower-quality white matter compared with their counterparts without ASD, which in turn may affect the communication between different brain regions (Schipul *et al.*, 2011). In other words, because of the integrity of the white matter in the brains of individuals with ASD, regions of their brain may not be efficiently transferring information. Therefore, when individuals with ASD process information, they process it quite differently to individuals without ASD.

Overgrowth in brain structures has been empirically studied in several regions of the brain in individuals with ASD, such as the prefrontal cortex (Carper and Courchesne, 2005). The prefrontal cortex is the outermost cortical layer of the frontal lobe, and is involved in social, language, communication, affective, and cognitive functions. Enlarged amygdala volume has also been found in children with ASD (Schumann *et al.*, 2004). The amygdala is responsible for processing emotional reactions. Abnormal hippocampal development from childhood through adolescence has also been established (Schumann *et al.*, 2004). The hippocampus plays a critical role in short-term and long-term memory. In addition, scientists have noted irregularities in the size, quantity, and internal organization of minicolumns in individuals with ASD (Casanova, Buxhoeveden, and Gomez, 2003). Minicolumns make up the neocortex, which is responsible for functions such as sensory perception, spatial reasoning, conscious thought, language, and the generation of motor commands. Scientists speculate that these irregularities may result in an overload of sensory stimulation (Casanova *et al.*, 2003). Taken together, differences in brain structure may help explain, in part, behavioral manifestations and cognitive processing difficulties experienced by individuals with ASD.

In addition to these anatomical differences, functional magnetic resonance imaging (fMRI) studies have demonstrated differences in brain functionality between individuals with and without ASD, which may further explain cognitive processing difficulties. Differences in functionality means that, compared with individuals without ASD, the brains of individuals with ASD often have areas of under- or over-activation, and differences in the location of activation (Minshew and Keller, 2010). For example, a recent study compared the ability to analyze information and solve problems using visual versus language-based reasoning skills in children with and without ASD with at least average intellectual quotient (IQ) scores (Sahyoun *et al.*, 2010). Results indicated that children with ASD had reduced connectivity and activation in frontal language areas and increased activation and intact connectivity of occipitoparietal and ventral temporal circuits. The children without ASD relied more on language skills, whereas the children with ASD relied more on visual spatial skills for solving both visual and verbal problems. This study provided evidence for the neural basis of visuospatial processing strengths among many individuals with ASD (Minshew and Keller, 2010). Other fMRI studies have demonstrated differences in brain functioning among individuals with ASD in the areas of face and emotion processing, and intrinsic mechanisms of behaving, thinking, and feeling (Minshew and Keller, 2010).

Although differences in brain structure and function have been documented among individuals with ASD, it is important to recognize that this body of research is complex and still evolving. Based on our current knowledge, it seems that if two people with ASD have the same structural difference in their brain, it doesn't mean that they will display exactly the same behavior (Grandin and Panek, 2013), but these studies demonstrate that the signs and symptoms of autism have a neurologic origin (Minshew and Keller, 2010).

As with all individuals, brain differences present areas of strength and areas of challenge for individuals with ASD. Areas of strength may include strong visual processing skills, rote memory abilities, and the ability to concentrate on narrow topics of interest and become an "expert." Particular areas of challenge make individuals with ASD vulnerable to accessing child pornography and explain why most individuals with ASD do not understand that downloading child pornography is illegal. These areas of challenge are described below and explain: (a) why individuals with ASD are attracted to computers; (b) why they seek alternative methods to explore sexuality; (c) how they get caught up in child pornography once they are on their computers; (d) why they do not understand the criminal responsibility of accessing child pornography; and (e) why they are rarely dangerous to children. The implications for understanding how these characteristics impact an individual with ASD's actions to view and download child pornography are also discussed.

COMPUTERS ARE ATTRACTIVE TO INDIVIDUALS WITH ASD

Computers are irresistible to individuals with ASD, because they provide an avenue to communicate and socialize with other people, which can be extremely challenging for them in person. Individuals with ASD have difficulty understanding the communications of others, which can impact their ability to comprehend and communicate effectively. Receptive verbal communication is challenging for them for several reasons. First, the speed of communication presents problems. People with ASD are often slow processors of language, so they need others to speak very slowly, clearly, and directly to them if they are to understand what is being said to them, especially if it is complex. Second, their visual skills are much stronger than their auditory skills, so the verbal emphasis on spoken language does not allow them to use their visual strengths. Frequently in secondary schools or colleges when they are allowed special accommodations for their differences, they are given extra time to take exams and visual outlines to follow during lectures so they can understand what is happening more easily. In addition, they also are quite literal and have difficulty with general phrases, idioms, or language that is not clear, direct, and specific. Interacting with more than a single person also can be challenging because the changes from one speaker to another are often hard for them to process and follow. School reports frequently mention problems with slow language-processing speed and difficulties with language comprehension. When using computers, however, individuals with ASD can process information at their own speed and take in information visually one piece at a time.

As more and more people with ASD are being educated in mainstream settings alongside their peers without disabilities, their interest in other people and desire for closer friendships and relationships has increased. Although their social skills are improving, the improvement is not sufficient for them to successfully achieve the kind of social interactions they desire, especially with members of the desired sex. As a result, they withdraw more and more into themselves. Over the past decade, the computer has become an important refuge for this group in general. As clumsy and inept as they seem to be in social relationships, the computer is something they can figure out and use because of the concrete, specific, and step-by-step linear thinking that it rewards. In other words, people with ASD think and reason in ways very similar to how computers think and reason. The internet has provided a means for people with ASD to engage in social interaction through email, discussion groups, and web pages. It provides a way of engaging with others without the confusion and subtlety of the nonverbal social messages that this group finds so difficult to understand in face-to-face interactions. The internet is excellent for these individuals, because they are intellectually intact and have good computer skills, but they are incredible naïve about how to act in social situations. The internet is often used by people with ASD as a tool for learning basic social skills and to gain information about sexuality through observing others engaging in social interactions and sex.

THE NEED FOR ALTERNATIVE METHODS TO EXPLORE SEXUALITY

Individuals with ASD are significantly delayed socially compared with their same-age peers, have few friendships, and have limited sexual knowledge. These challenges, described in detail below, often result in their searching for information about sexuality on the internet.

Social Delay

Individuals with ASD have significant deficits in social communication and interaction (APA, 2013). Their social-communicative skills may improve throughout adolescence and into adulthood; however, as they get older, increasing demands are placed upon them and their rate of improvement is not sufficient to accommodate for the new demands. Social and emotional limitations can greatly impact one's sexuality in the form of understanding the perspectives of others, forming relationships, expressing sexuality appropriately, and engaging in appropriate sexual behaviors. Even for individuals with ASD with average to above-average IQs, their social intellect is far behind their chronological and mental age. In fact, researchers found in a sample of children and adolescents with ASD with average to above-average IQ that their mean chronological age was 12.4 years, while their mean interpersonal social age was 3.2 years (Klin et al., 2007). These results indicate that while these children and adolescents have intact cognitive ability, they have significant social deficits. The data also indicated that, as these individuals age, the gap between the communicative and social abilities of individuals with ASD and of their peers without ASD increases. Although this does not mean that individuals with ASD are losing social skills over time, it does mean that the gap between individuals with ASD and their same-age peers without ASD widens as they move into adolescence and into adulthood (Klin et al., 2007). As individuals with ASD enter adolescence and become more aware of their social difficulties, anxiety and depression often worsen (Bellini, 2006). Experiencing anxiety and/or depression can greatly impact the interactions and relationships that individuals with ASD have with peers, which is concerning as these individuals often already have difficulties forming and maintaining friendships.

Difficulties with Relationships

Recent research indicates that individuals with ASD have reported fewer friendships and greater feelings of loneliness than their peers without disabilities, and have received more rejection nominations by their peers (Locke et al., 2010). Compared with individuals with other disabilities, adolescents with ASD have been reported as the least likely to see friends frequently outside of school, receive telephone calls from friends, and get invited to another student's social event (Wagner et al., 2004). Unfortunately, not only do adolescents with ASD often have limited social interactions with their peers, but they are frequently subjected to negative social interactions in the form of bullying. Because of their unique characteristics (e.g. social and communication deficits), quirky behaviors, and strange mannerisms, these individuals have been described as "perfect victims" of bullying (Klin, Volkmar, and Sparrow, 2000, p.6). Prevalence estimates of bullying victimization vary by study, but are extremely high, ranging from 29% (Twyman *et al.*, 2010) to 94% (Little, 2002) across prevalence studies (Sreckovic, Brunsting, and Able, in press). Individuals with ASD also have been reported to be victimized more frequently than their peers with and without disabilities (e.g. Humphrey and Symes, 2010; Twyman *et al.*, 2010). This corroborates the theory that there may be particular characteristics of individuals with ASD that make them especially vulnerable to being bullied. Individuals with ASD also have reported extreme rates of being ostracized (i.e. when the target is completely ignored). For example, in one study, participants with ASD were eight times more likely to report ostracism than participants without disabilities (Twyman *et al.*, 2010). Adolescents with ASD often struggle to adapt their behavior to "fit in" with the peer culture at their school and in their community. When adolescents with ASD do not adopt similar clothing, hair styles, and mannerisms to their peers, they may struggle to develop relationships with their peers and become vulnerable to victimization.

Unfortunately, individuals with ASD are vulnerable to peer victimization not only because of their often peculiar or nonconventional behaviors, but also because of their sexual orientation. It is well documented that individuals who identify as homosexual or bisexual are often victims of bullying (Berlan *et al.*, 2010), and in one study individuals with ASD reported higher rates of homosexual and bisexual interest, and asexuality, compared to the general population (Gilmour, Schalomon, and Smith, 2012). This may further increase their risk for victimization. Due to lack of positive social involvement with their peers, adolescents with ASD do not get many opportunities to develop social skills and casually learn about sexuality from their peers. Further, even if these individuals had the opportunity to talk with their peers about sexuality, they might feel restrained for fear of being teased or bullied.

Limited Sexual Knowledge

Throughout adolescence individuals learn about sexuality through interactions with peers, observing others, through the media (Koller, 2000), by reading books and magazines, and through school-based sexual education programs. Because individuals with ASD often have limited interactions with their peers, their primary sources of sexual knowledge typically include observing others, exploring on the internet, and school-based sexual education curriculums. This often results in inaccurate or incomplete sexual knowledge. Indeed, researchers have found that individuals with ASD demonstrate limited sexual knowledge compared with their counterparts without ASD (Mehzabin and Stokes, 2011).

Individuals with ASD have unique learning needs; they are literal thinkers and therefore require very direct and explicit instruction on what is and is not appropriate social and sexual behavior. Although it is not typical for adolescents and young adults with ASD to have abnormal sexual desires, they may tend to express or pursue normal interests in a manner that might be considered outside social convention for someone of their chronological age. Their blunt language and gestures may make them appear to be hyper-sexual, when they are just unaware of the social conventions (Mahoney, 2009). When this occurs, very specific instruction about appropriate behavior in specific situations is effective because, as a group, these individuals can be very rule-bound when they have the benefit of clear explanations and the chance to practice and rehearse appropriate behaviors. Unfortunately, our society's discomfort with sexuality often results in many references to appropriate and inappropriate behaviors but not the kind of specific, structured direction and practice that these individuals need. Whereas typical teens can evaluate social mores and discuss sexuality with peers to figure out appropriate behaviors within parameters that our society considers normal, children and adults with ASD need more specific and direct discussion, instruction, and practice than they typically receive. Most individuals with ASD have not had this kind of instruction available to them in the area of sexuality. Rather, most parents and teachers correct inappropriate sexual and social behaviors, rather than proactively teaching these behaviors before an issue occurs (Griffiths, 1999). Further, it may be difficult or uncomfortable for caregivers to teach their children with ASD about sexuality, because they may not be used to teaching such content so explicitly. Therefore, the combination of significantly delayed social skills, limited sexual knowledge, and difficulties learning about sexuality drive individuals with ASD to explore sexuality in a format that is more comfortable to them: the computer.

COMPUTERS AS A VEHICLE TO LEARN ABOUT SEXUALITY

Exploring sexuality on the internet is a way of satisfying biological urges, but for individuals with ASD, it is also a way for them to try to understand relationships and sexuality. Individuals with ASD often view child pornography as a means to understand sexuality in the very visual and concrete way they learn best, rather than as a precursor to attacking young children. Their desire for this material can become excessive and compulsive, as is the case with many things that interest and engage them.

Intense Absorption in Circumscribed Topics

An intense absorption in circumscribed topics is a characteristic of ASD involving restricted, repetitive, and stereotypical patterns of behavior, interests, and activities. These can include restricted patterns of interest that are abnormal in intensity or focus. With adolescents and adults with ASD, the most common of these behaviors is the restricted and intense absorption in narrow topics. These can be common everyday topics such as the weather or idiosyncratic interests in things like TV stations, railway tables, or deep fat fryers. Individuals with ASD may collect volumes of detailed information on these narrow topics without necessarily having a genuine understanding of the broader area or even strong interests in that. For example, an individual might obsessively memorize and collect camera model numbers without caring about photography, or continually draw and collect pictures of buses, without ever wanting to ride on one. As individuals with ASD involve themselves with these narrowly circumscribed interests, they often become overly obsessed. Unfortunately, some of the objects individuals with ASD often become obsessed with are now made into pornographic images and videos, and made freely available on the internet. For example, many individuals with ASD develop an intense interest with Thomas the Tank Engine from an early age and many adolescents and adults with ASD are intensely interested in anime. Both Thomas the Tank Engine and anime pornography are available on the internet. Therefore, this may be one avenue through which they are exposed to child pornography (e.g via pop-ups).

This intensity with narrow and circumscribed interests is one of the many reasons that they can become alienated from their peers.

Sometimes adolescents can be very obsessed with pop culture, but adolescents with ASD typically focus on topics that do not interest their peers. For example, in his chapter, Nick Dubin discusses his unique interest in maps. He likes to figure out where roads begin and end, and commented that when on a family trip, if his parents deviated from the route he mapped out, he would throw a tantrum. He is also very interested in TV game shows and mentioned how he would memorize all their catchphrases. This intensity with narrow and circumscribed interests can negatively impact peer relationships. Further, these social limitations make dating less likely, so the computer becomes their main vehicle for receiving information and satisfying their curiosity about matters such as relationships and sexuality.

For people with ASD, the internet in conjunction with sexuality can result in what Mark Mahoney calls a "lethal combination" (Mahoney, 2009). These individuals often have considerable technical skills about how things like computers work and a tremendous naivety about the larger picture, such as whether they are sharing or transferring the files with others. Their naivety also extends to our culture's attitudes and rules about sexuality. Child pornography is one of those topics that many adults with ASD have more recently become involved with. Some individuals with ASD may accumulate large amounts of pornographic material and keep what they collect as part of their ritualistic nature. This does not mean that they are more likely than the general population to approach young children or engage in sexual exploitation of them—in fact, the data are clear that they are much less likely to engage in these behaviors than typical adults and, in fact, very rarely do so (Mahoney, 2009; Tantam, 2003). Once they access child pornography (whether they access it trying to learn about sexuality, meeting their sexual needs, or by clicking on a pop up), the individual with ASD likely accumulates large amounts of pornography without focusing on broader issues like where and how they got those files, who else has access to them, and what the implications might be for the children who are posing.

Incomplete Understanding of Computers

Although, as a group, adults with ASD have good technical skills for using computers, their technical skills with computers are not always accompanied by a thorough understanding of all aspects related to how these machines work. Rather, as previously discussed, these individuals have very narrow interests and often become consumed with one piece of a larger puzzle and therefore do not understand how the whole puzzle works—just like a compulsive interest in maps does not always lead to an ability to find different streets or places, or a strong interest in kitchen appliances is not necessarily accompanied by knowing how to cook a meal. Individuals with ASD collect files and pass them on to others without realizing that is what they are doing because they often are narrowly focused on the complicated computer activities that they are initiating and the large amount of data they are collecting, and not on the larger issue that the files they are accumulating might be passed on to other people, through an automatically downloaded Trojan horse, as was the case with Nick Dubin.

Further, given that individuals with ASD often follow rigid routines, they are likely to continue to find images and download them in the same format each time they explore on the internet. So the user with ASD may not even have intended to look for child pornography in the first place, but if that is what showed up on the screen from that point forward, s/he will follow the same routine. Moreover, because of their naivety, when pop-up boxes appear on the computer screen asking the user to "click here," they are likely to click the box. As a group, these individuals are often very trusting and naive and it would not occur to them that clicking a link that asks them to click on it would lead to something illegal. In fact, given their literal and trusting nature, many individuals with ASD would probably ask, "Why would someone say to click on the link if it is illegal?" Throughout this process, it is very unlikely that the individual with ASD understands that downloading child pornography is a crime for several reasons, which are described below.

UNDERSTANDING THE CRIMINAL RESPONSIBILITY OF CHILD PORNOGRAPHY

Individuals with ASD have difficulty understanding the criminal responsibility of child pornography for many reasons. First is their intent to search for and download child pornography. These adolescents and adults may search for child pornography as a learning tool to understand more about sexuality in the comfort and privacy of their own home. Once they access the pornography, they may become obsessed with accumulating large amounts of it, because of the compulsivity that accompanies most of their routines. Therefore, an adult with ASD with an average to extremely above-average IQ may be intensely focused on one narrow topic, downloading as many files as they can, without even thinking about the broader picture of what they are doing and how it impacts the children in the images. Second is the way their brain processes information. As previously described, individuals with ASD often have disruptions in communication between different regions of the brain. Understanding the criminal responsibility of child pornography requires a person to understand that the children in the images did not give consent and do not want to participate, the people taking the videos/pictures are harming the children, and by viewing the children in the videos/pictures the viewer is harming the children. This requires a person to be able to understand the intentions of others and how other people are feeling (also known as ToM). As previously mentioned, neuroimaging studies have indicated that the communication between frontal and posterior ToM regions of the brain is lower in individuals with ASD compared with individuals without ASD (e.g. Kana *et al.*, 2009), which would clearly impact their ability to intuitively understand that viewing and downloading child pornography is illegal. Finally, individuals with ASD view the world very literally and it would not cross their minds that something so freely available on the internet would be illegal. In their naive and trusting minds, if it is wrong, then it should not be available. The social immaturity of these individuals, coupled with deficits in ToM, make it difficult for them to understand that their actions are wrong.

Social Immaturity

The social immaturity of adolescents and adults with high-functioning ASD, despite their average intelligence and biological development for their age, often makes them interested in knowing about younger girls/boys because they are of about the same age emotionally and socially as these children. Moreover, for the individual with ASD, the demarcation between observing an adult and observing a child is often unclear. Clinical observations confirm that individuals with ASD are poor judges of character and age. Many individuals with ASD are unclear about the moral and legal line between the two as well.

Further, the media is constantly marketing materials with risky images of teenage models or making older models look "barely legal." These images can cause great confusion for individuals with ASD, making the line between legal pornography and illegal pornography very blurry. Unfortunately, most parents would not think to discuss that distinction with an adolescent or adult with ASD, and most teachers would probably not think of it either. Even if a teacher did think that the legal distinction between observing a minor and observing an adult was important, this teacher very often would still not follow up on this with their students because of the possible social repercussions of discussing something so sensitive with them. Again, this information would need to be presented explicitly, concretely, and visually because individuals with ASD are such concrete learners. It would also need to be presented repeatedly, as these individuals have difficulty transferring new information to other situations. For example, understanding that a principal is an adult and a student is a child would not necessarily translate to an individual with ASD that a 30-year-old is an adult and a 12-year-old is a child.

What is often presented explicitly in the sexual education curriculum for adolescents and adults with ASD is masturbation. In fact, many curriculums provide visuals and explicit directions on how to masturbate. Keep in mind this may be one of the only modes for these individuals to achieve sexual gratification. They are taught that it is acceptable to masturbate in the privacy of their own home and bedroom. Rules about the distinction between public and private are repeatedly taught in these curriculums. This is relevant as individuals with ASD have been known to masturbate in public. However, they typically are not being explicitly taught what they cannot do in private. Because individuals with ASD are rule-governed and need explicit directions, if they are not explicitly taught behaviors that are inappropriate to engage in while masturbating in private (e.g. viewing child pornography), they likely do not recognize they are engaging in illegal behavior. Rather, because they are in the privacy of their own home or bedroom, they think all behaviors related to masturbation are acceptable.

Theory of Mind

Individuals with ASD have limited ability to empathize, often referred to as their problem with ToM, which makes it hard for them to intuit or understand how their viewing an image on the internet can be promoting the victimization of the child on the screen. The person who doesn't understand the intentions and emotions of others has considerable difficulty in perceiving when a child is being victimized, even though they might have the technical skill to find and collect the child's images on the internet. In addition, because their maturity level and moral understanding is the equivalent of a young child's, they do not fully appreciate the morally reprehensible aspects of what they are viewing and the illegality of downloading these images. Although pedophiles or antisocial personalities usually understand the repercussions of their criminal actions when observing illegal child pornography on the internet, unless explicitly and repeatedly told, coached, and rehearsed, an individual with ASD would not understand that the mere viewing of child pornography or even the mere act of clicking on a link can be a serious criminal act.

In prosecuting child pornography cases, a critical premise is that the person viewing such images understands that the children might not have given informed consent for participating in the pictures and are being exploited and perhaps psychologically and physically abused. Whereas individuals without ASD would likely be attuned to the possibilities of exploitation and the potential for harm, adults with ASD frequently lack the empathetic understanding and sensitivity to the perspectives of others to make these deductions and connections. When asked why they sometimes watched children involved in child pornography, a common answer of teens and adults with ASD is because they could relate better to younger girls/boys because their social-emotional age is at about that level (which in fact it is). Not only is their social and emotional age well below their chronological age, but many individuals with ASD view themselves as younger than their chronological age, which is the case with Nick Dubin, as described in Chapter 10. Typical adults observing child pornography usually understand that an observer is morally and legally culpable for promoting that victimization. Living in a narrower and very literal world, however, a person with ASD is usually unable to make these connections and deductions, and it would be very hard for them to fathom all of the negative consequences for the child in question.

Further, while individuals without ASD can likely recognize that the children in videos or pictures look upset, distressed, or anxious, individuals with ASD have extreme difficulties reading meaning in eye gaze, facial expressions, body language, gestures, and prosody. Individuals without ASD can look at a picture/video and recognize a child's emotion by observing their facial expressions (tilted eyebrows, squinting eyes, mouth in a neutral or downward position), gestures (where the child's hands are positioned), body language (if the child is shrugging their shoulders or in a tense position), and prosody. Individuals with ASD, on the other hand, have extreme difficulties recognizing these features in other people and determining how the other person is thinking or feeling. In other words, individuals with ASD have difficulties gathering enough information to work out the many possible ways a person could be feeling or thinking. This likely can be explained by anatomical and functionality differences of the brain described earlier in this chapter. To understand that the children in the videos are being victimized, individuals with ASD need to be taught how to recognize verbal and nonverbal cues related to sexuality and understand what consent means and that it is always needed prior to any sexual behaviors.

Despite these challenges, individuals with ASD can learn that child pornography is illegal if they have been explicitly taught; however, the availability of illegal materials like those on the internet are very recent developments, so few programs or families have had time to adjust and make this specific teaching a part of school curriculums or home learning activities. Further, current school-based sexual education programs teach students about the facts. Individuals with ASD can memorize these facts, but often have difficulty translating the facts into meaningful actions, because unless explicitly taught, they have difficulty generalizing the content they learn to other situations, contexts, and people. Therefore, if individuals with ASD are not explicitly and repeatedly taught how and why child pornography is illegal, they likely will not know it is illegal. Katz and Zemishlany (2006) describe such concrete thinking in a case report of a man with Asperger's syndrome who assaulted his father and sister. The man stated, "Maybe if the judge had explained to me that it was not permitted to beat up people, I wouldn't have done it" (p.169). Something with a consequence as serious as accessing child pornography needs to be explicitly and repeatedly taught to individuals with ASD, and alternative acceptable behaviors need to be clearly defined and practiced. However, no sexual education curriculum designed for individuals with ASD, to the authors' knowledge, addresses child pornography.

It is clear that the consequences of this neurological disorder present several challenges to the ability of an individual with ASD to recognize the legal responsibility of child pornography. In review, these challenges include having the same social and sexual maturity level as a child, not being able to discriminate a child from an adult, having extreme difficulties understanding the perspectives and emotions of others, and simply lacking skills and knowledge because they have not been provided with the explicit instruction they need to recognize that viewing and downloading child pornography is a crime. Taken together, these individuals are not observing child pornography to abuse; rather, they are observing to learn and are rarely dangerous to children.

PEOPLE WITH ASD ARE RARELY DANGEROUS TO CHILDREN

People with ASD who view child pornography are rarely dangerous to children during their contacts with them for several reasons. First, as already explained in this chapter, by and large they do not have the criminal mindset of those who are dangerous. There is rarely anything in their motivation or perception of the situation to incline them toward sexual deviance. Second, they typically lack the pedophile's interpersonal skills and ability to deceive that are essential for physically separating and directly exploiting children. Dangerous child pedophiles have skills that enable them to isolate children from their caregivers, build up trust, find children who are vulnerable in vulnerable situations, and then plan and execute complicated sequences to separate, isolate, and abuse these children. This is well beyond the skill set of most people with ASD who have problems with EF (executive functions are brain activities responsible for setting goals, organizing, and completing tasks). As mentioned previously, several EF constructs are often impaired in individuals with ASD, making organizing and implementing complex sequences, such as exploiting a child, beyond their skill levels.

Existing data supports the notion that individuals with developmental disabilities are much more likely to be the victims of sexual crimes than the perpetrators (Griffiths and Marini, 2000). Recent literature indicates that there is no evidence to support an association between violence and individuals with ASD; in fact, most individuals with ASD are law-abiding citizens who are no more likely to commit crimes than neurotypical people (Bjorkly, 2009). The claim of many adults with ASD that their interest in younger girls/boys reflects their developmental level rather than any criminal mindset supports that notion. Understanding how the characteristics of ASD greatly affect how and why individuals with ASD access child pornography, why they do not understand the legal consequences of viewing and downloading it, and why they are rarely dangerous to children is important during the criminal justice process. However, it is also important to recognize that the criminal justice system presents significant challenges for individuals with ASD, which are briefly described below.

INDIVIDUALS WITH ASD AND THE CRIMINAL JUSTICE SYSTEM

Beginning with the pre-arrest, the criminal justice system presents an array of problems for individuals with ASD. First, the way the FBI enters the residence of an individual with ASD creates great havoc and confusion for the individual with ASD. As Nick Dubin describes in Chapter 10, the intensity of the situation and overstimulation of noises and behaviors can be overwhelming to the individual with ASD. People with ASD, who have difficulty quickly processing information and responding to requests and questions, will have extreme challenges defending themselves and will often volunteer answers to leading statements that the FBI asks, often without giving Miranda warnings. In Nick Dubin's case, he was in custody for hours in his apartment and vigorously questioned and he was not given his Miranda warnings. Even if Miranda warnings are given, the overstimulation of noises and behaviors coupled with difficulties processing information can result in the individual with ASD not understanding their rights. Being naive and suggestible, there is great danger for false confessions during the pre-arrest, interrogation, and trial. People with ASD often confess immediately to the offense (Attwood, 2007), because they feel their actions were justified and do not think they did anything wrong. They may additionally share more information than individuals without ASD out of fear, which may be used against them later in court, thus incriminating themselves (Sperry *et al.*, 2014).

During the interrogation process, it can be difficult to determine if the offender with ASD is relaying accurate information, because people with ASD often have difficulties with the abstractness of time and deficits in sequencing events. This presents difficulties in remembering the timing of events, and therefore they may not be able to accurately recall information about the offense (Burdon and Dickens, 2009). Additionally, because of marked communication deficits, individuals with ASD may have difficulty effectively communicating with lawyers, prosecutors, judges, and juries. Further, these individuals are often compliant with the requests of others, because they have learned that if they say "yes" they are likely to get out of a situation (Taylor, Mesibov, and Debbaudt, 2009). In Chapter 10, Nick Dubin describes how he pleaded with the FBI, saying, "I'll do anything you want me to do," in order to ameliorate the situation. Additionally, people with ASD often yearn for friends and may agree with an interrogator, because s/he wants to make their new "friend" happy. Therefore, they may just give an affirmative answer, regardless of whether it reflects any truth (Taylor et al., 2009).

Individuals with ASD also may have difficulty understanding broad legal concepts (Mayes and Koegel, 2003). Indeed, Ericson and Perlman (2001) reported significant differences in knowledge of legal terms between adults with mild developmental disabilities (DD) and adults without delays. More specifically, 28 out of 34 legal terms were conceptually understood by at least 85% or more of the participants without delays and only eight legal terms were conceptually understood by at least 75% of the participants with DD. Additionally, individuals with ASD may have difficulty comprehending auditory information if visual supports are not provided to aid in understanding, which often they are not, and during times of stress and heightened anxiety it is more difficult for individuals with ASD to comprehend what is being said (Sperry et al., 2014).

Throughout the entire criminal justice process, the unique behaviors displayed by individuals with ASD may give the wrong impression to lawyers, prosecutors, judges, juries, and interrogators. For example, in the courtroom, individuals with ASD may speak in a monotone voice, laugh at inappropriate times, display negative affect, and misread subtle cues from professionals, such as a judge making a facial expression to signal for people to quiet down (Taylor et al., 2009). This demeanor may be understood by the judge and jury as someone being disrespectful, rude, and maybe even guilty. Because of this, they may receive harsher sentences: the affective control theory suggests that offenders who are positively perceived by people in charge of sentencing are given a less harsh sentence than those who are negatively perceived (Tsoudis, 2000).

Finally, the academic ability and vast language and vocabulary skills of offenders with high-functioning ASD may make them appear independent and capable (Taylor *et al.*, 2009). This may make them appear more capable than they actually are, especially in relation to communication and social deficits. The prosecutors, judge, and jury may misinterpret their academic intelligence and believe that if the individual demonstrates such academic capabilities, then s/he must have understood the consequences of the offense (Taylor *et al.*, 2009). Altogether, an individual with ASD can be poorly misunderstood in the context of the criminal justice system, because of the key diagnostic features of ASD which make social interaction and communication so difficult. It is imperative that criminal justice professionals consider the key features of ASD and how they affect the way an individual with ASD presents him/herself in the criminal justice process.

IMPLICATIONS FOR CRIMINAL JUSTICE OFFICIALS
Prison Can Be Disastrous for Someone with ASD

Prison is a well-accepted part of our jurisprudence system and a well-accepted form of punishment; however, it is often very hard on people with ASD because it can be especially cruel and dangerous for them. There are no special prisons or sections of prisons for people with ASD in the United States, and a diagnosis of ASD does not make one eligible for housing in a psychiatric facility. If arrested for child pornography, those with ASD are also ineligible for placement in a camp or minimum-security prison. Their problems in prison settings are many; their direct manner, unusual behaviors, and characteristics are interpreted by others as invitations to exploit, bully, and control. The same characteristics that make this population extremely vulnerable to being bullied in school will likely make them vulnerable to being victims in prison settings; however, the prison climate is much harsher than the school climate. These characteristics include communication challenges (Cappadocia, Weiss, and Pepler, 2012), severe social skills deficits (Sterzing *et al.*, 2012), gullibility (Sofronoff,

Dark, and Stone, 2011), internalizing mental health problems and depression (Cappadocia *et al.*, 2012; Zablotsky *et al.*, 2013), limited social support from peers (Humphrey and Symes, 2010), and few friendships (Cappadocia *et al.*, 2012; Hebron and Humphrey, 2013). Correctional workers often view them as rude and incorrigible, when they are actually just oblivious to social cues. Moreover, individuals with ASD are likely to be victims in prisons. Their failure to detect manipulation by others, combined with their high degree of social anxiety and inability to defend themselves effectively or to control to any extent social interactions, leads these individuals to be especially vulnerable. In prisons, where domination and regulation among prisoners plays an important role in inmate survival, a socially fragile individual such as one with ASD is an easy target for physical and sexual abuse.

Such a case was described by Dr. Tony Attwood in his book *The Complete Guide to Asperger's Syndrome*. Attwood described the case of a man with Asperger's syndrome who had committed robbery to get money to buy new items related to his special interest. While in prison, he was subjected to sexual assault almost daily. The sexual assaults continued even after he reported them to the authorities. Knowing that he had few options, he opted to start a small fire in the industrial workshop in the hope that he would be sent to solitary confinement. However, the fire spread and the entire workshop burned down. He then faced an arson charge, but once the circumstances were explained to the judge, the charges were dropped (Attwood, 2007). Prison sentences are not needed to protect the public from an individual with ASD who has downloaded child pornography, because the individual with ASD presents an extremely low risk of harming a child.

Being Labeled as a Sexual Offender

In response to some horrific crimes committed by convicted sex offenders, jurisdictions throughout the United States have enacted exclusionary zoning laws prohibiting sex offenders from residing or working in close proximity to schools, local parks, day care centers, or school bus stops. Sex offender laws enacted in many states essentially ban sex offenders from urban areas. These restrictions assume that anyone who views child pornography is also likely to physically approach and possibly abuse a child if given an opportunity. This logic clearly does not apply to an individual with ASD who does not have the compulsive desire, interest, social manipulation skills, or sexual sophistication of a non-ASD pedophile. Moreover, individuals with ASD have a very clear record of not contacting, approaching, or harming children in any way. Sexual predator restrictions frequently force family members to either relocate with the offender or be separated from their family member with ASD, a separation that deprives the individual of the family support that is so crucial in helping him/her to have a successful community experience and life. Being listed on the sexual offender registry makes finding employment difficult, which is already a challenge for many individuals with ASD. Being forced to relocate, being denied family support, and being asked to leave places of employment or study, which can be another consequence of a forced relocation, can place a person with ASD in a "whirlwind of destabilizing forces" (Mahoney, 2009). Positive case studies of families and people with ASD tell us about the enormous odds they must overcome, so the last thing that these individuals and families need is another series of obstacles placed in their way because of being labeled as sex offenders and subjected to the very restrictive registration and relocation requirements that go with this label but do not apply to their inclinations, behaviors, or crimes.

Individuals with ASD will not respond in the same manner as others likely will during prosecution, conviction, and imprisonment. Individuals with ASD are more vulnerable to experiencing post-traumatic stress disorder (PTSD), as was the case with Nick Dubin. Research indicates that following trauma individuals with ASD experience "deterioration in social and communicative abilities, increase in stereotypes, aggression, distractibility, sleep disorders, agitation, hyperactivity, self-injury, and loss of self-care skills" (Mehtar and Mukaddes, 2011, p.539). As Larry Dubin mentioned in Chapter 1, these individuals already have so much to overcome daily that further impeding them with imprisonment when they are not a harm to children is unnecessary. Instead, individuals with ASD need training on the proper use of computers as an alternative to incarceration, which can be taught during diversion programs.

SCREENING TOOLS AND DIVERSION PROGRAMS

In the case of an individual with ASD, criminal prosecution and labeling the individual as a sex offender is not necessary to protect the public, because the individual is very unlikely to harm children. Conviction and imprisonment are simply not needed. If prosecutors are hesitant, a tiered approach can be used to determine the level of risk of an individual with ASD harming a child, the need for a prison sentence, and the need to be labeled as a sex offender. First, screening tools are available to measure the likelihood that a sexual offender reoffends and the risk of pedophilia. These tools can be used to gauge the likelihood a person with ASD will commit a sexual offense and harm a child. These tools should be used, and the information gathered should be considered, when determining the need to prosecute, convict, and imprison a person with ASD.

For attorneys working with a client who shows some of the characteristics of ASD, consideration should be given to referring this person for a full evaluation. The gold standard for an evaluation for ASD is the Autism Diagnostic Observation Schedule, Second Edition (ADOS-2; Lord *et al.*, 2012). An experienced evaluator should be able to administer this test along with obtaining other necessary information, including a thorough early history from the parents or someone who knew the person when they were very young. The most comprehensive early history assessment is the Autism Diagnostic Interview, Revised (ADI-R; Rutter, Le Couteur, and Lord, 2003); other standardized assessments that could be used include the Vineland Social Maturity Scale (Sparrow, Cicchetti, and Balla, 2005) and the Social Communication Questionnaire (Rutter, Bailey, and Lord, 2003).

A diagnosis of ASD can be useful for adolescents and adults facing child pornography charges because it establishes that many of the characteristics and much of the data that have been described in this chapter are applicable. Probably most significant is the substantial data demonstrating that there is a very limited likelihood that youngsters with ASD will be predators and of any danger to young children. Research tells us that individuals with ASD, whose only offense is child pornography, present far fewer risks of other forms of criminal activity compared with other sex offenders or sex offenders without ASD (Eke, Seto, and Williams, 2011). Webb, Craissati, and Keen (2007) reported that 18 months post-offense none of those in their study, who only observed child pornography, later committed a contact sexual offense. Wollert, Waggoner, and Smith (2009) followed a sample for four years post-child pornography observation and found that none of this sample committed a contact offense against a child and only 1% reoffended with child pornography possession. Other investigators have found similarly low recidivism rates in those whose only offense was observation or possession of child pornography (Saris *et al.*, 2013).

Because of the very low incidence of contact offenses by those with ASD arrested for observing or possessing child pornography, many professionals do not think any risk assessment measures are needed because the risk is so minimal. There are, however, some risk assessment measures that are available. Included among these are some general risk assessment tools that can provide a good indication of whether a client with ASD is at risk for any forms of dangerous behavior that may endanger lives and impose risks for those who come in contact with them. Historical Clinical Risk Management, Version 3 (HCR-20V3; Douglas *et al.*, 2013), provides specific scenarios and gives information about how likely dangerous behaviors are to occur and, if they are occurring, what might be some precipitating and triggering factors. Another widely used measure is the Short-Term Assessment of Risk and Treatability (START; Webster *et al.*, 2009). More recently, the Structured Assessment of Protective Factors for violence risk (SAPROF; de Vogel *et al.*, 2009) has found some favor for identifying protective factors to decrease violence risk. Another risk assessment measure is the STATIC 99-R. This measure is useful in predicting future sex offending. It has not been designed or normed for identifying future offending in those whose only offense is viewing or possessing child pornography, but some have reported that it is useful for this purpose.

Once the screening tools are administered and if minimal risk is determined, prosecutors can choose to use a "pretrial diversion" program. A pretrial diversion program places offenders in a supervision program. Individuals who complete the program and do not reoffend are either not charged or have their charges dismissed. For individuals with ASD, diversion programs provide them with the opportunity to learn the moral and legal consequences of child pornography, something they most likely have previously not been taught. During this time, if the individual with ASD does not reoffend, the legal system can feel assured that the individual is not harmful to children; rather, because of their unique characteristics and lack of knowledge about child pornography, they never had the knowledge to understand that child pornography is illegal.

During the diversion program, individuals with ASD should be provided with explicit training on the consequences of child pornography. This training will look different from typical treatment programs designed for child pornography offenders, because the person with ASD sees the world differently. Not only are treatment programs for those convicted of child pornography inappropriate for adolescents and adults with ASD but, in fact, they can be harmful. A treatment program offering concrete rules and explicit instructions that are tailored to the level of understanding, ways of thinking and learning, lifestyle, and environment of a person with ASD is what is needed. The goal of a treatment program should be to ensure that the person with ASD does not view child pornography again. As has already been discussed, they are not sexual predators and do not require rehabilitation. Instead, they require education that is different from the typical sex offender program. Typical programs are generally rehabilitative, seeking to return sexual expression to a state of dignity so that it follows appropriate social mores. The problem for someone with ASD is not sexually deviant behavior but rather a lack of active, intensive, and autism-specific training for dealing with the possibility that child pornography might enter their room through their computer. Remember, it is not that individuals with ASD cannot understand why child pornography is illegal and why they should not download it; it is that they have not been taught or they have not been taught in a way that they can understand and process the information effectively. They need a thorough understanding of the subtle distinctions that must be made and practice making them. Not only would a typical sex offender treatment program be inappropriate for people with ASD but it could be damaging by further confusing them about the law, their privacy rights, and what and how they are supposed to deal with certain situations that present themselves when they are using their computer in their home.

A treatment team from Yale University has summarized five points for a comprehensive treatment program for a child pornography offender with ASD as follows: they need to be instructed very concretely, literally, and firmly that this behavior is unacceptable; they need instruction on the concept of underage females and males; they need instruction on how to distinguish between pornography that is everywhere and child pornography; they need instruction on explicit sanctions for viewing child pornography; and most of all they need instruction on how not to violate the rule that has been taught (Klin, n.d.). Further preventive action could include putting blocks on computers and computer monitoring by the individual's parents and a therapist to ensure appropriate usage while a program of this kind is being implemented. Treatment provided in this manner should be sufficient to prevent individuals with ASD from accessing child pornography in the future. With that said, it is unnecessary to label individuals with ASD as sex offenders, because it has severe implications for those with ASD who are not a threat to children and who, with appropriate instruction, can be taught not to access child pornography.

SUMMARY AND CONCLUSIONS

Individuals with ASD and their families often deal with much adversity because of the many challenges presented by ASD. They endure problems with school officials and personnel who often have limited understanding of individuals with ASD and their strengths and needs. As individuals with ASD enter middle and high school, lack of understanding among other students frequently leads to cruel bullying and rejection. They are significantly delayed socially and emotionally. Many families persevere through many difficult obstacles and work diligently to help their child become a contributing member of society in many areas. Individuals with ASD have many strengths and abilities, which should be recognized by the community at large. Unfortunately, the characteristics of ASD also make this population uniquely more vulnerable to accessing and sustaining interest in child pornography. By definition, people with high-functioning ASD are of average intelligence but cannot always understand or recognize the deviance of their behaviors, especially when it comes to our penal system and the circumstances involving child pornography. The situation is indeed tragic when an individual with ASD who, because of greater skills with and trust of the world of computers combined with obliviousness to many social mores and legal taboos, gets caught in the social and legal issues involving the world of child pornography. Individuals with ASD are most susceptible to the marketing schemes on computers surrounding the pornography industry and are naive about the social mores that lead to very harsh punishments. This naivety about all aspects related to how their computers share information and to how their computers are, in fact, opened to the world is also why people with ASD are easily caught.

Once involved in the criminal justice process, the interrogation process is extremely unfriendly to a person with ASD given the social, communication, and cognitive differences of these individuals— namely, several interrogators talking quickly with no visual supports or checks on the person's responses to be sure the person understands what was being said, vague insinuations, the mixing of real evidence with deceit and misinformation, and indirect references to the person's rights without clarifying precisely what these rights really are and, more importantly, exactly how the person can exercise them. Thus, the rights designed to protect individuals during the interrogation through the Miranda warning are very poorly understood and usually not protected. The consequence is that individuals with ASD face possible criminal conviction and very harsh penalties that can negatively affect the person's entire life. The unique features of ASD combined with the strong emotional reactions surrounding child pornography create a "perfect storm."

It is important to consider that the many differences in brain functioning among people with ASD make it hard for these individuals to understand the implications of watching child pornography on their computer in the privacy of their home; the reasons individuals with ASD do this is very different from typical people. Individuals with ASD, however, with appropriate teaching, can be taught not to access child pornography. Also, the difficulties individuals with ASD often have in understanding and exercising their rights are a major issue, as is the fact that the punishments for those convicted of this crime are especially harsh because they result in inappropriate treatments and conditions that make it virtually impossible for them to maintain all the hard-earned progress that they have made despite incredible obstacles. With proper instruction, individuals with ASD can be taught not to view and download child pornography. Alternative treatments that explicitly teach this information using instructional methods consistent with the learning needs of individuals with ASD should be used as an alternative to imprisonment and labeling these individuals as sex offenders. We recognize that courts have the difficult task of determining if the symptoms of ASD play a causal role in viewing and downloading child pornography. We hope that the evidence presented in this chapter is clear in demonstrating that the characteristics of

ASD make this population extremely vulnerable to accessing child pornography and that current approaches are ruining many lives that otherwise could be productive, meaningful, and useful for the individuals themselves and their families.

REFERENCES

American Psychiatric Association (2013) *Diagnostic and Statistical Manual of Mental Disorders*, Fifth Edition. Arlington, VA: American Psychiatric Association.

Attwood, T. (2007) *The Complete Guide to Asperger's Syndrome*. London: Jessica Kingsley Publishers.

Bellini, S. (2006) "The development of social anxiety in adolescents with autism spectrum disorders." *Focus on Autism and Other Developmental Disabilities 21*, 138–145.

Berlan, E.D., Corliss, H.L., Field, A.E., Goodman, E., and Austin, S.B. (2012) "Sexual orientation and bullying among adolescents in the growing up today study." *Journal of Adolescent Health 46*, 4, 366–371.

Bjorkly, S. (2009) "Risk and dynamics of violence in Asperger's syndrome: A systematic review of the literature." *Aggression and Violent Behavior 14*, 306–312.

Burdon, L. and Dickens, G. (2009) "Asperger syndrome and offending behaviour." *Learning Disability Practice 12*, 9, 14–20.

Cappadocia, M.C., Weiss, J.A., and Pepler, D. (2012) "Bullying experiences among children and youth with autism spectrum disorders." *Journal of Autism and Developmental Disorders 42*, 266–277.

Carper, R.A. and Courchesne, E. (2005) "Localized enlargement of the frontal cortex in early autism." *Biological Psychiatry 57*, 126–133.

Casanova, M.F., Buxhoeveden, D., and Gomez, J. (2003) "Disruption in the inhibitory architecture of the cell minicolumn: Implications for autism." *Neuroscientist 9*, 6, 496–507.

Courchesne, E., Karns, C.M., Davis, H.R., Ziccardi, R. *et al.* (2001) "Unusual brain growth patterns in early life in patients with autistic disorder: An MRI study." *Neurology 57*, 245–254.

de Vogel, V., de Ruiter, C., Bouman, Y., and de Vries Robbé, M. (2009) *SAPROF: Guidelines for the Assessment of Protective Factors for Violence Risk. English Version*. Utrecht: Forum Educatief.

Douglas, K.S., Hart, S.D., Webster, C.D., and Belfrage, H. (2013) *HCR-20V3: Assessing Risk of Violence User Guide*. Burnaby, Canada: Mental Health, Law, and Policy Institute, Simon Fraser University.

Eke, A.W., Seto, M.C., and Williams, J. (2011) "Examining the criminal history and future offending of child pornography offenders: An extended prospective follow-up study." *Law and Human Behavior 35*, 6, 466–478.

Ericson, K.I. and Perlman, N.B. (2001) "Knowledge of legal terminology and court proceedings in adults with developmental disabilities." *Law and Human Behavior 25*, 5, 529–545.

Gilmour, L., Schalomon, P.M., and Smith, V. (2012) "Sexuality in a community based sample of adults with autism spectrum disorder." *Research in Autism Spectrum Disorders 6*, 313–318.

Grandin, T. and Panek, R. (2013) *The Autistic Brain: Thinking Across the Spectrum*. Boston, MA, and New York, NY: Houghton Mifflin Harcourt.

Griffiths, D. (1999) "Sexuality and Developmental Disabilities: Myths, Conceptions and Facts." In I. Brown and M. Percy (eds) *Developmental Disabilities in Ontario*. Toronto: Front Porch Publishing.

Griffiths, D. and Marini, Z. (2000) "Interacting with the legal system regarding a sexual offence: Social and cognitive considerations for persons with developmental disabilities." *Journal on Developmental Disabilities 7*, 1, 76–121.

Hanson, R.K., Babchishin, K.M., Helmus, L., and Thornton, D. (2013) "Quantifying the relative risk of sex offenders: Risk ratios for Static-99R." *Sexual Abuse: A Journal of Research and Treatment 25*, 5, 482–515.

Hebron, J. and Humphrey, N. (2013) "Exposure to bullying among students with autism spectrum conditions: A multi-informant analysis of risk and protective factors." *Autism 18*, 6, 618–630.

Humphrey, N. and Symes, W. (2010) "Perceptions of social support and experience of bullying among pupils with autistic spectrum disorders in mainstream secondary schools." *European Journal of Special Needs Education 25*, 1, 77–91.

Just, M.A., Cherkassky, V.L., Keller, T.A., and Minshew, N.J. (2004) "Cortical activation and synchronization during sentence comprehension in high-functioning autism: Evidence of underconnectivity." *Brain 127*, 1811–1821.

Kana, R.K., Keller, T.A., Cherkassky, V.L., Minshew, N.J., and Just, M.A. (2009) "Atypical frontal–posterior synchronization of theory of mind regions in autism during mental state attribution." *Journal of Neuroscience 4*, 135–152.

Katz, N. and Zemishlany, Z. (2006) "Criminal responsibility in Asperger's syndrome." *Israel Journal of Psychiatry and Related Science 43*, 166–173.

Klin, A. (n.d.) "Five points for a comprehensive treatment program for a child pornography offender with ASD." Unpublished note.

Klin, A., Saulnier, C.A., Sparrow, S.S., Cicchetti, D.V., Volkmar, F.R., and Lord, C. (2007) "Social and communication abilities and disabilities in higher functioning individuals with autism spectrum disorders: The Vineland and the ADOS." *Journal of Autism and Developmental Disorders 37*, 748–759.

Klin, A., Volkmar, F.R., and Sparrow, S.S. (eds) (2000) *Asperger Syndrome.* New York, NY: Guilford Press.

Koller, R. (2000) "Sexuality and adolescents with autism." *Sexuality and Disability 18*, 2, 125–235.

Little, L. (2002) "Middle-class mothers' perceptions of peer and sibling victimization among children with Asperger's syndrome and nonverbal learning disorders." *Issues in Comprehensive Pediatric Nursing 25*, 1, 43–57.

Locke, J., Ishijima, E.H., Kasari, C., and London, N. (2010) "Loneliness, friendship quality and the social networks of adolescents with high-functioning autism in an inclusive school setting." *Journal of Research in Special Educational Needs 10*, 2, 74–81.

Lord, C., Rutter, M., DiLavore, P.C., Risi, S., Gotham, K., and Bishop, S.L. (2012) *Autism Diagnostic Observation Schedule, Second Edition (ADOS-2) Manual (Part 1): Modules 1–4.* Torrance, CA: Western Psychological Services.

Mahoney, M. (2009) *Asperger's Syndrome and Criminal Law: The Special Case of Child Pornography.* Available at www.harringtonmahoney.com/content/Publications/Aspergers%20Syndrome%20and%20 the%20Criminal%20Law%20v26.pdf (accessed January 12, 2017).

Mayes, T.A. and Koegel, R.L. (2003) "Persons with autism and criminal justice: Core concepts and leading cases." *Journal of Positive Behavior Interventions 5*, 2, 92–100.

Mehtar, M. and Mukaddes, N.M. (2011) "Posttraumatic stress disorder in individuals with diagnosis of autistic spectrum disorders." *Research in Autism Spectrum Disorders 5*, 1, 539–546.

Mehzabin, P. and Stokes, M.A. (2011) "Self-assessed sexuality in young adults with high-functioning autism." *Research in Autism Spectrum Disorders 5*, 614–621.

Minshew, N.J. and Keller, T.A. (2010) "The nature of brain dysfunction in autism: Functional brain imaging studies." *Current Opinion in Neurology 23*, 2, 124–130.

Rutter, M., Bailey, A., and Lord, C. (2003) *Social Communication Questionnaire (SCQ).* Los Angeles, CA: Western Psychological Services.

Rutter, M., Le Couteur, A., and Lord, C. (2003) *Autism Diagnostic Interview-Revised (ADI-R).* Los Angeles, CA: Western Psychological Services.

Sahyoun, C.P., Belliveau, J.W., Soulières, I., Schwartz, S., and Mody, M. (2010) "Neuroimaging of the functional and structural networks underlying visuospatial vs. linguistic reasoning in high-functioning autism." *Neuropsychologia 48*, 1, 86–95.

Saris, P.B., Carr, W.B., Jr., Jackson, K.B., Hinojosa, R.H., *et al.* (2013) *Report to Congress: Federal Child Pornography Offenses—Chapter 11.* Available at www.ussc.gov/sites/default/files/pdf/news/congressional-testimony-and-reports/sex-offense-topics/201212-federal-child-pornography-offenses/Chapter_11.pdf (accessed March 3, 2017).

Schipul, S.E., Keller, T.A., and Just, M.A. (2011) "Inter-regional brain communication and its disturbance in autism." *Frontiers in Systems Neuroscience 5*, 1–11.

Schumann, C.M., Hamstra, J., Goodlin-Jones, B.L., Lotspeich, L.J., *et al.* (2004) "The amygdala is enlarged in children but not adolescents with autism; the hippocampus is enlarged at all ages." *Journal of Neuroscience 24*, 28, 6392–6401.

Sofronoff, K., Dark, E., and Stone, V. (2011) "Social vulnerability and bullying in children with Asperger syndrome." *Autism 15*, 3, 355–372.

Sparrow, S.S., Cicchetti, D.V., and Balla, D.A. (2005) *Vineland Adaptive Behavior Scales: Second Edition (Vineland II) The Expanded Interview Form.* Circle Pines, MN: Pearson Assessments.

Sperry, L., Mesibov, G., Milford, T., Roberts, J., *et al.* (2014) *Criminal Justice and ASD.* Unpublished manuscript.

Sreckovic, M.A., Brunsting, N.C., and Able, H. (2014) "Victimization of students with autism spectrum disorder: A review of prevalence and risk factors." *Research in Autism Spectrum Disorders 8,* 9, 1155–1172.

Sterzing, P.R., Shattuck, P.T., Narendorf, S.C., Wagner, M., and Cooper, B.P. (2012) "Bullying involvement and autism spectrum disorders: Prevalence and correlates of bullying involvement among adolescents with an autism spectrum disorder." *Archives of Pediatrics and Adolescent Medicine 166,* 11, 1058–1064.

Tantam, D. (2003) "The challenge of adolescents and adults with Asperger syndrome." *Child and Adolescent Psychiatric Clinics of North America 12,* 1, 143–163.

Taylor, K., Mesibov, G., and Debbaudt, D. (2009) *Asperger Syndrome in the Criminal Justice System.* Available at www.aane.org/asperger-syndrome-criminal-justice-system (accessed January 12, 2017).

Tsoudis, O. (2000) "Relation of affect control theory to the sentencing of criminals." *Journal of Social Psychology 140,* 4, 473–485.

Twyman, K.A., Saylor, C.F., Saia, D., Macias, M.M., Taylor, L.A., and Spratt, E. (2010) "Bullying and ostracism experiences in children with special health care needs." *Journal of Developmental and Behavioral Pediatrics 31,* 1, 1–8.

Wagner, M., Cadwallader, T.W., Garza, N., and Cameto, R. (2004) "Social activities of youth with disabilities." *NLTS2 Data Brief 3,* 1, 1–4.

Webb, L., Craissati, J., and Keen, S. (2007) "Characteristics of internet child pornography offenders: A comparison with child molesters." *Sexual Abuse: A Journal of Research and Treatment 19,* 4, 449–465.

Webster, C.D., Martin, M.L., Brink, J., Nicholls, T.L., and Desmarais, S. (2009) *Manual for the Short-Term Assessment of Risk and Treatability (START)* (Version 1.1). Port Coquitlam, BC: Forensic Psychiatric Services Commission and St. Joseph's Healthcare.

Wollert, R., Waggoner, J., and Smith, J. (2009, October) *Child pornographer offenders do not have florid offense histories and are unlikely to recidivate.* Poster session presented at the annual meeting of the Association of the Treatment of Sexual Abusers, Dallas, TX.

Zablotsky, B., Bradshaw, C.P., Anderson, C., and Law, P.A. (2013) "The association between bullying and the psychological functioning of children with autism spectrum disorders." *Journal of Developmental Behavior Pediatrics 34,* 1, 1–8.

CHAPTER 3

Representing an Autism Spectrum Disorder Individual Charged with Possession of Internet Child Pornography

A Case Study

Kenneth M. Mogill

Litigators often take on representations that present unfamiliar issues. Whether the new aspect of a particular case is related to its issues of law or to its particular facts, or both, addressing something new is part and parcel of litigation. The uniqueness of a case can, in fact, be an appealing challenge for the litigator as well as a diversion from the familiar. In this writer's experience, though, representing an individual with an autism spectrum disorder (ASD) charged with the extremely serious offense of using the internet to possess child pornography presented issues of law and fact that, combined with the human story of the client's life, were singularly challenging and entirely engrossing.

Over the course of this representation I learned just how unique representing an individual with ASD can be:

- To those who are unfamiliar with ASD—including litigators who have previously represented clients with other, qualitatively different mental status issues—developing a sufficient understanding of ASD and how one's client fits on the spectrum requires educating oneself about complex, highly individualized, and, at times, counterintuitive neurological, emotional, and social circumstances.

- To communicate effectively with the client's treater and/or potential expert witnesses, educating oneself about ASD also requires developing a basic understanding of the profound differences, including differences in appropriate treatment methods and modalities and the risks to the client of being treated by a therapist utilizing the wrong modality, between neurologically based and non-neurologically based conditions.

- Even though the client may be highly intelligent in terms of cognitive functioning, communicating with the client requires considering the ASD-related limits of the client's capacity to understand the ways of the world around him or her.

- Respecting and addressing the client's fears presents unusual challenges, including not just the client's different ways of understanding the world in general and the legal system but also the client's ASD-related tendencies to obsess about details and to be extremely uncomfortable with shades of gray.

- The client's fears and lesser ability to handle stress may profoundly affect overall case strategy, as these limitations may preclude counsel from proceeding to trial even where a viable defense exists.

- Opposing counsel are often ignorant about ASD, unaware of its neurological basis, unfamiliar with the significant implications of its neurological basis (in contrast with conditions that are not neurologically based), and potentially uninterested in becoming educated about ASD and its implications for the case.

- To date, with some notable exceptions, the legal system in general, including the criminal law system, has failed to develop a meaningful understanding of what ASD is, or how it is related to issues of criminal responsibility and sentencing policy. Very few judges, prosecutors, or defense attorneys have received either the necessary training or developed the necessary experience to address cases involving individuals with ASD appropriately.

These observations, and others discussed below, grew out of my experiences representing an individual with ASD charged with possessing internet child pornography in the U.S. District Court for the Eastern District of Michigan.

* * *

On October 6, 2010, I received a panicked telephone call from Larry Dubin, a long-time friend and law professor at the University of Detroit Mercy Law School. Larry's adult son, Nick, whom I had never met, had just been arrested by FBI agents for possession of internet child pornography, and a court appearance was scheduled for the next day. As Larry related the situation to me, investigating agents had obtained a search warrant for Nick's condominium, and agents had appeared there in force that morning, had interviewed Nick and taken a statement from him, and had seized his computer. Even though the agents had chosen not to take Nick into custody—on his and Larry's promise to appear in court the next day—Nick was terrified. His fears were well grounded, as he was potentially facing a lengthy sentence in a federal prison; the local United States Attorney's office routinely sought and obtained sentences of at least five years' imprisonment in internet child pornography cases.

At the time of Larry's call, I had been practicing for 39 years, and I had previously represented many individuals in federal court, including some charged with internet pornography crimes. I had also represented many individuals with mental health problems and had worked on many occasions with psychiatrists, psychologists, and social workers. I had never represented an individual with ASD, however, and I knew virtually nothing about ASD, particularly the form of ASD then categorized separately as Asperger's,[1] and I did not know how different it is from the kinds of mental health issues with which I had experience. Moreover, from my own experiences and those of colleagues, I knew that the prosecution took a hard line on these cases; the office was committed to what it viewed as policies necessary for the protection of the child victims appearing in the videos accessed online. As I was about to find out, though, to the extent that there is a "normal" internet child pornography case, this was not one.

Larry explained to me that Nick, who was then 33 years old, had received special services beginning in childhood but had not been diagnosed as having Asperger's until 2004, and that Nick was and had been in therapy for an extended period. Larry and his wife,

---

1   Because Asperger's was considered as a distinct diagnosis prior to the adoption of DSM-5 which now includes it as an autism spectrum disorder, I will most frequently refer to Nick's condition as being Asperger's, as that was the term in use at the time.

Kitty, were deeply committed to making sure that Nick received the services and treatment he needed, and they had helped Nick achieve an amazing degree of success in his life. Although he had great difficulty navigating the day-to-day world, Nick was living on his own, albeit with a great deal of support. Nick was also very active in the Asperger's community nationally and had become a prolific writer, using his own life experiences to help others on the spectrum. He was, however, also quite asocial; he was very uncomfortable around most other people. Larry and Kitty were devastated by Nick's arrest and, like Nick, terrified at what he was now facing.

As I came to learn, one central aspect of Nick's Asperger's is asynchronous development; that is, unlike in most individuals, intellectual development at a different rate from physical and emotional development. Nick vividly illustrates this phenomenon, as he is a very intelligent individual in terms of his cognitive functioning; he had been able to earn a Psy.D. in psychology from a local private graduate school (although the school had to waive the clinical component of its degree requirements as an accommodation to Nick's Asperger's). With respect to psycho-social and psycho-sexual development, however, Nick has never progressed beyond pre-adolescence. This seeming incongruity is unquestionably difficult to grasp for one not familiar with Asperger's.

As I also came to learn, a second central aspect of Nick's Asperger's is what is called mindblindness, an inability to be aware of others' mental states, to conceptualize or understand others' emotional states. This limitation is reflected, in part, in a deficit in social insight. With respect to Nick, even though he is an extremely sensitive, caring, and empathic individual who was devoting a large portion of his time to helping others with his condition, because of his neurologically based condition, he literally didn't realize the reality of what was involved in watching images of child pornography on the internet.

Per the affidavit in support of the application for a search warrant in the case, about five weeks earlier an undercover FBI agent had logged onto the internet and had connected to a computer using a particular IP address which had filenames consistent with and appeared to depict child pornography. Based on this information, the agent traced the service and billing address for the computer through the internet service provider for the address being investigated and identified it as being that of Nick's condominium. Nick lived alone, and there was really no question either that he had been the person using the computer or that he had knowingly accessed the forbidden images. As co-counsel and I were later to learn in a very telling session with the case agents, however, unlike in other child pornography cases I had seen, the images in this case were in many ways consistent with the curiosity of a young child playing "doctor." Seeing the differences between these images and the images I had seen in connection with other cases dramatically underscored for us the extent to which Nick was, in fact, pre-adolescent in his psycho-social and psycho-sexual development. This understanding, in turn, reinforced for us that Nick did not deserve to be imprisoned for even a day.

When we appeared in court the day after Nick's arrest, we secured his release with the government's consent, albeit subject to an electronic tether, regular reporting to the court's Pretrial Services Agency, and other conditions. In an informal conversation with Matthew Roth, the assistant U.S. attorney assigned to the file, Matt made it clear that, as seriously as his office took the case, he was going to agree to us having the time we needed to marshal and submit to him and his superiors whatever information we wanted to present to demonstrate why, in our opinion, Nick's case was qualitatively different from most other internet child pornography cases his office handled.

Given my lack of familiarity about Asperger's, one of my first tasks was to make sure that I asked the right questions: What is Asperger's? How is it related to other autism spectrum conditions? How is it similar to and different from non-neurologically based mental health circumstances? How do I find the right expert? What have various federal and state courts done in similar cases? How have prosecutors and defense attorneys prepared in such cases? Given that there is no question that Nick had accessed child pornography on the internet (and that the images appeared to be those of real children as opposed to computer-generated images, possession of which would not be a crime[2]), were there any possible defenses in the case? What is the relationship between Asperger's and issues of criminal responsibility? What is the relationship between Asperger's and the application of the federal sentencing guidelines?

In pursuing answers to these questions, I was greatly helped by numerous circumstances. First, as a part of Nick's long-time activism in

---

2   Cf. *Ashcroft v. Free Speech Coalition*, 535 U.S. 234 (2002).

the national Asperger's community, he had written extensively about his experiences. Also, Kitty and Larry had been extremely involved in helping Nick throughout his life; both are highly educated and articulate individuals, and not only did they provide me with relevant materials, but they were, at all times, immediately available to answer my questions. As such, in addition to having a wealth of material about Nick in his own words available to me, I was able to be directed to useful material very efficiently. Because Nick had been receiving special services since childhood, there was also an extensive documentary history available to review and absorb.

In addition, my law clerk at the time, Kristina Saleh, happened to be simultaneously pursuing both a law degree and a master's degree in social work at the University of Michigan; her familiarity with a broad range of individual circumstances faced by mental health professionals enabled her to review and distill relevant information for me that saved me many hours of research time. She was also very well positioned to serve as a sounding board for many of the questions I had. Nick's treater, a highly regarded therapist with a great deal of experience in treating individuals charged with sex offenses and someone I coincidentally knew from a prior case in which he had treated my client, was also an extremely valuable, consistently available resource.[3]

Finally, early in the representation, Larry suggested bringing in Alan Gershel as co-counsel. Alan, who was then a professor at Thomas M. Cooley Law School, had spent most of his career in the U.S. Attorney's office in the Eastern District of Michigan, rising to the position of Chief Assistant U.S. Attorney (and, on multiple occasions, interim U.S. Attorney). He and I knew each other well from working on the opposite sides of cases over the years, and we worked together very well on the same side in Nick's case. Alan's experiences inside his former office also frequently provided important insights as we anticipated the government's concerns and prepared to address them.

With the defense team in place, we set out to find appropriate experts while simultaneously continuing our self-education about Asperger's and searching for useful precedents and/or illustrative cases from our own or other federal districts. We quickly learned that, with few exceptions, most cases involving an Asperger's individual did not involve a case record that suggested a meaningful understanding

---

3   At the therapist's request, the therapist is not identified by name in this chapter.

of Asperger's or its implications for the proper handling of the case. There was simply little to go on from others' experiences. As we later learned in our discussions with Matt Roth, he was simultaneously canvassing the experiences of his colleagues in other districts, and he, too, found very little guidance from those cases, other than that the exercise of discretion we would soon be requesting was not the norm, to say the least.

With respect to experts, we considered using someone from out of the area, and we did have Nick evaluated by Fred Volkmar, M.D., the director of the Yale Child Study Clinic and a national authority on Asperger's. We ultimately decided, however, that it would be preferable, if possible, also to identify someone locally, as it would be much more practical to have an expert who could easily meet with Nick in person as needed. After considering approximately half a dozen experts, we decided to retain Andrew Maltz, Ph.D., a local therapist with the relevant knowledge about and experience in dealing with Asperger's individuals. Importantly, we also felt that Dr. Maltz was someone who would be able to communicate about Asperger's effectively to the U.S. Attorney's office. Throughout the litigation of the case, Dr. Maltz provided astute insights, thoughtful and carefully prepared reports, and ready access to answer our many questions.

In addition to referring Nick to Dr. Volkmar and Dr. Maltz, we worked with Nick's therapist, who was instrumental during the lengthy pendency of the case in helping Nick to try to manage his extreme fears. As Nick's long-time treater, he was also an important source of critical information about Nick's condition, his attitude, and the risk of repetition. We also developed secondary sources of information that we hoped would be relevant to the U.S. Attorney's office's consideration of our submission. Of particular value among these resources were the "Principles for Prosecutors Considering Child Pornography Charges Against Persons with Asperger's Syndrome," sponsored by Ami Klin, Ph.D., then the director of the Autism Program at the Yale University School of Medicine Child Study Clinic, Dr. Volkmar, the Organization for Autism Research, the ASPEN Asperger Education Network, the Connecticut Autism Spectrum Resource Center, and the Asperger's Association of New England, among other individuals and organizations (Carley *et al.*, 2008).

On another track, it was important to us to address the government's concern—a concern present in every internet child pornography case regardless of the circumstances—as to whether Nick posed a risk of either repeating his viewing of internet child pornography or of committing a "touch" offense. To our experts and us, the risk of repeating his internet misconduct was extremely low for the reasons detailed in both Dr. Maltz's and Nick's therapist's reports, and there was no risk whatever that Nick would engage in a "touch" offense. Neither Matt Roth nor his superiors or the case agents knew Nick, however, so one of our tasks was to explain the nature of Nick's condition and the arc of his life experiences in a way that addressed these questions. We did so through developing three threads of information:

- In discussing Nick and how he lived his life, we noted that all his social contacts had been entirely respectful of others. As two examples, we explained that he had been a youth tennis coach, a role in which he had succeeded without socializing with his students; and, when speaking to groups about his Asperger's experiences, virtually his only interactions with others were at a podium while presenting, as he otherwise kept entirely to himself.

- We made sure that Nick's therapist addressed these questions in his report, including explaining Nick's response to therapy.

- We obtained character reference letters from many people who knew Nick well, had known him for many years in many different circumstances, and were in appropriate positions to comment not only on his character in general but also on the absence of risk that he would ever commit a "touch" offense.

After gathering all the information we could, including reviewing the guidelines in the U.S. Attorneys' Manual regarding the circumstances appropriate for pretrial diversion in lieu of prosecution, we determined that our specific proposal to the prosecution should be not just that the case be resolved without Nick being incarcerated but that Nick should be placed on pretrial diversion, with relevant conditions, for an extended period. We then set about organizing the information we had gathered and presenting it to Matt Roth in what we hoped would be the most persuasive package possible. In March 2011, we were finally ready to make our submission.

The process of preparing our submission involved not only deciding what information to include and how to organize it but also guarding against an inappropriate tone. Given Nick's life story and the looming risk of a lengthy jail sentence, the situation was laden with intense emotions. A submission that relied on an emotional appeal would be weaker than one based on logic and could even be counterproductive. It was, therefore, critical for us to strive for a consistently business-like tone.

We began the submission with a detailed review of Nick's background, noting that he was by then 33 years old, he had no prior criminal history whatever, he had never exhibited any aggressive or manipulative behavior, there were no issues involving substance abuse, and he was and had consistently been fully compliant with all conditions of release. We then moved on to addressing the question noted above—that is, what we knew would be the government's concern about future conduct. To respond to this question, we noted not only that the charged offense did not allege any contact with or attempt to contact a minor, but also that Nick had never had or attempted to have any inappropriate contact with a minor and that, as explained above, his social habits effectively ruled out any such risk.

We next explained what Asperger's is and then addressed in detail Nick's diagnostic and treatment history. Quoting from the "Principles for Prosecutors," we stressed that it is a neurologically based condition:

> an "Autism Spectrum Disorder" (ASD) typified by extreme social and emotional immaturity, the inability to "read" others or respond appropriately in social settings, lack of intuitive awareness of social/ moral/legal constraints, and intense and narrowly directed repetitive activities... These are intellectually intact people, with good computer skills but extraordinary brain-based naivete, acting in social isolation, compulsively pursuing interests which often unknowingly take them into forbidden territory. (Carley *et al.*, 2008, p.1)

Tying this general statement to Nick's condition in particular, we noted that Nick had received special education services throughout his school years and had been diagnosed with Asperger's in 2004. We also stressed from Dr. Maltz's report that while Nick's level of intelligence was at average levels, his social and sexual development lagged behind at a pre-adolescent stage of development.

We then addressed the likelihood of treatment being successful, quoting again from the "Principles for Prosecutors." An Asperger's individual's viewing of child pornography may arouse their curiosity. At these times AS is directly involved in the individual's obliviousness to the social and legal taboos surrounding child pornography, and the inability to intuit that the visual depictions are the product of any kind of abusive relationship. This behavior is not predictive of future involvement with child pornography or offenses against children. (Carley *et al.*, 2008, pp. 1–2)

We further noted that the absence of risk of a future offense was corroborated by Nick's basic morality, his desire to always do what is "right," the dramatic impact of his arrest on him, his ongoing participation in therapy, and the strong evidence of his good character as reflected in the character reference letters we attached.

With respect to our request for pretrial diversion instead of prosecution, we quoted yet again from the "Principles," which encourage prosecutors

to defer criminal prosecution in cases involving young first offenders with AS who have no history of directly offending against children, or having produced or distributed child pornography, no clinical indications of pedophilia (other than accessing child pornography), nor history of prior offenses involving child pornography. (Carley *et al.*, 2008, p. 4)

Tying this request to the prosecutor's determination as to how to exercise discretion in this case, we quoted relevant language from the U.S. Attorneys' Manual. Diversion is disfavored in child pornography cases, but it is not prohibited, and we noted that "innovative approaches are strongly encouraged" (U.S. Attorneys' Manual, § 9-22.000, Criminal Resources Manual 712). Finally, we included in our proposal specific suggested conditions of diversion designed to address particular prosecution concerns. In addition to the usual requirement of periodic reporting to the court's Pretrial Services Agency, we proposed that Nick be required to continue receiving mental health treatment with a treater knowledgeable about Asperger's, that Nick's treater be required to confirm Nick's compliance with the treatment requirement, and that Nick be subject to random unannounced home visits and computer searches by a Pretrial Services Agency officer.

As it turned out, this submission was just the beginning of a lengthy series of discussions, further forensic interviews, and supplemental submissions. As the process dragged on and Nick's emotional condition remained extremely delicate, we also met regularly with Nick, Larry, and Kitty to keep them up to date, answer their many questions, and try to help Nick cope with the stresses of the situation. Nick's Asperger's-related difficulty in handling uncertainty complicated these efforts and made our roles as attorney-counselors particularly complex. As challenging as this aspect of the representation was, it was a necessary part of it. It also repeatedly gave us a first-hand opportunity to see how Asperger's affected Nick's day-to-day life. We were also highly motivated to meet Nick's communication needs, as he is such a gentle, thoughtful, sympathetic, and trusting soul.

Following receipt of our submission, after clearly giving a great deal of thought to our submission and seeking to understand what, if anything, is different about Nick's circumstances from the circumstances of individuals with emotional problems who view child pornography and who are treated harshly by his office, Matt Roth posed a number of astute questions to us: What distinguishes Nick, as an Asperger's individual, from an individual who is also socially isolated and is suffering from a mental illness, such as depression or some other mental illness? Stated another way, what is it, if anything, about Asperger's that is different in terms of the impetus to view child pornography, rather than why an Asperger's individual may decide to view internet child pornography; what, if anything, about Asperger's renders such a decision beyond the individual's control?

To respond to Matt's questions, we asked both Dr. Maltz and Nick's therapist to prepare supplemental reports focusing specifically on these questions. These reports enabled us to quote from them at length in our late July 2011 response to Matt. As stated by Dr. Maltz:

> Asperger's Syndrome is not a mental illness: It is a developmental disability...[that] begins at birth, although causality most likely occurred congenitally... Each stage [of development] is a foundation for the next stage. If a particular stage of development is not completed successfully or if something has an effect on the stage such that there is an arrest in the progression of the stage, future stages will be distorted, as well...
>
> The difference between mental illness and developmental disabilities is based on the difference in how the symptoms develop. Individuals with mental illness do not have a specific impairment from birth which affects their development. Their symptoms become manifest at later points in their life when certain biological triggers set off neurochemical processes that result in the symptoms that we

associate with their mental illness... In individuals with Autism/ Asperger's Syndrome, their development is affected from birth and it permeates all later stages of development, with a primary effect on their capability to communicate effectively secondary to an inability to process pragmatics.

Linking these points to the asynchronous development that is central to Asperger's, our response also noted that, while Nick functions at a high level in certain aspects of his life, he remains at a pre-adolescent level in many other aspects of his life. Returning to the apparent incongruity of Nick's condition to someone unfamiliar with Asperger's, we stressed that "someone unfamiliar with Asperger's can easily fail to appreciate the extent of this disparity and, therefore, of his disability," and then returned once more to Dr. Maltz's report:

> Mr. Dubin's cognitive levels fell in the average range. However, his adaptive skills fell in the significantly impaired range (i.e. four to five standard deviations below the Mean). His adaptive skills relate to his ability to apply his knowledge to the requirements of day-to-day activities. While his ability to respond to questions fell at a level consistent with his age, individuals with his developmental disability are incapable of applying their seemingly average intelligence to overcoming their adaptive deficits because this deficit, in general, and in Mr. Dubin's case specifically, is a function of a biologically determined developmental disability and not a function of emotional compromise, environmental impact, or early childhood experiences.

Moving from discussion of Nick's condition to the legal implications of that condition, we addressed a point not discussed in our initial submission—the significance of Nick's disability in relation to criminal responsibility.[4] Under federal law, an individual is not criminally responsible if, at the time of the act at issue, "the defendant, as a result of a severe mental disease or defect, was unable to appreciate the nature and quality or the wrongfulness of his acts" (18 U.S.C. § 17. We also noted that federal law treats an individual as a juvenile until they have reached their eighteenth birthday (18 U.S.C. § 5031). We then asserted that, even though it is in some ways difficult to plug Asperger's syndrome into traditional categories of criminal responsibility, Nick should not be held criminally responsible for having viewed the images

---

4   Eligibility for diversion does not require a lack of criminal responsibility.

in issue because, whether considered in the context of 18 U.S.C. § 17 or of 18 U.S.C. § 5031, as a result of his Asperger's he was "unable to appreciate the…wrongfulness of his acts," and, even though he was chronologically an adult, his ability to appreciate the wrongfulness of his acts was at the level of a pre-adolescent.

Developing these points further, we argued that because of a developmental disability and not a mental illness Nick has never progressed in his social development beyond the age of a pre-adolescent.

Lest Matt Roth and his colleagues view our request as being one that would let Nick avoid any consequences for his conduct, we addressed this point, too, linking the notion of age-appropriate consequences to Nick's developmental age and to our initial request for pretrial diversion:

> In urging that Nick not be held to adult standards of criminal responsibility, we are not suggesting that there be no consequences for his conduct. Rather, we propose that the consequences be appropriate for someone of his developmental age. Continuing treatment with his therapist, under the supervision of the Pretrial Services Agency as part of a pretrial diversion agreement, would be a developmentally and legally appropriate consequence in this case.

There was one more point we were able to address in this submission, and it was both important and sensitive: Expanding on a point made in our initial submission, we noted that even though Nick had been in treatment with his therapist prior to the time of his offense and his therapist is a very competent therapist with a great deal of experience treating sex offenders, his therapist came to realize that his lack of experience treating Asperger's individuals in particular had been problematic in his treatment of Nick. To his great credit, his therapist candidly acknowledged that, given Nick's Asperger's status, he should have treated him with a different modality and that, if he had done so, there was a significant likelihood that Nick would not have committed an offense.

Around the time of this submission, Matt Roth indicated to Alan and me that his office was not going to seek a custodial sentence for Nick, but they were not willing to resolve the case without a guilty plea to possession of internet child pornography. As relieved as we were to have the issue of jail time off the table—and this was a huge relief, as we were extremely concerned that Nick would, quite literally, not be able to survive a prison sentence—we remained very concerned about the plea offer. Not only did the offer strike us as not adequately considering the role of Asperger's in Nick's behavior and level of culpability, but the fact that a guilty plea to possession of internet child pornography would result in placement on the sex offender registry even in the absence of incarceration presented substantial problems. The reality of being placed on the sex offender registry is that it brings with it a level of stigma and practical day-to-day restrictions that would be very difficult for Nick to cope with. We therefore continued to press our arguments in support of pretrial diversion or, as a fallback, a guilty plea to an offense that did not require placement on the registry.

Following further conversations with Matt, we mutually agreed that Nick would be interviewed by an in-house psychologist at FBI headquarters in Washington. In November 2011, accompanied by Larry, Nick traveled to Washington for what turned out to be an extremely lengthy interview with Steven J. Porter, an FBI neuropsychologist knowledgeable about and experienced with ASD and Asperger's. Although Dr. Porter did not prepare a written report, we learned from Matt that he accepted Dr. Maltz's analysis of Nick's condition and was not opposed to the case being resolved by placing Nick on pretrial diversion. Despite this evaluation by its own expert, however, the government remained unwilling to move from its offer of a plea agreement that required a plea to possession of internet child pornography.

Our efforts to identify other cases in which the defendant was an Asperger's individual and their case was resolved on terms consistent with our proposal in Nick's case continued to be unavailing. Despite extensive research and contacts with attorneys in federal defender offices around the county, we were only able to identify one other Asperger's internet child pornography case in which prosecutorial discretion had been exercised to avoid a registry offense conviction.[5] The absence of any such cases to note weakened our negotiating power. Our bargaining leverage was further limited by the fact that it was clear to Alan and me that Nick's emotional state was such that going to trial was not a viable option, even though a trial would provide us with an opportunity to argue, supported by very substantial evidence, that Nick lacked criminal responsibility.

---

5   *United States v. Rubino*, WD NY #08-cr-06021 (defendant pled guilty to an obscenity charge; no incarceration; obscenity is not a registry offense).

After additional back-and-forth negotiations in which we continued to press for at least a plea to a non-registry offense, we agreed to make Nick available for an October 2012 forensic interview by another expert of the government's choosing, Charles R. Clark, Ph.D. Although Dr. Clark had a great deal of forensic experience, we had preferred that the government select someone with more direct experience in dealing with Asperger's individuals. Clark acknowledged that Nick's Asperger's may be related to his viewing pornography on the internet. Dr. Clark's overall findings were also very understanding of Nick's condition and sympathetic toward Nick. He concluded that Nick does not present "even at [sic] appreciable risk of" becoming a contact sex offender in the future, that his Asperger's disorder "should not be seen as...a condition that puts him at risk of committing a sexual offense (or even using child pornography again)," and—of particular note in relation to our attempt to secure a plea to a non-registry offense—that

> [i]t is worthwhile, from all points of view, for him to continue without the imposition of new impediments, particularly ones that would limit his access to social support and opportunities for social learning. His path is hard enough as it is.

Since any resolution of Nick's case that resulted in a criminal conviction would constitute a substantial "new impediment," we argued that Dr. Clark's conclusion should be read as supporting our request for pretrial diversion. We were also able to note that Dr. Clark's conclusion as to an appropriate outcome was consistent with that of every expert who had evaluated Nick about this matter, whether for the government or for the defense, that diversion was an appropriate result here.

After further discussions, including meetings with Matt and his superiors in the office, including U.S. Attorney Barbara McQuade, the government determined that it would not revise its plea offer, and it was clear that we had exhausted our negotiating opportunities. Nick and his parents agreed that Nick would accept the government's offer, and after negotiating the language of a Rule 11 Plea Agreement, Nick eventually entered an agreement that called for him to plead guilty to possession of internet child pornography and be placed on both supervised release and the sex offender registry. In January 2013, Nick pled guilty before Hon. Arthur J. Tarnow, and in April 2013, after reviewing both the government's sentencing memorandum and the defense sentencing submission, Judge Tarnow accepted the plea agreement and placed Nick on supervised release for a period of five years.

* * *

As expected, Nick was fully compliant with all terms of his supervised release, and in 2016 the government stipulated for early release from supervised release after approximately three years. Judge Tarnow accepted the parties' stipulation and amended the judgment accordingly. The requirement that he be listed on the sex offender registry, a requirement that cannot be waived for ten years under current law, has taken and continues to take a great emotional toll on Nick, however, in the many ways in which being on the registry affects his day-to-day life beyond the substantial stigma inherent in being on the registry. Being on the registry affects, for example, where Nick can live, whether he can travel to another state for a speaking engagement, and whether he can even be in the presence of family members who are minors. Nick is writing about his experiences, but he remains very traumatized by this experience and haunted by its consequences.

I am very grateful that Nick has avoided incarceration following conviction for an offense that regularly results in a lengthy prison sentence, but I am also disappointed that the system did not have the capacity to address the relationship between his Asperger's and issues of criminal responsibility and sentencing in what I submit would have been the appropriate manner. I am also left with several questions I cannot answer: Would the government's position have changed if we could have shown that the resolution we were seeking had been deemed acceptable in other cases involving Asperger's individuals, so that this particular U.S. Attorney's office would not have been essentially breaking new ground? Would the government's position have changed if we could have expressed a willingness to take the case to trial, where, despite the risks, we believed that the testimony of the experts on both sides would have been favorable to our argument regarding criminal responsibility and where Nick's life story would have provided a sympathetic counterbalance to the allegations of the case?

In our discussions and negotiations with Matt and his superiors in the U.S. Attorney's office, they consistently appeared to be interested in learning about Asperger's, and they were invariably open to considering our arguments and submissions. As disappointed as we were and are at the ultimate outcome of the case, we also understood that they have a very difficult responsibility. They regularly see cases of awful people committing horrific acts, including, at times, individuals who have been given a break on an earlier occasion, and these other experiences, coupled with the office's obligation to protect the public, necessarily color their view of what is an appropriate exercise of prosecutorial discretion in any case. Further, as noted above, we were asking for an exercise of prosecutorial discretion that is outside the norm.

Ultimately, though, in my opinion, the system did Nick a disservice. Everything about his background and life, including the opinions of all the experts who examined him, strongly supports the conclusion that he would not have engaged in this misconduct but for his Asperger's and his consequent failure to understand what he was doing, that he presents no risk of repeating this behavior or other criminal behavior, and that, in fact, a conviction that places him on the registry is damaging to him and interferes with his ability to help others with Asperger's. From this perspective, the outcome of this case reflects poorly on the criminal justice system, and we should be able to expect more from the system. Finally, I am also very concerned that, if Nick had been someone who lacked the family resources to ensure that all of the relevant mitigating (and potentially exonerating) information was gathered and presented to the government, he might well have ended up in prison.

Based on this experience, I believe that the criminal justice system should take several specific steps to improve the investigation, prosecution, and disposition of cases involving ASD individuals viewing child pornography via the internet. In particular:

1. Prosecutors, defense attorneys, investigating officers and agents, judges, pretrial services officers, and probation officers need specific training that educates them about ASD and ASD individuals, their challenges, and the differences between developmental disorders and mental illnesses.

2. Defense attorneys representing ASD individuals need to take the time and make the effort to become competent at representing individuals with this very particular diagnosis,

and they need the financial and other resources necessary to enable them to do so.

3. Defense attorneys representing ASD individuals charged with possession of internet child pornography need to know how to identify the right experts to assist in the development of their clients' defenses, and they need the financial and other resources necessary to be able to retain these experts.

4. Consistent with the "Principles for Prosecutors" discussed above, prosecutors need to develop appropriate guidelines for exercising discretion in cases involving ASD individuals so that they are able fully to meet their responsibility to protect the public while taking into account the impact of ASD on an individual's level of criminal responsibility on a case-by-case basis, as well as, in many cases, the disproportionate and unwarranted impact on the individual of a criminal conviction, incarceration, and/or placement on a sex offender registry. These guidelines should include, *inter alia*, consideration of when prosecution, if a case is to be prosecuted, should be by federal authorities and when it should be by state or local authorities.

5. Federal and state sentencing guidelines should be reviewed so that, in those cases in which there is a prosecution and a conviction, the sentencing process adequately considers the defendant's developmental disability, the likely impact of appropriate treatment, the degree of risk of recidivism, and the impact on the defendant of incarceration, especially for an extended period.

These steps would materially improve the system and would benefit not just the Nick Dubins of this world but all others on the autism spectrum who run afoul of the law in what are now all too frequently circumstances that are inadequately understood.

REFERENCE

Carley, M.J., Gerhardt, P., Jekel, D., Klin, A., *et al.* (2008) *Principles for Prosecutors Considering Child Pornography Charges against Persons with Asperger's Syndrome.* Available at www.harringtonmahoney. com/content/Publications/Principles%20for%20Prosecutors%20-%209-14-08.pdf (accessed January 12, 2017).

CHAPTER 4

Forensic Assessment of Individuals on the Autism Spectrum Charged with Child Pornography Violations

Dennis P. Sugrue

INTRODUCTION

Child pornography (CP) violations committed by an individual on the autism spectrum present two important issues for our legal system. First, sentencing for CP-only offenses has become highly controversial. Every child pornographic image documents a child being sexually exploited, often in a cruel and inhumane fashion. In response, federal and, to a lesser extent, state courts (von Dornum, 2012) have aggressively prosecuted not only producers of child pornography but also any consumer of child pornography, often with penalties that exceed sentences given to perpetrators of contact offenses against a child (United States Sentencing Commission [USSC], 2012). A debate has arisen as to whether sentencing guidelines for CP consumers are misguided and overzealous (Specter and Hoffa, 2012; Sulzberger, 2010), especially in light of research showing that CP-only offenders present the lowest risk of recidivism compared with perpetrators of any other sexual offense (Seto, 2012). Assumptions that CP consumers encourage CP production, that they have likely committed contact offenses in the past, and that they are likely to commit contact offenses in the future have been seriously challenged due to a lack of supporting empirical evidence (von Dornum, 2012).

The issue of how our legal system should respond to CP-only offenses becomes further complicated when the offender is on the autism spectrum. Individuals who have been diagnosed with an autism spectrum disorder (ASD) have a neurological condition that in some cases can call into question the extent of their criminal responsibility (Mahoney, 2009). Further, ASD can predispose individuals to be drawn to pornography in general and child pornography in particular. Thus, sentencing for CP-only offenses, already challenging and controversial for neurotypical (non-ASD) offenders, is further complicated by questions regarding criminal responsibility and mitigation in cases involving individuals with ASD.

In cases where an individual with ASD is charged with a child pornography offense, an appropriate forensic evaluation can provide valuable assistance for defense attorneys, prosecutors, and judges to better understand the offender, the extent of his neurological disability, his motivation for accessing CP, his recidivistic risk, mitigation, and what constitutes an optimal disposition and intervention.

ASD, CHILD PORNOGRAPHY, AND LEGAL ISSUES
What We Know about ASD

Although we can find references to autism in the scientific literature going back for more than a century, our understanding of this condition has been continually evolving. Early in the 20th century, people who had severe deficits in communication and social interaction were labeled *autistic* and were assumed to be suffering from schizophrenia (Kuhn and Cahn, 2004). Starting in the late 1950s/early 1960s, autism was no longer viewed as a manifestation of schizophrenia but, instead, as a profound developmental disorder due to neurologic abnormalities (Rimland, 1964). During that era, the prevalence of autism was estimated to be five children out of every 10,000 births (Newschaffer *et al.*, 2007). Only during the past two or three decades have we come to appreciate that autism is a spectrum, with profound cases marked by an inability to communicate or interact with others, while in milder cases individuals can communicate but have difficulty maintaining a reciprocal conversation and are challenged when trying to decipher how to respond in social situations. Until recently, these milder cases, viewed as being at the high-functioning end of the autism spectrum, were assigned the unique diagnostic label *Asperger's syndrome* (American Psychiatric Association [APA], 1994). In 2013 the American Psychiatric Association, in its 5th Edition of its *Diagnostic and Statistical Manual of Mental Disorders* (DSM-5; APA, 2013), merged the diagnosis of Asperger's syndrome with the more classic concept of autism under the umbrella diagnosis autism spectrum disorder (ASD). In 2014, the Centers for Disease Control and Prevention (CDC, March 28) estimated the prevalence for ASD to be one out of every 68 children aged eight years old.

Individuals with ASD appear to be neurologically "wired" differently to people not on the spectrum (the latter group referred to as *neurotypicals*). Although no definitive cause for ASD has been identified, researchers have been able to observe distinct differences in neuroanatomy (Carper and Courchesne, 2005; Casanova, Buxhoeveden, and Gomez, 2003; Kana *et al.*, 2009; Schipul, Keller, and Just, 2011; Schumann *et al.*, 2004), neurophysiology (Minshew and Keller, 2010; Sahyoun *et al.*, 2010), and neuropsychological functioning (Hughes, Russell, and Robbins, 1994; Tager-Flusberg, 2007) between ASD individuals and neurotypicals. As reflected in a large body of literature (e.g. APA, 2013; Attwood, 2007; CDC, 2014), ASD individuals present in varying degrees with many of the following characteristics:

- childhood history of delays in motor development (e.g. clumsiness) and repetitive behaviors such as arm flapping or whole body movements

- sensory dysfunction such as being hypersensitive to tactile stimulation and easily distracted by bright lights and loud sounds

- problems with *central coherence*—that is, they become hyper-focused on details and have difficulty stepping back to see the "big picture"; this often manifests as black-and-white thinking

- problems with *fluid reasoning*—that is, they find it difficult applying principles or lessons previously learned to solve new problems

- tendency to adhere rigidly to rules and to be concrete and moralistic in their understanding of right and wrong

- *mindblindness*, often referred to as *theory of mind*—ASD individuals have a difficult time appreciating what others might be thinking or feeling

- lack of empathy, largely the result of their mindblindness; it is difficult to feel empathy for another's misery if a person has little ability to discern their misery

- being oblivious to the emotional context of a discussion or situation

- difficulty responding emotionally in an interpersonal relationship

- communication deficits—in severe cases of autism, the person may have limited or no language ability; high-functioning individuals on the spectrum, on the other hand, are capable of verbal communication, but speech may be stilted, non-spontaneous, or at times idiosyncratic

- social isolation due to repeated rejection and ridicule as a result of their idiosyncrasies

- often a childhood history of being bullied

- problems with eye contact; facial expressions and body posture may seem odd or out of context

- compulsive, repetitive behaviors and self-stimulation

- difficulty with impulse control

- restricted interests, behaviors, activities, and concepts

- tendency to be over-focused or preoccupied with a single topic

- inability to catch the subtleties of sarcasm or humor and a tendency to take a figure of speech literally

- difficulty being flexible in their routines and rituals; finding change very difficult

- extreme social and emotional immaturity and naivety

- comorbid conditions including ADHD, anxiety, depression, and obsessive-compulsive disorder (OCD).

Depending where the individual falls on the spectrum, his or her level of disability in communication, socialization, and adaptation to the demands of daily living can vary from significant to profound. Individuals at the higher end of the spectrum can have average to superior intelligence (Frith, 2004). Despite their marked disabilities, they often have areas of ability that stand in sharp contrast to their other deficits (Happe and Frith, 2009; Howlin *et al.*, 2009). For example, an individual with high-functioning ASD can be a mathematical genius yet be unable to complete a simple tax return, or can have advanced graduate degrees yet be unable to carry on a conversation beyond the initial greeting. Individuals at the severe end of the spectrum, on the other hand, may be intellectually impaired, incapable of speech (or at least conventional communication), and unaware of or indifferent to the presence of other people.

Unless otherwise stated, references to ASD in the remainder of this chapter will refer to individuals at the higher-functioning end of the autism spectrum, individuals previously diagnosed with Asperger's syndrome.

ASD and Child Pornography

Sexuality is a core component of human existence that extends beyond the biology of sex—it is the complex interaction of hormones, sexual physiology, sensory capacity, emotional maturity, social competence, cultural influence, and moral awareness. In the process of sexual maturation, human beings face the challenge of contending with strong sexual urges; new, intense physical sensations; feelings of attraction; vulnerability when attempting courtship; mixed cultural messages about eroticism and shame; and decisions about what constitutes sexual propriety.

These challenges are difficult enough under the best of circumstances, but the characteristics of autism described above further complicate this already difficult developmental task. For example, the tactile hypersensitivity often observed in ASD individuals can paradoxically produce uncomfortable rather than pleasurable sensations when aroused or engaged in physical contact. Mindblindness can make it difficult to interpret subtle cues about whether another person is interested in pursuing a relationship. Problems with fluid reasoning and central coherence can leave the ASD individual oblivious to what constitutes appropriate sexual behavior in novel situations.

Research has demonstrated that even though individuals on the spectrum experience considerable challenges in their sexual development, the intensity of their sexual interest is nevertheless similar to that of the neurotypical population (Hénault, 2006). Unlike the neurotypical population, however, individuals on the spectrum rarely have opportunities to learn from peers or exploratory sexual experiences, and they find it difficult or impossible to develop socially acceptable outlets for sexual gratification. Individuals on the spectrum often do not have the skills to make friends, let alone lovers, and their eccentric or odd behavior more often repels rather than attracts a potential sexual partner. To make things worse, if they were identified as being developmentally disabled or emotionally impaired as they were growing up, chances are they were placed in special education classrooms and not afforded the same sex education offered to neurotypical students. All too often sex education was reduced to a teacher, when finding a child with ASD touching himself in the classroom, instructing the child to do that in the privacy of his own room. Even their parents might have assumed that because their ASD child was asocial, he or she was also asexual, or that it would be dangerous to provide explicit sexual instruction because their child would be unable to handle the information or apply it in a responsible fashion (Gougeon, 2010). As a result of the above, when considering ASD and sexuality, we are often talking about people with strong sexual impulses, little or no information about healthy sexual behavior, and few suitable outlets for sexual gratification. In such cases, where do these individuals turn for information and a sexual outlet?

For many adolescents and adults on the spectrum, the internet becomes the ideal solution because it has already become their preferred conduit to the outside world (Attwood, 2007). Threatened by interaction with others, they find online activity a comfortable way to engage faceless individuals for gaming purposes or discussing shared quirky interests. By means of their trusted computer they are also able to explore their sexual interests. The internet becomes their primary sex educator, albeit a misleading and incompetent educator. They encounter pornography that excites them and provides them with satisfaction, without risking the ridicule and rejection that can occur in real life. The compulsivity of their ASD may cause them to become obsessed with the material, prompting them to spend more and more time online searching for explicit erotica. Inevitably, their compulsivity will lead them to extreme sexual content including, in many cases, child pornography. Their characteristic naivety and lack of social maturity prompts them to disregard any warning that certain pornography is wrong or inappropriate. Instead, in classic black-and-white thinking, they easily conclude that if it is allowed on the internet, it must be OK, or at least must not be so bad. And given their characteristic lack of empathy and inability to discern what other people are thinking or feeling, they have little or no awareness of what reality lurks behind the pictures and videos—that real children are experiencing horrible abuse.

Why do people, including individuals on the spectrum, view CP? For some, the novelty of the material sates their curiosity; for others, the outrageousness of the material excites them or distracts them from feelings of boredom, emptiness, or internal distress. In some cases, the person, despite his chronological age, has the psycho-sexual maturity of a 10- or 12-year-old and finds it natural to focus on minors, even if in fantasy only. Such fantasies can feel safer and far less threatening than imagining sex with an adult.

Some people, neurotypicals and ASD individuals alike, have a predominant sexual interest in minors. There is no clear understanding about what causes such interest, but there is growing evidence that pedophilia may be largely rooted in biology—more specifically, neurodevelopmental disorders (Seto, 2008). Whatever the cause of pedophilia, such interest can be a strong motivator for viewing child pornography. It is important to note, however, that having pedophile interests does not mean a person necessarily has any intention to harm a child. The research has been clear that not all pedophiles are child molesters, nor are all child molesters pedophiles (Mohnke *et al.*, 2014).

Legal Issues Associated with ASD and CP Offenses

When an individual on the spectrum is discovered viewing, possessing, and even distributing child pornography, an important question is raised—what impact, if any, did his ASD have on his appreciation of the wrongfulness of his actions? To explore this question, compare and contrast Norman and Albert. Both men are 32, college graduates, single, and sexually inexperienced. Albert, however, is on the autism spectrum, whereas Norman is neurotypical. Both Norman and Albert have found the internet to be a convenient outlet for their frustrated sexual urges. Over time, both have become obsessed with internet pornography, devoting considerable time to viewing and downloading erotic material. Over time both discover child pornography and become intrigued with it, either out of morbid curiosity or inherent sexual interest. Up to this point, both cases are essentially identical. It is only when we examine these cases more closely that we start to find important distinctions.

Norman's compulsive pattern of viewing pornography is likely due to what is frequently referred to as a *sexual addiction* (Carnes, 2001). The repetitive pattern of pornography use has been reinforced by the associated sexual pleasure or the decrease in stress levels due the distraction provided by the pornography. For Albert, on the other hand, due to his ASD, he is predisposed to become obsessive in response to many things in his life, not because they produce pleasure or reduce stress, but because that's how he's "wired." He will easily become preoccupied with the material, which will interfere with any possibility of stepping back and looking at the potential consequences of his behavior or the relationship between his behavior and the abuse of minors depicted in the pornography.

Do Albert and Norman know that what they are doing is wrong and illegal? Both have likely seen and read news stories about CP offenders. Both have likely been informed that such behavior is wrong. Norman fully understands he is breaking the law when viewing child pornography, but he dismisses the risk of being caught as negligible. Albert knows it is wrong or shameful, but, unlike Norman, he fails to have a full understanding of the wrongfulness or consequences.

People on the spectrum process information differently to neurotypicals. They can be told something, hear something, or read something, but without constant repetition and numerous examples that expand the range of applications for newly learned information, there is often a flawed understanding. Problems with *central coherence* and *fluid reasoning,* the classic characteristics of ASD described above, make it difficult for Albert to fully understand the illegality of his behavior or the consequences of his actions. What he was told about illegal pornography can't apply to what he is looking at because how bad can this pornography be if it is readily available, often at no charge, on the internet? Will he keep his internet activity covert? Yes, he has learned that anything involving sex tends to be shameful and embarrassing. But as for breaking a law that can have severe consequences, this often does not fully register.

And what about the children depicted in the pornography? Norman prefers not to dwell on the obvious—it would only ruin his arousal. Afterwards he may feel ashamed and promise himself to discontinue this pattern of behavior, but invariably he returns to the illegal material again and again. Albert, on the other hand, has little or no empathy for the children he views because their distress is not evident to him. It does not occur to him to put himself in their situation. On the contrary, due to his mindblindness and lack of empathy, he naturally assumes that, because he somehow finds the depictions arousing, why wouldn't the depicted children do the same?

In the above examples, Albert is at the high-functioning end of the spectrum and his lack of appreciation for the wrongfulness of his actions is subtler and less dramatic than what would be observed in more severe cases of ASD. Regardless, a point could be argued that even a high-functioning individual like Albert lacks criminal capacity, or his capacity to fully appreciate the wrongfulness of his behavior is diminished when compared with a neurotypical like Norman.

THE FORENSIC ASSESSMENT

Considering the potential impact that ASD can have on an offender's appreciation of the wrongfulness and consequences of his behavior, it can be valuable to have input from a psychologist or psychiatrist who has experience working with both sex offenders and individuals on the spectrum. There are few mental health professionals who have both skill sets, and it may be necessary to obtain a consultation from more than one professional. A neuropsychological assessment of the offender will help establish the ASD diagnosis and highlight the extent of deficits in cognition, communication, socialization, and impulse control. Additional psychological exploration and testing that are routinely used for the assessment of sex offenders will provide insight into factors contributing to the instant offense, the current level of psychological adjustment, comorbid conditions, recidivistic risk, disposition issues, and optimal treatment options.

Establishing or Confirming the ASD Diagnosis

If an offender has not already been formally diagnosed with ASD but displays characteristics suggesting that this neurologic disorder is present, screening instruments are available to provide an initial working diagnosis. Two commonly used self-report instruments that have good psychometric properties are the Autism-Spectrum Quotient (AQ; Baron-Cohen et al., 2001) and the Empathy Quotient (EQ;

Baron-Cohen and Wheelwright, 2004). Both instruments have been shown to have good *sensitivity* (correctly classifying individuals with ASD) and *specificity* (correctly screening out non-ASD individuals).

For a more definitive diagnosis and assessment of where an individual with ASD functions in reference to socialization, communication, cognition, and impulse control, a neuropsychological evaluation can be performed. Such an evaluation should include a thorough clinical interview, a reliable developmental history, and psychometric measures (Haskins and Silva, 2006). For the developmental history, a review of medical, educational, and treatment records is vital, as well as interviews with informed historians such as parents or caregivers. For the latter, instruments such as the Autism Diagnostic Interview-Revised (ADI-R; Lord, Rutter, and Le Couteur, 1994), facilitates a structured interview of an informed historian. Other commonly used psychometric instruments can include the AQ and EQ referenced above; the Autism Diagnostic Observation Schedule-2 (ADOS-2; Lord *et al.*, 2012), often considered the "gold standard" for diagnosing ASD; the Wechsler Adult Intelligence Scale-IV (WAIS-IV; Wechsler, 2008; see also Holdnack, Goldstein, and Drozdick, 2011); and a standard battery of neuropsychological tests. Neuropsychological testing will often highlight deficits in *executive functioning*, especially planning, sequencing, and self-regulation (Haskins and Silva, 2006). Assessment batteries may also include tests of language and communication; sensory processing and integration; achievement; attention; learning; memory; and visual/perceptual motor skills (see Educational Testing Service, 2013).

Frequently, an ASD individual's adaptation to the demands of independent living is not commensurate with his or her chronological age or level of intellectual functioning (Klin *et al.*, 2007). The Vineland Behavior Rating Scale-II (VABS-II; Sparrow, Cicchetti, and Balla, 2005), is a well-validated test of adaptive behavior (daily living skills, communication, and social competence) that can help establish an ASD diagnosis and document the extent of social impairment despite normal or above-average intelligence.

Sexual History

In addition to the detailed clinical history described above, a thorough sexual history is vital for developing an understanding of the instant offense and risk for sex offending in the future. The sexual history can be obtained from multiple sources, including an interview of the client; an interview of a parent, spouse, or other informed historian; a review of treatment records; and administration of questionnaires designed to elicit a sexual history, such as the Psychosexual Life History (Nichols and Molinder, 2000).

For a thorough understanding of the client's sexual history and adjustment, the following areas should be explored:

- history of sexual abuse and trauma

- family attitudes about sex and sexual behavior

- sources and extent of sex education

- early childhood sex-play

- first masturbatory experiences and masturbatory fantasies

- group masturbation

- first experience of sexual feelings towards a female; towards a male

- first sexual touch of another person

- first coital experience

- number of lifetime sexual partners

- sexual attraction to another male

- sexual orientation and any associated confusion or shame

- history of ongoing sexual relationships

- confidence and competence as a sexual partner

- sexual performance problems

- experience with sex workers

- history of sexually transmitted infections

- use of pornography, past and present

- evidence of sexual preoccupation

- evidence of high-frequency sexual behavior that has been out of control

- sexual fantasies

- sexual boundary crossings (incest, molestation, etc.)

- paraphilic interests (voyeurism, exhibitionism, pedophilia, etc.).

Personality Testing

ASD does not exist in a vacuum, and people on the spectrum can and often do suffer from comorbid conditions such as ADHD, anxiety, depression, and OCD (Mazzone, Ruta, and Reale, 2012). Personality tests are essential tools to help identify and quantify the presence of both personality characteristics and symptoms of psychological distress. The two most commonly employed personality tests utilized in forensic evaluations are the Minnesota Multiphasic Personality Inventory-2 (MMPI-2; Butcher *et al.*, 2003) and the Millon Clinical Multiaxial Inventory-III (MCMI-III; Millon *et al.*, 1994). Although neither of these tests is designed to diagnose ASD, people on the spectrum will often display predictable characteristics on these tests, including low self-esteem, social isolation, depression, and interpersonal conflict (e.g. Ozonoff *et al.*, 2005). Other features that may be detected by these and other personality tests include impulsive tendencies, bipolar symptoms, psychoticism, suicidal risk, antisocial features, rigidity, symptoms of trauma, somatization, and substance abuse.

Sexual Interest and Deviance

To understand a CP offender's behavior, assessment of his sexual interests is important. Although it is tempting to assume that anyone who looks at CP must be a pedophile, the research does not support this assumption. Seto, Cantor, and Blanchard (2006), in a study of 100 CP users who were administered a test measuring their physical response while viewing pictures of children, found that only 61% showed a preference for child stimuli over adult stimuli. This finding suggests that while many viewers of CP have pedophile interests, some access underage material for other reasons. Curiosity, a quest for novelty, the draw of the taboo, compulsivity, attempts to work through the effects of past trauma, and accidental acquisition are examples of reasons other than pedophile interest for people to access or possess CP (McCarthy, 2012). It has also been suggested that in some cases involving ASD individuals, the draw to pedophile themes or other deviant sexual topics are not an accurate reflection of their sexual interest but, rather, a byproduct of naive exploration. This latter example is referred to as *counterfeit deviance* (Hingsburger, Griffiths, and Quinsey, 1991; Mahoney, 2009)—that is, behavior that is considered deviant but is motivated by factors other than deviant sexual interests.

Other than documented behavior and self-report, the two most common means of assessing a person's sexual interest are penile plethysmography (PPG) and viewing time (VT). For tests utilizing PPG, the evaluee is presented pictures of children and adults, both males and females, while wearing a pressure-sensitive gauge around his penis. Physical reaction to the pictures is compared based on the age and gender of the depicted models, providing insight into the person's sexual orientation and possible attraction to minors. Although this procedure has *face validity*—that is, at first glance it appears to be a reasonable and valid approach—several criticisms have prevented PPG from passing Daubert and Frye tests for admissibility in state and federal courts (Tong, 2007). For individuals with ASD, the use of PPG has an additional drawback: strapping a gauge on the penis, found to be highly invasive by most neurotypicals, is often experienced as intolerable by people on the spectrum. This intolerance is due to the extreme social awkwardness and hypersensitivity to tactile stimulation so often characteristic of ASD.

VT assesses sexual interest from a different perspective. Rather than focusing on how the body responds to sexual cues, it measures how long a person views the sexual cue. The principle behind this procedure is that we visually linger in response to sexually attractive cues in comparison with cues in which we have little or no sexual interest. The most frequently utilized VT application is the Abel Assessment of Sexual Interest-3 (AASI-3; Abel et al., 2001), which includes sexual slides of preschool, grade school, adolescent, and adult males and females. The AASI has met Daubert and Frye standards for admissibility in a number of federal and state jurisdictions (Abel Screening, n.d.). It should be noted that this test by itself does not diagnose pedophilia, but provides data that combined with information derived from other sources (history, interview, additional testing results, etc.) can assist the clinician in rendering informed diagnostic and prognostic opinions.

In addition to VT, the AASI-3 has a 400-plus-item questionnaire that explores the evaluee's sexual behaviors in the past and present, fantasy themes, paraphilic tendencies, cognitive distortions associated with sexual molestation, and the probability of previous and future sex offending.

The Multiphasic Sex Inventory-II (MSI-II; Nichols and Molinder, 2010a) is a 560-item, self-report instrument that assesses the presence of paraphilias and sexual dysfunctions as well as comparisons with scores obtained by known child molesters and rapists. The MSI-II has been admitted under Daubert and Frye as acceptable evidence in both state and federal jurisdictions (Nichols and Molinder, 2010b).

When assessing an evaluee's use of child pornography, it can be helpful to explore his point of view (POV). Some CP users identify with the adults depicted in the picture or video: the erotic value comes from perceiving oneself in a position of power or dominance. Some users will identify with the child; this identification may reflect a longstanding desire for adult attention, or it may represent a symbolic reenactment of the user's history of being a victim. For individuals on the spectrum, we often observe that they gravitate to child pornography that depicts minors posing naked or sexually interacting with each other. What the evaluee will often report is a POV where they experience the playfulness and acceptance of their peers—an experience that had eluded them during their own childhood and adolescence. Another POV reported by some CP users is one of a voyeur. They find viewing the material sexually stimulating even though they neither identify with the participants nor have any desire to engage in such behavior in real life. Understanding the evaluee's POV can help us to better understand what has driven their use of CP and what unmet needs and unresolved conflicts need to be addressed in treatment.

Risk Assessment

Actuarial risk assessment has been an important element in forensic evaluations of sex offenders. Static and dynamic factors empirically identified and validated to predict recidivism have been used to place offenders in low-, moderate-, and high-risk categories. Instruments such as the STATIC-99R (Hanson *et al.*, 2013) and the Vermont Assessment of Sex Offender Risk-2 (VASOR-2; McGrath *et al.*, 2014) assess the presence of static (historical) factors such as age, previous criminal history, previous sex offending, relationship history, and victim characteristics. Research has shown that the greater the number of these predictive factors present, the more likely a future sexual or violent offense will occur. Other instruments, such as the Sex Offender Need Assessment Rating (SONAR; Hanson and Harris, 2015), assess the presence of dynamic (changeable) risk factors such as intimacy deficits, negative social influences, attitudes tolerant of sexual offending, sexual self-regulation, general self-regulation, substance abuse, negative mood, anger, and victim access. Research has shown that considering static and dynamic risk factors in combination will enhance predictive accuracy for future offending.

Unfortunately, none of these actuarial risk assessment instruments have been normed for people on the spectrum, nor, for that matter, have any of them been normed for individuals whose only offense is viewing child pornography. Due to the latter point, conventional actuarial risk assessments are usually not included in the forensic assessment of an offender whose only offense is receipt, possession, or distribution of child pornography.

In the absence of validated instruments for assessing recidivistic risk, we are forced to turn to existing research literature, which, unfortunately, is sparse when it comes to CP use and people on the spectrum. Instead, we are forced to rely on research based on neurotypicals (summarized below) and extrapolate based on what we know about ASD.

Polygraph

A polygraph examination can be a helpful tool to support or challenge a CP offender's insistence that he has never committed a touch offense against a child. It is also a useful tool post-adjudication to help ensure compliance with terms of probation (Branaman and Gallagher, 2005). Unfortunately, there is no substantive research on the accuracy of polygraphs when administered to individuals on the autism spectrum. The very nature of their neurological condition predisposes people on the spectrum to be far more reactive to a polygraph examination than is the case for the neurotypical population. Classic ASD characteristics include repetitive movements (flapping, fidgeting, etc.), especially when stressed; vulnerability to sensory overload (extreme reactivity to loud sounds, bright lights, etc.); and touch aversion (ASD individuals are so distracted by tactile stimulation that they will remove tags from their shirts and wear loose-fitting clothing made of soft material). If required to take a polygraph, it is unknown how a person with ASD will respond physiologically when strapped in a chair (forced restriction of movement) in a room most likely lit with fluorescent lighting (causing sensory overload) while pneumographs, galvanometers, and a blood pressure cuff are attached to his body (triggering touch aversion).

To further complicate matters, people with ASD often have a very rigid conscience. They are guilt prone and often truthful almost to fault. They are prone to be what some polygraphers informally term a "guilt grabber"—an innocent person who fails a polygraph test not because he or she is actually guilty of having done anything wrong, but because he or she feels guilty at the mere thought of doing something wrong. Lilienfeld (2009) describes this phenomenon in greater detail:

> The polygraph or so-called "lie detector" test is, as most scientists acknowledge, badly misnamed. It's a detector of autonomic arousal, not of lies. As a consequence, people who become highly aroused in response to the relevant (or "Did you do it?") questions, but not in response to the other questions, will tend to fail the test. In some cases, this arousal almost surely reflects actual guilt stemming from commission of a crime—and for this reason there's general consensus that the polygraph test probably does somewhat better than chance at detecting lies. But in many cases, this arousal just as surely reflects emotions other than guilt stemming from malfeasance, such as understandable anxiety at the prospect of failing the test, indignation at being accused of a crime one didn't commit, and—perhaps… guilt at the mere thought of having once fantasized about having committed a crime.

For the reasons stated above, without further research validating the use of polygraphs with the ASD population, use of this tool should be avoided in such cases.

Forensic Report

A comprehensive written report is the final work-product after completion of the interviews, review of discovery material, and psychological testing. Forensic reports will typically convey the following information:

- charges and summary of the evidence leading to the arrest

- a list of the discovery material reviewed by the examiner

- psycho/social/sexual history that includes information about the evaluee's family of origin, education, work history, sexual history, legal history, medical history, substance abuse history, and mental health history

- summary of information emerging from the interviews

- psychological testing results that verify the ASD diagnosis, document strengths and degree of impairment, and assess psychiatric status, comorbid conditions, and sexual interests

- a summary of the evaluee's mental status that describes his affect, mood, communication style, cognitive function, and behavioral idiosyncrasies during the interview

- formal psychiatric diagnoses

- a conclusions and recommendations section that integrates the above information into a narrative description of factors contributing to the instant offense, recidivistic risk, treatment prognosis, issues of responsibility and mitigation, and other disposition issues and recommendations.

KEY FORENSIC ISSUES

An appropriate forensic evaluation of an ASD individual who has committed a child pornography offense will provide the court with insight into the offender as a person rather than merely as an offense category. It will also provide valuable insight into the key forensic issues discussed below.

Recidivistic Risk

Research tells us that individuals whose only offense is possession of CP represent far lower risks for further criminal activity when compared with other sex offenders (Eke, Seto, and Williams, 2011). Webb, Craisatti, and Keen (2007) reported that, after 18 months post-offense, 0% of CP-only offenders committed a contact sex offense. Wollert, Waggoner, and Smith (2009; see Wollert, 2012) reported that, four years post-offense, 0% committed a contact offense against a child, and 1% reoffended with CP possession. Eke *et al.* (2011) reported that, 4–6 years post-offense, 1.3% of CP-only offenders were later arrested for a contact sex offense, and 4.4% were later discovered further accessing child pornography. The U.S. Sentencing Commission (Saris *et al.*, 2013), in a study of 610 CP-only offenders, reported that 3.6% committed a contact offense and 2.3% accessed CP during an average follow-up period of 8.5 years after the offenders' re-entry into the community.

Some critics have called the above findings into question, pointing out that child sexual abuse is an underreported crime. No doubt there were repeat offenses that were not detected in the studies described above, but the same is true for any study of recidivism. What is significant about the above findings is that compared with recidivism studies for any other sexual offense, CP-only offenders have extremely low rates of recidivism. Also, estimates of unreported cases of child molestation should not be applied indiscriminately to adjudicated CP-only offenders. It stands to reason that the likelihood of undiscovered sex offending by adjudicated CP-only offenders who have experienced arrest, possible incarceration, probationary supervision, restrictions on their access to minors, sex offender treatment, etc. will be far less than for unidentified, non-monitored, untreated sex offenders.

Although the studies reported above did not single out ASD individuals, based on our knowledge of ASD, it is reasonable to conclude that these findings of low recidivistic risk will also apply to the ASD offender. Research has demonstrated that ASD individuals in general tend to adhere rigidly to rules they adequately understand and are less likely to break the law compared with the general population (Howlin, 2004; Woodbury-Smith, 2014). They are also far less likely to commit violent crimes (Ghaziuddin, Tsai, and Ghaziuddin, 1991; Isager *et al.*, 2005). Their likelihood of victimizing children is limited because their social awkwardness will not make them attractive to children and their naiveté will make them inept in any effort to manipulate a potential child victim (Mahoney, 2009). It is therefore reasonable to conclude that risk of further offending by an ASD individual, especially after appropriate intervention, is less than the risk posed by a neurotypical offender.

There has been an inaccurate assumption that risk is related to the number of images in the offender's possession or the nature of the content. The logic for this assumption is that the more obsessed an individual is with children, the more images he will collect, and the more likely he will act on these urges. Research, however, fails to support this assumption (Stabenow, 2011), and it is even more inaccurate in cases of ASD because it fails to appreciate the association between the volume of collected pornography and the compulsivity characteristic of ASD. Likewise, research fails to support the contention that extreme sexual content predicts future dangerousness (Osborn et al., 2010). More specific to the ASD population, viewing extreme sexual material does not necessarily reflect deviant sexual interests but, rather, some form of *counterfeit deviance* such as naive curiosity (Hingsburger et al., 1991; Mahoney, 2009).

Treatment Recommendations

Conventional sex offender treatment relies heavily on group therapy and focuses on the offender understanding his offending pattern, learning about thinking errors, practicing empathic responses to the victims, and stopping deviant thoughts and fantasies. There is a growing consensus that this approach to sex offender treatment, which often benefits neurotypical individuals, is contraindicated for ASD individuals (Griffiths and Fedoroff, 2009; Ray, Marks, and Bray-Garretson, 2004).

Conventional sex offender treatment is inappropriate for ASD individuals on several accounts. First, a group setting, while offering many advantages for the neurotypical offender, is threatening for most ASD individuals. Their capacity for receptive communication (understanding the meaning behind the words being spoken) is often impaired, so they have trouble following what is being discussed. Unable to relate to many of the experiences discussed by other group members, they will often retreat into silence (Mahoney, 2009). In addition, whether in group or individual therapy, when encouraged to understand thinking errors or show empathy for victims, ASD individuals will often become confused and frustrated because they think differently and empathy is a difficult emotion for them to understand (Bolton, 2005).

Instead, ASD individuals require specialized treatment with very explicit sex education and an emphasis on learning specific responses to specific situations (Bolton, 2005; Griffiths and Fedoroff, 2009). Rather than attempting uncovering and repairing—classic psychotherapy techniques—therapists need to utilize cognitive/behavioral interventions to address the cognitive rigidity and literalness that often shape the ASD individual's reactions to daily events. Appreciating that the ASD individual will focus on details rather than grasping the "big picture," the therapist needs to provide very specific direction for specific situations rather than general guidelines that are to be applied whenever indicated. And because ASD individuals do not readily grasp abstract concepts, repetition is standard throughout treatment (Klin and Volkmar, 1995).

As suggested above, individuals with ASD respond well to explicit instruction and tend to conform slavishly to rules and guidelines they understand. These characteristics combined with appropriate supervision and treatment should make the risk of recidivism low and the prognosis favorable.

Responsibility and Mitigation

An important function of the forensic evaluation is to assess to what degree, if any, the ASD individual's neurologic condition has compromised his ability to appreciate the wrongfulness of his actions. As discussed above, it can be difficult for some people on the spectrum to appreciate that their use of child pornography continues the abuse of innocent victims. Although some offenders have difficulty making this connection and subsequently assume they are doing nothing terribly wrong, even if it is something shameful or embarrassing, others on the spectrum can indeed have sufficient awareness of the illegality of their behavior, but opt to offend regardless. Simply because an individual is on the spectrum does not automatically establish lack of or diminished responsibility. Evidence derived from interview data, clinical history, and psychological testing can help mental health professionals assess the degree of neurological compromise in regard to the offender's instant offense and provide valuable guidance for the court.

Even if the offender had sufficient appreciation of the illegality of his behavior, there may be important mitigating factors identified during the assessment that can have relevance for the final disposition of the case. A history of being sexually abused or bullied as a child, the presence of a comorbid psychiatric condition such as an anxiety disorder, depression, or a bipolar disorder, the influence of an overwhelming compulsion to collect pornography, or characteristic naiveté could have influenced the offender's decision to commit the instant offense. When these factors are identified and addressed with appropriate treatment, the prognosis is usually favorable, thus making these factors mitigating rather than aggravating. Amenability to treatment, need for specialized treatment not available in most prisons, low recidivistic risk, absence of dangerousness, and unusually high vulnerability in a prison setting are additional examples of potential mitigating factors.

Disposition

Penalties for possession, receipt, and distribution of child pornography tend to be severe. In 2012, non-contact child pornography offenders were sentenced 132 months on average in federal courts, exceeded only by sentences for murder and kidnapping (USSC, 2012). And we are not talking about career criminals—over 84% of these cases in 2012 were rated Criminal History Category 1 (no more than one previous sentence of 60 days or less) (USSC, 2012). Current federal sentencing guidelines for CP offenses fail to adequately reflect the "spectrum of criminal culpability," as highlighted in a 2009 federal court ruling (*United States v. Cruikshank*). Due to mandatory minimums, sentencing in most cases is driven by one or two factors such as number and content of images and is largely unaffected by the seriousness of the offense or the dangerousness of the offender. Thus, a growing number of defense attorneys, prosecutors, and judges have supported the position that sentencing guidelines for non-contact CP offenses are too severe and fail to reasonably distinguish among offenders (von Dornum, 2012).

This problem with sentencing guidelines has particular relevance in cases involving individuals on the spectrum. When the ASD offender is interviewed by pretrial services for determining the sentencing range, the court worker will score heavily the large number of pictures and videos as well as the extreme content sometimes depicted in that material (BDSM, children under 12, etc.). To make things worse, the offender's furtive eye contact and detached or cavalier attitude may lead the worker to assume there is a lack of remorse. It is unlikely that any consideration will be given to the fact that the large number of pornographic items might have been due to the compulsivity characteristic of ASD and that the extreme material may be due to *counterfeit deviance* rather than actual deviant sexual interests. The very low risk of recidivism and lack of dangerousness will have little or no impact on the final computation, and it is highly unlikely any question about the degree of criminal responsibility will be raised.

Sentencing takes on an additional level of significance in these cases because ASD individuals are far less psychologically equipped than a neurotypical individual to adapt to and survive in a jail or prison setting. His direct style, inability to read social interactions, eccentric behaviors, and communication deficits will make the ASD individual a target for inmate exploitation and violence and will prompt correction officers to misperceive him as arrogant and disrespectful (Taylor, Mesibov, and Debbaudt, 2009). Given the ASD individual's difficulty dealing with change, his hypersensitivity to loud sounds and bright lights, and his inability to decipher behavior going on around him, confinement can be sufficiently stressful and disorienting to lead to decompensation, a possible psychotic break, or a suicide attempt.

Upon release, there is the problem of the ASD offender being placed on a sex offender registry (SOR). A growing body of literature suggests that sex offender registries fail to afford the public additional protection from sex offending. For example, a 2008 report funded by the Department of Justice concluded that, "Despite wide community support for these laws, there is little evidence to date, including this study, to support a claim that Megan's Law is effective in reducing either new first-time sex offenses or sexual re-offenses" (Zgoba et al., 2008). In some cases, the negative impact of being registered (lack of housing, unemployment, difficulty accessing higher education, public taunts and ridicule, physical assault, etc.) can contribute to recidivism (Freeman-Longo, 1996; McCaghy and Capron, 1994; Presser and Gunnison, 1999). Thus, sex offender registries, originally intended to be a protection for society, have become largely a form of additional punishment for the sex offender (Tewksbury, 2005; Tewksbury and Lees, 2006; Zevitz and Farkas, 2000). Unfortunately, not only the offender himself suffers because of being on the registry, but also family members (parents, spouse, and children) often suffer housing discrimination, public humiliation, social ostracism, and economic hardship due to the offending relative's public exposure (Levenson and Tewksbury, 2009).

As discussed above, the SOR presents significant, and arguably unnecessary, challenges for individuals when they attempt to rebuild their lives post-adjudication. The challenges described above are amplified even further for ASD individuals. For example, some ASD individuals are challenged by independent living and are forced to live with their parents. If the parents reside in proximity to a school, upon being placed on the SOR, the ASD individual would not be allowed to continue living with the parents. In addition to housing challenges, ASD individuals are far less equipped than neurotypicals to psychologically cope with social ostracism and possible community harassment. In terms of future employment, ASD individuals are quite restricted in the type of employment they can contend with, and being on the SOR reduces options to the point that employment becomes virtually impossible.

Considering the above issues regarding degree of responsibility, disproportionate challenges associated with incarceration, low risk of dangerousness, and unwarranted negative consequences associated with the sex offender registry, some lawyers are now advocating that provisions for pretrial diversion be made for select CP-only offenders (Long, 2014). Pretrial diversion is rarely applied in federal child pornography cases, but has been successful in multiple state jurisdictions. Pretrial diversion combined with appropriate treatment and supervision represents an optimal solution for both protecting the public and affording a just disposition for an impaired individual. These provisions allow an ASD individual to avoid incarceration, receive appropriate supervision and intervention, and be spared the negative and unnecessary consequences of sex offender registration.

CONCLUSION

High-functioning ASD is a fairly new concept; it didn't exist as a diagnosis when the author was in graduate school in the 1970s, and research continues to increase our understanding of this neurological condition. As the behavioral sciences work toward expanding our understanding of the unique aspects of thinking and decision-making in ASD individuals, it will be important for the law to address how to deal with this phenomenon in a just manner. In the past, the law has evolved in how it handles other select groups. Youthful offenders, for example, were at one time prosecuted and punished in the same manner as adult offenders. In time, however, legal systems throughout the world came to acknowledge that juveniles should be treated in a fashion less harsh than for adults due to their inexperience and immaturity. Likewise, there are many examples of the law applying special safeguards and protections for the developmentally disabled, making provisions to identify those who are unfit to stand trial, determine competency to confess, discern criminal responsibility, or, in select cases, divert from the criminal justice system altogether. Similarly, the uniqueness of the neurological functioning of people on the spectrum should warrant special consideration in legal situations.

For cases involving child pornography violations by a person on the autism spectrum, a comprehensive forensic assessment can be invaluable in helping the court to understand the offender, the degree his neurological condition influenced his behavior, and what disposition best serves justice and the public interest.

REFERENCES

Abel, G.G., Jordan, A., Hand, C.G., Holland, L.A., and Phipps, A. (2001) "Classification models of child molesters utilizing the Abel Assessment for sexual interests." *Child Abuse & Neglect: The International Journal 25*, 5, 703–718.

Abel Screening (n.d.) "Use & acceptance." Available at http://abelscreening.com/use-acceptance (accessed January 16, 2017).

American Psychiatric Association (1994) *Diagnostic and Statistical Manual of Mental Disorders*, Fourth Edition. Arlington, VA: APA.

American Psychiatric Association (2013) *Diagnostic and Statistical Manual of Mental Disorders*, Fifth Edition. Arlington, VA: APA.

Attwood, T. (2007) *The Complete Guide to Asperger's Syndrome*. Philadelphia, PA: Jessica Kingsley Publishers.

Baron-Cohen, S. and Wheelwright, S. (2004) "The Empathy Quotient: An investigation of adults with Asperger syndrome or high functioning autism, and normal sex differences." *Journal of Autism and Developmental Disorders 34*, 2, 163–175.

Baron-Cohen, S., Wheelwright, S., Skinner, R., Martin, J., and Clubley, E. (2001) "The Autism-Spectrum Quotient (AQ): Evidence from Asperger syndrome/high functioning autism, males and females, scientists and mathematicians." *Journal of Autism and Developmental Disorders 31*, 1, 5–17.

Bolton, W. (2005) "Developmental Theory and Developmental Deficits: The Treatment of Sex Offenders with Asperger's Syndrome." In J. Hiller, H. Wood, and W. Bolton (eds) *Sex, Mind, and Emotion*. London: H. Karnac.

Branaman, T.F. and Gallagher, S.N. (2005) "Polygraph testing in sex offenders treatment: A review of limitations." *American Journal of Forensic Psychology 23*, 1, 45–64.

Butcher, J.N., Graham, J.R., Ben-Porath, Y.S., Tellegen, A., and Dahlstrom, W.G. (2003) *MMPI-2: Minnesota Multiphasic Personality Inventory-2*. Minneapolis, MN: University of Minnesota Press.

Carnes, P. (2001) *Out of the Shadows: Understanding Sexual Addiction*, Third Edition. Center City, MN: Hazelden.

Carper, R.A. and Courchesne, E. (2005) "Localized enlargement of the frontal cortex in early autism." *Biological Psychiatry 57*, 126–133.

Casanova, M.F., Buxhoeveden, D., and Gomez, J. (2003) "Disruption in the inhibitory architecture of the cell minicolumn: Implications for autism." *Neuroscientist 9*, 6, 496–507.

Centers for Disease Control and Prevention (2014) "Autism spectrum disorder (ASD): Signs and symptoms." Available at www.cdc.gov/ncbddd/autism/signs.html (accessed January 16, 2017).

Centers for Disease Control and Prevention (2014, March 28) "Prevalence of autism spectrum disorder among children aged 8 years—Autism and Developmental Disabilities Monitoring Network, 11 sites, United States, 2010." *Morbidity and Mortality Weekly Report 63*, SS02, 1–21. Available at www.cdc.gov/mmwr/preview/mmwrhtml/ss6302a1.htm?s_cid=ss6302a1_w (accessed January 16, 2017).

Educational Testing Service (2013) "ETS policy statement for documentation of autism spectrum disorder in adolescents and adults—First edition; Appendix III: Tests for assessing adolescents and adults." Available at www.ets.org/s/disabilities/pdf/documenting_asd.pdf (accessed January 16, 2017).

Eke, A.W., Seto, M.C., and Williams, J. (2011) "Examining the criminal history of future offending of child pornography offenders: An extended prospective follow-up study." *Law and Human Behavior 35*, 6, 466–478.

Freeman-Longo, R.E. (1996) "Feel good legislation: Prevention or calamity." *Child Abuse & Neglect 20*, 2, 95–101.

Frith, U. (2004) "Emanuel Miller lecture: Confusions and controversies about Asperger syndrome." *Journal of Child Psychology and Psychiatry 45*, 672–686.

Ghaziuddin, M., Tsai, L., and Ghaziuddin, N. (1991) "Brief report: Violence in Asperger syndrome—A critique." *Journal of Autism and Developmental Disorders 21*, 349–354.

Gougeon, N. (2010) "Sexuality and autism: A critical review of selected literature using a social-relational model of disability." *American Journal of Sexuality Education 5*, 328–361.

Griffiths, D. and Fedoroff, J.P. (2009) "Persons with Intellectual Disabilities Who Sexually Offend." In F.M. Saleh, A.J. Grudzinskas, J.M. Bradford, and D.J. Brodsky (eds) *Sex Offenders: Identification, Risk Assessment, Treatment, and Legal Issues*. New York, NY: Oxford University Press.

Hanson, R.K. and Harris, A. (2015, January 22) "The Sex Offender Need Assessment Rating (SONAR): A method for measuring change in risk levels 2000–1." Public Works and Government Services Canada. Available at www.publicsafety.gc.ca/cnt/rsrcs/pblctns/sx-ffndr-nd/index-eng.aspx (accessed January 16, 2017).

Hanson, R.K., Babchishin, K.M., Helmus, L., and Thornton, D. (2013) "Quantifying the relative risk of sex offenders: Risk ratios for Static-99R." *Sexual Abuse: A Journal of Research and Treatment 25*, 5, 482–515.

Happe, F. and Frith, U. (2009, April 12) "The beautiful otherness of the autistic mind." *Philosophical Transactions of the Royal Society B 364*, 1359–1367.

Haskins, B.G. and Silva, A. (2006) "Asperger's disorder and criminal behavior: Forensic-psychiatric considerations." *Journal of the American Academy of Psychiatry and the Law Online 34*, 3, 374–384. Available at www.jaapl.org/content/34/3/374.full.pdf+html (accessed January 16, 2017).

Hénault, I. (2006) *Asperger's Syndrome and Sexuality: From Adolescence through Adulthood*. Philadelphia, PA: Jessica Kingsley Publishers.

Hingsburger, D., Griffiths, D., and Quinsey, V. (1991) "Detecting counterfeit deviance: Differentiating sexual deviance from sexual inappropriateness." *The Habilitative Mental Healthcare Newsletter 10*, 51–54.

Holdnack, J., Goldstein, G., and Drozdick, L. (2011) "Social perception and WAIS-IV performance in adolescents and adults diagnosed with Asperger's syndrome and autism." *Assessment 18*, 2, 192–200.

Howlin, P. (2004) *Autism and Asperger Syndrome: Preparing for Adulthood*, Second Edition. London: Routledge.

Howlin, P., Goode, S., Hutton, J., and Rutter, M. (2009, April 12) "Savant skills in autism: Psychometric approaches and parental reports." *Philosophical Transactions of the Royal Society B* *364*, 1359–1367.

Hughes, C., Russell, J., and Robbins, T.W. (1994) "Evidence for executive dysfunction in autism." *Neuropsychologia 32*, 4, 477–492.

Isager, T., Mouridsen, S., Rich, B., and Nedergaard, N. (2005, September) "Autism spectrum disorders and criminal behavior: A case control study." Paper presented at the First International Symposium on Autism Spectrum Disorder in a Forensic Context, Copenhagen, Denmark.

Kana, R.K., Keller, T.A., Cherkassky, V.L., Minshew, N.J., and Just, M.A. (2009) "Atypical frontal–posterior synchronization of Theory of Mind regions in autism during mental state attribution." *Social Neuroscience 4*, 135–152.

Klin, A. and Volkmar, F.R. (1995) *Asperger's Syndrome: Guidelines for Treatment and Intervention.* Pittsburgh, PA: Learning Disabilities Association of America. Available at https://medicine.yale.edu/childstudy/autism/information/asdiagnosis_tcm339-34860_tcm339-284-32.pdf (accessed January 16, 2017).

Klin, A., Saulnier, C.A., Sparrow, S.S., Cicchetti, D.V., Volkmar, F.R., and Lord, C. (2007) "Social and communication abilities and disabilities in higher functioning individuals with autism spectrum disorders: The Vineland and the ADOS." *Journal of Autism and Developmental Disorders 37*, 4, 748–759.

Kuhn, R. and Cahn, C.H. (2004) "Eugen Bleuler's concepts of psychopathology." *History of Psychiatry 15*, 361–366.

Levenson, J. and Tewksbury, R. (2009) "Collateral damage: Family members of registered sex offenders." *American Journal of Criminal Justice 34*, 1–2, 54–68.

Lilienfield, S. (2009, July 21) "The polygraph strikes—and strikes out—again." *Psychology Today*, The Skeptical Psychologist. Available at www.psychologytoday.com/blog/the-skeptical-psychologist/200907/the-polygraph-test-strikes-and-strikes-out-again (accessed January 16, 2017).

Long, S.J. (2014) "The case for extending pretrial diversion to include possession of child pornography." *University of Massachusetts Law Review 9*, 2, Article 4. Available from http://scholarship.law.umassd.edu/umlr/vol9/iss2/4 (accessed January 16, 2017).

Lord, C., Rutter, M., DiLavore, P.C., Risi, S., Gotham, K., and Bishop, S.L. (2012) *Autism Diagnostic Observation Schedule, Second Edition (ADOS-2) Manual (Part 1): Modules 1–4.* Torrance, CA: Western Psychological Services.

Lord, C., Rutter, M., and Le Couteur, A. (1994) "Autism Diagnostic Interview-Revised: A revised version of a diagnostic interview for caregivers of individuals with possible pervasive developmental disorders." *Journal of Autism and Developmental Disorders 24*, 5, 659–685.

Mahoney, M. (2009) "Asperger's syndrome and criminal law: The special case of child pornography." Available at www.harringtonmahoney.com/content/Publications/Aspergers%20Syndrome%20and%20the%20Criminal%20Law%20v26.pdf (accessed January 12, 2017).

Mazzone, L., Ruta, L., and Reale, L. (2012) "Psychiatric comorbidities in Asperger syndrome and high functioning autism: Diagnostic challenges." *Annals of General Psychiatry 11*, 16. Available at www.ncbi.nlm.nih.gov/pmc/articles/PMC3416662 (accessed January 16, 2017).

McCaghy, C.H. and Capron, T.A. (1994) *Deviant Behavior: Crime, Conflict and Interest Groups.* New York, NY: Macmillan.

McCarthy, J. (2012, February 15) "Testimony before the United States Sentencing Commission public hearing on child pornography sentencing." Available at www.ussc.gov/sites/default/files/pdf/amendment-process/public-hearings-and-meetings/20120215/Testimony_15_McCarthy.pdf (accessed January 16, 2017).

McGrath, R.J., Lasher, M.P., Cumming, G.F., Langton, C.M., and Hoke, S.E. (2014) "Development of Vermont Assessment of Sex Offender Risk-2 (VASOR-2) Reoffense Risk Scale." *Sexual Abuse: A Journal of Research and Treatment 26*, 3, 271–290.

Millon, T., Millon, C., Davis, R., and Grossman, S. (1994) *Millon Clinical Multiaxial Inventory-III.* San Antonio, TX: Pearson.

Minshew, N.J. and Keller, T.A. (2010) "The nature of brain dysfunction in autism: Functional brain imaging studies." *Current Opinion in Neurology 23*, 2, 124–130.

Mohnke, S., Müller, S., Amelung, T., Krüger, T.H., et al. (2014) "Brain alterations in paedophilia: A critical review." Progressive Neurobiology 122, 1–23.

Newschaffer, C.J., Croen, L.A., Daniels, J., Craig, J., et al. (2007) "The epidemiology of autism spectrum disorders." Annual Review of Public Health 28, 235–258.

Nichols, H.R. and Molinder, I. (2000) Psychosexual Life History—Adult Male Form. Tacoma, WA: Nichols & Molinder Assessments.

Nichols, H.R. and Molinder, I. (2010a) "Multiphasic Sex Inventory II." Available at www.nicholsandmolinder.com/sex-offender-assessment-msi-ii.php (accessed January 16, 2017).

Nichols, H.R. and Molinder, I. (2010b) "Sex offender legal issues and forensic information." Available at www.nicholsandmolinder.com/sex-offender-legal-issues.php (accessed January 16, 2017).

Osborn, J., Elliott, I.A., Middleton, D., and Beech, A.R. (2010) "The use of actuarial risk assessment measures with UK internet child pornography offenders." The Journal of Aggression, Conflict, and Peace Studies 2, 3, 16–24.

Ozonoff, S., Garcia, N., Clark, E., and Lainhart, J.E. (2005) "MMPI-2 personality profiles of high functioning adults with autism spectrum disorders." Assessment 12, 86–95.

Presser, L. and Gunnison, E. (1999) "Strange bedfellows: Is sex offender notification a form of community justice?" Crime & Delinquency 45, 3, 299–315.

Ray, F., Marks, C., and Bray-Garretson, H. (2004) "Challenges to treating adolescents with Asperger's syndrome who are sexually abusive." Sexual Addiction & Compulsivity 11, 265–285.

Rimland, B. (1964) Infantile Autism: The Syndrome and its Implications for a Neural Theory of Behavior. Upper Saddle River, NJ: Prentice Hall.

Sahyoun, C.P., Belliveau, J.W., Soulières, I., Schwartz, S., and Mody, M. (2010) "Neuroimaging of the functional and structural networks underlying visuospatial vs. linguistic reasoning in high-functioning autism." Neuropsychologia 48, 1, 86–95.

Saris, P.B., Carr, W.B., Jr., Jackson, K.B., Hinojosa, R.H., et al. (2013) "Report to Congress: Federal child pornography offenses—Chapter 11." Available at www.ussc.gov/sites/default/files/pdf/news/congressional-testimony-and-reports/sex-offense-topics/201212-federal-child-pornography-offenses/Chapter_11.pdf (accessed January 16, 2017).

Schipul, S.E., Keller, T.A., and Just, M.A. (2011) "Inter-regional brain communication and its disturbance in autism." Frontiers in Systems Neuroscience 5, 1–11.

Schumann, C.M., Hamstra, J., Goodlin-Jones, B.L., Lotspeich, L.J., et al. (2004) "The amygdala is enlarged in children but not adolescents with autism: The hippocampus is enlarged at all ages." Journal of Neuroscience 24, 28, 6392–6401.

Seto, M.C. (2008) "Pedophilia." In D.R. Laws and W.T. O'Donohue (eds) Sexual Deviance—Theory, Assessment, and Treatment (Second Edition). New York, NY: Guilford Press.

Seto, M.C. (2012, February 15) "Testimony before the United States Sentencing Commission public hearing on child pornography sentencing." Available at www.ussc.gov/sites/default/files/pdf/amendment-process/public-hearings-and-meetings/20120215-16/Testimony_15_Seto.pdf (accessed January 16, 2017).

Seto, M.C., Cantor, J.M., and Blanchard, R. (2006) "Child pornography offenses are a valid diagnostic indicator of pedophilia." Journal of Abnormal Psychology 115, 610–615.

Sparrow, S.S., Cicchetti, D.V., and Balla, D.A. (2005) Vineland Adaptive Behavior Scales: Second Edition (Vineland II), the Expanded Interview Form. San Antonio, TX: Pearson Assessments.

Specter, A. and Hoffa, L. (2012) "A quiet but growing judicial rebellion against harsh sentences for child pornography offenses—should the laws be changed?" The Champion 33, 6. Available at www.nacdl.org/champion.aspx?id=22897 (accessed January 16, 2017).

Stabenow, T. (2011) "A method for careful study: A proposal for reforming the child pornography guidelines." Federal Sentencing Reporter 24, 2, 108–136.

Sulzberger, A.G. (2010, May 21) "Defiant judge takes on child pornography law." The New York Times. Available at www.nytimes.com/2010/05/22/nyregion/22judge.html (accessed January 16, 2017).

Tager-Flusberg, H. (2007) "Evaluating the theory-of-mind hypothesis in autism." Current Directions in Psychological Science 16, 6, 311–315.

Taylor, K., Mesibov, G., and Debbaudt, D. (2009) "Asperger syndrome in the criminal justice system." Available at www.aane.org/asperger-syndrome-criminal-justice-system (accessed January 12, 2017).

Tewksbury, R. (2005) "Collateral consequences of sex offender registration." *Journal of Contemporary Criminal Justice 21*, 1, 67–82.

Tewksbury, R. and Lees, M. (2006) "Consequences of sex offender registration: Collateral consequences and community experiences." *Sociological Spectrum 26*, 3, 309–334.

Tong, D. (2007) "The penile plethysmograph, Abel Assessment for Sexual Interest, and MSI-II: Are they speaking the same language?" *The American Journal of Family Therapy 35*, 187–202.

United States Sentencing Commission (2012) "Sourcebook of Federal Sentencing Statistics, Table 14." Available at www.ussc.gov/sites/default/files/pdf/research-and-publications/annual-reports-and-sourcebooks/2012/Table14.pdf (accessed January 16, 2017).

United States v. Cruikshank, 667 F. Supp. 2d 697, 701 (S.D. W.Va. 2009).

von Dornum, D. (2012, February 15) "Testimony before the United States Sentencing Commission public hearing on child pornography sentencing." Available at www.ussc.gov/sites/default/files/pdf/amendment-process/public-hearings-and-meetings/20120215-16/Testimony_15_vonDornum.pdf (accessed January 16, 2017).

Webb, L., Craissati, J., and Keen, S. (2007) "Characteristics of internet child pornography offenders: A comparison with child molesters." *Sexual Abuse: A Journal of Research and Treatment 19*, 4, 449–465.

Wechsler, D. (2008) *Wechsler Adult Intelligence Scale—Fourth Edition.* San Antonio, TX: Pearson.

Wollert, R. (2012, February 15) "Testimony before the United States Sentencing Commission public hearing on child pornography sentencing." Available at www.ussc.gov/sites/default/files/pdf/amendment-process/public-hearings-and-meetings/20120215-16/Testimony_15_Wollert_2.pdf (accessed January 16, 2017).

Wollert, R., Waggoner, J., and Smith, J. (2009, October) "Child pornography offenders do not have florid offense histories and are unlikely to recidivate." Poster session presented at the annual meeting of the Association for the Treatment of Sexual Abusers, Dallas, TX.

Woodbury-Smith, M. (2014) "Asperger Syndrome and Forensic Issues." In J.C. McPartland, A. Klin, and F.R. Volkmar (eds) *Asperger Syndrome: Assessing and Treating High-Functioning Autism Spectrum Disorders.* New York, NY: Guilford Press.

Zevitz, R.G. and Farkas, M.S. (2000) "Sex offender community notification: Managing high risk criminals or exacting further vengeance?" *Behavioral Sciences & the Law 18*, 2–3, 375–391.

Zgoba, K., Witt, P., Dalessandro, M., and Veysey, B. (2008) "Megan's Law: Assessing the practical and monetary efficacy." Available at www.ncjrs.gov/pdffiles1/nij/grants/225370.pdf (accessed January 16, 2017).

CHAPTER 5

Sex Offenses, Lies, and Politics

The Web of the Registry

Emily Horowitz

> *Sex offenders are the safest and easiest people to hate. Politicians, a category that certainly includes judges, never lose by condemning them and never win by coming to their defense. To argue too forcefully even for core legal protections afforded in other types of criminal cases is, in many contexts, to risk ostracism and raise suspicion.*

(Goetting 2015, p.2)

Widespread state and federal sex offender laws emerged swiftly in the 1990s after a series of highly publicized, horrific child abductions and murders involving repeat sex offenders. Little evidence existed then that sex offenses would decrease with public sex offender registries, but they were instituted as a result of mass public anger and fear. After 20 years, social science research overwhelmingly demonstrates the ineffectiveness and purely punitive nature of the laws, and legal scholars have continually challenged the constitutionality and fairness of post-conviction restrictions, although courts have upheld them. Sex offenders on registries face not only public shaming but also profound barriers to societal reintegration. This chapter outlines the political context of 1996 federal legislation leading to public sex offender registries, presents key findings from post-1996 research about the effects of the laws, and examines why sex offender laws continue to receive public support—despite decades of research and evidence showing they primarily function to excessively and permanently punish and publicly shame one subset of offenders.

In this volume, the chapters by Nick Dubin and Larry Dubin, describing the case of an autistic defendant convicted of a non-contact offense at virtually no risk of reoffense, with no allegations of sexual contact, highlight the way these laws are irrational and have unintentional and devastating consequences for defendants and their families. In this book, Nick Dubin tells the story of his arrest and conviction for viewing child pornography, and his father, law professor Larry Dubin, describes the arrest and conviction from the perspective of a parent and law professor. The story they tell is horrifying: not only is it the story of an autistic defendant with no criminal history suddenly being arrested and convicted of a crime, and the horror of a father realizing his son will be thrust into the criminal justice system that quickly destroys even the strongest and most resilient defendants, but one about an arrest and conviction for a sex offense, a crime viewed by outsiders as the very worst type of crime. Nick Dubin and Larry Dubin also share the experience of shame and humiliation that accompanies an arrest for a sex offense: Larry Dubin starts hanging his head in shame, after being a once proud and confident law professor, and Nick Dubin is banished by the autism community that once embraced him, and shunned and vilified by his own neighbors.

This chapter seeks to unravel how we got to a place where the criminal justice system functions to banish, punish, humiliate, and ruin those labeled as "sex offenders."

HOW DID WE GET SEX OFFENDER REGISTRIES?

Since the passage of federal sex offender registration and community notification laws in 1996, social scientists and legal scholars have published a significant amount of research and commentary regarding their ineffectiveness. After nearly 20 years of widespread sex offender registration and notification laws in the U.S., these measures continue to receive political and popular support—even as substantial research exists about how, in practice, the laws fail to protect the public. Most notably, research conclusively shows the following: that the vast majority of all sex offenses, and 93% of sex offenses involving children, are committed by non-strangers (e.g. family/friends/acquaintances); most new sex crimes are committed by people not on the sex offender registry, because sex offenders have much lower recidivism rates than all other groups of offenders, with the exception of homicide (Bureau of Justice Statistics, 1994); and that rates of all sex crimes, and particularly child sex abuse, started to continually decline before the widespread implementation of public registries. Overall, child sex offenses began to steadily decline in 1992, but that varies by state; for instance, in New Jersey, the decline in sex abuse cases started in 1985 (Veysey, Zgoba, and Dalessandro, 2008). In many states, even juvenile offenders are on public registries and subject to lifetime registration requirements—even though juvenile sex offenders have even lower recidivism rates than adult sex offenders. A decade ago, a study in ten states found that implementing sex offender registration and notification had no effect on the number of rapes committed after the implementation of the law—and one state had an increase after sex offender registry (Walker *et al.*, 2005). In practice, the laws serve solely to punish excessively and shame publicly one group of offenders even after they have completed lengthy criminal sentences. Child sex offenders are also not necessarily pedophiles—over one-third of sex offenders with child victims are themselves children, and the most frequent age of all juvenile sex offenders is 14 (Finkelhor, Ormrod, and Chaffin, 2009). Nonetheless, discourse about sex offenders centers on the notion that they are "hardwired" to commit sex crimes, and constitute an incurable, homogenous group of pariahs unable to reintegrate.

The first part of this chapter describes the lightning speed with which state and federal sex offender laws were passed, without substantial research or legal scrutiny, because of hysteria and justifiable public anger over a few instances of high-profile child murders (proven or perceived to be perpetrated by convicted repeat sex offenders). From the start, these laws were based on the flawed premise, voiced loudly and repeatedly by political supporters and victim advocates, that all sex offenders were predatory, uncontrollable, and incurable—and thus different from all other types of offenders, and thus deserving of post-conviction public shaming and monitoring. The chapter also examines the frequent and key findings of post-1996 peer-reviewed social science research and legal commentaries since passage of such measures. In addition, this chapter offers an analysis of why myths about sex offenses and sex offenders persist despite overwhelming research and evidence. This chapter suggests that researchers and legal scholars should work closely with advocates for sex offender law reform, in a way similar to advocates for reform of drug laws and the death penalty. Research about problems with drug laws and the death penalty did not influence change; the reforms occurred only when activists and researchers built effective organizations that publicized evidence and pressured political and legal actors. Additionally, researchers and legal scholars are particularly needed in the fight for rational sex offender policies, because of the unique and profound stigmatization faced by sex offenders and their families.

METHODS

This chapter utilizes direct quotations by political leaders, elected officials, law enforcement sources, victims' rights and anti-crime advocates, newspaper editorial boards, and reports by state commissions, as well as the texts of state and federal bills and legislative acts, to highlight the explicit premises and goals for the passage of sex offender registration and notification policies culminating with the 1996 passage of Megan's Law. In addition, I analyze the few available social science and legal articles preceding the passage of the laws, to determine the extent to which support for the laws existed outside of the political and activist realm.

I also examine the timing, frequency, and key findings from social science and legal literature about the effects of sex offender policies following passage of the 1996 federal law. Sources were obtained through keyword searches using EBSCO databases, and included peer-reviewed law review and research articles (research articles appeared primarily in criminal justice, criminology, psychology, and sociology journals), addressing the impact and effectiveness of the federal sex offender registries and community notification laws instituted in 1996.

FROM REGISTRATION TO COMMUNITY NOTIFICATION

In August 2015, *The New York Times* published an editorial denouncing civil commitment policies for sex offenders who had completed their criminal sentences. It read: "The essence of the American criminal justice system is reactive, not predictive: you are punished for the crime you committed. You can't be punished simply because you might commit one someday" (New York Times Editorial Board, 2015). Over two decades earlier, an editorial in the same paper, by New York Assembly member Daniel Feldman, calling for sex offender registration in New York, voiced a very different perspective. Feldman argued that requiring sex offenders to register with police after completing their criminal sentences would "become a medium to solve crimes," and that "registration laws prevent crimes because the police can intervene before a potential victim is harmed" (Feldman, 1994).

Feldman was writing about a month after the tragic murder of seven-year-old Megan Kanka in New Jersey by a convicted sex offender. Immediately following her murder, activists in New Jersey and elsewhere began calling for sex offender registration and notification; a terrified public believed Megan would be alive had her family been notified that a convicted, repeat child sex offender was living on her block. The push for public notification provisions for sex offenders emerged at a rapid pace; only days after Megan's murder, neighbors in her community started petitions calling on their New Jersey legislators to pass laws requiring notification of local law enforcement agencies when convicted sex offenders move into their jurisdictions and requiring that they notify those residing within 1000 feet of them (Barron, 1994). In the fall of 1994, Megan's Law was passed in New Jersey, requiring community notification, despite some drowned-out concerns voiced by the ACLU and others that it might invite vigilante justice. Only a few months later, in January 1995, a New Jersey community was notified that a sex offender on parole was moving into a specific address—and two men broke into the home and tried to assault him (Nordheimer, 1995).

The passage of Megan's Law in New Jersey did not emerge totally out of the blue; in 1994, Congress passed the Jacob Wetterling Crimes Against Children and Sexually Violent Offender Registration Act, the first federal law to establish state-level guidelines for sex offender tracking. In his history of registration laws, Wayne Logan (2009) describes how registration for various types of crimes has existed in multiple forms since as early as 1930. California was the first state to have a registration law for sex offenders, passed in 1947; other states followed, including Arizona (1951), Nevada (1961), Alabama (1967), Illinois (1986), Arkansas and Utah (1987), and Montana and Oklahoma (1989).

Washington State in 1990: First Community Notification Law

After a heinous violent sexual assault of a seven-year-old boy in 1989, by a repeat violent child sex offender in Washington State, a massive public outcry resulted in the first passage of community notification laws. The 1990 Washington State law was thus significant, because it was the first time sex offender laws included a provision for publicizing the names and addresses of convicted sex offenders; according to Logan, the 1990 law was also the first instance of the now-familiar term "sexual predator" in a legislative context (Logan, 2011).

A 1996 evaluation of the Washington law found that it did not decrease instances of sex crimes against children (Logan, 2009). The community notification provision of the 1990 Washington law, along with the related incorporation of the term and notion of the "sexual predator," highlights a profound shift in sex offender laws: first, it bifurcates the "sex offender" and non-sex offenders, creating one distinct group subject to public identification; and, second, the "sex offender" is not only distinct from other offenders but predatory, and thus differentiated further as more dangerous and more uncontrollable than non-sex offenders. The Washington Act justified the differential treatment of sex offenders, and the need for public notification, by arguing that a high risk of recidivism by sex offenders existed and that the "reduced expectation of privacy because of the public's interest in public safety will further the governmental interests of public safety and public scrutiny of the criminal and mental health systems" (Matson and Lieb, 1996).

The Washington Act emerged after a task force was put together and developed a list of recommendations to address sexual violence. The task force report highlights how a group that included politicians, a victim of sexual assault, a business owner, lawyers, a psychiatrist who researched effects on victims, and a psychologist who treated juvenile and adult offenders prompted the first sex offender notification provisions in the U.S. While the task force offered recommendations for victim services, the primary emphasis focused on dealing with convicted sex offenders. The task force recommended longer sentences for all sex offenders, including juveniles, and also notifying law enforcement of the whereabouts of a sex offender after release from prison. The report and recommendations were not grounded in research; in fact, the task force noted that little research was available because "research on sex offenders which meets rigorous, scientific criteria is difficult and expensive" (State of Washington, 1989, II-1).

The task force report relied largely on comments made in public hearings and provides evidence that attitudes towards sex offenders were already virulent and exceptional: for instance, the report states that sex offenders are different to other offenders, and shouldn't be eligible for reduced time for good behavior, and decisions about supervision should be based on risk assessment rather than the legal conviction category. At the same time, contradictions underlying the reasoning for the harshest punishment for offenders are also voiced, with the report noting that relatives and others known to the family often molest children, not only "strangers offering candy." However, the key premise for Megan's Law and the public registry is included in the report, which is that

> [b]ecause it is difficult to cure sex offenders, their potential for future offenses is a major concern. If law enforcement representatives knew the names and addresses of convicted sex offenders in their area, they could monitor the area more closely and use information for investigative purposes if a reported assault occurs. (Governor's Task Force, 1989, II-29)

Thus, it is argued, a registry is needed because sex offenders are incurable, and police can solve crimes more easily with a registry because new offenses are likely committed by someone with a past sex offense conviction.

Task force members acknowledge that there is not necessarily research showing this is the case, and even note that it is easier to increase prison terms than to fund research about decreasing sex offenses. The research cited in the report includes only one study of sex offender recidivism, and interestingly this study (Furby, Weinrott, and Blackshaw, 1989) does not support the conclusion in the report that sex offender recidivism is particularly or universally high, and notes differences among types of offenders and whether offenders receive treatment or not. The report highlights comments from citizens at hearings and via surveys, and a summary of the public comment on punishment for sex offenders notes many themes that persist today:

> [Punishment] recommendations included longer prison terms, life imprisonment on a second offense, lifetime supervision, chemical or surgical castration, and death. The public wants to see offenders face severe and long-term personal consequences for their behavior. It was frequently suggested that violent, juvenile sex offenders should be tried in adult court, and that bail for all sex offenders awaiting trial be eliminated. The expressed consensus was that current sentences and sanctions under the Sentencing Reform Act should be increased

and that some sexually-motivated misdemeanors should be classified as felonies. (Governor's Task Force, 1989, IV-70)

The Push for Federal Legislation

After the 1990 Act, in 1992 Louisiana passed a registration law that included a provision for public notification, also after a child murder by a repeat sex offender; three other high-profile child murders by convicted sex offenders took place in 1993 in Indiana, Texas, and California. In 1994, Tennessee and Alaska passed notification laws, and in 1994 Megan's Law was passed in New Jersey.

The push for sex offender legislation after Megan's murder was not limited to New Jersey; in New York, lawmakers immediately seized on the incident to blame those who had not voted for a recently proposed sex offender registration act. Thus, Democrats joined Republicans in a push to pass a bill—with Democrats going even further than Republicans by including the step of making the sex offender registry public (the Republican version of the bill allowed only police to view the registries). By May 1995, the New York State Senate passed, by a vote of 52 to 1, a bill requiring sex offenders to register with law enforcement (Nordheimer, 1995). In this early version of New York's sex offender registry, citizens could access it via a special phone number, and, in the most serious cases, local police would be notified when offenders moved into their jurisdictions, and the photos and addresses of offenders would be posted in police stations. A provision of the bill also gave law enforcement the option of notifying residents when a sex offender moved into their neighborhood—but this was not a requirement. Only one Democrat, New York State Senator Franz Leichter, a Democrat from Manhattan, opposed the 1995 bill, because he questioned the potential effectiveness of the registry.

The registry is a prime example of emotion-driven legislation. In the (albeit very limited) debate over the 1995 New York bill, advocates for the bill repeatedly invoked high-profile child murders in their push for the legislation. A month after the Senate passed the bill, in June 1995, the parents of Megan Kanka (murdered at age seven by a convicted sex offender) and Polly Klaas (murdered at age 12 by a violent career criminal) joined New York Assembly Republicans to push Democrats to support the bill. When the Assembly Democrat leader, Sheldon Silver, stated at a press conference that he supported a public sex offender registry but wanted to be sure that it could face constitutional challenges and was designed carefully, he was interrupted by Mr. Kanka, Mr. Klaas, and other parents of murdered children who demanded he quickly and immediately pass the bill. Mr. Klaas dismissed the issues of constitutionality, and shouted, according to *The New York Times*, "The rights of children to be protected have to override the rights of the perverts" (Sack, 1994).

The key Republican supporter of the bill in the Senate, Dean Skelos, co-sponsor of the legislation with Democrat Daniel Feldman, also dismissed concerns raised during the debate about constitutionality, saying that sex offenders were different from all other offenders, and required special monitoring even after prison and parole. He told reporters that "the harsh reality is, 'once a pedophile, always a pedophile'" (Dao, 1995). In July 1995, the New York State Assembly passed the sex offender registry bill. The New York law primarily focused on the registration with a state databank for ten years for non-violent offenders and lifetime registration for violent offenders. The data would be accessible to the public via a special phone number, and callers would have to provide details about a specific person to have access to the information. The law also gave police the ability to notify communities about those classified as "high risk" by judges.

New York, like most other states in the mid-1990s, quickly passed Megan's Law without testimony regarding the facts and data about sexual abuse and sex offender recidivism, and input from sex offender treatment providers. The political debate about civil liberties concerned almost exclusively the ability of the law to withstand constitutional tests, and not the civil rights of sex offenders or the potential effectiveness of the law. The passage of the flawed legislation is hardly surprising, given the vocal presence of the parents of murdered children in the legislative chambers.

Federal Sex Registration and Community Notification Laws

One month after the murder of Megan Kanka, Congress passed the Federal Violent Crime and Control Act of 1994 which included the Jacob Wetterling Crimes Against Children and Sexually Violent Offender Registration Act. Supporters of the federal registration requirements were already referring to this provision as "Megan's Law" (Manegold,

1994). Jacob Wetterling was 11 when he was abducted in 1978, and his case has never been solved. His mother, Patty Wetterling, became a staunch advocate for sex offender registration laws and believed it would have helped police solve the case (and possibly find her son) if they had had ready access to data about released sex offenders no longer under state supervision. The Wetterling Act emphasized law enforcement registration provisions for sex offenders. The initial version of the Act targeted sex offenders who victimized minors, but the final version included anyone convicted of a "sexually violent offense" and classified by the court as a "sexually violent predator."

In May 1996, the Wetterling Act was updated to include a version of Megan's Law and was signed into law by President Bill Clinton. The key change related to community notification. A Congressional report clearly stated that the update to the 1994 Wetterling Law "would make the disclosure of registration information necessary to protect the public mandatory rather than permissive under the Act's standards" (Committee on the Judiciary, 1996). Thus, the Megan's Law update incorporated guidelines requiring all states to have processes for notifying the public about released sex offenders.

At the signing ceremony, President Clinton voiced his explicit support for a shift to community notification, stating:

> From now on, every State in the country will be required by law to tell a community when a dangerous sexual predator enters its midst. We respect people's rights, but today America proclaims there is no greater right than a parent's right to raise a child in safety and love. (Clinton, 1996)

President Clinton, himself an attorney, clearly was unconcerned about constitutional issues such as civil liberties, the right to privacy, and the possibility that notification was a form of "cruel and unusual punishment" that subjected registrants to vigilantes, and recognized that the political climate was ripe for singling out sex offenders as pariahs and the primary threat to child safety. Clinton further remarked that notifying the public about sex offenders is in fact necessary, dismissing concerns about public shaming, because "widespread public access is necessary for the efficacy of the scheme, and the attendant humiliation is but a collateral consequence of a valid regulation" (Clinton, 1996). The Pam Lychner Act was also passed in 1996, which set up a national sex offender database and mandated certain types of sex offenders to lifetime registration and community notification.

Early Criticism of Registration and Notification

Prior to the passage of the 1996 notification requirement, legal scholars did express reservations about the growing popularity of registration publicizing sex offenders. In a *California Law Review* article published in May 1995, Abril Bedarf questions the potential effectiveness of notification, and further notes that it has the potential to promote hysteria and fear, making it more difficult for offenders to reintegrate after incarceration; Bedarf also argues that publicly branding sex offenders is a form of cruel and unusual punishment (Bedarf, 1995). Other legal scholars raised similar concerns about cruel and unusual punishment and the right to privacy; a 1996 article in the *Loyola University Chicago Law Journal* also notes the possibility for vigilante justice (as seen in New Jersey immediately following the implementation of Megan's Law), and suggests that the stress of notification and public humiliation could deter reintegration efforts and could thus lead to reoffense (Ball, 1996).

Similarly, in 1995, the journal *Criminal Justice Ethics* published an issue questioning the ethics underlying increasing popularity of community notification laws; a philosopher and a psychologist authored substantive essays strongly opposing the laws. A lawyer writing in the issue noted that the public registry laws signaled a profound shift in the legal landscape, which now allows "prioritizing protection and safety over civil liberties" (Brooks, 1995). Nevertheless, scholarly voices were limited and marginalized (and often mocked by politicians, characterizing concern for civil liberties as akin to advocating for "perverts" over innocent children). Various factors explain this relative silence by scholars. First, the laws emerged so quickly that there was little time for serious scholars to consider the potential impact of the laws; and, second, the concept of registration and notification was largely the result of politicians working closely with the parents of murdered children who pushed for immediate and decisive action. Primarily, however, these laws were profoundly difficult to critique in an emotion-driven setting. Additionally, the image of the "sex offender" was now solidified in the public imagination as a violent, uncontrollable predator indelibly linked to the tragic murders of innocent children, and dehumanized and unworthy of objective concern or compassion.

Increasing Federal Sex Offender Legislation

In 2006, Congress passed a further enhancement to these laws with the Adam Walsh Child Protection and Safety Act (named for Adam Walsh, a six-year-old kidnapped and murdered in 1981). The Walsh Act further enhanced registration and notification requirements. Most significantly, the Walsh Act requires anyone convicted of any sex offense to register, requires juveniles 14 and older to register, and requires sex offenders to register in person at law enforcement agencies at regular intervals. Although not all states have implemented the Adam Walsh Act due to costliness, most states already have similar provisions, including registration requirements for juvenile offenders—the issue of juvenile offenders is particularly problematic, given that a Human Rights Watch report (Pittman, 2013) found that about one-quarter of the registrants committed sex offenses as juveniles.

Today, because of the web of state and federal laws mandating community notification, the identities of all sex offenders are now easily accessible on the internet to all citizens, via state and federal registry websites. In addition, there are also private websites and apps that further publicize information on sex offenders, making the toll-free numbers and even the distribution of signs, flyers, or mailings of the 1990s seem relatively minor. There are differences in public registration requirements by state; in New York, for example, those convicted of sex offenses as juveniles or classified as low-risk or "Level One" offenders are not listed on the internet, whereas other states post data about all convicted sex offenders, and many include juvenile offenders on public internet registries.

Politicians continue to propose new laws to further monitor and expose convicted sex offenders. An "International Megan's Law" passed in the Senate in December 2015, to little notice or news coverage in any major outlet, which provides advance notification of travel by convicted sex offenders to governments of destination countries (114th Congress, 2015). The bill has been proposed in the past, and legal scholars have criticized it on the grounds that domestic Megan's Law is problematic and ineffective (Hamilton, 2011; Newburn, 2010; Viera, 2011). An article in the *CUNY Law Review* notes that there is far from an international consensus about sex offender policies, so this law is deeply flawed, and although some countries have certain registration requirements for some types of sex offenders, there is little support for community notification; the author further notes that this bill will potentially cost $252 million over a four-year period (King, 2011). As early as 2008, the Department of Justice published a study that found that after ten years in New Jersey, Megan's home state and a bastion of support for the law, Megan's Law had no effect on sex offenses, including no effect on reducing the number of sex offense victims; yet this key study, and many others just like it, seems to have had no effect on public or legislative enthusiasm for creating new laws based on the very same premises (Zgoba *et al.*, 2008).

SEX OFFENDER MYTHS INFILTRATE JUDICIAL AND LEGAL DECISIONS

The comments from politicians about Megan's Law in the mid-1990s highlight how myths about sex offenders and their recidivism created swaths of purposeless state and federal laws. Ira and Tara Ellman, in a 2015 paper, dissect how courts have also used flawed data and myths about sex offenders that influence judicial decision-making in profound ways. They note that in 2002 the Supreme Court ruled that a convicted sex offender could be punished for not completing a form as part of his prison-based sexual treatment program detailing his sexual history, "including any that might constitute an uncharged criminal offense for which he could then be prosecuted" (Ellman and Ellman, 2015, pp.1–2). Justice Kennedy justified the ruling on the basis that recidivism rates for "untreated offenders" is "as high as 80%," and thus the program is helpful because it allows inmates to examine what causes them to have "such a frightening and high risk of recidivism" (Ellman and Ellman, 2015, p.2).

While legislators, politicians, and victim advocates often use rhetoric about high recidivism rates to push the passage of new sex offenders, judges too rely on this mistaken idea of a "frightening and high" recidivism rate; 91 judicial opinions, as well as briefs in 101 cases, cite this untrue statistic (Ellman and Ellman, 2015, pp.495–496). Most troublingly, they describe how even the Supreme Court is willing to use questionable sources to justify any punishment for sex offenders; Justice Kennedy, they argue, found the 80% recidivism rate figure in a 1988 U.S. Department of Justice publication, which quoted from a 1986 *Psychology Today* article written by a counselor discussing a program he directed in one prison (Ellman and Ellman, 2015, p.497). In other words, they conclude, the evidence used in numerous opinions, including a Supreme Court decision, is based on the "unsupported assertion of someone without research expertise who made his living selling such counseling programs to prisons" (Ellman and Ellman, 2015, p.498).

The counselor Robert Longo was recently interviewed about sex offender registries and the impact his quote in the March 1986 article had had on the public consensus—as well as landmark legal decisions—that sex offenders almost always reoffend. In an interview with *The Sentinel* (Vaughn, 2016), a local Pennsylvania newspaper, Longo told the reporter that he's against public registries. Longo also said he doesn't believe that treating sex offenders is pointless, and says that in his experience treatment works and can result in low recidivism rates, and that his words were misunderstood. Longo was then quoted in a 1988 U.S. Department of Justice field practitioner's guide, written by Barbara K. Schwartz; not only does Longo oppose the registries, but Schwartz herself was also interviewed in *The Sentinel* article, and said that, after working in sex offender treatment since 1971, she too opposes registries.

The problem with the "frightening and high" comment from Kennedy, along with the remarks by legislators and politicians, and the text of various state laws, is that there is no research that shows that the sex offender recidivism rate is anywhere close to 80%. Numerous studies, along with data from the Department of Justice, now exist showing low rates of sex offender recidivism, particularly when compared with recidivism rates for other offenders; for instance, one recent (2014) study, which examined 7740 sex offenders across 21 samples, found rates of 1% to 5% for low-risk offenders over time, and 22% for high-risk offenders—but, importantly, the recidivism rate for even high-risk offenders decreased to 4.2% after ten years of non-offending (Hanson *et al.*, 2014).

It is understandable that in 1994 the Wetterling Act included language that erroneously argued the "high rate of recidivism" of sex offenders (103rd Congress, 1994, pp.246–247), and, in 1996, while remarking on Megan's Law, Clinton wrongly noted that "study after study has shown us that sex offenders commit crime after crime" (Clinton, 1996). At the time Megan's Law was passed in 1996, there were few studies or critiques of recidivism rates for sex offenders.

Now we have over 20 years of research and data examining the need to reform post-conviction laws for sex offenders, yet support for the laws remains.

THE INEFFECTIVENESS OF SEX OFFENDER LAWS

As of June 1, 2015, the National Center for Missing and Exploited Children listed 843,260 registered sex offenders in the United States (2015, p.495). With the advent of the internet, and the 1996 "public dissemination" provisions of Megan's Law, anyone has access to details about convicted sex offenders, including photographs, physical descriptions, details about the crimes, and home addresses. The 1994 Wetterling Act seems mild by comparison, only requiring even the most violent sex offenders to register with law enforcement for ten years. Indeed, some advocates for sex offender reform are now pushing for a return to the now humane-seeming law-enforcement-only registry, which would be a relief after the public humiliation and shaming of internet listings. Additionally, with almost 900,000 on the registry and subject to notification, it is impossible for the public, or law enforcement, to adequately assess the risk of the small number of sex offenders who will recidivate and pose a real danger to the public.

For my recent book (Horowitz, 2015), I interviewed dozens of sex offenders living life on the registry. A few themes emerged: virtually all of them experienced harassment and humiliation because of the public registry, in various forms; each described barriers to securing housing and finding and maintaining employment; most acknowledged that they had made serious mistakes and agreed that they should have been punished and incarcerated, but viewed the registry as the key barrier to their ability to reintegrate into society and live normal and productive lives. Many had experienced homelessness, and those with children experienced unique challenges, such as not being allowed to attend school events.

Research not only undermines the myth of high sex offender recidivism, and thus the very basis of registration and notification laws, but also shows these measures do not improve child safety. As journalist Judith Levine notes, children themselves might be the ones most harmed by sex offender legislation, because hundreds of thousands are on the sex offender registries: 14-year-olds are the group having committed most sex offenses processed in the criminal justice system (Levine, 2014). Indeed, the growing discussion about the impact of mass incarceration shows increasing interest in collateral consequences and the barriers to re-entry following a conviction. Yet initiatives aimed at helping the formerly incarcerated rarely address sex offenders, or the barriers faced by those listed, *inter alia*, because of constantly updated mugshots on readily accessible sex offender registries. In addition to the constant humiliation of being branded publicly as sex offenders, those on the registry confront additional restrictions that vary from state to state, including limitations on where they may live, work, shop, or even attend religious services. Not surprisingly, some researchers have found that the registry itself can lead to recidivism, because the inability to integrate into society after a conviction undermines the desire to reform (Prescott and Rockoff, 2011).

CONCLUSIONS
How We Got Here

Patty Wetterling, the mother of Jacob Wetterling, an early and vocal advocate for sex offender registration, is herself now questioning the laws, based on the irrefutable evidence that they do far more harm than good. In a 2013 interview, Wetterling explained, "We've been elevating sex offender registration and community notification and punishment for 20-some years, and a wise and prudent thing would be to take a look at what's working. Instead we let our anger drive us" (Bleyer, 2013). She also acknowledged that most people on the registry, such as juveniles and non-violent statutory offenders, are clearly not individuals such as those who abducted her son or many other children whose victimization led to the passage of other registration and notification laws. The most recent FBI statistics (from 1999) show that 115 children a year are abducted by strangers, and less than half are murdered by their abductors; moreover, teenagers—not young children—were the most frequent victims of abductions (Finkelhor, Hammer, and Sedlak, 2002).

There is increasing awareness about the unintended consequences and draconian nature of the laws, such as the groundswell of support for Zach Anderson in 2015. Anderson, a 20-year-old who had consensual sex with a 14-year-old who lied about her age, was sentenced to 25 years on the sex offender registry in Michigan and Indiana (he traveled to Michigan to meet the girl, who lived in Indiana). Mainstream news outlets, including *The New York Times*, highlighted how the registry forbade Anderson from having a smartphone or using the internet, staying out past 8 p.m., living with his family because they resided too close to a public boating facility (where children might congregate), and talking to minors outside of his family; it was observed that the internet restrictions effectively ended his ability to pursue his planned career in computer science. Anderson was eventually taken off the registry in Michigan, but he is still working on getting his name off the Indiana list.

Anderson's story went viral because his parents publicized his ordeal, and the alleged victim in the case backed Anderson and openly acknowledged that she lied about her age. However, most sex offenders, and their families, are too fearful to speak up because of the shame surrounding the issue. To roll back sex offender registration and notification laws, the formerly incarcerated and their families cannot lead advocacy and awareness efforts. Yet the personal stories of offenders, such as Anderson, who challenge the stereotypes, are key to changing attitudes.

More importantly, it's time to recognize that there exists sufficient research about the failure of the registry, and that publicly humiliating and labeling one subset of offenders is disastrous and inhumane; youth on the registry have shockingly high rates of depression and suicide, as documented by Human Rights Watch (Pittman, 2013). The term "sex offender" itself is thus tainted, with recent research showing that the very terms "sex offender" and even "juvenile sex offender" reinforce support for public registries and other restrictions (Socia and Harris, 2014).

A 2008 study found that advocates of Megan's Law are aware that it has not reduced recidivism and acknowledge that it subjects those on the registry to harassment, yet they don't believe it creates challenges to employment (Schiavone and Jeglic, 2008). Those who support the law, therefore, are similar to the political sponsors of the bill, who crafted the policy out of emotion, anger, and vengeance, and substantial unwillingness, and indifference, to recognize the collateral consequences because of revulsion for those labeled as sex offenders.

What We Can Learn from the Treatment of Autistic Defendants

The example of Nick Dubin's experience highlights the expanse and corruption of what civil liberties attorney Bill Dobbs has coined the "sex offense legal regime." This "regime" ignores virtually all mitigating factors before sentencing, such as the fact, in Nick Dubin's case, that he had no criminal history, that there were no allegations of a contact offense, and no likelihood of reoffense, and, after the criminal sentence is served, that those convicted of these offenses are then slammed with a lifetime of consequences that have no effect on public safety yet further ruin their lives via public shaming and a web of laws that ensure that they can never recover or overcome terrible mistakes. The sex offender registry undermines the very premise of a just justice system, which should function as a place to punish people for things they have done and rehabilitate them so they don't do them again. The registry does the opposite: it defines people forever by crimes they have committed and mistakes they have made, by punishing them over and over after they have been punished for whatever they have done. The never-ending punishment of the sex offender registry undermines any efforts at rehabilitation and reintegration, because the registry functions as a form of banishment and humiliation.

The next step is for researchers and legal scholars to focus on changing policies and influencing efforts to reform the laws. While over two decades of evidence and data undermining the laws should suffice for researchers to focus on policy changes, sex offenders and their families are worse off than ever because of the same period of fear-mongering and hysteria whereby politicians portray them as the ultimate embodiment of evil. Sex offenders and their families encounter hurdles not confronted by advocates of other kinds of criminal justice reform, such as those personally affected by draconian drug laws and mass incarceration policies; they face genuine threats of violence and harassment when they publicly identify as sex offenders. Researchers and scholars have a particularly significant role to play in efforts to change these unjust laws and must work to create a voice for those lumped together as sex offenders. Producing more nuanced and specific characterizations of the diverse nature of sex offenses must be a key part of the reform process. Social scientists, legal scholars, and journalists should model organizing efforts in the mold of reforms of drug laws and the death penalty, by emphasizing both the pointlessness of the measures as well as the devastating effects on individuals and families. Currently, there are small, scattered movements for reform of sex offender laws, led by offenders and families, including national groups such as Reform Sex Offender Laws, as well as its affiliate groups in many states; particularly active and successful ones in Texas, Virginia, and California have taken the first steps to organize and change the perceptions of sex offenders.

However, they require outside support from the research community in order to legitimize and speed reform efforts; there is a need for groups such as the Death Penalty Information Center, run by a board of attorneys who "promote informed discussion of the death penalty by preparing in-depth reports, conducting briefings for journalists, and serving as a resource to those working on this issue" (Death Penalty Information Center, 2015); or the Drug Policy Alliance, which similarly provides facts and information on a website, and also serves to "advance policies that reduce the harms of both drug use and drug prohibition, and seek solutions that promote safety while upholding the sovereignty of individuals over their own minds and bodies" (Drug Policy Alliance, 2017). Special laws that single out sex offenders undermine human rights, and those of us with access to status, resources, and power—specifically academics in the fields of law and the social sciences, attorneys, and investigative journalists—need to organize and speak loudly on behalf of the most stigmatized to change perceptions and policies.

REFERENCES

103rd Congress of the United States of America. 1994. Violent Crime Control and Law Enforcement Act of 1994. H.R. 3355.

114th Congress of the United States of America. 2015. International Megan's Law to Prevent Child Exploitation and Other Sexual Crimes Through Advanced Notification of Traveling Sex Offenders. H.R. 515.

Ball, J. (1996) "Public disclosure of America's secret shame: Child sex offender community notification in Illinois." *Loyola University Chicago Law Journal 27*, 2.

Barron, J. (1994) "Vigil for slain girl, 7, backs a law on offenders." *The New York Times*, August 3. Available at www.nytimes.com/1994/08/03/nyregion/vigil-for-slain-girl-7-backs-a-law-on-offenders.html (accessed January 16, 2017).

Bedarf, A.R. (1995) "Examining sex offender community notification laws." *California Law Review 83*, 3, 55.

Bleyer, J. (2013) "Patty Wetterling questions sex offender laws." *City Pages*, March 20. Available at www.citypages.com/news/patty-wetterling-questions-sex-offender-laws-6766534 (accessed January 17, 2017).

Brooks, A.D. (1995) "The legal issues." *Criminal Justice Ethics 14*, 2, 5.

Bureau of Justice Statistics (1994) "Recidivism of Prisoners Released in 1994." Table 10: Rearrest rates of State prisoners released in 1994, by most serious offense for which released and charge at rearrest. Available at http://bjs.gov/content/pub/pdf/rpr94.pdf (accessed January 17, 2017).

Clinton, B. (1996) "Remarks on Signing Megan's Law and an Exchange with Reporters."

Committee on the Judiciary (1996) House Report 104-555, edited by 2nd Session 104th Congress. Washington, DC: U.S. Government Publishing Office.

Dao, J. (1995) "Relatives of slain children join Albany lawmakers to push for bills aimed at violent crime." *The New York Times*, June 15. Available at www.nytimes.com/1995/06/15/nyregion/relatives-slain-children-join-albany-lawmakers-push-for-bills-aimed-violent.html (accessed January 17, 2017).

Death Penalty Information Center (2015) "Death Penalty Information Center: About DPIC." Available at www.deathpenaltyinfo.org/about-dpic (accessed January 17, 2017).

Drug Policy Alliance (2017) "About the Drug Policy Alliance." Available at www.drugpolicy.org/about-us/about-drug-policy-alliance (accessed March 3, 2017).

Ellman, I.M. and Ellman, T. (2015) "'Frightening and high': The Supreme Court's crucial mistake about sex crime statistics." *Constitutional Commentary*, Fall 2015. Available at http://nationalrsol.org/wp-content/uploads/2015/08/Frighteninghigh.pdf (accessed January 17, 2017).

Feldman, D.L. (1994) "Letter: On sex offenders; New York, too, needs registration law." *The New York Times*, August 29. Available at www.nytimes.com/1994/08/29/opinion/l-letter-on-sex-offenders-new-york-too-needs-registration-law-092959.html?pagewanted=print (accessed January 17, 2017).

Finkelhor, D., Hammer, H., and Sedlak, A. (2002) "Nonfamily Abducted Children: National Estimates and Characteristics." In *National Incidence Studies of Missing, Abducted, Runaway, and Throwaway Children*. U.S. Department of Justice, Office of Juvenile Justice and Delinquency Prevention.

Finkelhor, D., Ormrod, R., and Chaffin, M. (2009) "Juveniles Who Commit Sex Offenses Against Minors." In *Juvenile Justice Bulletin*. U.S. Department of Justice, Office of Juvenile Justice and Delinquency Prevention.

Furby, L., Weinrott, M.R., and Blackshaw, L. (1989) "Sex offender recidivism: A review." *Psychological Bulletin 105*, 1, 3–30.

Goetting, N. (2015) "Moral panic over sex offenses results in cruel and self-defeating over punishment." *National Lawyers Guild Review 71*, 3.

Hamilton, M. (2011) "The child pornography crusade and its net-widening effect." *Cardozo Law Review 33*, 1679.

Hanson, K.R., Harris, A.J.R., Helmus, L., and Thornton, D. (2014) "High-risk sex offenders may not be high risk forever." *Journal of Interpersonal Violence 29*, 15, 2792–2813.

Horowitz, E. (2015) *Protecting Our Kids? How Sex Offender Laws Are Failing Us*. Santa Barbara, CA: Praeger.

King, C. (2011) "Sex offender registration and notification laws at home and abroad: Is an International Megan's Law good policy?" *CUNY Law Review 15*, 117.

Levine, J. (2014) "The sex offender regime is cruel and unusual punishment." Counterpunch, October 24. Available at www.counterpunch.org/2014/10/24/the-sex-offender-regime-is-cruel-and-unusual-punishment (accessed January 17, 2017).

Logan, W.A. (2009) *Knowledge as Power: Criminal Registration and Community Notification Laws in America*. Stanford, CA: Stanford Law Books.

Logan, W.A. (2011) "Prospects for the international migration of US sex offender registration and community notification laws." *International Journal of Law and Psychiatry 34*, 3, 233–238.

Manegold, C. (1994) "Quiet winners in House fight on crime: Women." *The New York Times*, August 25. Available at www.nytimes.com/1994/08/25/us/quiet-winners-in-house-fight-on-crime-women.html (accessed January 17, 2017).

Matson, S. and Lieb, R. (1996) "Sex offender registration: A review of state laws." Washington State Institute for Public Policy. Available at www.wsipp.wa.gov/ReportFile/1227 (accessed January 17, 2017).

National Center for Missing and Exploited Children (2015) "Registered sex offenders in the United States and its territories per 100,000 population." Available at www.missingkids.com/en_US/documents/Sex_Offenders_Map.pdf (accessed January 17, 2017).

Newburn, K. (2010) "The prospect of an international sex offender registry: Why an international system modeled after United States sex offender laws is not an effective solution to stop child sexual abuse." *The Wisconsin International Law Journal 28*, 547.

New York Times Editorial Board (2015). "Sex offenders locked up on a hunch." *The New York Times*, August 15. Available at www.nytimes.com/2015/08/16/opinion/sunday/sex-offenders-locked-up-on-a-hunch.html?_r=0 (accessed January 17, 2017).

Nordheimer, J. (1995) "'Vigilante' attack in New Jersey is linked to sex-offenders law." *The New York Times*, January 11. Available at www.nytimes.com/1995/01/11/nyregion/vigilante-attack-in-new jersey is linked to sex offenders law.html (accessed January 17, 2017)

Pittman, N. (2013) *Raised on the Registry: The Irreparable Harm of Placing Children on Sex Offender Registries in the US*. New York, NY: Human Rights Watch. Available at www.hrw.org/sites/default/files/reports/us0513_ForUpload_1.pdf (accessed January 17, 2017).

Prescott, J.J. and Rockoff, J.E. (2011) "Do sex offender registration and notification laws affect criminal behavior?" *Journal of Law and Economics 54*, 1, 161–206.

Sack, K. (1994) "Political notes; road from stooge to running mate." *The New York Times*, July 10. Available at www.nytimes.com/1994/07/10/nyregion/political-notes-road-from-stooge-to-running-mate.html (accessed January 17, 2017).

Schiavone, S. and Jeglic, E. (2008) "Public perception of sex offender social policies and the impact on sex offenders." *International Journal of Offender Therapy and Comparative Criminology 53*, 6, 679–695.

Socia, K. and Harris, A. (2014) "What's in a name? Evaluating the effects of the 'sex offender' label on public opinions and beliefs." *Sexual Abuse: A Journal of Research and Treatment*, 1–19.

State of Washington (1989) Governor's Task Force on Community Protection. State of Washington Department of Social and Health Services, Office of the Secretary. Norm Maleng, Chairman.

Vaughn, J. (2016) "Closer look: Finding statistics to fit a narrative." *The Sentinel*, March 21. Available at http://cumberlink.com/news/local/closer_look/closer-look-finding-statistics-to-fit-a-narrative/article_7c4cf648-0999-5efc-ae6a-26f4b7b529c2.html (accessed January 17, 2017).

Veysey, B.M., Zgoba, K., and Dalessandro, M. (2008) "A preliminary step towards evaluating the impact of Megan's Law: A trend analysis of sexual offenses in New Jersey from 1985 to 2005." *Justice Research and Policy 10*, 2, 1–18.

Viera, D. (2011) "Try as they might, just can't get it right: Shortcomings of the International Megan's Law of 2010." *Emory International Law Review 25*, 1517.

Walker, J.T., Maddan, S., Vasquez, B.E., Van Houten, A.C., and Ervin-McLarty, G. (2005) "The influence of sex offender registration and notification laws in the United States." Arkansas Crime Information Center Working Paper.

Zgoba, K., Witt, P., Dalessandro, M., and Veysey, B. (2008) *Megan's Law: Assessing the Practical and Monetary Efficacy*. Office of Policy and Planning, New Jersey Department of Corrections. U.S. Department of Justice.

CHAPTER 6

Tilting at Windmills

The Misplaced War on Child Pornography Offenders

Mark H. Allenbaugh

"Do you see over yonder, friend Sancho, thirty or forty hulking giants? I intend to do battle with them and slay them. With their spoils we shall begin to be rich for this is a righteous war and the removal of so foul a brood from off the face of the earth is a service God will bless."
"What giants?" asked Sancho Panza.

Part 1, Chapter VIII. Of the valorous Don Quixote's success in the dreadful and never before imagined Adventure of the Windmills, with other events worthy of happy record.

INTRODUCTION: THE QUIXOTIC CRUSADE AGAINST CHILD PORNOGRAPHY

No other offense elicits such visceral reactions as the possession, receipt, and distribution of child pornography[1]—save, perhaps, its actual production.[2] This chapter focuses primarily on those federal offenses involving the possession, receipt, and distribution of child pornography since those offenses constitute the bulk of federal child pornography prosecutions,[3] and, as discussed herein, have been the primary focus of concern over the past several years.

---

1   Possession of child pornography generally is prosecuted under 18 U.S.C. § 2252(a)(4) and 18 U.S.C. § 2252A(a)(5); receipt and/or distribution is prosecuted under 18 U.S.C. § 2252(a)(1–3) and 18 U.S.C. § 2252A(a)(1–4, 6).

2   In contrast, production of child pornography generally is prosecuted under 18 U.S.C. § 2251.

3   According to Table 17 of the U.S. Sentencing Commission's *2015 Sourcebook on Federal Sentencing Statistics*, in fiscal year 2015, there were 1557 individuals sentenced for child pornography possession, receipt, or distribution. In contrast, there were only 415 individuals sentenced for production of child pornography.

With respect to child pornography, some depictions are so graphic as to transcend any connotation of eroticism conveyed by the pornography nomenclature; some depictions are nothing less than the intentional documentation of horrendous crimes: the rape of children and often infants. Terms like "child sexual abuse images," therefore, now are gaining favor as a more accurate nomenclature for such offenses.

That there are people who would "consume" such offensive images for their own sexual gratification speaks of a depravity so base as to shock even the most callous conscience. In short, just the simple possession of child pornography readily connotes both a revolting offense and an exceedingly deviant offender.

Thus, for the past generation, the many states, led by the federal government, have advanced an unofficial but quite real War on Child Pornography. This war, however, has not primarily been fought against the producers, but rather the consumers and traders of child pornography. In other words, the War on Child Pornography more aptly is described as a War on Child Pornography *Possession*. Like the official War on Drugs, state and federal governments have dedicated enormous resources to uncover, investigate, prosecute, and imprison such possessors of child pornography (like consumers of illicit drugs) ostensibly to eradicate the direct sexual exploitation of children through its production.

And, as with most crimes, that child pornography quickly migrated from the backrooms of seedy novelty stores to the internet necessarily has created more opportunities to obtain and distribute such contraband. Advances in technology, moreover, have made it cheap and easy to acquire and distribute, and even have created a novel subgenre of actual production offenses known as "sexting,"[4] and novel methods of remote production[5] via the inducement of minors through social media sites. By its ubiquity, like illicit drugs, child pornography presents both an increasingly challenging offense to combat from a technological perspective, and one that is morally far more repulsive than most other offenses.

---

4   See e.g. *United States v. Broxmeyer*, 699 F.3d 265, 268 (2nd Cir. 2012) (affirming 30-year sentence for attempting to induce minor to transmit sexually explicit image of herself).

5   See e.g. *United States v. Garden*, 2015 U.S. Dist. LEXIS 88575, *4 (D. Neb.) (defendant posed as fictitious juvenile in order to persuade other juvenile to produce sexually explicit images).

But is this War on Child Pornography premised on sound suppositions? Because of the visceral nature inherent in such an offense and often reflexively imparted to the offender, this chapter asks whether the War on Child Pornography is more a quixotic crusade against mythic monsters than a realistic and just effort at protecting children.

In this chapter, I identify the three principal suppositions that underlie the War on Child Pornography Possession, which, due to their hyperbole, largely have gone unchallenged, and thus have misdirected efforts to eradicate the sexual exploitation of children, and, like the War on Drugs, have concomitantly led to gross miscarriages of justice. After arguing that these suppositions are more myth than reality, this chapter concludes that the War on Child Pornography Possession is, indeed, a misadventure against windmills.

Section 1 provides a statistical overview of the War on Child Pornography, focusing primarily on federal efforts and policies. The rate of prosecution for child pornography offenses is growing faster than any other major offense category, and the sentences imposed also are higher than for any other major offense category despite a concerted backlash by the federal judiciary. This has resulted in a swelling inmate population in the Bureau of Prisons such that inmates serving time for sex offenses (of which child pornography possession constitutes the clear majority of such offenders) now compose the fourth largest segment of the inmate population, a segment that is growing faster than any other. And this in a system already overcrowded and growing. Included in Section 1 is a review of the U.S. Sentencing Commission's 2012 report, *Federal Child Pornography Offenses*, and the Commission's call for fundamental reform of sentencing for non-production offenses.

Section 2 identifies the three primary suppositions-*qua*-myths underlying the prosecution and sentencing policies of the federal government with respect to the simple possession of child pornography, which also underlie the receipt, distribution, and transportation of such contraband (collectively "non-production offenses"). Section 2A discusses the most fundamental myth: the Market Theory. The Market Theory holds that the possession of child pornography contributes to the general market for it; in short, possession creates a demand, which promotes supply. The Market Theory suggests that by reducing demand through increased prosecution and severe sanctions, supply-

qua-production likewise will be reduced. Not only has this simplistic theory not worked for the War on Drugs, but it is even less applicable in the context of non-consumables such as images of child pornography. Section 2A argues that even eliminating all production will have little to no effect on consumption, and vice versa. The Market Theory simply is a myth without foundation.

Section 2B discusses the Cross-Over Myth, which often goes hand-in-hand with the Market Theory as a justification for severe sanctions even in simple possession cases. Here it is argued that there is some correlation between possession of child pornography and actual contact offenses such that a possession offender is believed, for sentencing purposes, to have a likelihood toward committing future contact offenses (and is presumed to have committed undetected prior contact offenses), thereby justifying a longer period of incarceration. The scientific literature is at best ambiguous on this position, and even if this myth turned out to have some veracity, there are less onerous and far fairer vehicles already available to address the issue than simply imposing longer terms of incarceration.

Section 2C discusses the Harms Myth. Here the hypothesis is that every time an image of pornography is disseminated and viewed, the victim depicted in the image is harmed yet again by the knowledge and shame associated with knowing others are (yet again) exploiting the victim for self-gratification. The scientific literature, however, is also far from definitive on this matter. Indeed, any additional harms suffered by a victim through dissemination likely are more a result of being notified by the prosecutor of another prosecution of child pornography possession than anything else. Recent developments in the law of restitution in these cases are discussed with respect to issues involving proximate causation and victim compensation.

Section 3 proposes an overhaul to the sentencing scheme for child pornography offenders that considers the various matters previously canvassed.

This chapter concludes that the War on Child Pornography Possession offenses should be declared over, and certainly should be done so before the same mistakes made in the War on Drugs exacerbate its well-intended but misguided approach. Regardless of rhetoric, to combat child sex offenses, including the documentation and distribution of child rape and solicitation of child prostitution, resources are better spent on preventing and quickly identifying those who perpetrate such heinous crimes, rather than on those who possess and/or trade in *images* of the crimes. This is not to say that the criminalization and prosecution of child pornography possession, receipt, distribution, and transportation should be abandoned. Far from it. But like the War on Drugs, locking up consumers of child pornography for lengthy prison sentences has a net negative effect on society with little to show for it, especially when, as here, the reasons for doing so are fundamentally flawed. Those who possess child pornography by and large are not the mythic monsters many uncritically believe them to be. So, let's fight the real monsters and not windmills.

1. A STATISTICAL OVERVIEW OF THE WAR ON CHILD PORNOGRAPHY

When it comes to federal crime, five offense types and their corresponding sentencing guidelines constitute nearly 78% of the criminal docket in any given year. They are, in descending order, drug trafficking (2D1.1; 30.6%), immigration offenses (2L1.2; 24.5%), fraud (2B1.1; 12.2%), firearms (2K2.1; 8.2%), and child pornography (2G2.2; 2.4%) (Table 6.1). Accordingly, this chapter primarily focuses on these offense types and guidelines when making comparisons.

According to former FBI Director Robert S. Mueller, III, in a statement before the U.S. Senate Judiciary Committee, "From 1996 to 2009, child exploitation investigations in the FBI increased more than 2,500 percent" (Mueller, 2011). As Table 6.1 indicates, the annual number of sentences under USSG § 2G2.2 grew at a far higher rate than for any other major offense category.

Table 6.1: U.S. Sentencing Commission, 2015 Federal
Sentencing Statistics, Table 17 (1996 and 2015)

Guideline	No. of Sentences in 1996	No. of Sentences in 2015	Percentage Increase
2D1.1	16,196	19,773	22.1%
2L1.2	2543	15,815	521.1%
2B1.1	3024	7858	159.9%
2K2.1	2204	5325	141.5%
2G2.2	**98**	**1557**	**1488.8%**
Overall	40,739	64,622	58.6%

During the same period, while the median sentences for some major
offense types also grew, some actually declined, as did sentences
overall. As Table 6.2 shows, sentences for child pornography offenses
again grew far higher than for any other offense category.[6]

Table 6.2: U.S. Sentencing Commission, Federal
Sentencing Statistics, Table 13 (1996 and 2015)

Offense Category	Median Sentence in 1996	Median Sentence in 2015	Percentage Increase
Drug Trafficking	60	50	−16.7%
Immigration	15	9	−40%
Fraud	8	14	75%
Firearms	41	58	41.5%
Child Pornography	**15**	**96**	**540%**
Overall	24	21	−12.5%

Thus, given the dramatic increases in both the number of child
pornography cases prosecuted and the sentences imposed on such
offenders, it is not surprising that sex offenders (who primarily are

---

6   See U.S. Sentencing Commission, Federal Sentencing Statistics, Table 13 (1996 and 2015).
    Prior to 2010, the Commission only reported data on "Pornography/Prostitution" cases,
    which included some non-child pornography cases. Starting in 2010, the category was
    renamed "Child Pornography" and includes all and only child pornography offenses—
    that is, possession, receipt, distribution, and production.

child pornography offenders) constitute the fourth largest group of inmates according to data reported by the U.S. Bureau of Prisons.

Table 6.3: Inmates by Offense Type in U.S. Prisons

Offense Group	No. of Inmates	% of Inmates
Drug Offenses	85,124	46.3%
Weapons, Explosives, Arson	31,082	16.9%
Immigration	16,925	9.2%
Sex Offenses	**14,643**	**8.0%**
Extortion, Fraud, Bribery	12,089	6.6%
Total Population	196,134	100%

In 2005, the U.S. Supreme Court ruled that the U.S. Sentencing Guidelines were unconstitutional if applied in a mandatory manner (*United States v. Booker*). Since that time, the guidelines have been considered "merely advisory" and are just one of many factors for sentencing judges to consider when imposing a sentence. Judges have clearly been exercising this discretion in child pornography cases more so than for any other major offense category.

As the ten-year post-*Booker* sentencing trend analysis in Figure 6.1 demonstrates, courts have significantly decreased the rate in which they have been imposing within guidelines sentences ("Within FSG" (Federal Sentencing Guideline)) from 66.2% to a mere 30.8%. In other words, shortly after the *Booker* decision, courts were imposing sentences within the applicable guidelines range nearly two-thirds of the time; now, courts are following the applicable guideline range less than one-third of the time.

At the same time, the government has increased the rate at which it has sought downward departures below the guidelines range from 8.6% in 2006 to 23.6% in 2015 ("Below FSG by Gov't"). More pertinently, pursuant to the now-advisory nature of the guidelines, courts have increased the rate at which they have imposed below-guidelines sentences from 20.8% to 43.6% ("Below FSG by Court"). Thus, over two-thirds of all child pornography sentences are being sentenced below the applicable guidelines range.

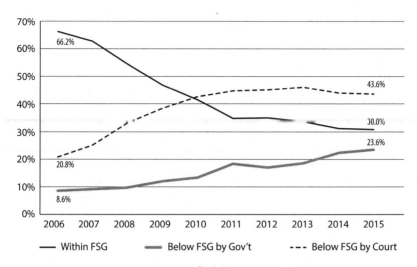

Figure 6.1: Percentage of Child Pornography Sentences
Within and Below the Advisory Guidelines
Source: U.S. Sentencing Commission, 2006–2015 Sourcebooks of Federal Sentencing, Table 27

And as Figure 6.2 further demonstrates, the rate of court-sponsored "below guidelines" sentences is significantly greater in cases involving child pornography offenses than for any other major offense category. Indeed, court-sponsored "below guidelines" sentences are being imposed in child pornography cases at over twice the rate (43.6%) of such sentences overall (21.3%).

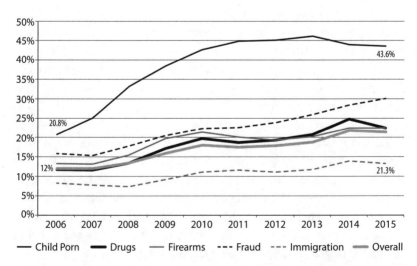

Figure 6.2: Rate of Non-Government-Sponsored Below-Guidelines Sentences
Source: U.S. Sentencing Commission, 2006–2015 Sourcebooks of Federal Sentencing, Table 27

Moreover, as reflected in Figure 6.3, when judges do decide to exercise their *Booker* discretion in child pornography cases to impose a sentence below the guidelines range, the magnitude of such a downward variance not only is larger than for any other major offense category, but is the only one that has continued to grow in magnitude. In 2006, when judges imposed a "below guidelines" sentence in child pornography cases, the median downward variance was 24 months. Now, the median downward variance has grown to 60 months, while the magnitude of downward variances has remained approximately the same for all other major offense categories.

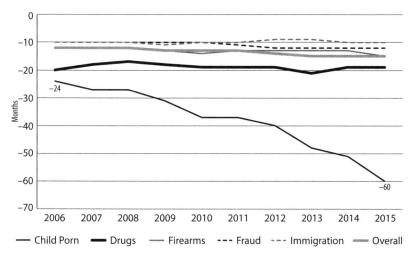

Figure 6.3: Median Decrease in Months for Non-Government-Sponsored Below-Guidelines Sentences
Source: U.S. Sentencing Commission, 2006–2015 Sourcebooks of Federal Sentencing, Table 31C

Thus, as reflected in Figures 6.4 and 6.5, it is rather surprising that the median and mean sentences for child pornography offenses have continued to increase even though the median and mean sentences overall have decreased from 2006 through 2015.

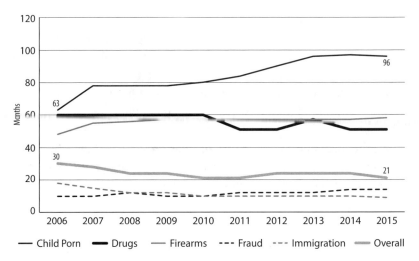

Figure 6.4: Median Federal Sentences for Major Offense Categories
Source: U.S. Sentencing Commission, 2006–2015 Sourcebook of Federal Sentencing, Table 13

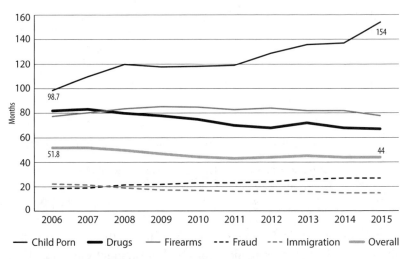

Figure 6.5: Average Federal Sentences for Major Offense Categories
Source: U.S. Sentencing Commission, 2006–2015 Sourcebooks of Federal Sentencing, Table 13

So, why do child pornography sentences continue to increase while, at the same time, the rate and magnitude of downward variances for such sentences continue to decrease? The answer is two-fold: first, the guidelines for non-production child pornography offenders simply are set far too high for typical offenders; and, second, because they are so high, even significant, frequent downward variances are not enough to offset the numerous enhancements increasingly applied in the typical case.

Figure 6.6 demonstrates the increasing frequency in the application of various specific offender characteristics contained within the guidelines for non-production child pornography offenses at USSG § 2G2.2.[7] As the internet has made the acquisition of child pornography all that much more readily obtainable, it is not surprising that the five-level enhancement for possessing more than 600 images of child pornography has rocketed from 7.8% in 2004 to 79.3% in 2014. And, as the prevalence of peer-to-peer file-sharing software has become far more available, the distribution enhancement has nearly doubled from 22% to nearly 42%. Of course, the two-level enhancement for the use of a computer continues to be applied in approximately 95% of cases.

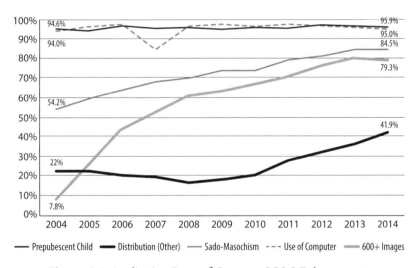

Figure 6.6: Application Rates of Common 2G2.2 Enhancements
*Source: U.S. Sentencing Commission, Use of Guidelines and
Specific Offense Characteristics 2004–2015*

What this speaks to is a desperate need to recalibrate USSG § 2G2.2 to remedy the overly punitive nature of that guideline. But before delving into suggested changes, it is worth first considering *why* the guidelines have been calibrated so high. It is because of three primary myths underlying non-production child pornography offenders.

---

7   The 2015 report is available at www.ussc.gov/sites/default/files/pdf/research-and-publications/federal-sentencing-statistics/guideline-application-frequencies/2015/Use_of_SOC_Guideline_Based.pdf (accessed March 3, 2017).

2. THE PRIMARY MYTHS UNDERLYING CHILD PORNOGRAPHY SENTENCING

There are three primary myths surrounding non-production child pornography offenders: (a) possession and distribution contribute to a market for the production of child pornography; (b) if an offender possesses child pornography, he must at least desire to engage in contact offenses or has engaged in such offenses; and (c) the mere possession of child pornography causes harm to the victims depicted victims.

A. The Market Myth

This supposition, sometimes referred to as the "market thesis," holds that "child pornography consumers increase the demand for production, leading to the sexual exploitation of more children" (Hamilton, 2012, p.1729). According to the market thesis, prosecuting and imposing harsh sentences on consumers will reduce demand, which in turn will reduce the production of child pornography. Although this thesis has intuitive economic appeal, it is in fact nothing more than unfounded conjecture. See, for example, von Dornum (2012, pp.47–48) (on behalf of the Federal and Community Defenders):

> Child pornography thrives in cyberspace independent of an organized market place... Because child pornography is free, widely available and easy to produce, it is not subject to the normal laws of supply and demand... For this reason, it is unlikely that harsh punishment of an end user will do anything to destroy the market for child pornography.

Hamilton (2012, p.1729) argues that "[t]he market thesis...is more speculative and ideological than supported by experiential data," and the United Nations Office on Drugs and Crime (2010) states:

> One of the risks associated with the growth of the Internet is that the greater accessibility of child pornography could lead to greater demand, and thus greater profitability in the production and sale of these materials... To date, this threat does not appear to have been realized.

To be sure, the "market thesis" may have had some import in the pre-internet era when obtaining child pornography was far more difficult and there in fact existed a commercial market for the same. Accordingly, as with any commodity, a greater demand from consumers will promote increased production; a depressed demand often will decrease production. Thus, it is not surprising that

> [i]n 1986, the Final Report of the Attorney General's Commission on Pornography was presented to Congress ("Meese Report"). The Meese Report found that the production and sharing of child pornography images causes serious harm and noted that "[i]f the sale or distribution of such pictures is stringently enforced, and if those sanctions are equally stringently enforced, the market may decrease and this may in turn decrease the incentive to produce those pictures." (U.S. Sentencing Commission, 2009)

As the Department of Justice has observed:

> In the 1980s the mail was the primary means of distributing child pornography. The Child Protection Act of 1984 expanded the U.S. Postal Inspector's role in investigating those who knowingly sent and received child pornography through the mail. Over the past two decades, the dramatic increase in Internet availability provided a relatively anonymous forum for instantaneous exchange of pornographic images that more easily circumvented authorities (Motivans and Kyckelhahn, 2007).
>
> By the mid-1980's [sic], the trafficking of child pornography within the United States was almost completely eradicated through a series of successful campaigns waged by law enforcement. Producing and reproducing child sexual abuse images was difficult and expensive. Anonymous distribution and receipt was not possible, and it was difficult for pedophiles to find and interact with each other. For these reason[s], child pornographers became lonely and hunted individuals because the purchasing and trading of such images was extremely risky. Unfortunately, the child pornography market exploded in the advent of the Internet and advanced digital technology. (U.S. Department of Justice Child Exploitation and Obscenity Section)

Thus, when the U.S. Supreme Court observed shortly thereafter in 1990 that states have an interest in seeking "to destroy a market for the exploitative use of children," it did so in an era wholly different from today in degree and kind (*Osborne v. Ohio*, p.109). In that era, a reduction in demand would, and did, correlate to a reduction in production. Thus, law enforcement strategies of that time recognized that much of the child pornography market has been driven underground; as a result, it is now difficult, if not impossible, to solve the child pornography problem by only attacking production and distribution. Indeed, [the] [s]tates have found it necessary to proscribe the possession of this material. (*Osborne v. Ohio*, pp.110–111)

But, as many commentators, including the Department of Justice, recognize, this is no longer the case in the internet era. Ultimately, there simply is no evidence that consumption of child pornography promotes, encourages, or is correlated with its production such that deterring mere possession will likely decrease its production to any measurable degree. The market thesis is, in short, a "myth"—a myth with intuitive appeal but wholly lacking in empirical foundation.

Indeed, after undertaking an exhaustive review of relevant sociological literature and studies, the U.S. Sentencing Commission itself also recognizes that there is no evidence in support of the market thesis:

To date, social science research has not addressed whether, or to what extent, criminal punishments have affected the commercial or non-commercial "markets" in child pornography since the advent of the Internet and P2P file-sharing. In view of the exponential growth in child pornography in recent years and the worldwide scope of offending, such research may be impossible to undertake. (U.S. Sentencing Commission, 2012, p.98)

B. The Cross-Over Myth

Numerous recent studies have assessed the question, and most have found that "there is no empirical support for a direct causal link between internet sex offending and the commission of contact offenses" (Basbaum, 2010, pp.1294–1295, footnotes omitted; reviewing recent scientific literature).

Indeed, in the oft-cited case of *United States v. Dorvee*

we are troubled by the district court's apparent assumption that Dorvee was likely to actually sexually assault a child, a view unsupported by the record evidence yet one that plainly motivated the court's perceived need to protect the public from further crimes of the defendant. We believe that this assumption, in the face of expert record evidence to the contrary, caused the district court to place unreasonable weight on this sentencing factor. (p.183; citation and internal quotation marks omitted)

These observations are echoed by the Commission: "Most current social science research suggests that viewing child pornography, in the absence of other risk factors, does not cause individuals to commit sex offenses" (FCPO, p.104; citation omitted). See *United States v. Marshall* (pp.491–492), rejecting the presumption that "those who view child pornography are indistinguishable from those who actually abuse children," finding instead that the "[e]mpirical data strongly suggests that viewing child pornography does not equate to child molestation"; *United States v. Kelly* (pp.1207–1208), rejecting the government's argument that the guideline range is appropriate because of the "chance that [the defendant] will molest children in the future, or that he has in the past," as this "speculation is directly contrary to submissions by Kelly's therapist and Kelly's psychiatrist," the defendant "has never been accused of hands-on abuse," "empirical testing disproves the fear that the typical child pornography defendant will go on to molest children," and "[a]ny Guideline based on unsupported fears, rather than actual evidence, is far more likely to render an unreasonable sentence"; *United States v. Cruikshank* (p.703): "Rarely able to catch the monsters that create the images, society reflexively nominates the consumers of this toxic material as proxies for the depraved producers and publishers"; *United States v. Phinney* (p.1045): "[C]ourts should not assume that a defendant has or will commit additional crimes without a reliable basis"; *United States v. Grober* (p.404): "[T]he Court cannot make [the Defendant] a surrogate for the monsters who prey on child victims through actual contact" (aff'd 624 F.3d 592 (3d Cir. 2010), 595 F. Supp. 2d 382, 404 (D.N.J. 2008).

As Judge Merritt of the Sixth Circuit Court of Appeals observed in a dissenting opinion:

> The problem in this pornography case is the gross disparity, inequality, and unfairness that exists in sentencing generally, but even more so in these child pornography viewer cases. It illustrates the continued sad dependence of federal judges on a harsh sentencing grid created by a distant bureaucracy. (*United States v. Overmyer*, p.866)

This harsh sentencing grid illustrates "how the Sentencing Commission got so far off track in this area and why so many judges and academic writers have opposed the pornography grid we must apply in this case" (p.866). Significant prison sentences, after all, should be reserved for the most serious forms of sex offenses and the most culpable offenders. See, for example, *United States v. Plachy* (pp.27–28): "A possessor of child pornography is the least culpable in the chain and is a marginal player in the overall child exploitation scheme."

C. The Harms Myth

The U.S. Supreme Court recently opined, without citation to any authority, that "[t]he demand for child pornography harms children in part because it drives production, which involves child abuse" (*Paroline v. United States*, p.1716). As discussed above, there is no empirical support for the market thesis. But where the Court was somewhat correct was in its observation that "[t]he harms caused by child pornography, however, are still more extensive because child pornography is 'a permanent record' of the depicted child's abuse, and 'the harm to the child is exacerbated by [its] circulation'" (*Paroline*, p.1717, quoting *New York v. Ferber*, p.759). "Because child pornography is now traded with ease on the Internet, 'the number of still images and videos memorializing the sexual assault and other sexual exploitation of children, many very young, has grown exponentially'" (*Paroline*, p.1717, quoting FCPO, p.3).

But what the Court overlooked in the Sentencing Commission Report it quoted from was the Commission's finding that the harm caused by the permanent record and circulation of child pornography is more a factor of victim notification than of anything inherent in the possession and distribution of child pornography itself.

> For child pornography victims who have opted into notification, it is not unusual to receive multiple court notifications each week informing them that their images have been recovered from child pornography offenders. One victim stated, "I can't tell you how many letters from the courts have come to me and how helpless they make me feel." A parent who opted to receive notification as the minor victim's representative has described receiving enough "notices to overflow a 55 gallon drum." Thus, even as the victims' rights laws have empowered victims and enabled them to be involved in the criminal justice process, the notification process itself can have the unintended and incidental effect of exacerbating the harms associated with the ongoing distribution of the images. (U.S. Sentencing Commission, 2012, p.116)

In *Paroline*, the Court grappled with the question of causation for the purposes of determining restitution in child pornography cases. A circuit split had developed over whether a victim of child pornography had to establish that a defendant's possession of child pornography proximately caused her harm, or it was enough to establish strict "but for" causation. The Fifth Circuit and other circuits had held that restitution was not limited "to losses proximately caused by the defendant, and each defendant who possessed the victim's images should be made liable for the victim's entire losses from the trade in her images, even though other offenders played a role in causing those losses" (*Paroline*, p.1718).

Ultimately, the Court disagreed with those circuits that had held proximate causation was not required. Per the Court in *Paroline* (p.1721):

> [P]roximate cause forecloses liability in situations where the causal link between conduct and result is so attenuated that the so-called consequence is more akin to mere fortuity. For example, suppose the traumatized victim of a [child pornography] offender needed therapy and had a car accident on the way to her therapist's office. The resulting medical costs, in a literal sense, would be a factual result of the offense. But it would be strange indeed to make a defendant pay restitution for these costs.

Thus, the Court held that "[r]estitution is therefore proper...only to the extent the defendant's offense proximately caused a victim's losses" (p.1722). In other words, district courts are to "[a]ssess...an individual defendant's role in the causal process behind a child-pornography victim's losses" (p.1728).

Accordingly, mere possession or even distribution of child pornography does not *ipso facto* imply that any harm has been caused to a particular victim. More is needed. And here, unfortunately, ignorance may provide some form of bliss. In no sense can it be said that any harm is caused to a victim of child pornography where some unknown, third-party defendant possesses or distributes child pornography depicting the victim *and the victim is completely unaware of such possession or distribution.* But as the Commission correctly recognizes, notification of such possession may in and of itself cause or even "exacerbate" the underlying harm caused by the original production of the child pornography.

This is not to suggest that victims should not be notified by the government that child pornography in which they are depicted has been found, but it does suggest that the manner of notification and frequency of such notification perhaps should be changed. The ultimate point, however, is that where it is beyond dispute that children necessarily are seriously and irrevocably harmed by the *production* of child pornography, it is not at all clear that they are necessarily harmed by the mere *possession* or distribution of child pornography in the abstract. As the *Paroline* decision and the Commission's report suggest, it is the awareness of such possession and distribution that causes additional harm to victims of child pornography, and not anything inherent in the conduct of child pornography possessors or distributors *per se*.

3. OVERHAULING USSG § 2G2.2

As reviewed throughout Section 2, USSG § 2G2.2 has significant issues. Indeed, as the U.S. Sentencing Commission itself recognizes:

> Several provisions in the current sentencing guidelines…in particular, the existing enhancements for the nature and volume of the images possessed, an offender's use of a computer, and distribution of images—originally were promulgated in an earlier technological era. Indeed, most of the enhancements, in their current or antecedent versions, were promulgated when offenders typically received and distributed child pornography in printed form using the United States mail. As a result, enhancements that were intended to apply to only certain offenders who committed aggravated child pornography offenses are now being applied routinely to most offenders. (U.S. Sentencing Commission, 2012, p.313)

Accordingly, the Commission has targeted these enhancements for "[p]otential amendments" (U.S. Sentencing Commission, 2012, p.xviii).

With respect to the two-level enhancement for use of a computer, as several district courts have recently observed, "Computer use is now so widespread that this enhancement 'is a little like penalizing speeding, but then adding an extra penalty if a car is involved'" (*United States v. Abraham*, p.731, quoting *United States v. Kelly*, p.1209; *United States v. Klear*, p.1308; *United States v. Westbrook*, p.12930). Accordingly, as "[t]his enhancement applies in nearly every case and no longer serves any reasonable purpose," "the enhancement for use of a computer (§ 2G2.2(b)(6)) should be rejected outright" (*Abraham*, p.731).

The Commission rightly has targeted this enhancement for deletion and to replace it with one that is "technologically neutral" (see FCPO, p.324, noting also "§2G2.2(b)(6) applies in virtually every case and, thus, fails to differentiate among offenders with respect to their" culpability). In fact, even the Department of Justice agrees that this enhancement should be withdrawn from the guidelines. In an Annual Report to the Commission, the Department has opined that "the enhancement for the use of a computer in §2G2.2(b)(6) is no longer useful and should be eliminated" (Wroblewski, 2013).

The same objections hold true for material involving a prepubescent minor (USSG § 2G2.2(b)(2)), distribution (USSG § 2G2.2(b)(3)(B)), sadistic or masochistic conduct (USSG § 2G2.2(b)(4)), and number of images (USSG § 2G2.2(b)(7)(D)). Figure 6.6 above illustrates the increasing frequency such specific offense characteristics (SOCs) occur, which results in courts rejecting outright application of the SOCs in USSG § 2G2.2.

In *United States v. Kelly*, the defendant pleaded guilty to one count of receiving child pornography pursuant to 18 U.S.C. § 2252(a)(2), and therefore was subject to a mandatory minimum term of imprisonment of five years, and a statutory maximum of 20 (p.1203). In imposing only the five-year mandatory minimum sentence, Judge Black rejected application of the enhancements for use of a computer, number of images, depictions of sado-masochism, and images involving prepubescent children (p.1211).

As Judge Black recognized, USSG § 2G2.2 necessarily violates the requirement that sentencing judges avoid unwarranted disparities (p.1210). This is so since USSG § 2G2.2 fails to distinguish between run-of-the-mill possession cases and those most culpable by "creat[ing] vastly different sentences for essentially identical conduct" (p.1210), as well as "creat[ing] similar sentences for starkly different offenses" (p.1210, n.17; *United States v. Klear*, p.1306, applying substantially revised methodology for sentencing child pornography offenders, rejecting USSG § 2G2.2 outright).

As Judge Black also observed, "[t]he child pornography Guideline has come under significant judicial criticism for being based on politics rather than data, and Circuit courts routinely find that § 2G2.2 is unworthy of serious deference" (*Kelly*, p.1205). "Because § 2G2.2

punishes the worst crimes no more severely than routine offenses, and small-scale offenders have no incentive to keep from escalating their crimes, the goals of sentencing cannot be met" (p.1206). Accordingly, "[a] district court need not defer to an irrational guideline that fails to meet the goals of sentencing and does not exemplify the Commission's expertise" (p.1206; *United States v. Westbrook*, replacing the USSG § 2G2.2 sentencing framework with one assessing different factors and assigning lesser weights to various SOCs).

Finally, as Judge Black correctly recognized, "[i]n the age of the computer," the disparity in punishment between possession and receipt cases "defies logic": "These two functionally identical crimes can seemingly only be distinguished in terms of which one the Government decides to charge in any given case" (p.1211).

Thus, as argued above, factors such as the use of a computer, the bare number of images, and the like are anachronistic and otherwise do not properly provide a sentencing court with a meaningful metric for assessing offense seriousness in non-production child pornography cases. Furthermore, as reflected in the statistical review in Section 1 above, § 2G2.2 is overly punitive and is in dire need of being calibrated downward. A revised § 2G2.2 thus should be calibrated so that most offenders receive a guidelines sentence that approximates the median sentences now imposed. This, after all, is how the guidelines were initially promulgated and calibrated.

With that in mind, and taking into consideration the Commission's suggestion that the quality of the offender's collection is an important factor, as well as the artificial distinction between possession and receipt cases, my proposal is based on the following principles:

1. Revise the alternative base offense levels to account for sentence differences between distribution and non-distribution cases.

2. Eliminate anachronistic enhancements such as use of a computer.

3. Revise other enhancements considering technological reality, such as number of images.

4. Ensure that the revised § 2G2.2 guideline results in most sentencing ranges encompassing current median sentences for such conduct.

Table 6.4 sets forth this proposal.

Table 6.4: Proposed New USSG § 2G2.2

USSG § 2G2.2 Subsection	Offense Level	Description
(a)(1)	20	Possession or receipt
(a)(2)	26	Distribution
(b)(2)(A)	1	Library is greater than 5 Gigabytes but not greater than 15 Gigabytes in size
(b)(2)(B)	2	Library is greater than 15 Gigabytes but not greater than 30 Gigabytes in size
(b)(2)(C)	3	Library is greater than 30 Gigabytes in size
(b)(3)(A)	2	The library *predominantly* contains depictions of sexual penetration of minors over 12 years of age
(b)(3)(B)	4	The library *predominantly* contains depictions of sexual penetration of minors 12 years of age or under, or *predominantly* involves depictions of pain, humiliation, or torture of minors
(b)(4)	2	The library *predominantly* contains depictions created within the past five years of the onset of the defendant's offense conduct

Currently, according to Commission reports, the majority of those sentenced under § 2G2.2 receive the guidelines calculation shown in Table 6.5.

Table 6.5: Current Enhancement Application Rates for USSG § 2G2.2

Guideline	Offense Level	Description	n	Application %
(a)(2)	22	Otherwise	920	55.6
(b)(2)	2	Prepubescent	1579	95.4
(b)(3)(F)	2	Distribution, other	678	40.9

Guideline	Offense Level	Description	n	Application %
(b)(6)	2	Use of computer	1571	94.9
(b)(7)(D)	5	600+ images	1297	78.3
3E1.1	−3	Acceptance		
Total	34			

At a total offense level of 34 in Criminal History Category I, the guidelines range is 151 to 188 months. However, the average sentence imposed is just 97 months and the median is only 78 months.

Under the overhauled § 2G2.2, a typical offender's guideline calculation most likely would look as shown in Table 6.6.

Table 6.6: Hypothetical Application of New USSG § 2G2.2

Guideline	Offense Level	Description
(a)(2)	26	Distribution
(b)(2)(B)	2	Library is greater than 15 Gigabytes but not greater than 30 Gigabytes in size
(b)(3)(A)	2	The library *predominantly* contains depictions of sexual penetration of minors over 12 years of age
3E1.1	−3	Acceptance
Total	27	

At a total offense level of 27 in Criminal History Category I, the guidelines range is 70 to 87 months, which encompasses the current median for the most frequent guidelines application.

CONCLUSION

No one disputes that child pornography is a serious problem, or that real children are harmed in its production… [W]hile those who traffic in or consume child pornography must be punished, *a spectrum of criminal culpability is involved in this crime.* Those who produce and distribute these images are at one end of the spectrum. They deserve the harshest punishment. At the other end of the spectrum are men... who view these disgusting images. Rather than physically harming a child, their criminal act is complete by entering a market with a few clicks of a mouse... While these men bear responsibility for the horrors created by child pornography, any system of justice must attempt to emotionally remove itself from natural instincts of revenge and retribution. These pathetic men make easy targets. There is nothing redeeming or even understandable about this crime. But judges must objectively consider whether the sentences imposed further the goals of punishment. To do so, we must differentiate between those who create child pornography and those who consume it. (*United States v. Diaz*, 720 F. Supp. 2d 1039, 1043 (E.D. Wisc. 2010); emphasis added, quoting *United States v. Cruikshank*, 667 F. Supp. 2d 697, 701–02 (S.D. W.Va. 2009))

Misinformed crusades like the current one against child pornography possession and distribution, and as the War on Drugs before it has unequivocally demonstrated, have little crime control effect and enormous unintended, diametrically opposed consequences. While morally and aesthetically the possession of child pornography is revolting and those possessing or trading such images should be held accountable, it nevertheless is critical not to lose sight of what the crime is, and, more importantly, what it is not. At bottom, the possessing and trading of child pornography is an obscenity offense and not a contact sex offense. There is no evidence that the simple possession and trading of such images contributes to increased production, that the same necessarily causes additional harm to victims above and beyond the original production, or that consumers of child pornography are likely to engage in contact offenses. Thus, there is no principled reason for such exceedingly long sentences. Accordingly, USSG § 2G2.2 should be overhauled and recalibrated to reflect these truths. Just as the conviction of the innocent is a manifest injustice, so too is the excessive deprivation of liberty.

REFERENCES

Basbaum, J.P. (2010) "Inequitable sentencing for possession of child pornography: A failure to distinguish voyeurs from pederasts." *Hastings Law Journal 61*, 1281, 1294–1295.

Hamilton, M. (2012) "The child pornography crusade and its net-widening effect." *Cardozo Law Review 33*, 1, 1679.

Motivans, M. and Kyckelhahn, T. (2007) "Federal Prosecution of Child Sex Exploitation Offenders, 2006." U.S. Department of Justice, Bureau of Justice Statistics Bulletin. Available at www.bjs. gov/content/pub/pdf/fpcseo06.pdf (accessed January 17, 2017).

Mueller III, Robert S. (2011) Statement Before the Senate Judiciary Committee, Washington, D.C., March 30, 2011. Available at www.fbi.gov/news/testimony/oversight-of-the-federal-bureau-of-investigation-1 (accessed January 17, 2017).

New York v. Ferber, 458 U.S. 747, 759 (1982)

Osborne v. Ohio, 495 U.S. 103, 109 (1990)

United Nations Office on Drugs and Crime (2010) *The Globalization of Crime: A Transnational Organized Crime Threat Assessment.* Vienna: UNODC.

United States v. Abraham, 944 F. Supp. 2d 723, 731 (D. Neb. 2013)

United States v. Booker, 543 U.S. 220 (2005)

United States v. Cruikshank, 667 F. Supp. 2d 697, 703 (S.D. W.Va. 2009)

United States v. Diaz, 720 F. Supp. 2d 1039, 1043 (E.D. Wisc. 2010)

United States v. Dorvee, 616 F.3d 174 (2d Cir. 2010)

United States v. Grober, 595 F. Supp. 2d 382, 404 (D.N.J. 2008)

United States v. Kelly, 868 F. Supp. 2d 1202, 1207–08 (D.N.M. 2012)

United States v. Klear, 3 F. Supp. 3d 1298, 1308 (M.D. Ala. 2014)

United States v. Marshall, 870 F. Supp. 2d 489, 491–92 (N.D. Ohio 2012)

United States v. Overmyer, 663 F.3d 862, 866 (6th Cir. Dec. 20, 2011)

United States v. Phinney, 599 F. Supp. 2d 1037, 1045 n.10 (E.D. Wis. 2009)

United States v. Plachy, 2013 U.S. Dist. LEXIS 65561, *27–*28 (D. Neb. 2013)

United States v. Westbrook, 2015 U.S. Dist. LEXIS 12930 (M.D. Ala. 2015)

U.S. Bureau of Prisons, Statistics: Offenses, June 6, 2016. Available at www.bop.gov/about/statistics/ statistics_inmate_offenses.jsp (accessed January 17, 2017).

U.S. Department of Justice, Child Exploitation and Obscenity Section. Available at www.justice.gov/ criminal-ceos (accessed March 3, 2017).

U.S. Sentencing Commission (2009) *The History of the Child Pornography Guidelines.* Washington, DC: U.S. Sentencing Commission. Available at www.ussc.gov/sites/default/files/pdf/research-and-publications/research-projects-and-surveys/sex-offenses/20091030_History_Child_Pornography_Guidelines.pdf (accessed January 17, 2017).

U.S. Sentencing Commission (2012) 2012 Report to Congress: Federal Child Pornography Offenses. Available at www.ussc.gov/research/congressional-reports/2012-report-congress-federal-child-pornography-offenses (accessed March 3, 2017).

U.S. Sentencing Commission (2015) Use of Guidelines and Specific Offense Characteristics: Guideline Calculation Based. Fiscal Year 2015. Available at www.ussc.gov/sites/default/ files/pdf/research-and-publications/federal-sentencing-statistics/guideline-application-frequencies/2015/Use_of_SOC_Guideline_Based.pdf (accessed March 3, 2017).

von Dornum, D. (2012, February 15) Testimony before the United States Sentencing Commission Public Hearing on Child Pornography Sentencing. Available at www.ussc.gov/sites/default/ files/pdf/amendment-process/public-hearings-and-meetings/20120215-16/Testimony_15_ vonDornum.pdf (accessed January 16, 2017).

Wroblewski, Jonathan, Director, Department of Justice Office of Policy and Legislation, Letter to the United States Sentencing Commission 12 (July 11, 2013).

CHAPTER 7

Egregious Flaws Discredit the *Butner Redux* Study

Effective Policies for Sentencing Federal Child Pornography Offenders Require Findings Based on Valid Research Principles

Richard Wollert and Alexander Skelton

Many professionals and laypersons believe that pedophiles, convicted contact child molesters, and undetected molesters are predisposed to watch pornographic depictions of children on the internet. It is also believed that those who have downloaded child pornography—that is, child pornography offenders (CPOs)—experience an increase in the intensity of deviant sexual fantasies and a decrease in inhibitions that result in recurrent sexual misconduct in the form of child molestation. This behavior is assumed to be resistant to treatment and punishment.

One corollary of this commonsense conception, which we call the Pornographic Attraction Theory ("PAT"), is that CPOs are mentally ill. Another is that they are sexually dangerous. Still another suggests that the internet sophistication of CPOs makes them more dangerous than convicted child molesters (Gelber, 2009; Heimbach, 2002).

The PAT was prominently paraphrased in an article by Drs. Michael Bourke and Andres Hernandez published in the *Journal of Family Violence* (*JOFV*; Bourke and Hernandez, 2009). Titled "The 'Butner Study' Redux: A report of the incidence of hands-on victimization by child pornography offenders," this article argued that CPOs under the supervision of Bourke and Hernandez at the Butner Federal Correctional Institution Sex Offender Treatment Program (SOTP) disclosed committing many undetected contact sex offenses that occurred prior to being convicted of a child pornography offense.

Some disclosures were verbal in nature, but a large number were recorded by program participants while completing a form called the "Personal History Questionnaire" (PHQ) on multiple occasions.

The Bourke and Hernandez article and an earlier similar conference presentation by Hernandez (2000a) are significant because they have been used as evidence by some (Allen, 2009, Gelber, 2009; Heimbach, 2002; Smith, Grassley, and Sensenbrenner, 2012) to influence the United States Sentencing Commission (USSC) to (1) increase or (2) retain CPO sentencing guidelines that others (Baron-Evans, 2008; Basbaum, 2010; Hansen, 2009; Specter and Hoffa, 2011; Stabenow, 2008, 2011; U.S. v. Dorvee, 2010; U.S. v. Grober, 2010) have characterized as excessively punitive and indiscriminate. Regarding issue (1), "sentences of imprisonment...have substantially increased...because of...amendments resulting from the PROTECT ACT" (U.S. Sentencing Commission, 2012, p.x; also see U.S. v. Grober, 2010) that Congress passed three years after Hernandez's first presentation in 2000. The impact of this and other amendments is underscored by the fact that the average sentence length for first-time CPOs, most of whom have been convicted for the "non-production" offenses of receiving, possessing, transporting, or distributing child pornography, is now more than three times what it was for both first-time and recidivist CPOs in 1994 (112 months vs. 36 months; see U.S. Sentencing Commission, 1996, Table 1; U.S. Sentencing Commission, 2008, Table 14; Wollert, Waggoner, and Smith, 2012, Table 2.1).

Regarding issue (2), several determinants of longer sentences—called "enhancements"—have come to be so commonly encountered that they "apply to the vast majority of offenders...and...fail to meaningfully distinguish among offenders in terms of their culpability and dangerousness" (U.S. Sentencing Commission, 2012, p.11). Over the last decade many federal judges have become concerned that such enhancements in the CPO sentencing guidelines undermine the principle of proportional sentencing (U.S. Sentencing Commission, 2010). These concerns, in turn, have given rise to a crisis where judges have increasingly resisted enhancements and the guidelines by making "downward departures" from the guidelines so that most non-production cases receive prison terms below those specified in the guidelines. Trying to reverse this trend, and apparently without input from well-qualified behavioral scientists, some legislators (Smith et al., 2012) and prosecutors (Gelber, 2009) have cited the Bourke and Hernandez (2009) article as an argument for steadfast adherence to the guidelines. The *Butner Redux* claims have also been treated as "legislative fact" (Larson, 2012)[1] in the absence of issue-specific expert testimony by some federal judges. One, for example, selected a 121-month guideline term of incarceration for a non-production defendant with no criminal history on the argument that CPOs "have appallingly high rates of recidivism" and "the *Butner Study*...certainly raises the prospect that a correlation exists between viewing deviant pornography and committing a hands-on offense" (*U.S. v. Cunningham*, 2010). Another picked a 97-month guideline sentence because the *Butner Study Redux* "suggests that most who appear to be lookers are, in fact, doers" and its "findings...justify...harsh punishments for child pornographers" (*U.S. v. Crisman*, 2014).

Hernandez's reports have also been cited by fellow psychologists at the Bureau of Prisons as a rationale for the preventive civil commitment, under the Adam Walsh Act, of a subset of federal prisoners who have fully completed their assigned sex offense sentences (Lee *et al.*, 2012). State legislation for the preventive detention of such individuals, referred to as "sexually dangerous persons" or "sexually dangerous predators," was first passed in 1990 (American Psychiatric Association, 1999). A huge volume of research has been carried out on these legal concepts since that time. Nonetheless, science has been unable to show that it is possible for professionals or laypersons to use them reliably to identify individuals who meet the criteria (Ewing, 2011; Prentky *et al.*, 2006; Wollert, 2007).

The methods that Hernandez (2000a) and Bourke and Hernandez (2009) used to elicit data from their supervisees and the findings they obtained have been criticized on various grounds from different quarters. Psychological researchers Seto, Hanson, and Babchishin (2011) characterized the contact sex offense rate reported in *Butner Redux* as an "outlier" (p.133) that far exceeded each of the rates in 23 other projects, including studies based on self-reports that examined the same issue (pp.128–130). CPOs who were Butner residents have disseminated a report accusing the study of being a "fraudulent execution of the Adam Walsh Act" (Neuhauser, Francis,

---

1   "A legislative fact," according to Larson (p.1256), "gets its name...because it relates to the 'legislative function' or policy-making function of the court... [T]he central feature of a legislative fact is that it 'transcends the particular dispute,' and provides descriptive information about the world which judges use as foundational 'building blocks' to form and apply legal rules."

and Ebel, 2011) and quoting psychiatrist Dr. Richard Krueger as alluding to the "SOTP's treatment participants' 'incentive to lie'" (p.8). When Dr. Gene Abel, another eminent psychiatrist, testified at a public hearing on CPOs held by the USSC (Abel, 2012), he was asked about the quality of the Butner data. He replied that "if you don't participate in that program, you're out ... so it's a very select group" (Bourke, 2012, pp.6–7; U.S. Sentencing Commission, 2012). Federal judge Robert Pratt, after hearing testimony from Iowa behavioral scientist Dr. Dan Rogers on the methodological inadequacy of the Butner procedures, held that the "Court can find no error in [the] conclusion that the Butner Study...'doesn't meet scientific standards for research, and is based upon, frankly, an incoherent design for a study'" (*U.S. v. Johnson*, 2008). Another federal judge who was told by government attorneys that civil commitment respondent Markis Revland "admitted" to 149 incidents of "hands-on sexual abuse" in his PHQs concluded that he "invented the 149 incidents" because he was fearful of being returned to a prison where he had been raped and stabbed. The judge further observed that Revland's PHQ was "unbelievable on its face" (*U.S. v. Revland*, 2011). Regarding the reason for this, journalist Rachel Aviv (2013) reported:

> At a professional workshop, Hernandez explained that he created a climate of "systematic pressure," so that inmates would "put all the cards on the table," abandoning a "life style of manipulation." Patients were required to compose lists of people they had sexually harmed, which they updated every few months. At daily community meetings, when offenders insisted they had nothing left to disclose, other prisoners accused them of being in denial or "resistant to change." If they failed to accept responsibility, they were expelled from the program.

Aviv was also told by former Butner participant Clyde Hall that he was encouraged by "patients who had been formally designated 'mentors'" to augment his confessions. He told Aviv he submitted his complete list of self-reported crimes to the Butner staff on three occasions but that "the third plan came back to me with basically the same note, saying, 'We want more information.'"

Members of our research team have repeatedly criticized the Butner studies in a technical report (Wollert, 2008), a presentation at the annual meeting of the Association for the Treatment of Sexual Abusers (ATSA; Wollert, Waggoner, and Smith, 2009), a book chapter

(Wollert *et al.*, 2012), and in testimony before the USSC (Wollert, 2012). Like Judge Pratt and others, we have argued that the methodology underlying the Butner projects does not meet standards for research to be considered "scientifically reliable" in federal courts of law (*Daubert v. Merrell Dow Pharmaceuticals, Inc.*, 1993). On the contrary, our view is that the validity controls in the Butner studies were inadequate, that their implementation produced a high error rate, and that the results have not achieved acceptance by the scientific community.

Butner Redux is also devoid of legal credibility because of ethical problems and inconsistencies with the Codes of Federal Regulation that govern the protection of Bureau of Prisons (BOP) research subjects and BOP research projects. Regarding the first issue, the National Institutes of Health's *Institutional Review Board Guidebook* states that

> the nature of incarceration may conflict with the ethical principle of **autonomy**, captured in the **Nuremberg Code** provision requiring that the subject "be so situated as to be able to exercise free power of choice, without the intervention of any element of...duress... or other ulterior form of...coercion." (Office for Protection from Research Risks, 1993; bold emphases in the original)

Hernandez's self-admitted creation of "a climate of 'systematic pressure'" (Hernandez, 2000b) is clearly at odds with this principle.

Several examples reflect the second problem. One is that all "research" supported by the BOP "must be approved...by an Institutional Review Board (IRB)" per 28 CFR § 101(a)(1). *Butner Redux*, however, has never been listed among the IRB-approved projects registered at Butner.[2] Another is that CFR § 512.16(a) requires researchers to "give each participant a written informed consent statement," but we have not found any reference to such a statement among the materials that describe the Butner projects. Still another is that the PHQ responses of Butner patients were used as SVP evidence even though CFR § 512.11(2) specifies that "research information identifiable to a particular individual cannot be admitted as evidence...in any...judicial...proceeding without the written consent of the individual."

Regarding the last issue, CFR § 512.20 clearly indicates that investigators of any IRB-approved research project have complete freedom to publish their results as long as they "acknowledge the

---

2   We verified this by accessing http://clinicaltrials.gov.

Bureau's participation," indicate their publication does not express the Bureau's views, and provide the Bureau's Office of Research with two copies of the publication, "for informational purposes only," before submitting it. Manuscripts for unauthorized projects will, of course, not speak to some of these points. Although *Butner Redux* included a disclaimer, it did not indicate that the BOP participated in the project or provide the Bureau with copies of the *Redux* manuscript before submitting it to *JOFV* (Garrett, 2007). These omissions are further evidence that *Butner Redux* did not have IRB approval and, in the words of BOP spokesperson Traci Billingsley, "was not a Bureau of Prisons study" (Vanderpool, 2011). This conclusion, in turn, provides a framework for understanding why Assistant BOP Director for Information Policy Judith Garrett (2007) attempted to recall *Butner Redux* in a letter to *JOFV*'s co-editors and Springer Publications because it "did not meet 'agency approval'" (Sher and Carey, 2007).[3]

Therefore, although *Butner Redux* has been published, its quality falls so far below that of the average professional journal article that *JOFV* should now publish a retraction or corrective article that adequately describes the study's unacceptable flaws. We submitted an original article with this end in mind to *JOFV*'s current editor, Bob Geffner, and negotiated with him for several years regarding its publication. He ultimately declined to publish it but indicated he would consider a "commentary" or "letter to the editor" in its stead.

We decided against further negotiations with *JOFV* and Springer Publications because it seemed to us that neither a comment nor a letter to the editor would stimulate further action by the psychological

---

3   Sher and Carey's article, published in the influential *New York Times*, implied that the BOP suppressed publication of *Butner Redux*. Our analysis of the CFRs, the content of the Sher and Carey article, and Ms. Garrett's letter, which we obtained with a FOIA request, is that this implication was unfair to the BOP and that well-justified objections to the publication of *Butner Redux* were likely silenced by political pressures that arose in the wake of Sher and Carey's article. The full text of Ms. Garrett's letter to *JOFV* co-editors Michael Hersen and Vincent Hasselt was as follows: "I respectfully request that you retract the Butner Redux manuscript submitted by [redacted], Director, Sex Offender Treatment Program, Federal Correctional Complex, Butner, North Carolina. As an employee of the Bureau of Prisons (BOP) writing about a BOP program, [redacted] is required to gain agency approval of a final manuscript prior to submitting for publication. [Redacted] failed to submit for agency review the version of the paper that he provided to you for publication. Accordingly we ask that you return the paper to [redacted]. If you have any questions or need additional information, please do not hesitate to contact me at [redacted]. Sincerely, Judi Garrett, Deputy Assistant Director for Information, Policy, and Public Affairs." A copy of the foregoing letter may be obtained from the authors.

or legal communities that might lead to a genuinely curative result. The remaining sections of this chapter are part of an alternative strategy for achieving this goal. The first describes the methodology and results of the Butner projects. The second explains how the results of these projects were produced by demand characteristics that fatally contaminated the procedures used by Bourke and Hernandez for data collection. The third and fourth sections review the results from credible research with federal and non-federal CPOs that show they are not as mentally ill or dangerous as the Butner results suggest. The discussion stresses the importance of relying on sound research methodologies to develop just and effective policies for sentencing and supervising federal CPOs in the future.

A DESCRIPTION OF THE BUTNER PROJECTS AND THE RESULTS THEY REPORTED

In his 2000 conference paper, Hernandez proposed that users of child pornography "can be equally predatory and dangerous as extrafamilial offenders" after he found that a group of 54 CPOs who completed PHQs and polygraph exams during sex offender treatment at the Butner SOTP disclosed more molestations than were reported in their federal pre-sentence investigation reports (PSRs). Bourke and Hernandez (2009) conducted a second study with a larger group of CPOs following Hernandez's earlier procedures. They assessed two outcome variables from a review of the records of 155 CPOs who voluntarily agreed to participate in the Butner SOTP, which Hernandez directed. One of the variables recorded by Hernandez and Bourke reflected the number of adjudicated and self-reported molestations reported in the PSR for each CPO. The other reflected the number of adjudicated and self-reported molestations disclosed by each CPO to staff members at Butner, who apparently expected all treatment participants to make new disclosures on an ongoing basis and to pass a polygraph indicating they had "fully disclosed" their sex offenses. Participants were also told that they did not have to "reveal any identifying information when listing their victims" (p.186).

Bourke and Hernandez (p.187) estimated that 26% of their subjects, who were not described as being different from federal CPOs in general, had previously committed either an adjudicated or non-adjudicated molestation per their PSRs, which described a total of

75 sex crimes. They also reported that the first figure grew to 85% when treatment disclosures were added in, while "the number of reported victims known at the end of treatment...was 1,777" (p.187). If disclosures made in treatment reflected the "true extent" (p.188) of the sex offense histories of CPOs, it was suggested (p.189) that the results of the Butner studies validated the theory that CPOs harbor "pervasive and enduring" pedophilic interests that cause them to access child pornography on the internet. This access, in turn, reinforces the "paraphilic lifestyle" of CPOs, and results in "behavioral disinhibition" that makes them likely to commit more child molestations. Bourke and Hernandez also asserted that "the findings of this study underscore the importance of prison-based sex offender treatment" (p.188) that could, of course, only be provided to CPOs given sentences long enough to accommodate it.

THE BUTNER RESULTS WERE ARTIFACTUALLY PRODUCED BY INADEQUATE RESEARCH METHODS

We criticized the Butner projects in our papers and presentations because they included many different methodological flaws. One very troubling feature was that the welfare of Hernandez's "subjects" was dependent on their standing in his program. From interviewing or counseling CPOs who had been at Butner, we learned they were fearful of program termination. If this happened, it was possible that they would be returned to the general population of prisoners from which they were referred, where they would be harassed as sex offenders. Another problem was that Hernandez's results were over-inclusive or misleading because he did not define what he meant by a "sex offense." Boyfriend–girlfriend relationships between 15-year-olds and 13-year-olds might therefore be counted in the same way as father–daughter relationships. It was also impossible to verify the accuracy of reports because CPOs were told not to identify victims, and treatment participation forms promised confidentiality. Still another problem that several Butner patients revealed was that staff members pressured them to overestimate their offenses or disclose new offenses on an ongoing basis. One former patient, for example, spontaneously wrote a letter to one of us (C.S., personal communication, 2010) stating that "when I got into the SOTP program I was instructed to count all incidents of sexual contact regardless of my age or the age of my 'victim.'"

Another was required to complete the PHQ on three occasions within the span of a single year. Finally, Butner patients were also expected to pass the full disclosure polygraph that Bourke and Hernandez (2009) described in the "Measures" section of their paper (p.186). This holds significant implications for a study based on self-report data because a technique that is widely used to pass this exam entails "overestimating the number of possible victims" (Abrams, 1991, p.259).

We also described how these circumstances interacted with one another to artifactually produce Hernandez's results. This explanation relied heavily on the fact that subjects in psychological experiments will act the way a researcher wants them to act if they know what the researcher hopes to find. Aspects of a data collection situation that tip subjects off to this agenda are referred to as "demand characteristics" (Fillenbaum, 1966; Orne, 1962). It was a simple matter for offenders in the Butner program to figure out what Hernandez wanted from them, and offenders who stayed in the program were likely to comply with this demand because its existence was reinforced by polygraph examinations, repeated PHQ administrations, and the fact that many participants were expelled after "we...put the heat on them," even though all admissions were "prescreened" and "went through me" (Hernandez, 2000b). Over-disclosure was also encouraged by the adoption of data collection procedures that made it impossible to verify the accuracy of disclosures.

This analysis led us to conclude that almost any offender faced with the pressures built into the Butner program would generate so many possible false disclosures as to make it very difficult to differentiate cohort members in terms of their treatment needs, culpability, or dangerousness. We also pointed out that Hernandez could have assessed whether his results were artifacts of his methods by changing his instructions in his second project. He could have, for example, told the second group of CPOs that they would not be placed in the general prison population under any circumstances, that they weren't expected to make ongoing disclosures or pass a polygraph, that they were only expected to be totally honest, and that he wanted to collect victim information to verify their truthfulness. Had he achieved his original results after exercising some of these options, he could have claimed that his results were not due solely to demand characteristics. He did not do so, however.

Although Bourke and Hernandez (Bourke, 2012, items 1, 10, and 11) have denied pressuring Butner inmates to over-disclose the number of victims or expelling anyone for "failing to disclose," the information we collected from different sources points to a conclusion that is diametrically opposed to their claim. Our initial concerns arose when one of us wrote a technical report (Wollert, 2008) after a couple of former Butner participants in the sex offender counseling program studied by Hernandez claimed they were pressured to make false confessions. After finishing that report, he discussed his findings with Dr. Jason Smith, who was the Director of the Iowa Civil Commitment Unit for Sex Offenders and supervised an outpatient program that provided counseling services to CPOs referred to him per a federal contract. Dr. Smith indicated he had heard similar allegations from some of his clients. We alluded to these disclosures in our ATSA presentation (Wollert et al., 2009) and subsequently received seven unsolicited confirmations that they were correct—one from C.S., two from other Butner inmates, one from a former Butner resident, and three from the authors of the "Fraudulent Butner Study" (Neuhauser et al., 2011). Prior to testifying before the USSC, one of us also had the opportunity to interview and evaluate two CPOs at Butner after reviewing several thousand pages of file materials. While carrying out these procedures, it became evident that one man was expelled for not disclosing more offenses after failing a polygraph. Although his counterpart completed the program, he spontaneously observed that "a lot of times you had stuff in the PHQ just to make the staff happy so they didn't kick you out... [T]hey dangled that over your head the whole time." Another psychologist who evaluated whether other Butner inmates met the SVP criteria had reached the same conclusion and told us that the number of sex offenses in the files of his evaluees "were all highly inflated, out of programmatic expectation... [I]n order to remain in the program, it was expected that you would disclose new victims on quarterly progress reports... [Y]ou can imagine how the numbers 'grew.'" Aviv, in her 2013 New Yorker article, also described how inmates "shared victim lists" to generate new confessions and kept "cheat sheets" in their cells so that they would not forget the ages of fictitious victims that they had disclosed.

Overall, we have periodically collected data for five years from many sources that point to the conclusion that at least 14 Butner participants felt compelled to over-disclose victims or were expelled from the program because their disclosures were considered inadequate. A number in this group have sworn, under penalty of perjury, that their allegations were inflated during court proceedings. This evidence, and Dr. Hernandez's admission about his "climate of pressure," confirms that overt demand characteristics had a clear and robust impact on the number of offenses reported in Bourke and Hernandez's article.

RECENT RESEARCH ON FEDERAL CPOS CONTRADICT THE BUTNER RESULTS AND RELATED EXPECTATIONS

In addition to our methodological criticisms, we argued that Hernandez's dependent measure—the number of past sex crimes reported under duress—was useless for estimating either the sexual dangerousness of federal CPOs or the chances that they would sexually recidivate after being released from prison. Regarding sexual dangerousness, one of the most accurate ways of assessing this issue is through the administration of a valid actuarial test for this purpose. Such tests place little weight on self-report, but focus instead on the number of charges or convictions for sex offenses and violent offenses that are recorded in their official criminal histories. They also do not attempt to weight undetected offenses because there is no reliable method for doing so (Wollert, 2006). Regarding sexual recidivism, the most direct way of studying this issue as it relates to federal CPOs is to simply compile recidivism data on a representative sample of federal CPOs who have been released from prison.

Several studies have been conducted since 2010 that are relevant to these issues. The first was the product of a joint effort among members of our research team (Wollert et al., 2012). Prior to this we had published articles on sex offender risk assessment (e.g. Wollert, 2006; Wollert et al., 2010) and diagnostic reliability (Wollert, 2007; Wollert and Cramer, 2011). We were also clinicians and, in that capacity, had personally counseled over 3000 sex offenders, evaluated over 1000 for treatment or sentencing, and consulted or testified in 200 sexually dangerous person proceedings. Most these referrals involved contact offenses, although a substantial number were for non-contact offenses such as exposing, peeping, or possession of child pornography.

Between 1999 and late 2009, one of us provided psychological evaluations and treatment to 55 CPOs under federal supervision in the Portland metropolitan area. Some clients were required to make nominal co-payments, but the federal contract under which these services were provided covered most treatment costs. Thus, supervisees who participated in the program represented a near exhaustive sample of federal offenders with child pornography index offenses in the local area.

All CPOs in this program were counseled with an approach called the "containment model." Per the USSC's 2012 Report to Congress, this "approach relies on therapy to address the offender's internal controls, supervision to provide external criminal justice control measures, and uses polygraph to monitor internal controls and compliance with external controls" (p.A-3). Although "widely considered to be a 'best practice' to be implemented in supervising sex offenders, including federal child pornography offenders" (U.S. Sentencing Commission, 2012, p.xiv), the containment model does not endorse the Butner Model of exerting extreme "systematic pressure" on clients to elicit as many sex offenses as possible. It concentrates instead on helping offenders disclose the range of illegal sexual behaviors they have enacted so that each of these possible problems may be addressed in treatment.

Our impression of federal CPOs, within the containment model perspective, was markedly different to the picture painted by Bourke and Hernandez. Only a handful seemed affected by compulsive urges. On the contrary, they generally struck us as ashamed of their pornography offenses, motivated to succeed, well educated, responsive to treatment, compliant with supervision, and unlikely to reoffend.

To further analyze the features of this group, we compiled a computerized spreadsheet in 2009 on all 55 CPOs who had participated in the program from documents in their files. These documents often included PSRs, police records, charging sheets, psychological evaluations, and treatment reports. We recorded each CPO's birthdate, date of program admission, and his status on ten possible offense-related risk factors that were included on the Static-99R, one of the most widely used instruments for assessing sex offender recidivism risk (Helmus et al., 2011). We also recorded the date whenever a client absconded from supervision, died, or was taken into custody. This made it possible to automatically calculate each person's time at risk in the community.

Another member of our team used the containment model to counsel 17 CPOs under a federal contract in Iowa. Data for these supervisees were added to the data for the Portland supervisees to increase the size of our data base. One supervisee in the Portland program was sentenced under § 2G2.1 of the USSC Guidelines for producing child pornography, and two supervisees with this background were placed in the Iowa program. All other supervisees were sentenced under § 2G2.2, which is applied to non-production CPOs.

Analyzing our survival data as of September 1, 2009, we found that two out of 72 CPOs were taken into custody and adjudicated for possessing child pornography over an average risk period of 4.0 years. Another CPO who was on active supervision was apprehended for the commission of a non-contact sex offense (peeping), two were apprehended for technical violations, and one absconded but was returned to continue his supervision. Most importantly, no one was arrested on charges of committing a contact sex offense or attempting to do so. Ninety-two percent of our clients succeeded in completing their supervision without being revoked, and no one who successfully completed supervision was charged with either a contact or a non-contact sex offense.

Tabulating data that pertained to the Static-99R, we found our clients were 48 years old on average, but that 35% had never been involved in a long-term committed relationship. Regarding contact offense data, 14% had previously been convicted of contact sex offenses, 8% were sentenced for a contact offense with their index pornography offense, and 3% had tried to meet with a minor for sexual reasons. Overall, 21% had contact offense convictions (n=15). Regarding non-contact offenses, 3% had prior convictions for possessing child pornography, 3% had prior convictions for public indecency, and 3% had prior convictions for peeping. Overall, 6% had prior non-contact offenses. Regarding targets of offending, 37% of the victims of contact and non-contact offenses were family members. Regarding other markers of criminality, no client was sentenced for a violent crime with his index offense, one had a prior conviction for violence, and two had four prior sentencing dates. A low level of risk for our cohort was reflected in the fact that 72% were negative for all of the sexual conduct problems we selected for analysis, except for being convicted of a pornography offense.

To examine this issue further we used the foregoing data to compute the total Static-99R score for each offender in our sample. The average score for our 72-person cohort was 1 point. Per the 99R's actuarial table (Helmus *et al.*, 2011), one would expect a five-year recidivism rate of 4% for a cohort having a score of 1. The average 99R score for the 11 CPOs with prior convictions for contact sex offenses was 3 points. In this case the 99R table leads to a five-year expected recidivism rate of 7.5%. These results, being overestimates of our obtained recidivism rate, support the advice of the instrument's developers (Harris et al., 2003) that Static-99R should not be used to estimate CPO recidivism risk among those with no contact offenses.

The PAT and the results of the Butner Study also propose that CPOs are "pedophiles." To evaluate this theory, it is useful to keep in mind that the diagnosis of pedophilia is characterized by a strong compulsive element. Those who meet the criteria must have longstanding "recurrent, intense sexually arousing fantasies [or] sexual urges" towards prepubescent children that cause sexual misconduct, marked distress, or interpersonal difficulty (American Psychiatric Association, 2013, p.697). It is also believed that "the disorder usually begins in adolescence" (American Psychiatric Association, 2000, p.571), because this is the developmental period when sexual orientations are established. The six-year recidivism conviction rate for "exclusive" and "non-exclusive" pedophiles released from prison after being convicted of child molestation is 13% (Eher et al., 2010), but exclusive pedophilia is associated with a recidivism rate that is four times as high (41%; Wollert and Cramer, 2012).

Applying these criteria and facts to the theory that CPOs are pedophiles, one would expect to find that the CPOs in our programs were young, had a history of contact sex offenses against children, had a four-year recidivism rate by arrest of close to 10%, viewed child pornography the first time they obtained sexually explicit material over the internet, and were unable to desist from viewing child pornography after being apprehended. This was not the case in that our clients, on average, were in their late forties. Although 20% had been convicted of offenses against children, none were rearrested for new contact offenses during a four-year follow-up period. This result may be attributable in part to the effects of the containment model, but our clients' history of pornography offending was still not suggestive of pedophilia. They usually viewed adult pornography when they began accessing sexually explicit materials on the internet. Then they accessed pornography depicting adolescents. Eventually, they viewed depictions of prepubescent children. Except for a few cases, their misuse of the internet also stopped after they were apprehended and sentenced.

These patterns do not support the theory that most CPOs are pedophiles. They are more consistent with the view that illegal use of the internet is a learned disorder that is "shaped" by a process that involves reinforcement, satiation, searching for more graphic material, and additional reinforcement (McCarthy, 2010, p.184; Young, 2001). This has important treatment implications because a learned disorder is amenable to psychotherapy, particularly "cognitive-behavioral" (U.S. Sentencing Commission, 2012) and "relapse prevention" (Hudson and Ward, 2000) modalities, whereas a preferential and compulsive paraphilia may require pharmacological as well as psychological interventions.

The impetus for the second relevant study was a memorandum by U.S. Judge Jack Weinstein that directed the U.S. Parole and Probation Office of the Eastern District of New York to prepare a report for him on the treatment and supervision of CPOs under the district's supervision (Stabenow, 2011). In response, Probation Officer Lawrence Andres, Jr., sent Judge Weinstein a memorandum in May 2011 indicating that the district had supervised a total of 108 CPOs since 1999 using the Containment Model. Officer Andres reported:

> Approximately 20%…disclosed a prior victim [sexual contact with a minor (under 18)[4] that occurred before the term of supervision which was never reported to law enforcement or another treatment agency] either via clinical polygraph examination or self-report during the term of supervision. It is the policy of the probation department and treatment provider to advise offenders that any such disclosure will not be used against them for the pursuit of new criminal charges, so long as they do not provide identifying information. As such, they are encouraged to *only* report the age, gender, and details of the sexual contact in an effort to gain the offender's trust and provide the basis for continued honesty in treatment.

Regarding the issue of recidivism, Officer Andres informed Judge Weinstein that "only 1" CPO had "committed a new sexual contact

---

4   During a personal telephone call with Mr. Andres we learned that anyone under 18 years old was considered a minor and thus a victim of a sex offense for the purpose of his review. Within this framework a 40-year-old CPO who had sex with a 16-year-old high school junior when he was a 19-year-old college student would be counted as having committed a prior contact sex offense. This is obviously not in the same category of misconduct as a 35-year-old man who molests his sister's five-year-old daughter. Researchers who wish to study undisclosed sex offenses should therefore differentiate sexual contacts between adults and prepubescent children from other types of sexual behavior. They will otherwise potentially mislead their audience.

offense while under the supervision of this department... [T]his offender admitted to current sexual contact of a 9-year-old female family member." Eighty-seven percent of the New York cohort also succeeded in not having their supervision revoked.

The timeframe for Officer Andres's review was almost the same as ours. The supervision success rate was also comparable. Although risk periods were not calculated using our methods, it seems safe to assume that the average risk period for CPOs in the New York cohort was about four years in length. It also seems reasonable to combine the New York cohort with ours on the assumption they come from the same underlying population. This resulted in an overall base rate of convictions for contact sex offenses over a four-year period of about 1% $(1/180 = .6\%)$.

The New York District program encouraged the disclosure of offenses within the context of participation in counseling and polygraph examinations. It was similar to our programs in these respects. It was also like our programs in that its director, to the best of our knowledge, has never endorsed the use of "systematic pressure" to elicit disclosures (McCarthy, 2012). It therefore used some of the self-report procedures that Bourke and Hernandez (2009) used, but not all of them. Twenty percent of the New York supervisees made new disclosures. This percentage stands in stark contrast to the Butner results, which reported that 59% of the cohort without previous convictions made disclosures. Statistical testing shows that the 20% New York rate is significantly smaller than the 59% Butner rate $(z=6.3, p<.0001)$.

Still more information is available on federal CPOs because of two studies that the USSC carried out and included in its recent Report to Congress. One, designed to map out the rates of "criminally sexually dangerous behaviors" (CSDB) among CPOs, tabulated data from the PSRs for three exhaustive samples of 2696 non-production offenders (U.S. Sentencing Commission, 2012, Chapter 7). Counting only prior convictions as offenses, the Commission assigned 9% of its sample (n=243) to the most serious category of child contact sex offenders, 2% (n=53) to the second most serious category of adult contact sex offenders, 2% (n=54) to a third most serious category of having convictions for a child pornography offense and a non-contact sex offense that involved a child, and 2% (n=56) to the least serious category of having a prior child pornography conviction.

Thirteen percent of all CPOs were classified as having engaged in CSDB when offenders who were assigned to more than one category were removed from less serious categories.

The Commission also conducted an alternative study that reassigned offenders to CSDB categories with a more inclusive method that counted prior convictions (n=406), PSR "Findings" without convictions (n=464), and PSR "Allegations" (n=88). Nineteen percent (n=499) were assigned to the first category with this method, 4% (n=110) to the second, 10% (n=270) to the third, and 3% (n=79) to the fourth.

Thirty-six percent of all CPOs were classified as being positive for having engaged in CSDB with this alternative definition. The 23% difference between this result and the result based on convictions shows how the magnitude of CSDB among CPOs may change as a function of a change in definitions. Nonetheless, even an inclusive definition did not lead the Sentencing Commission to classify most CPOs as having engaged in CSDB.

The Commission's second relevant study compiled recidivism rates on an exhaustive sample of 610 CPOs released in fiscal years 1999 and 2000, over a follow-up period that was 102 months in length on average and over 60 months in length for 95% of the group (U.S. Sentencing Commission, 2012, Chapter 11). Eleven members of this cohort were convicted of new contact sex crimes, nine were convicted of new non-production child pornography offenses, and 86% of all recidivistic outcomes occurred in the first four years after release. This suggests that about 1.5% of those in the follow-up group ($11 \times .86 = 9$; $9/610 = 1.5\%$) were convicted of new contact sex crimes in a four-year risk period, and 1.3% ($9 \times .86 = 8$; $8/610 = 1.3\%$) were convicted of new non-production child pornography crimes. The presence of CSDBs did not differentiate between general recidivists and non-recidivists (p.302) or sexual recidivists and non-recidivists (pp.303–309). It was also reported that those in the follow-up group were 41 years old on average in 1999 and 2000, had "some college" education, and were employed when they were arrested. These demographic characteristics matched the demographic characteristics of our cohort.

To extend this line of research as part of the chapter at hand we analyzed the criminal histories of all 504 defendants who were convicted of an "index" child pornography offense in New Zealand between

July 1, 2002 and June 30, 2012. All offenders were tracked for a minimum of three years and a maximum of 13 years. The follow-up period started from the date of conviction for those offenders given either a community-based sentence or a fine without a sentence. It started from the date of release for offenders who were sentenced to prison. We found that 19% (n=95) were previously or concurrently convicted of committing some type of contact sex offense. About 2% of the full sample committed contact sex offenses after their index offense, while this was also the case for the 95 offenders with a history of contact offenses against children. Four percent of the full sample recidivated with another child pornography offense and no other type of sex offense.

Taken together, the results of these other projects contradict the Butner studies by suggesting that only a small minority of federal CPOs are dangerous pedophiles. They are also at odds with the Butner view that almost all federal CPOs have committed contact sex offenses and that they are prone to recidivate. Finally, they show that disclosures of past sexual misconduct can be manipulated by incorporating strong demand characteristics into a research design, but that inflated estimates of past sexual misconduct are useless for predicting future misconduct by CPOs. The simplest and most reasonable explanation for this is that non-production CPOs are unlikely to recidivate because they are responsive to apprehension, sentencing, and treatment.

RESEARCH ON NON-FEDERAL CPOS IS CONSISTENT WITH RESEARCH ON FEDERAL CPOS

Assessing the characteristics of those who expose themselves to an emergent forensic condition like internet child pornography requires the introduction of the condition to a population and the identification of offenders. It also takes time to compile group data as well as case studies. The dissemination and clarification of research findings can occur only in the wake of these other endeavors.

Considering the relatively recent advent of the internet, it is not surprising that only a limited amount of research has been published on the recidivism rates and actuarial status of non-federal CPOs. The research that is available, however, is consistent with the results we have summarized about federal CPOs. Regarding the issue of recidivism, for example, Seto and colleagues (Seto *et al.*, 2011) averaged the results of nine published and unpublished follow-up studies of offenders who were primarily non-federal CPOs to derive estimates of sexual and violent recidivism. Observing that "most of the follow-up times were under 4 years" (p.135), they reported that "3.4%...of the online offenders recidivated with a contact sexual offense and 3.6% recidivated with a child pornography offense...4.2% recidivated with a violent offense." One Canadian study in their analysis (Seto and Eke, 2005), which included a large number of production offenders, found that CPOs with a history of contact sex offense convictions committed more new contact sex offenses over a 30-month follow-up period (9.2%) than CPOs with no contact offenses (1.3%). Taken together, such recidivism patterns led them to conclude that "there is a distinct group of online offenders whose only sexual crimes involve illegal (most often child) pornography... [O]nline offenders rarely go on to commit contact sexual offenses" (Seto et al., 2011, p.136).

Regarding the issue of actuarial scores, Wakeling and colleagues (Wakeling, Howard, and Barnett, 2011) obtained results that were also consistent with what we reported. They found that 99% of a large cohort of British CPOs did not have high scores on an actuarial instrument for sex offenders known as the Risk Matrix 2000. They also found that the sexual recidivism rate for this group was only 1.6%, but that it was four times higher—at 6.7%—for those with low scores who were classified as "Generalist Sexual Offenders" rather than internet sex offenders.

Research on non-federal CPOs, which we have reviewed in more detail in our book chapter (Wollert et al., 2012, pp.2-8 to 2-12), is also consistent with our clinical observations. Regarding the prevalence of paraphilias, for example, Wolak and colleagues reported that only 3% of several hundred suspects arrested primarily by state authorities for internet child pornography were known to have been diagnosed with a sexual disorder (Wolak, Finkelhor, and Mitchell, 2005). The same pattern was apparent in a sample of 33 Swiss CPOs, among whom "there were no hints of psychiatric treatment in the files" except for one person who "appeared to be paraphilic" based on interviews with his relatives (Frei et al., 2005, p.492).

A similar level of comparability is evident from research on the personality and demographic characteristics of diverse contemporaneous CPO samples. Comparing British child molesters with CPOs, Webb and colleagues reported that "child molesters were more likely to fail in all areas compared to the internet offenders... [I]nternet offenders appear to be extremely compliant with community treatment and supervision" (Webb, Craissati, and Keen, 2007, pp.462–463). McCarthy (2010) found that a group of U.S. CPOs, including 51 child molesters and 56 non-molesters, spent 21 hours per week viewing child or adult pornography; 55% had never been married, 67% had attended or completed college, and contact offenders were twice as likely as non-contact offenders to be diagnosed with pedophilia. Endrass and his research team (Endrass *et al.*, 2009) documented a similar pattern after studying an exhaustive sample of 231 CPOs from Zurich. They stated:

> Child pornography users are less likely to be married...[and] are well-educated... [O]nly 5% of the investigated sample held an unqualified job position... [O]ur results suggest that users of child pornography are probably well-integrated into Swiss society... [T]he consumption of child pornography alone does not seem to represent a risk factor for committing hands-on sex offenses in the present sample—at least in those subjects without prior convictions for hands-on sex offenses. (pp.48–49)

DISCUSSION

Sex offenders, as a group, are feared and hated by members of the public (Levenson *et al.*, 2007) and policy makers (Meloy, Curtis, and Boatwright, 2013). Research that reports glowing results in the development of effective methods for identifying or managing sex offenders may therefore encourage the adoption of laws or policies for achieving these goals. Studies that report the most sensational results may also have the greatest potential for impacting legislation and policies. This is sometimes the case even though the studies in question are unpublished, not replicated, or have a basis in procedures that are not accepted by the scientific community.

While lay persons, the courts, and legislators frequently cite behavioral research, perhaps more often when it supports a favored theory, psychology graduate students who take courses on statistics, measurement theory, and research methods learn that a host of issues threaten the validity of findings associated with behavioral research. Results obtained on a small and highly "selected" sample, for example, cannot be attributed to a more diverse group with any meaningful degree of certainty. Alternatively, a poorly defined outcome measure will overestimate the prevalence of a more specific outcome (Ackerman and Burns, 2016). Such errors of design, which include demand characteristics like those in the Butner Study, must be controlled to obtain findings that are interpretable and useful for the selection of sentences for those with disabilities and others. Table 7.1 describes and illustrates a number of procedures that are likely—in the absence of adequate controls—to produce erroneous estimates of prior contact sex offenses. It also describes methods of controlling these flaws.

Table 7.1: Research Design Flaws that Produce Artifactual Estimates of Prior Contact Sex Offenses (PCSOs) for Federal CPOs

Type of Flaw	Definition	Example (Artifactual Effects in Parentheses)	Possible Solutions
Misleading dependent measures	An outcome is underestimated by a narrow definition or inflated by a broad definition.	The definition of a PCSO includes sex between a 19-year-old and a 16-year-old. (This produces high rates in both offender and non-offender samples.)	Have experts specify definitions. Compare a full range of outcomes.
Nonrepresentative sampling	Data are collected from subjects who come from the extremes of a reference group.	An ad solicits interviews from "pedophiles" and the PCSO rate they report is attributed to federal CPOs. (The rate for CPOs is misestimated because a minority of CPOs are pedophiles.)	Carefully define the reference group. Use procedures to select representative samples.
Obvious demand characteristics	Research procedures are adopted that are so transparent that subjects know the results that researchers hope to obtain.	Counts of PCSOs are based on unverified self-reports from patients in treatment programs where a premium is placed on high levels of disclosure. (Clients give their therapists whatever they want.)	Minimize demands. Compile disclosure rates for different procedures. Verify disclosures.

Type of Flaw	Definition	Example (Artifactual Effects in Parentheses)	Possible Solutions
Masked effects	Data from different offender populations are averaged.	Four of 25 CPOs report a PCSO. Sixty of 100 convicted molesters do so. The data are pooled and a 51% rate is reported. (The high rate for the molesters hides the lower rate for the CPOs.)	Test if groups differ on the data. Report data separately if groups differ.
Overinterpretation	Data collected from a single group are treated as though they are valid and uniquely characterize the group.	A sample of CPOs is called "dangerous" after a 25% rate of PCSOs is obtained. (The rate may be seen in a different light if it is reported by non-sex offenders.)	Compare data for non-offenders and non-sex offenders with CPO data.
Lack of cross-validation	The accuracy of a test for detecting individuals with a target problem is calculated without replication.	A test identifies 80% of those CPOs with a PCSO in a developmental sample. (Accuracy is almost always overestimated when a test is developed.)	Collect data from other samples and compare accuracy rates.

Congress established the USSC when it passed the Sentencing Reform Act of 1984 (Public Law No. 98-473, Stat. 1987). The primary purpose of the Commission is to use empiricism and sound judgment to promulgate sentences and sentencing policies for federal crimes that are proportional to the "nature and circumstances" of each crime at the same time they achieve several other sentencing goals (U.S. Sentencing Commission, 2009, pp. 2–3). Disproportional sentences are unacceptable not only because they are unfair, but also because they potentially undermine respect for the law and exacerbate disciplinary problems among those who are incarcerated.

In 2009, after studying the history of the federal guidelines for sentencing child pornography offenders, the Commission concluded that the guidelines had reached a crossroads in their evolution (U.S. Sentencing Commission, 2009, p.54). On the one hand, it pointed out that Congress had a "continued interest" in increasing criminal penalties for child pornography offenses. Some of this interest, as we have suggested, is probably due to the dissemination via professional channels of sensationalized findings based on weak research designs such as those in Table 7.1. On the other hand, the Commission observed that the downward departure rates of sentencing courts signaled that many judges perceived the guidelines as too severe.

Having identified this conflict, the Commission "established a review of the child pornography guidelines as a priority" (U.S. Sentencing Commission, 2009, p.54). During the next several years it examined relevant laws and professional literature, analyzed recidivism and criminal history data for thousands of federal CPOs, and received testimony from researchers, treatment providers, attorneys, law enforcement officers, victim advocates, and judges during a two-day public hearing in Washington, D.C.

The Commission submitted a summary of its review to Congress. It concluded that "stakeholders, including the sentencing courts, increasingly feel that they 'are left without a meaningful baseline from which they can apply sentencing principles' in non-production cases" (U.S. Sentencing Commission, 2012, December, p.iii). "[T]he current guideline produces overly severe sentencing ranges for some offenders, unduly lenient ranges for other offenders, and widespread inconsistent application" (p.xxi). To address this problem, it is recommended that the length of the sentences imposed on non-production offenders should be determined by the content of their collections and the sophistication of their methods of offending, the extent of their involvement in internet communities dedicated to child sexual exploitation, and the presence of CSDB beyond a current child pornography offense (pp.xvii–xviii). Incorporating these ideas into a tentative guidelines framework, the Commission proposed (p.321):

> The presence of aggravating factors from any of these three categories, even without the presence of any aggravating factors from the other two categories, warrants enhanced punishment... The presence of

aggravating factors from multiple categories generally would warrant a more severe penalty than the presence of aggravating factors from a single category.

Will the child pornography guidelines of the future resolve the problems with the existing guidelines? The Commission's recognition that the guideline penalties are very severe in some cases, and its willingness to consider options that may address this issue, is a promising sign. Another is its recognition that many factors that have been used for sentencing enhancements are encountered so frequently that they are useless for discriminating offenders in terms of their culpability and dangerousness.

Nonetheless, compiling a just and useful set of guidelines that govern a set of crimes that are widely reviled is a daunting challenge, one that will most likely require much patience combined with a compelling set of arguments based on meaningful research results obtained with defensible methodologies. One finding that meets this standard is that the PAT is invalid and consequently lacks merit as an argument for retaining or changing any of the guidelines. Another is that CPOs without a prior history of contact convictions are unlikely to recidivate.

There is a risk, however, that the Commission's deliberations may be skewed in a counterproductive direction by invalid, emotionally appealing, and oversold conclusions that—like those in the Butner reports—proceed from unwarranted assumptions, vacuous constructs, unachievable goals, and speculative theories. This is a real concern because several claims or theories in the Commission's 2012 report lack strong justification. Furthermore, these points are repeated at various locations. Although repetition may be useful for emphasizing core conclusions and promoting their acceptance by lay audiences, it does nothing to actually validate them. It may, paradoxically, have the effect of impeding policy development because erroneous beliefs—like "all sex offenders recidivate"—often take years to dislodge once they are in place. Table 7.2 summarizes some of the most troubling claims and theories in this category, references their locations in the Commission's report, and explains why they are of concern and deserve careful scrutiny.

Table 7.2: Claims and Theories in the USSC's Report to Congress on Child Pornography Offenders that Lack Strong Justification

Claim and/or Theory (Locations in Parentheses)	Reasons for Concern
Criminally sexually dangerous behaviors (CSDBs) are relevant to Adam Walsh Act civil commitment proceedings against CPOs and revising the Sentencing Guidelines because it is a reliable construct that meaningfully differentiates between CPOs (xix, xxi, 174, 314, 319, 321, 325).	The reliability for identifying CSDBs is unstudied. No research indicates the CSDB construct is correlated with any external variable. CSDBs may not discriminate between CPOs who have accessed chat rooms. CSDBs should not be confused with the Adam Walsh concept of "serious difficulty controlling behavior."
Scientists agree that CPOs with CSDBs differ from CPOs with only one pornography sentence. One reason is the first group is more likely to recidivate (170, 303, 308, 314, 319).	The likelihood ratio (LR) of the CSDB construct for predicting recidivism does not differ from 1.0 (Fig. 11-4, p.302). This means it is invalid for picking out recidivists (Mossman, 2006). Convincing validity data need to be compiled for the construct to merit scientific acceptance.
The USSC's study that defines recidivism as RAP sheet arrests is credible because researchers agree that (1) arrests index recidivism better than convictions and (2) many offenses, being undetected, are not on offender RAP sheets (x, 295, 296, 315).	Reliability studies are more effective than surveys for picking recidivism definitions. Convictions are advantageous because they don't inflate recidivism. The temptation to attribute undetected offenses to CPOs should be tempered by the finding that 95% of all new sex crimes are committed by first-time offenders (Sandler, Freeman, and Socia, 2008).

Claim and/or Theory (Locations in Parentheses)	Reasons for Concern
Viewing pornography does not potentiate child molestation among typical CPOs but it may have a "tipping point effect" on some who may be susceptible to this if other risk factors are present (vii). An offender's noncriminal sexual behavior may estimate recidivism even if the behavior is not a criminal offense (x, 169).	The first view is a speculative reincarnation of the PAT, one that is contradicted by the finding that 84% of those CPOs who committed contact sex offenses did so before they began collecting pornography (McCarthy, 2010, p.193). The second thesis has never been empirically confirmed.
Researchers are developing actuarial instruments for use with CPOs (xiv). (Readers may thus anticipate that evaluators will soon be able to identify which CPOs will recidivate on the basis of their past behavior or other characteristics.)	CPOs have a recidivism rate that is below 5%. Past experience indicates that psychological tests for populations with such a low recidivism rate generate unacceptably high rates of error. The results of actuarial test development, in other words, are not worth the costs.

Overall, the USSC's report observed that "most stakeholders in the federal criminal justice system consider the non-production child pornography sentencing scheme to be seriously outmoded" (p.iii). Although the Commission has not yet promulgated a specific set of proposals for updating the guidelines, it has studied this issue extensively and has framed out some of the themes it intends to develop further. It is also hoped that the Commission will carry out further research on these themes and continue to submit frequent proposals to Congress for improving the guidelines.

The Butner studies illustrate how policy research can have serious negative effects when results-oriented (Rozelle, 2007, p.597) data collection is emphasized at the expense of methodological and ethical considerations. With this lesson in mind, we believe that future child pornography guidelines promulgated by the Commission will be optimized if it relies on replicated findings from projects with adequate subject protections, tests promising conceptions through the application of the questions posed in the *Daubert* decision, considers how well-intended research projects may be invalidated by the types of design flaws shown in Table 7.1, exercises caution in evaluating the weak claims and theories found in Table 7.2, and continues to invite input regarding its empirical efforts from a diverse range of behavioral scientists who are well versed in research design and methodology.

REFERENCES

Abel, G.G. (2012, February) "Child pornography offending." Testimony to the U.S. Sentencing Commission, Washington, D.C. Available at www.ussc.gov/sites/default/files/pdf/amendment-process/public-hearings-and-meetings/20120215/Transcript.pdf (accessed March 3, 2017).

Abrams, S. (1991) "The use of polygraphy with sex offenders." *Annals of Sex Research 4*, 239–263.

Ackerman, A.R. and Burns, M. (2016) "Bad data: How government agencies distort statistics on sex-crime recidivism." *Justice Policy Journal 13*, 1, 1–23.

Allen, E. (2009, October) Written testimony to the United States Sentencing Commission's Regional Hearing. Available at www.ussc.gov/sites/default/files/pdf/amendment-process/public-hearings-and-meetings/20091020-21/Allen_testimony.pdf (accessed March 3, 2017).

American Psychiatric Association (1999) *Dangerous Sex Offenders*. Washington, DC: APA.

American Psychiatric Association (2000) *Diagnostic and Statistical Manual of Mental Disorders* (4th edn). Washington, DC: APA.

American Psychiatric Association (2013) *Diagnostic and Statistical Manual of Mental Disorders* (5th edn). Washington, DC: APA.

Andres, L. (2011, May 16) *Memorandum to the Honorable Jack B. Weinstein*. New York, NY: Author.

Aviv, R. (2013, January) "The science of sex abuse: Is it right to imprison people for heinous crimes they have not yet committed?" *The New Yorker*. Available at www.newyorker.com/magazine/2013/01/14/the-science-of-sex-abuse (accessed March 3, 2017).

Baron-Evans, A. (2008) "Rita, Gall and Kimbrough: A chance for real sentencing improvements." Available at www.researchgate.net/publication/265121978_Rita_Gall_and_Kimbrough (accessed August 29, 2016).

Basbaum, J. (2010) "Inequitable sentencing for possession of child pornography: A failure to distinguish voyeurs from pederasts." *Hastings Law Journal 61*, 1281–1306.

Bourke, M.L. (2012, May 17) Letter to U.S. Sentencing Commission Chairperson Judge Patti Saris. Available at www.ussc.gov/sites/default/files/pdf/amendment-process/public-hearings-and-meetings/20120215/Testimony_15_Bourke.pdf (accessed March 3, 2017).

Bourke, M.L. and Hernandez, A.E. (2009) "The 'Butner Study' Redux: A report of the incidence of hands-on victimization by child pornography offenders." *Journal of Family Violence 24*, 183–191.

Daubert v. Merrell Dow Pharmaceuticals, Inc., 509 U.S. 579, 589, 113 S. Ct. 2786, 2795 (1993)

Eher, R., Rettenberger, M., Matthes, A., and Schilling, F. (2010) "Stable dynamic risk factors in child sexual abusers." *Sexual Offender Treatment 5*, 1, 1–12.

Endrass, J., Urbaniok, F., Hammermeister, L., Benz, C., *et al.* (2009) "The consumption of internet child pornography and violent and sex offending." *BMC Psychiatry 9*, 43–50.

Ewing, C.P. (2011) *Justice Perverted: Sex Offense Law, Psychology, and Public Policy*. New York, NY: Oxford University Press.

Fillenbaum, S. (1966) "Prior deception and subsequent experimental performance: The 'faithful' subject." *Journal of Personality and Social Psychology 4*, 5, 532–537.

Frei, A., Erenay, N., Dittman, V., and Graf, M. (2005) "Paedophilia on the internet: A study of 33 convicted offenders in the Canton of Lucerne." *Swiss Medicine Weekly 135*, 488–494.

Garrett, J.S. (2007, April) Letter to Springer Publications and *Journal of Family Violence* co-editors Michael Hersen and Vincent Hasselt. Copy with authors.

Gelber, A. (2009) *Response to "A Reluctant Rebellion."* Unpublished manuscript, U.S. Department of Justice Criminal Division at Washington, D.C.

Hansen, M. (2009, June) "A reluctant rebellion." *American Bar Association Journal 95*, 6, 54–59.

Harris, A., Phenix, A., Hanson, R., and Thornton, D. (2003) *Static-99 Coding Rules Revised—2003*. Unpublished manuscript. Ottawa, Canada: Solicitor General Canada.

Heimbach, M.J. (2002, May) "Internet child pornography." Available at http://commdocs.house.gov/committees/judiciary/hju79366.000/hju79366_0f.htm (accessed March 3, 2017).

Helmus, L., Thornton, D., Hanson, K., and Babchishin, K. (2011) "Improving the predictive accuracy of Static-99 and Static-2002 with older sex offenders: Revised age weights." *Sexual Abuse 24*, 64–101.

Hernandez, A. (2000a, November) "Self-reported contact sexual offenses by participants in the Federal Bureau of Prisons' Sex Offender Treatment Program: Implications for internet sex offenders." Paper presented at the Annual Conference of the Association for the Treatment of Sexual Abusers, San Diego, CA.

Hernandez, A. (2000b, June) *Special Needs Offenders: FCI Butner Sex Offender Treatment Program* (Parts One and Two). Part One, tape 1 available at https://archive.org/details/gov.ntis.ava20973vnb1.01; Part One, tape 2 available at www.youtube.com/watch?v=w8lada_gUKw; Part Two, tape 1 available at https://archive.org/details/gov.ntis.ava20973vnb4.01 (all accessed March 3, 2017).

Hudson, S.M. and Ward, T. (2000) "Relapse Prevention: Assessment and Treatment Implications." In D.R. Laws, S.M. Hudson, and T. Ward (eds) *Remaking Relapse Prevention with Sex Offenders: A Sourcebook*. Newbury Park, CA: Sage.

Larson, A.O. (2012) "Confronting Supreme Court fact-finding." *University of Virginia Law Review 98*, 1255–1312.

Lee, A.F., Li, N., Lamade, R., Schuler, A., and Prentky, R. (2012) "Predicting hands-on child sexual offenses among possessors of internet child pornography." *Psychology, Public Policy, and Law 18*, 644–672.

Levenson, J.S., Brannon, Y., Fortney, T., and Baker, J. (2007) "Public perceptions about sex offenders and community protection policies." *Analyses of Social Issues and Public Policy 7*, 1–25.

McCarthy, J. (2010) "Internet sexual activity: A comparison between contact and non-contact child pornography offenders." *Journal of Sexual Aggression 16*, 181–195.

McCarthy, J. (2012, February) "The assessment and treatment of child pornography offenders and the motivation to collect child pornography." Testimony to the U.S. Sentencing Commission, Washington, D.C. Available at www.ussc.gov/sites/default/files/pdf/amendment-process/public-hearings-and-meetings/20120215/Transcript.pdf (accessed March 3, 2017).

Meloy, M., Curtis, K., and Boatwright, J. (2013) "The sponsors of sex offender bills speak up: Policy makers' perceptions of sex offenders, sex crimes, and sex offender legislation." *Criminal Justice and Behavior 40*, 438–452.

Mossman, D. (2006) "Another look at interpreting risk categories." *Sexual Abuse 18*, 41–63.

Neuhauser, J.C., Francis, S., and Ebel, P. (2011, May) *The Butner Study: A Report on the Fraudulent Execution of the Adam Walsh Act by the Federal Bureau of Prisons*. Unpublished manuscript. Available at http://rsoresearch.files.wordpress.com/2012/01/butner_study_debunking_kit.pdf (accessed January 18, 2017).

Office for Protection from Research Risks (1993) *Institutional Review Board Guidelines*. Washington, DC: Author.

Orne, M.T. (1962) "On the social psychology of the psychological experiment: With particular reference to demand characteristics and their implications." *American Psychologist 17*, 776–783.

Prentky, R.A., Janus, E., Barbaree, H., Schwartz, B., and Kafka, M. (2006) "Sexually violent predators in the courtroom: Science on trial." *Psychology, Public Policy, and Law 12*, 357–393.

Rozelle, S.D. (2007) "*Daubert*, Schmaubert: Criminal defendants and the short end of the science stick." *Tulsa Law Review 43*, 597–607.

Sandler, J.C., Freeman, N., and Socia, K. (2008) "Does a watched pot boil? A time-series analysis of New York State's Sex Offender Registration and Notification Law." *Psychology, Public Policy, and Law 14*, 284–302.

Seto, M.C. and Eke, A. (2005) "The criminal histories and later offending of child pornography offenders." *Sexual Abuse 17*, 201–210.

Seto, M.C., Hanson, R.K., and Babchishin, K.M. (2011) "Contact sexual offending by men with online sexual offenses." *Sexual Abuse 23*, 124–145.

Sher, J. and Carey, B. (2007, July 19) "Debate on child pornography's link to molesting." *The New York Times*. Available at www.nytimes.com/2007/07/19/world/americas/19iht-19sex.6737195.html (accessed March 3, 2017).

Smith, L., Grassley, C.E., and Sensenbrenner, F.J. (2012, February 14) Letter to U.S. Sentencing Chairperson Judge Patti Saris. United States Congress, Washington, D.C.

Specter, A. and Hoffa, L. (2011) "A quiet but growing judicial rebellion against harsh sentences for child pornography offenses—should the laws be changed?" *The Champion 33*, 6. Available at www.nacdl.org/champion.aspx?id=22897 (accessed January 18, 2017).

Stabenow, T. (2008, July 3) "Deconstructing the myth of careful study: A primer on the flawed progression of the child pornography guidelines." Available at www.fpdvermont.org/downloads/3%20July%202008%20Edit.pdf (accessed March 3, 2017).

Stabenow, T. (2011) "A method for careful study: A proposal for reforming the child pornography guidelines." *Federal Sentencing Reporter 24*, 2, 108–136.

U.S. Sentencing Commission (1996) *Report to Congress: Sex Offenses Against Children. Findings and Recommendations Regarding Federal Penalties*. USSC. Available at www.ussc.gov/research/congressional-reports/1996-report-congress-sex-offenses-against-children (accessed March 3, 2017).

U.S. Sentencing Commission (2008) *Sourcebook of Federal Sentencing Statistics*. USSC. Available at www.ussc.gov/research/2015-sourcebook/archive/sourcebook-2008 (accessed March 3, 2017).

U.S. Sentencing Commission (2009) *The History of the Child Pornography Guidelines*. USSC. Available at www.ussc.gov/sites/default/files/pdf/research-and-publications/research-projects-and-surveys/sex-offenses/20091030_History_Child_Pornography_Guidelines.pdf (accessed March 3, 2017).

U.S. Sentencing Commission (2010, June) *Results of Survey of United States District Judges January 2010 through March 2010*. USSC. Available at www.ussc.gov/sites/default/files/pdf/research-and-publications/research-projects-and-surveys/surveys/20100608_Judge_Survey.pdf (accessed March 3, 2017).

U.S. Sentencing Commission (2012) *Report to Congress: Federal Child Pornography Offenses*. USSC. Available at www.ussc.gov/research/congressional-reports/2012-report-congress-federal-child-pornography-offenses (accessed March 3, 2017).

U.S. v. Crisman, 39 F. Supp. 3d 1189 (D. New Mexico, July 22, 2014)

U.S. v. Cunningham, 680 F. Supp. 2d 844 (N.D. Ohio, January 26, 2010)

U.S. v. Dorvee, 616 F.3d 174; 2010 App. Lexis 16288 (2d Cir., May 11, 2010)

U.S. v. Grober, 624 F.3d 592 (3d Cir., October 26, 2010)

U.S. v. Johnson, 588 F. Supp. 2d 997 (S.D. Iowa, December 3, 2008)

U.S. v. Revland, No. 5-06-HC-02212 (E.D. North Carolina, December 23, 2011)

Vanderpool, T. (2011, May 19) "Child pornography arrests and prosecutions are on the rise—and perhaps, on occasion, going too far." *The Tucson Weekly*. Available at www.tucsonweekly.com/tucson/defending-the-innocent/Content?oid=2832889 (accessed March 3, 2017).

Wakeling, H.C., Howard, P., and Barnett, G. (2011) "Comparing the validity of the RM2000 scales and OGRS3 for predicting recidivism by internet sexual offenders." *Sexual Abuse 23*, 146–168.

Webb, L., Craissati, J., and Keen, S. (2007) "Characteristics of internet child pornography offenders: A comparison with child molesters." *Sexual Abuse 19*, 449–465.

Wolak, J., Finkelhor, D., and Mitchell, K. (2005) "Child pornography possessors arrested in internet-related crimes: Finding from the Online Victimization Study." Available at www.missingkids.com/en_US/publications/NC144.pdf (accessed January 18, 2017).

Wollert, R. (2006) "Low base rates limit expert certainty when current actuarial tests are used to identify sexually violent predators: An application of Bayes's Theorem." *Psychology, Public Policy, and Law 12*, 56–85.

Wollert, R. (2007) "Poor diagnostic reliability, the Null-Bayes Logic Model, and their implications for sexually violent predator evaluations." *Psychology, Public Policy, and Law 13*, 167–203.

Wollert, R. (2008) *A Summary of the Treatment Offense Histories of Men Who Were Supervised by Federal Pre-Trial and Probation Services after Being Charged With or Convicted of Possession of Child Pornography*. Unpublished manuscript. Portland, OR.

Wollert, R. (2012, February) "The implications of recidivism research and clinical experience for assessing and treating federal child pornography offenders." Testimony to the U.S. Sentencing Commission, Washington, D.C. Available at www.ussc.gov/sites/default/files/pdf/amendment-process/public-hearings-and-meetings/20120215-16/Testimony_15_Wollert_2.pdf (accessed March 3, 2017).

Wollert, R. and Cramer, E. (2011) "Sampling extreme groups invalidates research on the Paraphilias: Implications for DSM-5 and sex offender risk assessments." *Behavioral Sciences and the Law 29*, 554–565.

Wollert, R. and Cramer, E. (2012, October) "Reverse Phi: A computerized spreadsheet for estimating Bayesian conditional probabilities from phi coefficients." Paper presented at the Annual Conference of the Association for the Treatment of Sexual Abusers, Denver, CO.

Wollert, R., Cramer, E., Waggoner, J., Skelton, A., and Vess, J. (2010) "Recent research (N=9,305) underscores the importance of using age-stratified actuarial tables in sex offender risk assessments." *Sexual Abuse: A Journal of Research and Treatment 22*, 171–190.

Wollert, R., Waggoner, J., and Smith, J. (2009, October) "Child pornography offenders do not have florid offense histories and are unlikely to recidivate." Poster session presented at the annual meeting of the Association for the Treatment of Sexual Abusers, Dallas, TX.

Wollert, R., Waggoner, J., and Smith, J. (2012) "Federal Child Pornography Offenders Do Not Have Florid Offense Histories and Are Unlikely to Recidivate." In B. Schwartz (ed.) *The Sex Offender, Volume VII*. Kingston, NJ: Civic Research Institute.

Young, K.S. (2001) *Tangled in the Web: Understanding Cybersex from Fantasy to Addiction*. Bloomington, IN: Authorhouse.

CHAPTER 8

Accessors and Distributors of Child Pornography

Not Who You Think They Are

Fred S. Berlin

In a court of law, judges sometimes need to determine the extent to which potential evidence may be probative versus prejudicial. That is done to try to ensure that decisions will be made objectively and fairly, absent the taint of potentially prejudicial bias. In general, legislators are under no mandate to eliminate such bias when enacting criminal statutes. Rather, the implicit theory is that vigorous advocacy from competing constituencies will result in balanced legislation that considers the best interests of all the relevant parties.

One of the relevant parties, with respect to legislation dictating sanctions for those who access child pornography, are those accessors themselves, and, of comparable importance, their families. In a court of law, those accused are often afforded numerous legal protections. In my judgment, when legislation is enacted to sanction the viewers of child pornography, balanced advocacy intended to ensure such fairness and protections is often lacking. In the face of the understandably intense feelings elicited by any perceived threat to our children, how many among us would likely step forward publicly to insist upon compassionate treatment of anyone who would be so "vile" as to access pornographic images of minors?

Of additional importance, legislation (especially legislation that mandates minimum mandatory sentences) does not ordinarily consider potential psychological vulnerabilities within individuals who may violate a particular statute. For example, if an individual accessing child pornography has previously been the victim of a traumatic brain injury, is suffering with mild mental retardation, or is afflicted with autism, the required imposition of a minimum mandatory sentence pays no heed to those realities. That begs the question, "Should individuals with documented mental impairments (or, perhaps, even with a sense of naive benign curiosity) be subjected by mandate to the same legal sanctions as those who may manifest a malicious disregard for the wellbeing of children?" It also begs the question, "What sorts of individuals are actually accessing child pornography, and in general do they pose a risk of becoming a 'hands-on' sexual offender?"

STIGMATIZED AND DEMONIZED

Historically, at the height of the so-called "War on Drugs," some individuals received lengthy prison sentences, often involving many years of incarceration, for the possession of a relatively small amount of a drug such as marijuana (Hari, 2015). Drug users were often dehumanized, labeled as "junkies," and even the small-time user was sometimes perceived as a grave threat to the wellbeing of the community. As an understanding began to emerge that many decent people were afflicted with a dependency on drugs, the publicly perceived "face of the drug user" began to change, and to some extent, along with that recognition, so did relevant legislation. Today, in many jurisdictions, there are specialized drug courts that factor into account the treatment needs, and the humanity, of those drug users who are facing legal sanctions (Gerra and Clark, 2010).

At this point in time, those who access child pornography are often perceived by society as a grave threat, just as many drug users were years ago perceived as immoral individuals deserving of stigma and scorn. Therefore, particularly in the federal system, the criminal sanctions for accessing child pornography (usually via the internet) are quite severe (Doyle, 2013). Most convicted of such an offense will find themselves facing sanctions of a far greater severity than they would likely have imagined.

In most federal cases, those sanctions will include a minimum mandatory sentence of about five years, ongoing status as a convicted felon, loss of voting rights, confiscation of one's computers and related electronics, loss of employment and additional financial burdens (e.g. fines/restitution), and placement on a sex offender registry (along with a stamped marker on that individual's passport [United States House of Representatives, 2015]).

For those convicted who are parents, there may be additional unintended consequences as well. For example, in one survey 47% of children of persons on a sex offender registry reported being harassed by others; over 50% said that they had been ridiculed or teased; 65% felt left out by other children; and 22% said that they had been attacked by others (Levenson and Tewksburg, 2009). Over 70% felt depressed and anxious. In some jurisdictions, an individual on a sex offender registry may be required to move if his home is located near a neighborhood school (Stop It Now, n.d.). The scope of potential consequences, legal and otherwise, associated with accessing and viewing child pornography, is indeed quite broad.

ACCESSORS OF CHILD PORNOGRAPHY

Who is accessing and distributing child pornography, and how are they doing so? In contemporary society, child pornography is most frequently accessed via the internet (Berlin and Sawyer, 2012). The internet offers free easy access to child pornography (access that is often far too easy for vulnerable populations, such as those with mild intellectual disability or autism). Because such access is so often free, contrary to claims that are sometimes made, it does not ordinarily "fuel the profit motive" to produce child pornography.

The internet affords those who might access child pornography an illusion of anonymity, with the sense that others are not going to be aware of their actions or their identities. That sense can be disinhibiting of sexual impulses. In addition, for many, the act of accessing child pornography via the internet may begin to feel more like a game than an activity with potential real-life consequences. Under such circumstances, it can be very easy for such individuals to rationalize that, because certain images are already on the internet, "nobody is going to be harmed" if they simply continue viewing them while alone in the privacy of their bedrooms.

Today, many people access child pornography via file-sharing networks (United States Government Accountability Office, 2003). Those systems can allow images to flow into and out of individual computers that have become linked to such networks. If a given individual has shared images by allowing them to flow out of his computer into another computer on such a network, he can be charged criminally with the "distribution" of child pornography. Thus, most individuals arrested for accessing child pornography via a file-sharing network can be charged with receiving, possessing, and distributing it.

CASE EXAMPLES

In recent years, as a mental health professional and forensic psychiatrist with a focus on sexual disorders, I, along with my colleagues, have seen significant numbers of individuals who have accessed child pornography via the internet. In most instances, these have been decent law-abiding citizens, with no prior criminal histories. Because they have differed so radically from common public misperceptions about accessors of child pornography, I will present a few brief examples below to illustrate that point. Others from differing professional perspectives have made similar observations. Douglas A. Burman, a professor at the Moritz College of Law at the Ohio State University, has stated: "What has caused concerns in courts across the nation is that we have a lot of relatively law-abiding individuals sitting in the basement downloading the wrong kind of dirty pictures facing not just prison sentences but incredibly long prison sentences" (Burman, 2015). In voicing his concerns about federal minimum mandatory sentencing requirements, and stating, "I don't approve of child pornography obviously," Federal Judge Jack B. Weinstein had gone on to state that "we're destroying lives unnecessarily. At most, they should be receiving treatment and supervision" (Sulzberger, 2010; see also Weinstein, 2016).

In detailing aspects of the seven cases presented below, I have taken care to ensure the anonymity of the individuals involved. These seven examples are representative of numerous other cases that exist in which the necessity, severity, and just nature of the criminal sanctions imposed are open to question.

Case #1

Mr. A. was a 78-year-old sophisticated gentleman who had been the primary care provider for his similarly aged wife. Somewhat debilitated himself, he had developed an interest in collecting various forms of erotica from both contemporary and past cultures. Some of those eroticized images had depicted children. Without appreciating that he had done anything criminal, or that he was placing himself into potential legal jeopardy, he had taken his computer, which had contained those images, to be repaired. As a mandatory reporter, the repair person had notified the legal authorities, and then Mr. A. was prosecuted for receiving and possessing child pornography. At the age of 78, he had been sent to prison and placed on a sex offender registry. His wife had then needed to be moved out of state to be cared for by other family members. There was no evidence that this decent elderly gentleman, with no prior criminal record, had posed any threat to children, as had been attested to by his own children and grandchildren.

Case #2

Mr. B. was a very affable 18-year-old gay male, who, like many young men his age, would periodically access pornography via the internet. As an 18-year-old gay man, some of the eroticized images of males that he had accessed had been of adolescents a few years younger than himself. Federal law defines a minor as anyone under the age of 18. As a consequence of having downloaded pornographic images of 15-, 16-, and 17-year-old males, he had been arrested and prosecuted for receiving and possessing child pornography. Mr. B. is now a convicted felon on a sex offender registry, and consequently his ambition to be an attorney in the future may be in jeopardy. Because of his young age, as an alternative to prison, he was court-ordered to be confined in a residential treatment facility for a couple of years, although why he even required treatment at all was unclear.

Case #3

Mr. C. was a young man in his early 20s, who at about the age of 19 had sustained a traumatic brain injury. One of the sequelae of that injury had been a mild disinhibition of his sexual impulses. Consequently, he began to spend several hours each day in the basement of his mother's home where, unbeknownst to her, he was viewing pornography via the internet. Some of those pornographic images had involved children, but because of his brain injury he had an impaired capacity to appreciate the significance of that fact. In time, he was prosecuted criminally for the receipt and possession of child pornography. That was in a state court that did not require a minimum mandatory sentence, and he has been placed on probation and ordered to receive treatment. Nevertheless, he is now a convicted felon on a sex offender registry.

Case #4

Mr. D. was a young adult on the autism spectrum. Autism is a neurodevelopmental disorder characterized by impaired social interactions, impaired verbal and nonverbal communication, and repetitive behaviors. Many persons with autism have trouble perceiving social cues and nuances. Consequently, they may experience difficulties in interacting socially, and sexually, with their peers. At the same time, they may have a fascination with inanimate objects such as computers. Mr. D., in his mid-20s, was still a virgin, and his way of having sex had become via masturbation while viewing pornography (including some child pornography) over the internet. Mr. D. had a diminished capacity for abstract reasoning of the sort that could have enabled him to more fully appreciate the significance of some of his actions. That said, he had been around numerous children in his life, and there was no evidence that he had ever attempted to approach any minors in an improper or sexual fashion. As a consequence of having accessed child pornography, Mr. D., a developmentally impaired individual with autism, is now a convicted felon on a sex offender registry.

Case #5

Ms. E. was a 16-year-old female, who had "sexted" naked pictures of herself to her 18-year-old boyfriend. After her parents found out about that and complained to the legal authorities, her boyfriend was charged with receiving and possessing child pornography. For unclear reasons, she was not charged with the production and distribution of child pornography, even though technically she could have been. In this case (unlike some others I am aware of), the charges against Ms. E.'s boyfriend had subsequently been dropped—although technically they could just as easily have been sustained (potentially resulting in severe sanctions of the sorts imposed in the cases noted above).

Case #6

Dr. F. was a 33-year-old male physician who, as a child, was placed into foster care following parental neglect. He attended numerous schools. He was exposed to pornography as a youngster and had been a victim of child sexual abuse. For reasons that are not well understood, in his case his "premature sexualization" may have predisposed the later development of a transient desire to view child pornography as an adult. Several months before being arrested at the age of 33, he became aware of its existence on the internet and had downloaded some such images. However, about one month prior to a search warrant of his home having been served by investigating authorities, he became disgusted with himself for having viewed it, and he stopped doing so.

Dr. F. never produced child pornography. He obtained it via a file-sharing network. He never paid to receive any of it, and in that sense he had not "fueled the market" for its production. His computer had been confiscated and analyzed forensically, and it was clear that he had never entered sites that cater to children on the internet. He had never "chatted" sexually with a child, and there was no evidence that he had ever attempted to use child pornography to "groom" a child for sexual purposes. His arrest generated a good deal of publicity locally, and no children (including his own) alleged being sexually abused by him. He also "passed" a polygraph examination regarding that matter.

Dr. F. had had no prior criminal record. When evaluated clinically, he had expressed guilt, shame, and embarrassment, as well as remorse, about having accessed child pornography. In my judgment, he was clearly an individual of good moral character, who had never meant to cause anyone to be harmed by his actions.

As a result of having accessed child pornography via the internet, and of his subsequent conviction, Dr. F.'s medical license was revoked; he was incarcerated in a federal detention center for a number of years; and he was placed on a sex offender registry for a period of 25 years. His children were deprived of the companionship and daily guidance of their father. His wife lost the financial support and ongoing presence of a loving and supportive husband, and his patients (all adults) lost access to a devoted and competent physician.

Case #7

As a final example, Mr. G. was a middle-aged professional male who was consistently a responsible and productive member of the community. In the context of his private sexual life, he had used a computer application (an "App") to morph the faces of actual female children onto images of the bodies of naked adult women. He felt perplexed about the origin of his strong atypical sexual urges to produce such images. He never expected or intended to show those images to anyone else, and despite his actions, during more reflective moments, he felt ashamed and conflicted about what he had done.

Mr. G.'s computer was set up in such a fashion that images contained in it would be backed up on the virtual "cloud," thereby preventing their loss. He had always believed that such images were maintained in privacy and with absolute confidentiality. They are not. The morphed images that he had maintained in the "cloud" were detected by regulatory authorities and reported as a form of child pornography. Mr. G. is now an incarcerated felon serving a lengthy prison sentence.

CRIMINAL SENTENCING IN CHILD PORNOGRAPHY CASES

Ordinarily, criminal sentencing is intended to serve several purposes. The first, particularly for those believed to constitute an ongoing threat to community safety, is incapacitation. The issue of whether incapacitation is needed to ensure community safety in most child pornography cases will be further discussed below. Second, particularly for those who have caused significant harm to others, retribution (punishment) for its own sake is often deemed necessary. Third, sentencing is intended both to deter the individual being sentenced from repeating his criminal acts in the future and to deter others from acting similarly. Fourth, sentencing may require some form of restitution. Finally, any treatment needs of the individual being sentenced may also be considered.

Federal minimum mandatory sentences require that most accessors of child pornography be incapacitated for a period, presumably, at least in part, as a form of punishment. Because such sentences are mandatory, in any given instance there is the risk that such incapacitation and punishment may be disproportionally harsh.

As noted above, sentencing is also intended to deter the individual being sentenced (as well as others) from attempting to access child pornography in the future. Any such deterrence may be less effective when an individual who is accessing child pornography is being "driven" to repeatedly do so by the presence of atypical sexual cravings—analogous to the way in which some drug addicts are "driven" to seek out illicit substances by their cravings. When such cravings are present, they cannot simply be deterred or punished away.

Instead, in such instances, the provision of appropriate treatment should also be a component of sentencing. In my professional experience, in many instances it is not.

When an individual accesses pornographic images of known victims that depict those victims being sexually abused as children, the person being sentenced may be required to pay restitution to those victims (United States Congress, 2014). Therefore, those victims are notified about the fact that the person being sentenced has viewed sexually explicit images of them. Whether making them aware of that fact serves the best interests of those previously molested individuals, or simply reopens or keeps open old emotional wounds, is debatable. Also debatable is the question of whether viewing such images privately actually causes additional harm to the persons depicted in those images.

DO CHILD PORNOGRAPHY ACCESSORS BECOME "HANDS-ON" SEXUAL OFFENDERS?

In my experience, in some instances, federal mandatory minimum sentences for those who have accessed child pornography have resulted in longer periods of incarceration than has been required of some "hands-on" sexual offenders in various local non-federal jurisdictions. That begs the question, "Are some individuals who are sentenced federally being sentenced for what they have actually done (e.g. for accessing and possessing child pornography) or for what it is feared they may do in the future (i.e. commit a 'hands-on' sexual offense)?"

Several studies have addressed the question of whether those who have been arrested for accessing child pornography (but who have had no known prior history of sexually molesting a child) are likely to become "hands-on" sexual offenders. An early retrospective study, utilizing polygraph reports from incarcerated child pornography accessors, had suggested that many of them had had previous unreported sexual activities with children (Bourke and Hernandez, 2009). The validity of that study has been questioned and debated (Citizens for Change, 2011). That aside, as a retrospective study, it did not prospectively track the activities of accessors of child pornography following conviction to determine as time passed whether they had subsequently been accused of a "hands-on" sexual offense.

Three relatively large prospective studies have addressed that issue. Canadian researchers tracked 2630 men convicted for having accessed child pornography, following them for a period of up to six years (Seto, Hanson, and Babchiskin, 2011). They reported that 3.4% of those 2630 individuals had had a new child pornography charge (as opposed to a "hands-on" sexual offense charge) during that follow-up period. More than 96% had not had such an allegation. Only 2% had been accused of a "hands-on" sexual offense.

Researchers in Switzerland tracked 231 men who were convicted of accessing child pornography over a six-year follow-up period (Endrass *et al.*, 2009). An individual was considered to have been a recidivist during that period if he was the subject of an ongoing investigation, if he had been accused of a new sexual offense, or if he had been convicted of a new sexual offense. Nine of the 231 men being followed (3.8%) were determined to be "hands-off" (as opposed to "hands-on") recidivists. The percentage of "hands-on" sexual recidivism during that follow-up period was 0.8% (2/231). One of the two men who had committed a "hands-on" sexual offense during that period had previously been a "hands-on" offender, in addition to having previously accessed child pornography. The researchers concluded that "consuming child pornography alone is not a risk factor for committing hands-on sex offenses—at least not for those subjects who had never committed a hands-on sex offense."

The United States Sentencing Commission prospectively followed 610 men convicted federally as a consequence of a "non-production" child pornography offense (United States Sentencing Commission, 2012). Those men had been sentenced in either 1999 or 2000, and the follow-up period had averaged approximately 8.5 years. Recidivism was defined as an arrest, a conviction, a registration violation, or a "technical" supervision violation. Total sexual recidivism was 7.4% (45/610). "Hands-on" (contact) sexual recidivism was 3.6% (22/610); 96.4% of those followed had had no known "hands-on" sexual offense subsequent to their child pornography conviction. Research such as this has led Canadian investigator Michael Seto to conclude that there is a "subgroup of online-only offenders who pose a relatively low risk of committing contact sexual offenses in the future" (Seto and Babchiskin, 2011, p.124). Several examples have been detailed above that likely fall into that category.

FUTURE CONSIDERATIONS

Society has a moral obligation to protect its children. In doing so, it is important that appropriate criminal justice sanctions and thoughtfully crafted legislation be fully supported. To the extent possible, the need for, and likely benefits of, such legislation should be evidence-based. At the same time, a public health, and treatment, perspective to the issue of child sexual abuse as well as to the issue of child pornography is also needed.

In recent years, at the Johns Hopkins Hospital in Baltimore, Maryland, where I am the Director of the Sexual Behaviors Consultation Unit, we have seen significant numbers of patients (and their family members) come forward in search of help because of a "compulsion," or recurrent urge, to view child pornography. Given that we are not mandatorily required to report such disclosures, in most instances we have been able to assist such individuals, sometimes with the aid of prescribed medication, to successfully bring their sexual behavior under good control. It is my understanding that the State of California has introduced legislation mandating the reporting of disclosures about accessing child pornography, which, in my professional opinion, will only serve to deter individuals and their families from seeking help (Friedersdorf, 2015).

In my judgment, significant numbers of individuals and families are inadvertently being needlessly harmed by some of the current legislation that is related to the accessing of child pornography. I believe that that is especially so with respect to mandatory minimum federal sentencing requirements. If there is going to be such severe mandatory sentencing (which, in my opinion, is not serving the best interests of a just society), that fact should at least be publicly and repeatedly made known. In my experience, most individuals arrested for accessing child pornography (as well as their families) had had no idea about the potential severity of associated penalties.

The mental health community should be doing more. One routinely hears public service announcements encouraging individuals to come forward for treatment if they have a drug problem, depression, or a variety of other mental health needs. One rarely, if ever, hears a public service announcement encouraging individuals who may be experiencing atypical sorts of sexual cravings (such as an urge to repeatedly access child pornography or to seek out sex with children) to come forward for help. In Germany, the Prevention Project Dunkelfeld (Dark Field) has been doing just that, reportedly with good success (Beier *et al.*, 2009).

In dealing with the issue of child pornography, it may be worth considering what values we want to instill in our children. Should we convey to them that those who access child pornography are invariably unworthy, deserving of punishment and scorn? Conversely, as has been documented here, should we educate them to the fact that many are worthy, though perhaps in some instances mentally challenged, deserving of understanding and kind care, and, when needed, also deserving of access to appropriate treatment?

REFERENCES

Beier, M., Neutze, J., Nundt, I., Ahlers, C., *et al.* (2009) "Encouraging self-identified pedophiles and hebephiles to seek professional help: First results of the Prevention Project Dunkelfeld (PPD)." *Child Abuse and Neglect 33*, 545–549.

Berlin, F. and Sawyer, D. (2012) "Potential consequences of accessing child pornography over the internet and who is accessing it." *Sexual Addiction and Compulsivity 19*, 30–40.

Bourke, M. and Hernandez, A. (2009) "The 'Butner Study' Redux: A report of the incidence of hands-on child victimization by child pornography offenders." *Journal of Family Violence 24*, 183–191.

Burman, D. (2015) Sentencing Class, Ohio State University Moritz College of Law, Law Professors Blog Network.

Citizens for Change (2011) "The Butner Study: A report on the execution of the Adam Walsh Act by the Federal Bureau of Prisons (BOP)." Available at https://rsoresearch.files.wordpress.com/2012/01/butner_study_debunking_kit.pdf (accessed January 19, 2017).

Doyle, C. (2013) *Federal Mandatory Minimum Sentencing Guidelines.* Congressional Research Service Report, Congressional Research Service, Washington, D.C., September 9, 2013.

Endrass, J., Urbaniok, F., Haammermeister, L.C., Benz, C., *et al.* (2009) "The consumption of internet child pornography and violent and sex offending." *BMC Psychiatry 9*, 43. Available at http://bmcpsychiatry.biomedcentral.com/articles/10.1186/1471-244X-9-43 (accessed January 19, 2017).

Friedersdorf, C. (2015) "Should therapists have to report patients who viewed child pornography?" *The Atlantic*, July 28, 2015.

Gerra, G. and Clark, N. (2010) *From Coercion to Cohesion: Treating Drug Dependence through Health Care, Not Punishment.* New York, NY: United Nations Office on Drugs and Crime.

Hari, J. (2015) *Chasing the Scream: The First and Last Days of the War on Drugs.* London: Bloomsbury.

Levenson, J.S. and Tewksburg, R. (2009) "Collateral damage: Family members of registered sex offenders." *American Journal of Criminal Justice.* Available at http://dx.doi.org/10.1007/s12103-008-9055-x (accessed March 3, 2017).

Seto, M., Hanson, R.K., and Babchiskin, K. (2011) "Contact sexual offending by men with online sexual offenses." *Sexual Abuse: A Journal of Research and Treatment 23*, 124–145.

Stop It Now (n.d.) "What is the legal distance a registered sex offender can live near a school or a park?" Available at www.stopitnow.org/advice-column-entry/what-is-the-legal-distance-a-registered-sex-offender-can-live-near-a-school-or-a (accessed March 3, 2017).

Sulzberger, A.G. (2010) "Defiant judge takes on child pornography law." *The New York Times* (N.Y. region), May 21, 2010. Page A1.

United States Congress (2014) The Amy and Vicky Child Pornography Restitution Improvement Act, 18 U.S.C. § 2259.

United States Government Accountability Office (2003) *Peer-to-Peer Networks Provide Ready Access to Child Pornography*. Washington, DC: GAO. Available at www.gao.gov/assets/240/237369.pdf (accessed January 19, 2017).

United States House of Representatives (2015) International Megan's Law to Prevent Child Exploitation and Other Sexual Crimes Through Advanced Notification of Traveling Sex Offenders. H.R. 515.

United States Sentencing Commission (2012) "Recidivism by child pornography offenders." Report to the Congress, Federal Child Pornography Offenses, 293–306.

Weinstein, J. (2016) "The Context and Content of *New York v. Ferber*." In C. Hessick (ed.) *Redefining Child Pornography Law: Crime, Language and Social Consequences*. Ann Arbor, MI: University of Michigan Press.

CHAPTER 9

Collateral Damage of Sex Offender Management Policies for Individuals with Asperger's Syndrome and Their Family Members

Erin Comartin

INTRODUCTION

This chapter discusses the different forms of child pornography falling under current federal policy. Once an individual has been convicted of this offense, they are labeled a "sex offender" subject to sanctions designed to manage sex offenders living in the community. Since the mid-1990s, a slew of federal and state-level sex offender management policies have been implemented across the United States (Terry and Ackerman, 2009). These policies were intended to protect the public, particularly children, from individuals who were likely to prey upon them. The unintended collateral damage from these policies has caused considerable harm to the individuals listed on public sex offender registries, and this harm has extended to their family members. More specifically, this chapter relates the cumulative collateral damage existing for individuals diagnosed with Asperger's syndrome (AS) who have been convicted as a sex offender for viewing child pornography. In addition, the substantial impact for family members of those with AS are also discussed. This chapter concludes with a discussion about what the criminal justice system and treatment providers can do to respond to individuals with AS who access illegal, yet available, sexually inappropriate images of children.

CHILD PORNOGRAPHY

Child pornography has become an increasingly important social problem with the advent of the internet. The internet-based pornography industry provides instant access to an endless amount of sexually explicit images. While pornography is legal for consenting adults under the U.S. constitutional right to free speech, issues are raised when these images include children under the age of 18 (18 U.S.C. § 2256 2003). The Protection of Children Against Sexual Exploitation Act was enacted in 1977 to criminalize the use of children in sexual images. The goal of this federal legislation was to protect one of society's most vulnerable populations from sexual experiences since they are not physically, psychologically, emotionally, socially, or developmentally ready to do so (Abel, Becker, and Cunningham-Rathner, 1984; Finkelhor, 1979). There are three types of offenders falling under child pornography laws: those who are physically present with the child when the pictures are taken; those who coax and manipulate a child to send pictures over the internet; and those who have no contact with the child, but view the images for sexual gratification. Although a child victim is involved in each of these cases, the severity of the crime varies. Offenders who are physically present to take the pictures are the most severe type of offender, as there is evidence that the majority (63%) also commit a contact sexual offense when the pictures are taken (i.e. touching, fondling, penetration, or sadistic act) (Wolak *et al.*, 2011) and they are producers of images that are often made available to others. Individuals who only view images produced by others commit a less severe offense as they have not had any sexual contact with the child, although legal sanctions for those in this category are often as severe as for those who produce images and/or commit contact offenses.

Researchers have questioned the distinction being made between different types of child pornography offenders: there are individuals who only look at images of child pornography, but have not in the past nor will go on to commit a contact sexual offense with a child. For example, a study commonly referred to as the "Butner Study" (Bourke and Hernandez, 2009; Hernandez, 2000) suggests viewers of child pornography are likely to have committed a contact sexual offense with a child. Using a prison-based sample, Bourke and Hernandez (2009) found 85% of child pornography viewers self-report previously committing a contact sexual offense with a minor. These offenses were disclosed over the course of a treatment program during their incarceration. What has been called into question is whether self-report offenses disclosed during treatment are ethically derived. A common determination of release from incarceration is successful completion of a treatment program, and treatment programs for those who sexually offend requires offenders to take responsibility for their crimes and to disclose and discuss any unreported offenses (Marshall *et al.*, 2008). To attempt to use a bigger sample with fewer limitations, Seto, Hanson, and Babchishin (2011) conducted a meta-analysis of similar studies to determine whether individuals charged with possessing/viewing child pornography previously had a contact sexual offense, and to determine whether, after they have served their sentence for viewing child pornography, they go on to commit a contact sexual offense with a child. In a sample of 4697 viewers of child pornography, using official records or self-reported measures, 17.3% (n=812) were known to have previously committed a contact sexual offense with an adult or a child—12.2% for studies using official records and 55.1% for studies that involved self-report measures. As reported in the Butner Study, this study also found that the use of self-report measures garners a higher incidence of contact offenses; however, the meta-analysis found the Butner Study to be significantly higher than other studies used in the meta-analysis. This same meta-analysis, using a sample of 1247 viewers of child pornography, determined that 2.0% (n=25) went on to have a future contact sexual offense (Seto *et al.*, 2011). Therefore, it is essential to point out that research evidence does not support the assumption suggesting most viewers of child pornography have committed a contact offense.

Research has shown that child pornography viewers are different to offenders convicted of a contact sexual offense. Another meta-analysis investigated the difference between individuals who viewed child pornography, compared with those whose sexual offense was committed in person (Babchishin, Hanson, and Hermann, 2011). They found viewers of child pornography had greater empathy for their victims, had higher levels of sexual deviancy, and were less likely to present themselves as excessively positive, compared with in-person sexual offenders. These authors suggest that "[m]any of the observed differences can be explained by assuming that online offenders, compared to offline offenders, have greater self-control and more psychological barriers to acting on their deviant interests" (p.92). As a result of these psychological barriers, this study noted that viewers of child pornography may be less likely to seek emotionally connected relationships. The authors reflected on the literature suggesting that there are individuals who avoid emotional closeness in relationships due to experiences in their childhood (Popovic, 2005), or based on their male gender (Buss and Schmitt, 1993). Although differences exist between offenders who view child pornography and those committing contact offenses, both are often given the same label as a sex offender, which triggers the same draconian policies designed to manage them in the community following incarceration and/or probation/parole.

SEX OFFENDER MANAGEMENT POLICIES

Individuals charged and convicted of a sexual offense may vary in the sentences they receive (Crow and Lannes, 2014), but what is likely similar in their case processing by the criminal justice system is their label as a sex offender (called "registrants" in the remainder of this chapter). Once an individual has been designated as a registrant, they are mandated by federal policy to register their personal information and picture with local law enforcement under Sex Offender Registration and Community Notification (SORCN) laws. In many states, the registrant is also required to have the address of their employer also posted on their personal profile. Although an attempt has been made by the federal government to create consistency in registration laws with the Adam Walsh Act in 2006, states still vary in the offenses leading to registration, the personal information that is reported for the individual's registration profile, and how the law is maintained (Lytle, 2015). Thus, some states only require a certain class of registrants to go on the public registry, whereas others go on a private registry. Additionally, some states require juvenile offenders to register, whereas others do not.

In addition to the label as a "sex offender" with the resulting registration and community notification requirements, additional laws are applied to some registered individuals, depending on the crime they committed and/or the state or town where they reside. These laws include: residency restrictions, presence and loitering laws, civil commitment, chemical castration, and other fringe laws. Residency restrictions typically prohibit individuals convicted of sex crimes from residing within 500–2500 feet of schools, parks, playgrounds, day care centers, bus stops, and other places where children are commonly present (Levenson, 2009). These laws have extended to places where registrants can be present, often called "presence or loitering" laws (Bains, 2007), and where they can work.

Civil commitment laws have been implemented in various states across the country, and are intended as an additional containment strategy for those with a mental health diagnosis believed to lead to future sexual reoffense (Harris, 2009). This law allows the justice system to retain individuals in a mental health or correctional facility for a period after their sentence is complete. The additional containment time is designed to provide treatment for their mental illness (Sims and Reynolds, 2007). This additional sentence, after already serving a prison sentence, is often for an indefinite period, and these offenders are released when the treatment providers deem the individual a low risk for reoffense (Harris, 2009; Sims and Reynolds, 2007).

Chemical castration is an additional management strategy given to some offenders upon their release from prison. The goal is to decrease the risk of future sexual offenses by altering the biological and chemical makeup of the offender to decrease sexual arousal (Scott and del Busto, 2009). This procedure is done using chemicals or surgically removing the testicles. Since 1996, at least nine states have had chemical castration laws, all of which vary in the type of offense that requires an offender to receive this additional sanction (Scott and del Busto, 2009).

Fringe laws are less common and are generally found at the county, city, or township levels. For example, some locations in the nation have banned registrants from entering public libraries (Ekblaw, 2010), having access to the internet (Tewksbury and Zgoba, 2010), and being able to participate in Halloween activities (Chaffin *et al.*, 2009). These fringe laws are designed to keep the public safe from registrants who may look for potential victims (i.e. children) in particular locations or on specific days of the year. The multiple laws applied to registrants have severely affected their lives to the point that many court cases have challenged the constitutionality of these laws (see Mancini and Mears, 2013, for a review of federal cases).

COLLATERAL DAMAGE RESULTING FROM SEX OFFENDER MANAGEMENT STRATEGIES

For over a decade, researchers have investigated the collateral damage that is caused by modern sex offender management policies. The impact these laws have on registrants, and those who reside with them, has noted economic, psychological, social, and physical damage resulting from an individual being listed on a public registry. In general, three out of every four registrants (73%) reported that their lives are greatly impacted by having their name and personal information listed on the public registry (Tewksbury and Lees, 2006a).

Collateral Damage for Registrants

Economic Damage

The first study of collateral damage for registrants, conducted by Tewksbury (2005), surveyed 121 registrants in Kentucky. He found that four out of every ten registrants had lost employment (42.7%) and housing (45.3%) because of registration. Additionally, almost a quarter of the sample had been denied a promotion at work (23%). Every follow-up study regarding collateral damage from registration has reported a significant number of registrants who have had negative economic consequences from registration. Reports of difficulties obtaining and maintaining employment (Tewksbury and Lees, 2006b) and loss of employment (Tewksbury and Lees, 2006a) are common.

Studies related to the consequences of residency restrictions (Levenson, 2008) and removal of internet access (Tewksbury and Zgoba, 2010) also find economic hardship for registrants. For residency restrictions, registrants found they often had to move to new homes further away from their place of employment. The cost of moving and the additional travel costs, among other burdens, caused financial hardship (Levenson, 2008). This same study also found difficulties in finding available, affordable housing. Lack of housing was exacerbated for young offenders because many are not allowed to move home with family due to homes being within the prohibited distance from a school or day care (Levenson, 2008). In a study related to registrants who have been banned from using the internet, 42% reported the greatest barrier has been their inability to find and apply for employment (Tewksbury and Zgoba, 2010).

Psychological Damage

Psychological hazards most often reported by registrants are high levels of stress, social isolation and stigmatization, and feelings of vulnerability. A study by Tewksbury and Zgoba (2010) assessed registrants' stress levels using the Perceived Stress Scale (PSS). The sample of 107 registrants in New Jersey showed a moderate level of stress over the entire sample, with an average score of 10 on a scale from 4 to 20. Higher stress scores were reported by individuals who coped with their stress through means of distraction and who had difficulty accepting the sanctions imposed on them due to their status as a registrant (Tewksbury and Zgoba, 2010).

Registrants also commonly report fears and feelings of vulnerability. Tewksbury and Lees (2006b) found in their qualitative study of 22 registrants that many feared being harassed or threatened by members of the public. They also reported they feared being "outed" at work. This population is particularly attuned to the public's view of their status as a registrant, noting that the public sees them as reprehensible and as having little to no value to society (Tewksbury and Lees, 2006b). These feelings of vulnerability and the experiences of harassment have resulted in registrants feeling isolated by society (Tewksbury and Lees, 2006a) and they have self-imposed their own isolation as a means of protection (Tewksbury and Lees, 2006b).

Social Damage

Studies of the collateral damage for registrants find harm to one's personal relationships and social damage coming from the general public. Tewksbury (2005) found that approximately half of registrants had lost a friendship (54.7%). Tewksbury and Lees (2006b) found that many are rejected by a close person in their lives and have difficulties finding a romantic relationship. Tewksbury (2005) also found that almost half experienced harassment by another person (47%). Likewise, four in ten reported being treated rudely in public (39.3%) because of their registration status. Similar to registration requirements, residency restrictions have caused registrants to lose social support networks, as being forced to move out of family homes can lead to a breakdown in support that may have existed if the registrant was allowed to live with or near their family members (Levenson, 2008).

Physical Damage

In rare instances, registrants have been reported as being physically harmed or killed because of their status on the registry. Tewksbury's (2005) study reported that 16% of registrants had been assaulted. There are additional reports of registrants being murdered by vigilantes attempting to seek their own justice outside of law enforcement and the courts (Fenton, 2016). In a study of 109 registrants in an outpatient treatment program, 17% reported becoming homeless because of residency restrictions for an average of 63 days. This same study showed 39% found themselves transient for a few days because of this law (Levenson, 2008). In one instance, a registrant was turned away from emergency shelter in Michigan and died outside in the frigid winter temperatures (Michels, 2009).

Collateral Damage for Family Members

The registry incurs collateral damage not only for registrants but also family members and those living with them at the address posted on the public registry. Family members, both those who reside with the registrant and those who do not, have also experienced economic, psychological, social, and physical damage.

Economic Damage

In an online survey of 584 family members of a registrant, Levenson and Tewksbury (2009) found a majority (82%) of family members of registrants had experienced financial hardship as a direct result of their family including someone on the registry. Comartin, Kernsmith, and Miles (2010) found specifically that having a financially dependent child on the registry was debilitating for family members. One individual in this study reported their child's inability to obtain and maintain employment resulted in the parents drawing all the funds out of their retirement accounts to pay for their child's housing and psychological needs. As previously reported in studies of registrants, family members are also forced to move along with registrants because of residency restrictions. Such moves were reported for one-third (31%) of family members (Tewksbury and Levenson, 2009), and 41% reported difficulties in finding affordable housing once they were forced to move (Levenson and Tewksbury, 2009).

Psychological Damage

As a result of having a family member on the public registry, a majority of family members (68%) report "very frequently experiencing stress" (Tewksbury and Levenson, 2009). In addition, family members report feelings of loneliness and isolation (Comartin *et al.*, 2010; Tewksbury and Levenson, 2009) as they experience the indirect feelings of shame the registrant faces. Tewksbury and Levenson (2009) also found high levels of stress, as measured by the PSS. Family members who live with a registrant have PSS scores more than double (average of 10.6) those found in the general public (average of 4.5). Reports of greater feelings of isolation, feelings of shame, and fear for their safety were likely to increase the PSS score for family members who lived with a registrant. Along with feelings of stress, parents reported feelings of fear and paranoia that their child would become non-compliant with registration requirements (which would lead to a felony charge) and may be falsely accused of another crime (Comartin *et al.*, 2010). These parents felt a persistent struggle to move forward with their lives, as their child's registration status was an overarching label on the family. Parents also reported feelings of powerlessness as their child's case went through the criminal justice process. This led parents to do all they could to protect their child. Parents reported going to a local high school after their child graduated to take down paper postings of their child's registration profile. Additionally, parents also reported attending their child's meetings with law enforcement officials to protect them from becoming non-compliant in their status (Comartin *et al.*, 2010).

Being the child of a registrant is also likely to cause psychological issues; Levenson and Tewksbury's (2009) study reported approximately three out of four children suffered from depression (74%), anxiety (73%), and anger (80%) due to having a parent on the sex offender registry.

Social Damage

The social hazards reported by family members are similar to those reported by registrants. Just under half (44%) of all family members of registrants report being harassed or threatened (Levenson and Tewksbury, 2009) and more than half reported the loss of a close relationship (Tewksbury and Levenson, 2009). Residency restrictions have also forced registrants and their family members to relocate to communities experiencing higher rates of social disorganization (areas with higher crime, poverty, etc.) (Burchfield and Mingus, 2008). These moves are generally accompanied by fewer social supports and community protection services (Tewksbury and Levenson, 2009).

Comartin *et al.* (2010) report that the impact of a family member's registration status extends to siblings and grandparents. Siblings often had feelings of resentment about the time, energy, and money spent on their sibling's court case and compliance with registration laws. Grandparents were reported as either becoming an advocate in the cause to help lessen the laws' impact on their grandchild, or refusing any discussion about their grandchild's registration status as a result of their shame. Children of registrants have also experienced social hazards from their parent's registration status. They have had classmates and teachers treat them differently, 78% report having their friendships impacted in some way, and over half have been teased and ridiculed by peers. Finally, three out of four children were not able to have their parents participate in their school activities because of their status (Levenson and Tewksbury, 2009).

Physical Damage

As with registrants themselves, physical hazards for family members are also rare. However, 7% of family members reported being assaulted because of a family member's registration status (Levenson and Tewksbury, 2009). In addition, the Associated Press (2007) reported on a story where two neighbors tried to scare a registrant out of their community by setting his house on fire. The registrant escaped from the flames; his wife, however, did not survive the fire.

The management policies designed to protect the public from individuals who commit sexual violence have good intentions; however, when applying these requirements to individuals who are convicted of solely viewing child pornography, it appears the punishment does not fit the crime, especially when one considers the collateral damage done to the registrant and their family members. The collateral damage of registration is particularly disturbing when these management policies are misapplied to individuals diagnosed with Asperger's syndrome.

CHARACTERISTICS OF INDIVIDUALS
WITH ASPERGER'S SYNDROME

Asperger's syndrome (AS) is a developmental diagnosis related to an individual's brain functioning (Khouzam *et al.*, 2004). The diagnosis, once separate but linked with autism in the *Diagnostic and Statistical Manual of Mental Disorders* (DSM), has now been combined on a continuum of related features, known as the autism spectrum disorder (ASD) (Happe, 2011). The hallmark characteristic of both disorders is the high level of social impairment for the individual (Khouzam *et al.*, 2004). It has been emphasized that ASD is not a diagnosis of social pathology. Individuals diagnosed with a spectrum disorder do not have features of callousness or maliciousness found in antisocial disorders or personality disorders, but there is a true developmental delay impairing their ability to understand and interpret social cues, as well as understanding socially acceptable behaviors and social norms. Two additional diagnostic features shared by ASD and AS are repetitive behaviors and intense and restricted interests. There are also two features generally not found in individuals diagnosed with AS, but commonly found in individuals diagnosed with ASD: delays in language development and lower cognitive capabilities (Mesibov and Shea, 2001).

Social impairments in individuals with AS are particularly important to consider when thinking about the way they interpret potentially criminal behavior, and in the way they deal with the consequences of sex offender management policies. Thus, a description of these features of the diagnosis are important. AS causes a delay in the individual's ability to understand others' needs, perspectives, and feelings. This is commonly noted as a lack of empathy on the part of someone with AS (Roth and Gillis, 2015). Generally, when noting that an individual lacks empathy, society commonly construes this as antisocial behavior, in that it is malicious in nature. For individuals with AS it is a function of their diagnosis, not antisocial. Clinical criteria suggest individuals with AS do not see, and cannot accurately interpret, social cues. They are not skilled in reading others' facial expressions, body language, or reactions (Mahoney, 2009). They also fail to appreciate socially acceptable behavior and social norms. For example, they do not understand that a lack of response from a message sent to a love interest means they do not want to continue a relationship. Finally, individuals with ASD are delayed in their social and emotional development, causing them to act and appear younger than their age. Their intense interests and repetitive behaviors cause them to be perceived by their peers as outcasts.

A defining difference between individuals with AS not commonly found for others diagnosed with ASD is their desire for social interaction. Both have deficits in this area; however, individuals with AS desire friendships and romantic relationships, whereas individuals with ASD generally do not desire social interaction (Mahoney, 2009). Since individuals with AS want and desire social interaction, but are isolated and shunned, they commonly experience depression because they do not have the skills to acquire such relationships (Whitehouse et al., 2009). A final AS characteristic is the lack of expressive use of language and the inability to carry out a conversation that is reciprocal in nature (Mahoney, 2009). Although their language skills are not delayed, the way they use language to communicate is concrete and explicit. Due to their repetitive and intensely focused interests, they are likely to dominate a conversation by discussing only the things they are interested in while leaving no time for what others wish to talk about. The social isolation they feel, combined with the social interaction they desire, leads many individuals with AS to turn to the computer for social relationships.

Although research has found individuals with AS to be more likely to be victims of crimes due to their social naivety (Sevlever, Roth, and Gillis, 2013), research has also checked to see if the clinical attributes of AS are linked to criminal offending. The most commonly reported form of perpetration is stalking, and some research has discussed public displays of sexually inappropriate behavior (i.e. masturbation) and, in more rare cases, sexual assaults (Allen and Evans, 2007; Haskins and Silva, 2006; Kalyva, 2010; Ruble and Dalrymple, 1993; Sevlever et al., 2013; Van Bourgondien and Reichle, 1997). These studies highlight the features of AS that are likely to be the cause of sexual offending. "Some have suggested that the lack of empathy characteristic of ASD, sexual frustration, a tendency to exhibit private sexual behavior in public (e.g., masturbation), intense interests in other individuals, and sexual preoccupations could potentially be contributing factors to victimizing behavior" (Roth and Gillis, 2015, p.135). Others have also noted that issues with impulse control, inability to pick up on social cues of sexual disinterest, and deficits in social-emotional reciprocity are further contributing factors to sexual offending (Sevlever et al., 2013).

Although there are reports of individuals with AS concurrently having a paraphilia diagnosis, instances of child sexual abuse in this population is rare (Tantam, 2003).

Recent investigations have reported individuals with AS being criminally charged for viewing child pornography. In the general population of sex offenders, those who offend by viewing child pornography have been shown to have greater self-control and more psychological barriers to acting on their deviant interests, and likely commit these offenses to "avoid emotional closeness in sexual relationships" (Babchishin et al., 2011, p.109). It can be argued in the case of individuals diagnosed with AS that it is likely not an avoidance of emotional closeness, but one of the only locations where they are able to access sexual relationships. Since the social world often excludes individuals with AS, these individuals are even more likely to turn to the internet to find relationships and explore their sexuality. Roth and Gillis (2015) studied the use of online dating services by individuals diagnosed with AS, and they note online dating offers a safe space to engage in romantic relationships. The appeal is that there are "fewer social demands than traditional face-to-face dating (e.g. eye contact), fewer nonverbal communication interpretation (e.g. body language), more time to process information, more control over self-presentation, and a slower pace of communication" (Nichols, 2009, p.285). However, the exploration of their sexuality may cause them to commit sexual crimes they likely do not understand to be offensive in nature. Mahoney (2009, p.1) writes about individuals diagnosed with AS who have been charged for viewing child pornography:

> Their curiosity, unrestrained by social or legal taboos, of which they are unaware, leads them to view images of "underage" (i.e., younger than 18-years old) girls who are nearly their own age and years older than the level of their own social adaptation skills.

This author further notes that the obsessional quality of their diagnosis may lead them to collect many images. Furthermore, individuals with AS take the world at face value, and thus they may believe that images of children are legal because they are easy to obtain. They have little understanding that one type of image (i.e. children) is more reprehensible than a similar image (i.e. adult) (Mahoney, 2009). Individuals diagnosed with AS have social impairments and characteristics that likely lead them to viewing child pornography without any malicious intent. Once they are charged with a sexual offense, the same collateral damage that results for non-diagnosed registrants is likely to happen to them as well; however, these individuals and their families are likely to experience an even greater cumulative impact than that experienced by registrants without the additional barriers of those diagnosed with AS.

COLLATERAL DAMAGE OF SEX OFFENDER MANAGEMENT POLICIES FOR INDIVIDUALS WITH ASPERGER'S SYNDROME AND THEIR FAMILY MEMBERS

Sex offender management policies were instituted across the country in the 1990s, requiring individuals charged with a sexual offense to periodically register their personal information and a picture with law enforcement. This information is then made available to the public for their use in protecting themselves from individuals who have committed sexual offenses. Law enforcement agencies then take steps to verify that the information the registrant provides is accurate. This is done through the mail or in face-to-face checks at the reported address (Center for Sex Offender Management, 1999). In addition to registration requirements, many jurisdictions additionally require offenders to comply with residency restrictions, presence and loitering laws, and other fringe laws.

As previously discussed, there are many kinds of harmful collateral damage resulting for individuals listed on the public registry and who are subject to residency restrictions. There are rare instances of physical damage, such as assault and murder. The social damage of public shaming, isolation, and ostracism by friends and the general public are far more pervasive. There is also psychological damage in the form of fear and feelings of vulnerability. Finally, there is likely to be economic damage related to employment and housing.

There is likely to be a greater cumulative impact of these different types of collateral damage for individuals diagnosed with AS who are required to register because they viewed child pornography. These individuals are already perceived by their peers as outcasts because of their awkward presentation and lack of social skills. As previously noted, they often desire social relationships but are unable to achieve them, which can often lead to depression and anxiety. Their additional status as a registrant is likely to keep them as an outcast in society, and will cause public shaming and ostracism, which will further exacerbate the severity of their depression and isolation.

In addition to their isolation, there are further problems resulting from the law enforcement registration verification processes. Individuals diagnosed with AS are known to successfully cope with their diagnosis by having daily routines (Henderson *et al.*, 2011). When these routines are interrupted, there can be resulting difficulties (Mahoney, 2009). Thus, when law enforcement stops by the home of a registrant unexpectedly, it can cause psychological harm because of the fear they experience as a registrant, in addition to the change in routine. This combination is likely to cause complications for their mental health. In addition, the fear and vulnerability they experience as a registrant along with obsessional preoccupation could result in a downward spiral into severe mental illness. Residency restrictions have caused registrants to move from their family's home, which is a barrier to the much-needed social support for both registrants and individuals diagnosed with AS. Some individuals with AS are incapable of living on their own due to financial concerns or because of their symptoms. The diagnosis alone causes barriers to employment, as they often have trouble during the interview process. For those who successfully obtain and maintain employment, once they become a registrant they are likely to have complications in this area of their lives. Sex offender management policies prohibiting a registrant from living in a home where a child resides could destabilize an individual with AS who is dependent on their family for daily living.

Family members of individuals with AS are not only financially burdened, but they also are psychologically tasked, as they often spend a considerable amount of time teaching their children social mores and interpersonal skills, and assisting them in their daily routines (Karst and Van Hecke, 2012). The social difficulties, dependence in daily activities, and need for long-term care of their children has been shown to significantly increase the level of distress experienced by parents of children with AS. Being a parent of a child diagnosed with AS is also related to having a negative outlook on life (Karst and Van Hecke, 2012) and to feeling less confident in one's ability to be a successful parent (Jones and Prinz, 2005). What results is an increase in mental and physical illnesses (Ekas, Lickenbrock, and Whitman, 2010) and higher rates of divorce (Freedman *et al.*, 2012) for parents of children with AS, compared with parents of children with developmental disabilities and those of neurotypical children. Thus, these families are already vulnerable due to their family member's diagnosis.

Research has shown that having a strong social support network can mitigate the stress levels that result from having a child on the spectrum (Ingersoll and Hambrick, 2011). In addition, community and social service supports have also been shown to decrease distress, reduce depression rates, and increase confidence in one's parenting (Weiss, 2002). When an individual with AS becomes a registrant, it can further exacerbate the already fragile nature of the person's family. Parents are already over-extended psychologically and financially by the nature of their child's diagnosis. Compound these burdens with the physical, psychological, social, and economic hazards experienced by family members of a registrant, and what results is a potentially immobilizing situation. These specific families need social support, yet the registration status causes people to ostracize not only the offender but their family members as well. These parents are also in need of social services and community supports to help manage their children's AS symptoms, yet the family member's label as a sex offender removes them from access to services that have daycare or a school. These two identities, when combined, cause considerable cumulative damage to both the individual with AS and their family members.

CONCLUSION

Societies have a responsibility to protect children from sexual exploitation, and therefore policies that sanction individuals for creating, distributing, and viewing child pornography are needed. While the sanctions for these crimes should be harsh enough to deter individuals from committing such acts, they should also be proportional to the crime committed. Non-contact offenses are not as severe as sexual offenses that include contact with a child, even if the law and mandatory sentencing guidelines do not reflect this reality. Although there has been debate about the likelihood that individuals charged with child pornography have committed a contact offense, a rigorous study showed that recidivism rates for individuals charged with child pornography are "substantially lower" than the recidivism rates of contact offenders (Seto *et al.*, 2011, p.137). These lower rates of additional sex crimes for individuals who viewed child pornography suggests that the strategies used to manage these individuals in the community can be less stringent than those that should be considered for individuals who commit contact offenses, especially when considering the economic, social, psychological, and physical damage caused for the registrant and their family members.

Furthermore, there must be special considerations made when an individual with AS has been viewing images of child pornography. The clinical criteria that classify someone with AS may lead law enforcement officials to misjudge their behaviors as malicious and sexually deviant, when they are likely attempting to explore their sexuality in a space they have been banished to or that makes them most comfortable. The criminal justice system needs to train and inform law enforcement on the "intent" behind the AS individual's behavior. Sex offender management policies were designed to deter individuals from offending, and seeks punishment for individuals who are trying to satisfy their sexual needs without concern for the victim's needs. The intent behind inappropriate sexual behavior for an individual with AS is likely not driven by a need for sexual gratification, but by a need for social interaction and sexual exploration. Education of this disorder is needed across all levels of the criminal justice system. Systems for appropriate referrals to psycho-social treatment groups should be how an individual with AS is diverted out of the criminal justice system.

If an individual with AS is charged with viewing child pornography, the current system is likely to subject them to time in prison, and upon their return to the community, they are likely required to register on the public sex offender registry. In addition, they may also be subject to residency restrictions and the other fringe laws previously discussed. These individuals are, in most cases, not a threat to individuals in their lives or to society. Taking the punitive/criminal route in these cases is harmful and malicious to the vulnerable individual with AS and makes their families suffer. The cumulative impact that results from being both a registrant and an individual with AS is detrimental for these individuals and their family members. Individually, both labels lead to hardship, but, when combined, the difficulties faced by the family supporting the registrant can be insurmountable. This special population needs compassion and support, not punishment.

Instead of harsh sanctions, it is suggested that a psychoeducational session be offered to individuals with AS with first-time charges of viewing child pornography. This educational session should go above the normal sexual education offered to deter unwanted pregnancies or sexually transmitted diseases and infections, and must spend a great deal of time explaining the different physical characteristics of children so they can discern child pornography from adult pornography. Additionally, this intervention should also explicitly explain why it is exploitive to view an image of a child, as opposed to pornography featuring adults. A presentation on consent and the specific laws that govern sexuality must be explicitly noted. Finally, in-depth discussions about social cues and norms governing sexual behavior must be outlined with great detail. As Mahoney (2009) writes, "The unspoken language of dating and sexuality is incredibly difficult for AS teens, and even adults, to read" (p.36). Once rules are explained and verbal and social cues are understood, AS individuals are quite likely to abide by the rules, as they are known to be reliable due to the rigidity commonly found with the diagnosis (Mahoney, 2009).

REFERENCES

Abel, G., Becker, J., and Cunningham-Rathner, J. (1984) "Complications, consent, and cognitions in sex between children and adults." *International Journal of Law and Psychiatry 7*, 1, 89–103.

Allen, D. and Evans, C. (2007) "Offending behaviour in adults with Asperger syndrome." *Journal of Autism Developmental Disorder 38*, 4, 748–758.

Associated Press (2007) "Police: Vigilante justice led to unintended death." *NBC News*, September 14, 2007. Available at www.nbcnews.com/id/20780983#.Vpafw0ZTeto (accessed January 20, 2017).

Babchishin, K., Hanson, R., and Hermann, C. (2011) "The characteristics of online sex offenders: A meta-analysis." *Sexual Abuse: A Journal of Research and Treatment 23*, 1, 92–123.

Bains, C. (2007) "Next-generation sex offender statutes: Constitutional challenges to residency, work, and loitering restrictions." *Harvard Civil Rights–Civil Liberties Law Review 42*, 483.

Bourke, M. and Hernandez, A. (2009) "The 'Butner Study' Redux: A report of the incidence of hands-on child victimization by child pornography offenders." *Journal of Family Violence 24*, 183–191.

Burchfield, K.B. and Mingus, W. (2008) "Not in my neighborhood: Assessing registered sex offenders' experiences with local social capital and social control." *Criminal Justice and Behavior 35*, 3, 356–374.

Buss, D. and Schmitt, D. (1993) "Sexual strategy theory: An evolution perspective on human mating." *Psychology Review 100*, 204–232.

Center for Sex Offender Management (CSOM) (1999) "Sex offender registration: Policy overview and comprehensive practices." Available at www.csom.org/pubs/sexreg.html (accessed January 20, 2017).

Chaffin, M., Levenson, J., Letourneau, E., and Stern, P. (2009) "How safe are trick-or-treaters? An analysis of child sex crime rates on Halloween." *Sexual Abuse: A Journal of Research and Treatment 21*, 3, 363–374.

Comartin, E., Kernsmith, P., and Miles, B. (2010) "Family experiences of young adult sex offender registration." *Journal of Child Sexual Abuse 19*, 2, 204–225.

Crow, M. and Lannes, P. (2015) "Risk, proportionality, and sentencing: Guideline circumvention in federal child pornography and sexual abuse cases." *Criminal Justice Policy Review 26*, 6, 575–597.

Ekas, N., Lickenbrock, D., and Whitman, T. (2010) "Optimism, social support, and well-being in mothers of children with autism spectrum disorder." *Journal of Autism and Developmental Disorders* 40, 1274–1284.

Ekblaw, J. (2010) "Not in my library: An examination of state and local bans of sex offenders from public libraries." *Indiana Law Review 44*, 919–956.

Fenton, J. (2016) "'Vigilante justice' leads to prison time in fatal beating of sex offender." *The Baltimore Sun*, January 13, 2016. Available at www.baltimoresun.com/news/maryland/crime/bs-md-ci-vigilante-justice-sentencing-20141030-story.html (accessed January 20, 2017).

Finkelhor, D. (1979) "What's wrong with sex between adults and children? Ethics and the problem of sexual abuse." *American Journal of Orthopsychiatry 49*, 4, 692–697.

Freedman, B., Kalb, L., Zaboltsky, B., and Stuart, E. (2012) "Relationship status among parents of children with autism spectrum disorders: A population-based study." *Journal of Autism and Developmental Disorders 42*, 539–548.

Happe, F. (2011) "Criteria, categories, and continua: Autism and related disorders in DSM-5." *Journal of the American Academy of Child and Adolescent Psychiatry 50*, 6, 540–542.

Harris, A. (2009) "The Civil Commitment of Sexual Predators: A Policy Review.' In R. Wright (ed.) *Sex Offender Laws: Failed Policies, New Directions*. New York, NY: Springer Publishing.

Haskins, B. and Silva, J. (2006) "Asperger's disorder and criminal behavior: Forensic-psychiatric considerations." *Journal of the American Academy of Psychiatry and Law 34*, 3, 374–384.

Henderson, J., Barry, T., Bader, S., and Jordan, S. (2011) "The relation among sleep, routines, and externalizing behavior in children with an autism spectrum disorder." *Research in Autism Spectrum Disorders 5*, 2, 758–767.

Hernandez, A. (2000) "Self-reported contact sexual offenses by participants in the Federal Bureau of Prisons Sex Offender Treatment Program: Implications for internet sex offenders." Poster session presented at the 14th Annual Research and Treatment Conference of the Association for the Treatment of Sexual Abusers, San Diego, CA.

Ingersoll, B. and Hambrick, D. (2011) "The relationship between the broader autism phenotype, child severity, and stress and depression in parents and children with autism spectrum disorders." *Research in Autism Spectrum Disorders 5*, 337–344.

Jones, T. and Prinz, R. (2005) "Potential roles of parental self-efficacy in parent and child adjustment: A review." *Clinical Psychology Review 25*, 3, 341–363.

Kalyva, E. (2010) "Teachers' perspectives of the sexuality of children with autism spectrum disorders." *Research on Autism Spectrum Disorders 4*, 3, 433–437.

Karst, J. and Van Hecke, A.V. (2012) "Parent and family impact of autism spectrum disorders: A review and proposed model for intervention evaluation." *Clinical Child Family Psychological Review 15*, 247–277.

Khouzam, H., El-Gabalawi, F., Pirwani, N., and Priest, F. (2004) "Asperger's disorder: A review of its diagnosis and treatment." *Comprehensive Psychiatry 45*, 3, 184–191.

Levenson, J. (2008) "Collateral consequences of sex offender residence restrictions." *Criminal Justice Studies 21*, 2, 153–166.

Levenson, J. (2009) "Sex Offender Residence Restrictions." In R. Wright (ed.) *Sex Offender Laws: Failed Policies, New Directions*. New York, NY: Springer Publishing.

Levenson, J. and Tewksbury, R. (2009) "Collateral damage: Family members of registered sex offenders." *American Journal of Criminal Justice 34*, 54–68.

Lytle, R. (2015) "Variation in criminal justice policy-making: An exploratory study using sex offender registration and community notification laws." *Criminal Justice Policy Review 26*, 3, 211–233.

Mahoney, M. (2009) "Asperger's syndrome and criminal law: The special case of child pornography." Available at www.harringtonmahoney.com/content/Publications/Aspergers%20Syndrome%20and%20the%20Criminal%20Law%20v26.pdf (accessed January 12, 2017).

Mancini, C. and Mears, D. (2013) "US Supreme Court decisions and sex offender legislation: Evidence of evidence-based policy." *Journal of Criminal Law and Criminology 103*, 4, 1115–1154.

Marshall, W., Marshall, L., Serran, G., and O'Brien, M. (2008) "Sexual offender treatment: A positive approach." *Psychiatry Clinics in North America 31*, 681–696.

Mesibov, G. and Shea, V. (2001) *Understanding Asperger Syndrome and High Functioning Autism*. New York, NY: Kluwer Academic/Plenum Publishers.

Michels, S. (2009) "Sex offender dies in cold after being denied from shelter." *ABC News*, January 30, 2009. Available at http://abcnews.go.com/TheLaw/story?id=6769453 (accessed January 20, 2017).

Nichols, S. (2009) *Girls Growing Up on the Autism Spectrum: What Parents and Professionals Should Know about the Pre-Teen and Teenage Years.* London: Jessica Kingsley Publishers.

Popovic, M. (2005) "Intimacy and its relevance in human functioning." *Sexual and Relationship Therapy 20*, 31–49.

Roth, M. and Gillis, J. (2015) "'Convenience with the click of a mouse': A survey of adults with autism spectrum disorder on online dating." *Sexual Disability 33*, 133–150.

Ruble, L. and Dalrymple, J. (1993) "Social/sexual awareness of persons with autism: A parental perspective." *Archives of Sexual Behavior 22*, 3, 229–240.

Scott, C. and del Busto, E. (2009) "Chemical and Surgical Castration." In R. Wright (ed.) *Sex Offender Laws: Failed Policies, New Directions.* New York, NY: Springer Publishing.

Seto, M., Hanson, R., and Babchishin, K. (2011) "Contact sexual offending by men with online sexual offenses." *Sexual Abuse: A Journal of Research and Treatment 23*, 1, 124–145.

Sevlever, M., Roth, M., and Gillis, J. (2013) "Sexual abuse and offending in autism spectrum disorders." *Sexual Disability 31*, 189–200.

Sims, B. and Reynolds, M. (2007) 'Sex Offender Registration, Notification, and Civil Commitment Statutes: Due Process vs. Community Safety.' In C. Hemmens (ed.) *Current Legal Issues in Criminal Justice.* Los Angeles, CA: Roxbury.

Tantam, D. (2003) "The challenge of adolescents and adults with Asperger's syndrome." *Child Adolescent Psychiatry Clinics of North America 143*, 147.

Terry, K. and Ackerman, A. (2009) "A Brief History of Major Sex Offender Laws." In R. Wright (ed.) *Sex Offender Laws: Failed Policies, New Directions.* New York, NY: Springer Publishing.

Tewksbury, R. (2005) "Collateral consequences of sex offender registration." *Journal of Contemporary Criminal Justice 21*, 67–81.

Tewksbury, R. and Lees, M. (2006a) "Sex offenders on campus: University-based sex offender registries and the collateral consequences of registration." *Federal Probation 70*, 3, 50–56.

Tewksbury, R. and Lees, M. (2006b) "Perceptions of sex offender registration: Collateral consequences and community experiences." *Sociological Spectrum 26*, 309–334.

Tewksbury, R. and Levenson, J. (2009) "Stress experiences of family members of registered sex offenders." *Behavioral Sciences and the Law 27*, 611–626.

Tewksbury, R. and Zgoba, K. (2010) "Perceptions and coping with punishment: How registered sex offenders respond to stress, internet restrictions, and the collateral consequences of registration." *International Journal of Offender Therapy and Comparative Criminology 54*, 4, 537–551.

Van Bourgondien, E. and Reichle, C. (1997) "Sexual behavior in adults with autism." *Journal of Autism and Developmental Disorders 27*, 113–125.

Weiss, M. (2002) "Hardiness and social support as predictors of stress in mothers of typical children, children with autism, and children with mental retardation." *Autism 6*, 1, 115–130.

Whitehouse, A., Durkin, K., Jaquet, E., and Ziatas, K. (2009) "Friendship, loneliness and depression in adolescents with Asperger's syndrome." *Journal of Adolescence 32*, 2, 309–322.

Wolak, J., Finkelhor, D., Mitchell, K., and Jones, L. (2011) "Arrests for child pornography production: Data at two time points from a national sample of U.S. law enforcement agencies." *Child Maltreatment 16*, 3, 184–195.

CHAPTER 10

An Alternative Universe

The Perspective of an Autistic Registrant

Nick Dubin

I am the only non-academic participant writing a chapter for this book. My dad approached me and asked if I would write a chapter about my experiences on the sex offender registry as an individual on the autism spectrum. Part of this chapter will address this new facet of my life. I will address both how the registry has impacted me and what Asperger's has done to magnify the impact. But I also feel obliged to address a larger issue that I believe makes the sex offender registry not only unconstitutional but a travesty of justice. The collateral consequences of the registry that are inflicted upon family members including spouses and children are medieval, while doing nothing to protect the public from sexual predators.

I don't condone the sexual abuse of children. I abhor child abuse, period. I can never bring myself to account for downloading child pornography in adequate speaking terms. I won't defend it and I can never justify it. But it does not make me someone who would hurt children directly and I greatly resent my own government saying that it does. One of the things that I had a very hard time getting used to after my arrest was the leap in logic that people made between what I did in looking at child pornography and their assumptions about me that I would directly hurt a child. I couldn't wrap my mind around it. To be viewed as a child molester is so alien a concept for me that I felt trapped in an alternative universe, and I still do. To hurt a child would go against every fiber of my being. It would be like abusing my own dog or any dog—a wholly unthinkable act. I have special contempt for sexual abusers of children, particularly because I know that autistic children are a vulnerable target. Many autistic children do not have the communication skills or the pragmatic awareness necessary to know what is happening to them and therefore cannot speak up against their abusers. I personally believe the full weight of the law should be brought to bear against someone who would actually sexually abuse a child. The criminal justice system should treat these people very harshly for the irreparable damage they will have inevitably caused their victims. At the same time, learning about the registry has made it clear that even those who harm children should not be placed on a sex offender registry after they have completed their prison sentences.

I believe that, if positive change is ever to be effectuated with regard to the registry, it will be because people see how it negatively impacts entire communities, not just individual registrants who might happen to be on the autism spectrum. Frankly, the average citizen doesn't care much about how the registry affects registrants. In most people's eyes, registrants are subhuman and unworthy of critical attention. The average citizen might care, though, if he or she understands how the families and children of registrants have the ground ripped out from underneath their feet because of this recent invention of the United States Government called the sex offender registry.

How has my family been affected? I'll never forget the look on my father's face on the day of my arraignment. In the courtroom, he hung his head low and wore sunglasses so as to not be recognized by fellow lawyers or reporters from the media. For a man who normally exudes supreme confidence in himself, I had never seen him so shaken to the core in my life. The first semester following my arrest, he barely spoke to any of his colleagues at school where he teaches for fear that they may be aware of our family secret. One day he left a textbook on top of his car and drove off, a textbook that contained all of the notes he had compiled over the years. He never found it. My mom fell and broke a toe in the midst of an emotional breakdown shortly after my arrest. She ran a stop sign and broke down emotionally when the officer approached her…so much so that the officer had to call for the city chaplain to come to the scene. For years, my parents hid in the shadows. However, unlike most people, they have started speaking out after seeing the way the criminal justice system treats those with Asperger's as well as those convicted of sex offenses. This is not typical of most family members who are in the situation my parents are in, and for this they should be given a tremendous amount of credit. Most family members try to avoid talking about what happened to their son or husband out of great shame, humiliation, and embarrassment.

Many family members are harassed or fired from jobs because of their familial relationship with the sex offender. The registry causes many divorces and family breakups where children never see their fathers again. We are lucky because the three of us are still together, intact. Many are not that fortunate.

Make no mistake, registrants' lives are ruined once they are placed on the registry. Terrorists and sex offenders are the two most hated and feared groups of people in the United States. Speaking for myself, being placed on the sex offender registry has ruined the life I had prior to my conviction. I have been put into a subhuman classification. I would feel the exact same way if my government labeled me a terrorist and people believed this was true because the government said so. All of my life, I have lived as a law-abiding person. At worst, I had a speeding ticket. My respect for the law matched that of your most upstanding citizen in the community. Once I was put on the sex offender registry, though, I have been continually reminded about how I am viewed as dangerous and different and corrupt, which gives my life an air of surrealism. Other states have actually refused to allow me there to vacation for a few days even with the assurance that my parents would be with me at all times. Florida gave the reason that, because I planned on playing tennis with another adult and tennis courts are a place where children congregate, they did not want to take the chance of having me in that setting. Imagine that. Arizona flat out denied my request with no explanation whatsoever. Traveling anywhere requires notifying the municipality you are visiting of your presence in the community. In other words, wherever you go, you must register as a sex offender while you are there. In Florida, after you leave the state, you remain on their registry for life and even one year after becoming deceased. It doesn't seem very likely that a sex offender could do much harm once deceased, but as I have come to learn over the past six years, these laws have nothing to do with logic.

My dad and I have had many conversations about the logic or lack of logic of these laws. Having autism tends to make me perseverate on the fact that the government has defined me as a sex offender, and therefore this is who I am. It is very hard for me to simply play a game of tennis, watch a movie, or enjoy any recreational activities without focusing on the fact that this horrible label applies to me and I have no redress or recourse to change the situation. My dad will simply tell me that the law is often not logical. He has said that in order to live with some semblance of peace for the rest of my life, I have to accept the illogical nature of what has happened. He has to continually remind me of my true nature: a flawed human being, who has made mistakes, certainly, but not a bad person unworthy of respect or acceptance. Realizing my true nature in the midst of being labeled something terrible is a harder task for me than one might realize. It is hard for me to accept that something "not true" could be not only accepted as fact by the public but decreed as "fact" by the United States Government. Even though I know I have never hurt another human being and most certainly not a child, because the government has labeled me predator, I walk around with a complete sense of shame about myself. My father and my therapist have been working hard with me to help me adapt a way of thinking about myself that rejects the label that the government has given me.

This isn't so easy. Let me provide an example of what I am referring to. I have lived in a variety of places by myself. In every apartment complex I have lived in prior to where I am living now, I have had friendly neighbors. They all reciprocated my hellos with smiles to match, wanted to pet my dog as I was walking her, and would engage in chit-chat. My current neighbors are the opposite. They avoid making eye contact with me, barely acknowledge my presence, and occasionally have been nasty towards me. One day as I was pulling out of my parking space, a neighbor told me to "f myself." Prior to being on the registry, I have never been subjected to that kind of unprovoked abuse from any neighbor in my life.

How is a person with Asperger's supposed to understand this alternative universe which seems so unreal? Being autistic presents me with a huge challenge in this regard. I can either completely turn inward, thus becoming even more isolated than I was before my arrest, or I can resist the way society has unfairly defined my identity by my malleable and impressionable mind. In other words, I have to balance out safety and security versus the constant fear of being rejected. Because I admit I'm malleable and impressionable, engagement with the world is extremely risky for me. Both choices are bad. Since engagement requires risk, and risk can easily backfire when one is on the sex offender registry, I have taken the path of least resistance in most situations. But here's a real-life example of someone both on the spectrum and the sex offender registry who has taken a more courageous path by engaging with the world.

The other day I was in the room when my dad received a phone call. It was from a young man with Asperger's syndrome who lives in Oregon. Many years ago he was convicted of possession of child pornography in his home state of Florida and he moved to the Pacific Northwest after he got out of prison to try to make a fresh start for himself. On this particular evening, this young man was in a horrible state of mind. He had finally made a new friend but this other person somehow found out about his status as a sex offender and wanted nothing to do with him. After a lonely childhood, a lifetime of struggling to make friends, and then an exile to Oregon in the hopes of a new start, this young man took a risk in engaging with the world. He hoped to make a friend and have that person see past the label that the government assigned him. When that didn't happen, his malleable mind convinced himself that he was as worthless as the government proclaimed him to be because the actions of this so-called "friend" reinforced this position. This same person tried joining two synagogues in Oregon, and when the rabbis of each temple found out about his sex offender status, he was told he was not welcome in either place of worship.

This social banishment that is all too often felt among individuals who are on the sex offender registry is magnified for me. I will be the first person to admit that I sometimes view my life through a black-or-white lens with very few shades of gray that can cause exaggerated thinking. This is, of course, a classic characteristic of Asperger's. This black-and-white thinking has caused me to believe that everyone hates me, even when some don't. I have avoided large family gatherings for fear that there would be extended family there who would judge me negatively. I feverishly try to avoid making eye contact with someone who might recognize me in public. After my arrest went viral on Asperger websites six years ago, I rarely left the house. When I did, I wore sunglasses and a cap. This feeling of unease that I have when I am in public has not abated much in six years. Perhaps it never will, though I am still working on it.

As to the man in Oregon, I can well relate to his tribulations. I commend him for taking the risks he took that would have been harder for me to take. As has been previously stated, I have taken a more passive path of least resistance because I don't want to go through the rejection and sorrow that he faced when being turned away from synagogues and having friends desert him. This man is not alone in the rejection he feels from society.

Consider the reality of what life is like for the typical sex offender. Sex offenders are routinely harassed in their communities, denied work and housing, and even forced out of homeless shelters and left to die on the streets in freezing cold temperatures. Some are murdered out of cold blood by vigilantes (just Google the name "Stephen Marshall" for an example of this). Depending on the state, many registrants are not allowed in libraries, schools where they have biological children attending, movie theaters, zoos, fast food restaurants with play structures, and other common places. These places where sex offenders are not allowed to be at are called "presence restrictions" in legal terms, which has an Orwellian ring to it. The government of the United States recently passed a law known as International Megan's Law, mandating that every sex offender must have his passport marked with the insignia "sex offender," which was signed into law by President Barack Obama. Need I remind the reader that there once was a country in the mid-twentieth century during the Second World War that forced Jews from all over Europe to walk around with marked identification meant to label them as inferior? We all know that experiment did not turn out so well. Most foreign countries today deny entry to sex offenders. Even when an offender gets off their probation or supervised release, they have to give the State Department 21 days' notice of their travels so the State Department can let that country know that a sex offender will be trying to gain entry. On Halloween in some municipalities, offenders have to report to their local sheriff's offices and remain detained until trick-or-treating hours are over. Some states such as Texas designate that an offender place a sign on his yard notifying the community of his presence as a sex offender. Others require the offender himself to go door-to-door and explain to families that he is a sex offender living in the neighborhood. In other localities, where it is a little less harsh, law enforcement will go door-to-door instead. Sometimes community notification is sent to all neighbors of an impending registrant moving into the zip-code through emails or the United States Postal Service. This is not Salem, Massachusetts, circa the late 1600s, or the Jim Crow South, but America in the 21st century for the registered sex offender.

The end result is that the offender can never truly feel reintegrated into his community and is ostracized and effectively banished. As an ostracized sex offender, an only child, and a person with Asperger's, I can't imagine what it will be like for me when one day I will have to navigate through this maze of laws without the help of my parents.

One day I will have to accept that I will be completely on my own in this world when my parents pass away, with no brothers or sisters, extended family, or friends to help guide me as I continually struggle. I try to stay in denial that this will one day become a reality for me.

This ostracism is not only true for the offender but for his entire family. Take, for example, what it must feel like to be the child of a sex offender. Through no fault of the child's own, he goes to school knowing that his classmates are going to mercilessly bully him because of his father's status. There isn't anything he can do about it: if the family decides to move, the father will have to register his new address immediately. Countless children have been victimized in this way. They have either been ordered to have no contact with their parent or they have been subjected to the same kind of community harassment that their family members experience. This is wrong.

I was a child in school during the pre-internet era. In many ways, I am thankful for this. Today social media allows bullies 24-hour-a-day access to their intended targets. However, bullies had no shortage of items in their tool chest to pick on me without the use of social media. I was gullible, very naive, had special interests way outside of the norm (like game shows and Frank Sinatra), and was confused about my own sexuality. But what if I had grown up in the era of social media? I try to imagine what my life might have been like if I had a parent who downloaded child pornography and was forced to register on the sex offender registry. I am fairly convinced the bullying would have been much, much worse. Like other children in this situation, I probably would have been slandered online. Most likely, I would have been told that I was a pervert myself. I would have been teased relentlessly and mercilessly about my dad and told that I wouldn't amount to anything. Perhaps like other kids with parents on the registry, I would have been physically assaulted. Politicians and those in law enforcement like to talk about how the sex offender registry is designed to protect children from predators, but they give very little consideration to the unintended consequences the registry has on those same children.

For the past six years, I've been thinking constantly about my childhood and my entire life. One thing that has always been consistent throughout most of my life is a feeling of being different and not wanting to be that way. Once I was diagnosed with Asperger's, the difference became somewhat normalized for me. I no longer felt as if I was the only person on the planet with this unique constellation of traits known as Asperger's syndrome. I was to learn that there were many others like me who had been bullied in school, felt socially isolated from their peers, had very little romantic or dating experience as adults, and struggled in the workplace. I also learned that a subset of individuals on the spectrum were considered to be geniuses and that fictional characters in the mold of Sheldon on *The Big Bang Theory* were created to celebrate these differences. The philosophy of neurodiversity, to which I became a subscriber, would constantly reinforce the value of autism and Asperger's by referring to historical figures like Albert Einstein, Isaac Newton, and Glenn Gould with the argument being that society greatly benefits from having a diverse gene pool and that we need to focus more money on services for individuals on the spectrum to support them instead of only seeking a cure.

For the first time in my life after having received a diagnosis, being a part of the autism community gave me a sense of belonging. Believing in neurodiversity helped "level the playing field" in my mind from all of the misunderstanding that I had felt over the years from teachers, peers, and society at large. While I agree that money for adult services is extremely important, I can now say that I no longer subscribe to the main tenets of the neurodiversity philosophy. I believe I took this philosophy to an extreme and it caused a major blind-spot for me. Let me explain.

After my arrest, I truly did not want to believe that my Asperger's or autism had anything to do with the offense I committed. I became defensive and protective of those in the autism community who did not want autism to be associated with something as grotesque as child pornography. As I was to learn, Asperger's and autism are not associated with predation or with being a danger to society and particularly children. Yet it does seem to present a vulnerability that can make one more susceptible to engaging in the behavior I engaged in. It took a lot of convincing to get me to the place I am today. Here are a few things that I considered when making the shift. Over the past six years, my dad has received close to 30 calls from parents all around the country of children with Asperger's who were charged with the exact same crime as I was. They tell almost identical stories. Their children had few friendships, rarely dated, and used the computer as a substitute for in-person socializing. All of the reports written by their experts concluded very low risk on the part of the Asperger defendants in each case, and a reasonable treatment plan was proposed that would help to facilitate recovery from this self-destructive behavior without the need for criminal prosecution and the sex offender registry. On top of that, I discovered that several Asperger organizations and highly prominent professionals working in the field had signed up to a document called "Principles for Prosecutors" which recognized that this problem had been an ongoing issue for the autism community and that it needed to be addressed by the Department of Justice. I subsequently learned that a former district attorney in North Carolina named Michael Parker had also written a document with the same name that put forth the same beliefs and conclusions as the prior "Principles for Prosecutors" did and Parker was totally unrelated to the first position paper.

Many people had apparently recognized that this problem existed. Except me. Aside from the inherent nature of the disability causing challenges to my ability to engage in appropriate forms of intimacy, I believe my adherence to neurodiversity caused me to only see the "good" in autism. Any problems that were more challenging for individuals with autism I had tended to write off as unfortunate byproducts of other strengths they may have concealed beneath the surface. Just so that no one will misunderstand me, I still believe in the dignity and worth of every human being on the spectrum. I don't believe individuals with autism should be cured if they don't want to be. But whereas before I would tend to minimize autism's role as the cause of my problems and blame it on society's response to my autism, I am able to see now that autism itself presented many obstacles in my life. Why did I minimize autism's role? Because I didn't want to feel different.

Because I have developed this new understanding, I have compassion for Asperger individuals who have been charged with the crime of possessing child pornography and have been sent to prison and placed on registries. My firm belief is that the vast majority of those individuals are not dangerous regarding their risk of harming children and that they now have a dual disability in life, for no good reason. On the one hand, they were born with a disability that they didn't ask to be born with. Speaking for myself, I did not choose to be born with a disability that caused me to have delayed speech, a very difficult time connecting with people and making friends, and a tremendous difficulty being intimate and reading the cues of intimacy, not to mention problems staying employed and living independently.

I would much rather have been born without Asperger's if given the choice prior to my birth. This statement may offend those in the neurodiversity camp, but my feelings have changed in the past six years and I don't apologize for my new views. I realize now that all of these impairments I had made it very difficult to remain employed and complete requirements such as being a student teacher or working in a radio station. Rather than blaming Asperger's for these failures, I simply recognize that having this disability played a role.

On the other hand, the same thing is true with Asperger's, with the possession of child pornography and registration adding on another disability to the challenges of an existing neurological disability. Without the understanding that Asperger's is a lifelong neurological disability that in many cases precludes employment, relationships, and independent living, it is impossible for those in the legal profession to estimate the damage done to an Asperger's person who is placed on the registry. The dual disability becomes both neurological and civil. If you consider that individuals on the spectrum are vastly unemployed or underemployed to begin with, it is not a stretch of the imagination to say that their odds of getting a job upon registering go down even further. When you consider that independent living is a huge challenge for individuals on the spectrum, how can residency restrictions or lack of a job make that prospect any easier?

What about the parents of the child with Asperger's who now has this dual disability? Think about how hard it is to raise a child with a disability that impacts almost every aspect of one's life, starting from birth: from digestion (intestinal issues) to navigation (hoping your child doesn't get lost), to tens of thousands of dollars for therapy because of relational issues, to meltdowns because the child isn't in touch with his emotions—the list could go on and on. Assuming the best-case scenario, the child becomes an adult and with proper help and guidance can live a successful and productive life, but not without a lot of assistance along the way. Parents of adults on the spectrum are very often more involved in their adult child's life than if that child were a neurotypical.

But let's not assume the best-case scenario. Let's assume this child gets sent to federal prison for possession of child pornography. This is a child who couldn't fend for himself in the most basic areas of his life: all of a sudden, he is thrust into an environment where sadistic guards, solitary confinement/protective custody, gangs, and prison politics are rules and life circumstances that this child is going to have to become accustomed to. It's unspeakable, isn't it? Tragically, this happens all too often. Our family has heard of cases where individuals on the spectrum have been sentenced to as many as 15 years in prison for possession of child pornography, with no evidence whatsoever that the person was at risk of actually harming a child.

Let's continue with our scenario. The adult with Asperger's gets out of prison, if he is lucky. He has nowhere to go because his parents live within 1000 feet of a school and that was the one place he was planning on going. His parents have to either sell their home or find a place for their child to live outside of a residency restriction zone, assuming the parents have the money to do this. Would an apartment work? Most apartments do not allow sex offenders to live there. In some cases, offenders end up homeless. Could an Asperger individual survive on the streets? It is very doubtful. The whole family is harmed in this scenario, not just the individual with Asperger's. The collateral damage is endless.

Even worse, the United States Government puts juveniles on the registry. It is horrifying to imagine an autistic juvenile being placed on the registry for the rest of his life for behavior he didn't understand the implications of. But this happens as well.

In the name of protecting children, the United States has upheld pointless laws that make some of the most naive, vulnerable, and truly innocent children and adults even more vulnerable to certain life conditions that they are simply not equipped to handle. Worse, in case after case that I have read, prosecutors take a laissez-faire and skeptical attitude towards the issue. Some view autism as a smokescreen. Some see it as an excuse and the behavior in question as an indicator of dangerousness and future predation towards children when this is simply a myth. The bottom line is that, in case after case, they decide to prosecute.

A few precautionary measures could be taken to account for whether the person is truly a risk to harm children. First, when the FBI does their forensic analysis of the hard drive in question, they would no doubt determine whether or not the defendant had any contact over the internet with children in an inappropriate way. If the defendant only has child pornography and has never actually tried to contact a child over the internet, this would be one indication that the person has never stepped beyond the bounds of his own imagination.

Second, psychological examinations by both defense and prosecution experts based on hard data (testing) could show whether someone has the personality profile of a sociopath or someone who would hurt a child with no regard or concern for that child. Third, the FBI or Homeland Security usually conducts undercover surveillance on someone for a period of time before they go through with their raid. They can usually get a sense of daily routines and behavior patterns simply by observing what a person does when they think no one is looking. Fourth, they could theoretically investigate by asking children who interacted with this individual whether anything improper ever took place. Since federal cases involving child pornography usually last for months if not years after an arrest is made (and before an arrest too, I might add), the FBI would have plenty of time to conduct these interviews with due diligence. Digital forensics, psychological testing, observing the defendant in his natural habitat, and interviewing those who knew him would give a lot of information to those in law enforcement about his level of risk.

It actually doesn't matter in the eyes of the law if an offender has never directly sexually abused a child. The law doesn't care. The law assumes that a possessor of child pornography will either go on to commit a contact offense against a child or has done so already. This is a false assumption that has been rebutted in a multidisciplinary way by psychologists, sociologists, lawyers, and even a sitting Federal District Judge named Jack B. Weinstein in New York City who routinely sentences defendants charged with these crimes. Federal child pornography sentences for non-contact offenders who are simple possessors can be much harsher and longer than state cases where actual molestation of a child has taken place. Trying to figure out the logic in this is a fool's errand.

What are the sentencing guidelines more concerned with? To be brief, they are concerned with the number of images one has on his computer. Instead of seeing this hoarding as a trait of Asperger's in the guise of the compulsive collector, the government uniformly sees it as more evidence of pedophilia. Also, if even one image is downloaded which is considered "sadistic" (and this includes any image of someone under 13), this increases the sentencing guidelines. But by upping the guidelines for even one picture categorized this way, the Sentencing Commission overlooked the fact that large quantities of images can be downloaded simultaneously. If there are only five images out of 500 in someone's collection that are sadistic, clearly sadistic images are not the preference of the downloader. Again, the government doesn't care about this. One image is enough to add years to an already long prison sentence.

This was true for me. When the FBI, the Assistant United States attorney, and my defense lawyers met to go over the discovery evidence in my case, one of the things that was agreed upon by all parties present was that I had one of the most non-sadistic collections of anyone that they had ever seen who was being charged with this crime. In other words, most of the pictures did not involve adults actually abusing children or pictures of sadism or masochism. I was not even aware that such pictures actually existed since I never looked for such pictures in the first place. Yet when a local television station put out their news exposé on me, they noted that there happened to be one of these pictures on my hard drive which I cannot at all recall downloading. From this news story, the public extrapolated that because I had downloaded one of these kinds of images, it must have meant I had this type of collection—which was completely false. More consequential than that, as a result of having even one of these pictures that I wasn't even aware of having, my sentencing guidelines were increased significantly.

One aspect of my case that could have had a devastating impact was that I was initially charged with distribution of child pornography. The law proscribes a five-year mandatory minimum prison sentence for this crime. When I first heard I was being charged with that, I was extremely confused and very much bewildered as to why that term was being applied to me. I had no idea that once I downloaded the images on my computer they automatically became available to others. I always assumed the basic principle that, in order for someone to receive something, you have to purposefully send it to them. If I had known then what I know today, I would never have wanted to make what I was downloading available to others. I wasn't involved in trading and I never said a word to another human being online while I was downloading. I didn't download to trade; I downloaded to download, period! Unfortunately, I had no understanding then of how peer-to-peer systems operated. At sentencing, the presiding judge in my case acknowledged that I was not a distributor of child pornography, and that if he had believed I was, I would have been given a very long prison sentence.

Another flaw in the charging process are the terms "receipt" and "possession," which mean the same thing in conversational parlance but entirely different things statutorily in a child pornography case. To give some context to this, everyone who is charged in a federal child pornography case is charged with at least possession, receipt, and distribution, and I was no exception to this. According to the statute, being found guilty of "receipt" imposes a five-year mandatory minimum prison term for the defendant, whereas with a mere "possession" charge, there is no mandatory minimum. Supposedly, the difference between the two rests with intent. The logic is as follows: If one downloads child pornography accidentally and never looks at it, they are in possession of the child pornography but they might not have intended to receive it. Theoretically, this could happen if someone accidentally clicks on a "pop-up" and unknowingly downloads an image of an underage person; digital forensics can prove the person never opened the file or intended to view it. It could also happen if someone accidentally downloaded the child pornography but never deleted it. However, the first example is not only an extremely unlikely scenario, but if it did happen, it describes a complete lack of criminal intent on the part of the internet user. In the second scenario, criminal intent could never be proven one way or the other unless you got inside a person's head. Common sense tells us in cases where a person has only two or three pictures, and it can be established that the person never opens those files, it would be incredibly unreasonable for a prosecutor to bring charges. True possession without intent to receive the pornography is almost impossible to conceive of on its face as a crime. In fact, there is no such criminal act as possession of child pornography without receipt.

I am dwelling on the semantics of this point because there is a five-year difference in mandatory minimum sentences between possession and receipt, and people's lives are horribly affected because of this bargaining game that prosecutors play. Congress has statutorily sanctioned a myth that there is a difference between the two charges and put it into law, when in fact there is a distinction without any substantive difference. Unless a person produces child pornography themselves (production is a much more serious charge), they must have received it from somewhere. It is possible to be legitimately charged with production and possession of child pornography but not receipt because the material originated with the producer. Being able to add "receipt" as a higher charge above possession, however, is a bargaining chip prosecutors typically use for leverage in pleading out cases. Defense attorneys feel good about themselves if they can drop both "distribution" and "receipt" for their client and end up with only possession. It still may result in a four- or five-year prison sentence, but the defense attorney feels like a hero who has saved his client from years in prison. Because possession without receipt doesn't exist in a practical sense, receipt should be removed as a charge available to prosecutors to avoid abusive overcharging. Likewise, distribution should only be reserved for cases when purposeful trading or sending of the illegal material to another person takes place.

If a person with Asperger's is charged with this crime, the system inherently does not understand how their characteristics could have made them vulnerable to committing the crime. Those in law enforcement also have little or no training on interacting with individuals on the autism spectrum. When the FBI came to make what is known as a pre-dawn raid (a raid made before the break of dawn) on my apartment, they showed up with a level of force one would expect if they had their sights set upon Lucky Luciano. They came into my bedroom with pure brute force as if I was an enemy military combatant in Afghanistan, even though they knew I had Asperger's syndrome and had thoroughly vetted my background prior to the raid and probably conducted undercover surveillance on me. Why was the shock and awe so necessary? Did it really require ten people to come storming into my bedroom screaming at me as loudly as they could, violently jolt me out of bed, and thrash me against the wall to place me in handcuffs so that the search would go without incident? I hardly posed any threat to these agents, and some simple investigation and background checks beforehand would have told them so. You don't kill a fly with an AK-47; you use a fly swatter. The level of force they used against me was totally disproportionate to the threat I posed to them, and they knew it. Just think about if this was your son or daughter with a developmental disability. Would you want the highest-ranking law enforcement agency in this country treating him or her that way?

This is the way the FBI treats disabled people when they conduct these raids. One might assume that the type of raid they conducted on me is a statistical outlier if they know the person has a developmental disability in advance, but that is not true. It is conducted this way on everyone who is suspected of committing this crime, including the most impaired autistic individual one can possibly imagine. My parents have heard horror stories of other raids you would not believe. One raid in particular traumatized the younger sister of an individual with Asperger's when the FBI stormed in because everyone in the family (including the parents) was put in handcuffs and treated like criminals. Ask yourself what the little sister, who had nothing whatsoever to do with her brother's crime, did to deserve this trauma. The sister (who was a child herself) was brutally traumatized, and for what? Because she could have aided her brother in helping him escape from the FBI? Not a chance. There is no rational justification for their use of quasi-military aggression when they conduct these raids on disabled people.

After being forced out of bed, thrown against the wall while handcuffed, and then dragged to my couch in the living room by ten people charging at me like I was an enemy combatant at 6.30 in the morning, I was shocked, awed, and traumatized. The sheer force of their presence left me in an entirely helpless state of being where I literally did not know what to do. After being thoroughly traumatized, they calculatingly commenced the interrogation with impeccable timing. At the beginning of the interrogation, I was given what seemed like a firm promise by the FBI that the more I helped them, the more they would help me. In other words, if I answered their questions and gave them useful information, they would tell the prosecutors not to go so hard on me. This is a line and a lie they use on everyone. I believed it like a child who believes in the Tooth Fairy.

I was never read my Miranda rights and was never given the impression by any of the agents that I could leave if I wanted to. If I was told that I could leave, there is absolutely no doubt in my mind that I would have driven to my parents' house immediately, which would have foreclosed their ability to ask me any more questions. It is interesting to note that in the criminal complaint filed against me, nowhere is it to be found that they Mirandized me. Also nowhere to be found was a statement by them indicating that they let me know that I could leave my residence during the time of my interrogation. In fact, outside of my apartment I saw many police cars with flashing lights and I asked one of the FBI agents why they were there. I was told "in case you made a run for it." This very statement implied to me that I was not allowed to leave. The truth is that if they had Mirandized me and told me that I could leave if I wanted to, you can count on the fact that they would have put both of these facts in the criminal complaint.

In essence, I was interrogated while being detained in my apartment without the courtesy of Miranda, and detainment is usually what happens when an arrest is made. Let me explain further why this is important.

When law enforcement detains a suspect, they must be read their Miranda rights and arrested immediately if further questioning is to proceed. A person is not supposed to be detained when a search is being conducted unless they are under arrest; otherwise, anything said by a defendant can be deemed inadmissible in court without Miranda being given. I maintain that I was not Mirandized and also not told that I could leave because the FBI knew that a suspect is more likely to talk when he doesn't feel prejudged and it helps if you do not arrest a person while you are interrogating him. To have been read my Miranda rights would have given me reason to ask for a lawyer, which did not even occur to me (in spite of the fact my father is a law professor). It also helps the FBI immensely to have the suspect physically there to ask him questions; if you tell him that he can leave, he just might do so and talk to a lawyer in the interim. The FBI must have repeated at least three times, "We are not here to judge anything that you did; you are not under arrest; we just want to know the facts." They were trying to exude a sense of rapport, understanding, and empathy in that moment, as if they didn't know what I was about to say to them and were merely investigating something of which they had no knowledge. The FBI knew very well that they were going to arrest me and they had the facts they needed. They had probable cause at the time to arrest me right then and there, and they could have if they wanted to. Telling me that I was not under arrest was stressed so many times as a technique, a deliberate way to get me to open up to them—and it worked. Also, they know that the average citizen is not at all aware of the intricacies of what constitutes admissible or inadmissible statements in a court of law, and this was certainly true for me. Lastly, they know that the evidence is so overwhelming in the vast majority of child pornography cases that any technically inadmissible statements made in an interrogation will not be challenged in an evidentiary pretrial hearing or on appeal because the case will most likely not go to trial. The person will probably plead guilty and waive all of his rights in the end.

Why do they want to talk to a person that much if they have all of the evidence they need? Because they want a confession, to give that extra bit of assurance of a conviction. The name of the game for these guys is a conviction. After all, someone else could have downloaded the pornography that ended up on my computer or I could have been hacked. A confession in the law, even a false one, is a nearly ironclad way of sealing that coveted conviction. The more convictions they amass, the more funding they receive from the federal government.

Once the FBI started interrogating me, the first question they asked was "Is there anything you want to tell us about what is on your computer?" Up until that point I had no idea why the FBI was there, so it occurred to me that the only thing possible was the child pornography images and I foolishly said so. "You are here because I have child pornography on my computer?" I asked in a whimper. By uttering that one sentence, I confessed. Having admitted to that, one of the agents then asked me, "So you knew then that what you were doing was wrong?" I agreed and answered, "Yes." Since I promised to be cooperative, I was obviously doing my best to tell them what I thought they wanted to hear. The truth is, I did know on some level it was wrong, but the smart thing to do would have been to politely say that I wanted an attorney to be present before answering any more questions.

Later on, this single answer that I gave them was then retooled in the media by rephrasing it to mean that I knew it was illegal. It was even presented that way in the criminal complaint. For the record, I never told the FBI that I knew it was illegal. This was a gross inaccuracy. This inaccurate statement was used against me at every turn—from those who trashed me online to the prosecutors who were trying to determine my criminal intent. At my allocution/plea hearing, when I was asked under oath if I knew what I was doing was illegal at the time, I told the judge the truth: That I knew it was wrong but that I did not know it was illegal. Prior to my arrest, I had never heard of someone in the news getting in trouble for this crime because I did not watch or read much news. Unfortunately, I was not aware that I was contributing to a culture of abuse when I looked at those horrible images. I felt deep shame and an uneasiness about my actions, but I couldn't imagine I was committing one of the most serious federal crimes on the books. I simply saw myself as a passive participant who had nothing to do with what had taken place 10 or 20 years ago. I now see how deeply flawed and incorrect this reasoning was, but it was how I saw it at the time. Every day of my life, I wish I could have understood the harm I was causing these children so that I could have immediately stopped or never started in the first place.

I was arrested the day after my interrogation. This is what one would expect for such a serious crime. I was lucky I was arrested the next day. It does not work this way for most families and I am personally stupefied by this. Even though the FBI has probable cause and the evidence they need to make an arrest on the day of each raid they conduct, many people wait years before they are finally arrested. My father has heard from countless families who report that these traumatic raids occur and then the family goes years without knowing the status of their case.

What are the practical implications of this? It means that individuals the government claims they consider so dangerous that they need to be sentenced to years in prison and be placed on a sex offender registry after their cases are concluded are allowed for years to have no conditions of bail placed on them while the government takes their time in conducting a forensic analysis of their computers. They are essentially totally free individuals to do whatever they please, until it is time to pay the piper. Think about this for a moment: If a person was suspected of committing a murder and the police had probable cause, would law enforcement wait years while sealing their investigation before arresting that person? Can you imagine the FBI waiting years to arrest someone who was suspected of robbing a bank if they had probable cause? Do you think the police would hold out for six months, a year, or two years if they had probable cause to arrest someone who was suspected of involuntary manslaughter for a hit and run? Wouldn't law enforcement consider these crimes as presenting an extreme risk to public safety, even with the presumption of innocence? In fact, can you, the reader, think of any crime of a serious magnitude where the FBI or police would let someone roam the streets with no restrictions whatsoever for years before arresting them? Again, one has to ask in good faith why the FBI and the U.S. Attorneys would do this. If they really believe they are prosecuting individuals who present such a high risk for molesting children, why do they wait so long to arrest them? If the individual can remain free for years before their arrest, why is there even a need for the registry many years later for those who possess child pornography if there was no need to keep them under supervision while the computer forensic analysis was taking place? It is a stunning inconsistency that boggles the mind.

What is just as concerning is that it is a documented fact that the FBI took over and ran one of the largest internet child pornography websites in the world for two weeks, according to this *USA Today* article: www.usatoday.com/story/news/2016/01/21/fbi-ran-website-sharing-thousands-child-porn-images/79108346. According to the article, this apparent takeover was the third time in recent years that the FBI had done this that has been made public. After all, it was classified information. The Justice Department itself now has been forced to acknowledge that the FBI operated a site on the dark web known as Operation Playpen. Keep in mind that these websites contained lots of sadistic images with children as young as Kindergarteners being abused by adults. You may ask why the FBI did this. It is the old "the ends justify the means." In order to catch the people who would hurt children, the FBI says, they needed to take over these websites to entice possessors so they could later identify them. Are we to judge this reasoning as sound and just?

No, it is simply wrong by any standard. Those websites should have been taken down immediately once they were discovered. In fact, once any child pornography file is flagged online by law enforcement, it should come down at once. The FBI has failed to—or apparently doesn't want to—take into account the harm that they themselves are causing by distributing these images in the first place. They were co-conspirators in re-victimizing these children in their search for sexual predators. If their goal and endgame is the complete eradication of child pornography on the internet (as it should be), is it right and just to be engaged in the same re-victimization of these children that they themselves prosecute individuals for intentionally distributing their images? Is it right and just that the same victims being called to make victim impact statements at sentencing hearings by U.S. Attorneys across the country are the same victims whose images the FBI deliberately distributed on the internet? Is it right and just to subject non-dangerous individuals on the autism spectrum to years in prison and a lifetime on the sex offender registry because the FBI feels it necessary to catch anyone who might have the inclination to look at child pornography? I would answer in the negative.

Of course, after any raid, arrest, conviction, and prison time comes the sex offender registry. The civil disability of registration cannot be underestimated. If a registrant is lucky enough to find a job, it will usually be in the area of construction or manufacturing, or possibly working as a short order cook. Perhaps they might find a job as an electrician. The obvious reason for this is that these are jobs where children would typically not be present. But there is also a further liability. The address of where a sex offender works is publicly listed on the sex offender registry, which would, of course, be embarrassing to any employer and a good reason not to hire someone. Unfortunately, this narrow field of job prospects has shut the door on any future career I might have had. Even if I tried with every bone in my body to learn these manufacturing skilled trades, I would fail miserably. I simply do not have the coordination or the fine motor skills to work in a factory making equipment or building structures. I don't have the skills to be a short order cook due to my horrible multi-tasking and lack of ability to work under pressure. Other than volunteering, I simply don't have the skillsets that equip me to be able to handle the jobs that registrants typically get if they are lucky. My only skill is being able to teach tennis. Children are the primary consumers of tennis lessons and thus no tennis club would hire me.

I had big career dreams a long time ago. As a child, I wanted to be the next Bob Barker hosting *The Price is Right*. Later on, I wanted to be the next Bud Collins as a tennis announcer on a major network. After that, I wanted to be like Casey Kasem. When I finally came to my senses and realized that none of those things were possible, I would have settled for a job as a radio disc jockey at some local radio station. When I went to a radio station and actually saw what the job would have entailed, I decided upon trying to become a special education teacher. When I failed student teaching due to Asperger-related issues, I tried becoming a psychologist. After I was told by the school that it would be in my best interests not to go into clinical psychology, I obtained a Psy.D. so that I could help to advocate for those on the autism spectrum. At this point, my goal was to teach at a university. But before that possibility could emerge, I was finally offered my first real job: I would be a consultant at a school for individuals on the spectrum for both administration staff and teachers who were totally unfamiliar working with this population. One month into that job, all prospects for any future jobs went out the window.

People ask my parents all the time: "When will Nick find work again?" If they only knew it just isn't that simple. When I hear that another person has made that inquiry of my parents, it actually angers me a little bit. The implication is that I am lazy, or if I only was a little more motivated and less depressed, I could find success again. What people don't understand is that it was hard enough to find any kind of work before being placed on the registry. Now it is not in the cards and I unfortunately have to live with that, but it is not an easy thing to live with.

I suppose I am in a more fortunate position than other people on the registry who are also on the spectrum. I have parents who can financially support me—not extravagantly but enough to meet my daily needs. But I think of those individuals who cannot find work or a place to live, or who do not have family members who have the means to support them. What will they do? It pains me to even think about it. When I become an orphan after my parents die, I shudder to think about how this will affect me as well.

Just like autism impacts every area of my life, so too does being on the registry. I will never be able to use an online dating service if I want to meet someone as they forbid registrants from using their sites. I will never be able to teach at a college or university, which is one of the few jobs I think I would have been capable of. I have to think twice about going to walk my dog around a lake for fear that it might be considered a place "where children congregate." Again, just like autism affects every aspect of my internal reality, the registry affects every aspect of my external reality.

There is a bit of irony to the registry. After all, the goal of any probation department that supervises sex offenders is to get them socially reintegrated. The feeling is that it is not good for a sex offender to be alone too much. Left to his own devices, his behavior will only turn self-destructive and perhaps he will reoffend. As social isolation is one of the risk factors almost all probation departments uniformly look at for recidivism, the registry has actually created the conditions for higher risk. How can we honestly tell ourselves that ostracizing a group of individuals does anything to help socially reintegrate them? The most ironic thing of all is that while probation departments talk a good game when it comes to social reintegration, they actually do whatever they can do to hinder it by their protectionist policies. They will refuse to let a registrant go to a family gathering if there are going to be children there, even with adequate adult supervision. They will not let someone get a job where there is access to a computer, which nowadays is just about anywhere. They will turn down your requests for vacation time simply because the probation department in the jurisdiction you want to travel to doesn't want you there. They will issue no-contact orders against registrants who want to date someone with a child, even with adequate supervision. I ask again the following question: How does isolation from family, loss of job prospects, inability to travel, and limiting opportunities to date actually help a registrant socially reintegrate himself?

Just as disturbing: If a person on probation actually submits a motion to try to terminate their supervised release early, the probation officer is required to take a position of opposition if the person is a sex offender. It doesn't matter how well they have behaved or how much progress they have made. It is simply a matter of policy. So much for believing that a person can rehabilitate themselves. To put this in perspective, if a bank robber who served time in federal prison behaves well, a probation officer is not likely to object to this motion and may even support it.

Federal supervised release is a terrible experience for someone on the spectrum. Probation officers routinely come to your home and conduct unannounced home visits where you are constantly asked invasive and extremely embarrassing questions. Your home is routinely ransacked in their everlasting search for more child pornography. For me, my home is my sanctuary, and to have people show up unannounced at any time is a terribly unsettling feeling. Once they are at your home, they make no secret about the fact that they view all sex offenders as a high risk for not only reoffending but actually molesting children, and therefore they make conditions of probation much more restrictive than for any other category of felon. They believe anyone who looks at child pornography will hurt a child eventually—it is just a matter of time.

Some registrants on probation are required to take what is called a penile plethysmograph test on a routine basis. This test actually measures the volume of one's penis based on blood flow, which depends on how a person responds to visual stimuli—in other words, erotic pictures of both children and adults. Based on how one scores on this test will determine whether the leash or noose should be tightened even more so than to begin with. The fallacy of this test is that a person's response to pictures is not a reliable indicator as to their future behavior. A person can be aroused by the wrong set of pictures and still not be a child predator in the slightest way, shape, or form. What actually matters most is if the person has antisocial or sociopathic tendencies.

Due to these horribly restrictive policies, I almost didn't attend my own grandmother's funeral because there were children there. I've missed important family gatherings like bar and bat mitzvahs and Thanksgiving dinners. In the meantime, one of my probation officers was worried about my risk factor of social isolation. Did she ever stop and consider that perhaps the Asperger's along with these oppressive policies were part of the reason I was socially isolated to begin with? And maybe being on the registry has something to do with it as well?

What does the registration process actually entail? The registrant goes to a police station and gives information such as their address, make and model of their car with license plate, any internet identifiers such as email addresses or screen names, place of work (if they are employed), and then, to add insult to injury, one has to pay for the privilege of being on the registry—in my state, I have to pay $50 each time I register. All of this information goes on the sex offender registry and is also transferred to other public websites such as Homefacts. com which easily show up on Google searches. The actual visit to a police station to register is a mortifying experience. Once you tell the police that you are there to register, you begin to notice a very different tone and expression they have towards you compared with when you first walk in and they have no idea why you are there.

One of the things I have learned about sex offenders in general since I have been placed on the registry is that these crimes have among the lowest recidivism rates of any crime. This is counterintuitive to what we all believe since we've been conditioned to think the opposite, but statistics do bear it out. Also, since most sexual abuse actually takes place within one's family or with close friends and acquaintances, the registry doesn't actually fulfill the promise it sets out to achieve. Stranger danger happens, but it is in fact rare and greatly exaggerated by the media and politicians. Almost all sex offender laws are named after abductees. However, there is a greater chance that a child will be struck by lightning than be abducted by a stranger.

The reader should also keep in mind that the Supreme Court has stated as justification for the sex offender registry that it is not a punishment, only a civil regulatory process. In this way of thinking, you could equate being on the registry as doing what is necessary to drive a car by making a trip to the department of motor vehicles to update your car's registration. This ridiculous reasoning has allowed for new restrictions to be placed on registrants all of the time without the registrant being able to challenge the restrictions on the grounds of *ex post facto*. If these new restrictions were considered to be "punishments," they would constitute retroactivity and would not be allowed. For example, if a new state law were passed that said a sex offender could not live less than 2000 feet from a school and the current law was 1000, anyone living within 2000 feet would be forced to move. The move would not be considered punishment since the Supreme Court said so. Does anyone actually believe that the sex offender registry is not a punishment?

My feeling for individuals on the autism spectrum is that the sex offender registry is totally inappropriate for someone who has downloaded child pornography and is not a risk to children. It is a red herring to assume that just because someone has downloaded child pornography it means he wants to hurt children. What one does in private versus what one could actually do are two separate things altogether.

Diversion programs and mental health courts should be set up for this particular population with this crime in mind so that proper treatment and care can be given to this population, rather than placing them on a registry where they don't belong. I strongly concur with every author in this book who feels that the criminal justice system should let the mental health system handle these cases. Just as society has the innate instinct to protect children because they represent vulnerability, so too should we have that innate instinct when it comes to the most vulnerable adults among us.

During my intensive post-arrest therapy, I have truly come to see the horrendous nature of my actions. I unknowingly watched children being unspeakably abused without getting rid of the pictures immediately. At the beginning of my post-arrest therapy when it was explained to me the ramifications of what I had actually done, I was mortified. I always considered myself to be an extremely ethical person, or at least tried to be. Yet I could see what I had done was not only unethical but also morally reprehensible. As I stated previously, there hasn't been a day that has gone by where I haven't meditated upon the horror of my own behavior in looking at those pictures.

An 18-month diversion program would have allowed me to understand the horrific nature of my actions without society prejudging me as a threat to their children, which I am not. A felony conviction and life on the sex offender registry hasn't accomplished what the legislators intended when they created these laws. My neighborhood isn't any safer with the public knowing about the horrible mistake I made than if they didn't know. They are just more scared and, in my case, they are afraid of a boogeyman.

I wrote this chapter to help protect those on the autism spectrum from ending up on the sex offender registry and in the criminal justice system. Parents need to know that the stakes of following the human sexuality aspect of their child's development is a matter of life and death. The registry is social death. Its restrictions are limitless; I couldn't name them all in this chapter if I tried. Our brutal and dangerous prisons are not equipped for the autism population, or even for those with serious mental or emotional issues. Too many of us are thrown in solitary confinement or are placed in prisons with potential predators who would like nothing more than to harm a sex offender. If this chapter can help parents take preventive action or enlighten professionals as to the damage that the registry inflicts upon whole communities, I will feel I have accomplished something.

As it stands now, my life as I once knew it is no more and never will be. I often feel as if I have died an early death. I take ownership for what I did. Yet I wish I had received a second chance in life from those in power who had the authority to grant me one. The one comfort life offers me is the fact that, when I die, I'll be free from this dreaded label that I have been condemned to live with for the rest of my life. On that day, my soul will smile again.

CHAPTER 11

Navigating Judicial Responses for Those Caught in the Web

Catherine Carpenter

The image of the violent pedophile haunts us. Notable high-profile cases play across our television screens and disturbing images of child rapists and murderers are seared into our minds. We recall Phillip Garrido who abducted 11-year-old Jaycee Dugard and held her captive for 17 years. We were shocked to learn that Jerry Sandusky, a respected coach with the Penn State football team, established a children's charity in order to gain the trust of vulnerable young boys so that he could sexually abuse them. We remember Ariel Castro who kidnapped and held three young women captive in his ramshackle home in Chicago in plain sight of family and neighbors. We cannot forget Megan Kanka's murderer, Jesse Timmendequas, a convicted sex offender, who lured seven-year-old Megan into his home across the street from where she lived in order to rape her. And we are heartbroken by the rape and murder of nine-year-old Jessica Lunsford at the hands of John Evander Couey, also a previously convicted sex offender who lived behind the Lunsfords.

It is human nature to want to control what seems scary. Enter sex offender registration laws. Established in an effort to protect children from those we fear most, sex offender registration laws are designed to track those strangers to our children who have previously committed sex offenses. This is especially interesting given that the vast majority of the sexual abuse of children is committed by family members. But fear is motivating, and the appeal to our peace of mind—even if it might result in a false sense of security—fuels the public's desire to monitor sex offenders.

This chapter traces the evolution of sex offender registration laws from inception through modern day to trace the myriad changes that have taken place during that time. It invites examination of the legitimacy and value of sex offender registration laws, especially in light of their serial expansion. Further, and juxtaposed to the emotionally charged rhetoric that drives the discussion, the chapter presents statistical evidence to challenge the notion that sex offenders pose a threat of future dangerousness. Finally, because emotional rhetoric drives the issue, the courts serve as neutral arbiters of an issue firmly in the grasp of the legislators. Therefore, this chapter explores viable legal challenges to the inherent imbalance these laws have created.

THE EVOLUTION OF SEX OFFENDER REGISTRATION LAWS
How the National Movement Began

Although sex offender registration laws have been in effect since the 1940s, they rose to national prominence in the 1990s. And here is where the story begins: with the tragic and unrelated abductions and murders of three young children. Six-year-old Adam Walsh was abducted and murdered in 1981, 11-year-old Jacob Wetterling was abducted at gunpoint and presumed murdered in 1989, and seven-year-old Megan Kanka was sexually assaulted and murdered in 1994 by a neighbor who, unbeknownst to Megan's family, had prior convictions for sexual assault against children. These deaths took place states apart and over a number of years. Yet they shared a common tie: grief-stricken parents who galvanized the nation to demand a change in laws to address crimes against children.

Anguish led to action. As one justice acknowledged, "The societal pressure for legislation designed to prevent terrible tragedies such as befell Megan Kanka and her parents is hydraulic" (*E.B. v. Verniero*, 1997). The national conversation moved Congress in 1994 to pass the Jacob Wetterling Crimes Against Children and Sexually Violent Offender Registration Act. The Wetterling Act included the Sex Offender Registration Act (SORA), and focused on the creation of a national law enforcement database through the registration of sex offenders. The law required the states to adopt sex offender registration laws under SORA within three years of the Act's passage or Congress could withhold 10% of certain grants the state would ordinarily receive for a variety of crime prevention and interdiction programs. Within a relatively short period of time, every jurisdiction had complied with the Act's provisions.

However, the Act did not address the concern expressed specifically by Megan Kanka's parents that the community had a right to be notified of a known sexual offender living in its neighborhood. In what has become known as "Megan's Law," Congress amended the Jacob Wetterling Act in 1996 to include community notification statutes. With the addition of Megan's Law, the Act expanded its focus from informing law enforcement agencies to alerting the community to the convicted sex offender's location.

SORA: The First Generation of Sex Offender Registration Laws

By today's practice, SORA was a modest effort that was limited in governmental reach. Indeed, initially, because sex offender registration laws were designed solely for law enforcement agencies, registry records were kept confidential. Under SORA, registration was required of any person convicted of a "criminal offense against a minor" including "criminal sexual conduct toward a minor[,] solicitation of a minor to engage in sexual conduct[, and] use of a minor in a sexual performance" (42 U.S.C. § 14071).

When first passed, federal guidelines only required a limited number of offenses to trigger registration. The seriousness of the crime corresponded with the length of time the registrant was obligated to register, with a minimum of ten years required for registration. Indiana's first sex offender regime serves as an excellent example. When enacted in 1994, eight crimes triggered status as a sex offender, and registration involved providing limited information to law enforcement agencies. By comparison, today in Indiana, more than 20 offenses trigger registration; in New York, offenses requiring registration have swelled to over 40.

Risk assessment defined initial sex offender registration schemes. That is, the regime was divided into tiers, with those convicted of sexual offenses assigned levels of risk according to their perceived risk of reoffending. And depending on the assigned risk, the registrant faced varying degrees of burdens associated with registration. For example, many registrants were required to register for a limited period of ten years, while only the most dangerous were subjected to lifetime registration and in-person notification.

Similarly, community notification laws under Megan's Law in the 1990s looked very different than they do today. Under the terms of Megan's Law, "[t]he State or any agency authorized by the State… shall release relevant information that is necessary to protect the public concerning a specific person required to register under this section" (42 U.S.C. § 14071(e)(2)). In practice at the time, notification laws only provided notice to a select group of people within the community and only via in-person viewing at the police station. The internet had not yet come to play the prominent role that it does now in notifying the community, indeed the world, about the offender's status. Again, Indiana provides an excellent example where notification involved the distribution of a paper registry, updated twice per year and sent to a few select agencies. Other entities could receive the registry on request, but the home addresses of the registrants were withheld (Indiana Code §§ 5-2-12-1–5-2-12-13).

Nonetheless, even in 1994, registration and notification requirements were not inconsequential. Federal guidelines required that each registrant provide local law enforcement with their name, address, a photograph, and fingerprints (42 U.S.C. § 14071(a)(1)–(3)). Despite limiting the persons who received the particular information, community notification laws required that a registrant provide a host of information including name, aliases, address, photograph, physical description, description of motor vehicles, license numbers of motor vehicles, and vehicle identification numbers of motor vehicles, place of employment, date of birth, crime for which convicted, date of conviction, place and court of conviction, and length and conditions of sentence.

The offender was required to register in the state where employed or attending school, report any change in address, and also notify the proper authorities of the intention to move to another state (42 U.S.C. § 14071(b)(1)(A)(ii–iii)). In some states, and depending on the perceived level of dangerousness of the offender, the act of registration might only require the completion of a form that verified the registrant's current residential and employment addresses. For those who were deemed the most serious of offenders, in-person registration might be required.

How frequently offenders were required to register generally depended upon the classification of the offender. In most states, sexually violent predators and/or sexually violent offenders are required to reregister every 90 days, whereas non-violent offenders are to reregister annually. The failure to register, reregister, or verify the registrant's current address subjects the registrant to serious penalties. When first introduced, registration requirements continued for a minimum of ten years if the offense was considered a non-aggravated sex crime, up to registration for life if it was an aggravated sex crime. Residency restrictions were gaining popularity as well. Some states prohibited the registered sex offender from living within a certain distance of a school, day care center, or any place where minors congregate.

2003: A Watershed Year

With eight years of settled implementation of SORA, the battle over its constitutionality played out in 2003 when the United States Supreme Court heard two separate, but interrelated, challenges to the registration and community notification schemes. In *Smith v. Doe*, Alaskan petitioners challenged the state's authority to require registration of those convicted prior to the enactment of the laws (538 U.S. 84, 89 (2003)). Registration, they argued, would be unconstitutional according to *ex post facto* principles under the Eighth Amendment because they had already served their sentences for sex offenses prior to the enactment of Alaska's registration scheme. To resolve the question, the Court faced the fundamental issue of whether registration schemes are criminal penalties governed by the Eighth Amendment or only civil regulations designed to protect the public.

In a related issue, in *Connecticut Department of Public Safety v. Doe*, Connecticut sex offenders challenged Connecticut's practice to post the information of all registrants on a public website under Megan's Law without first determining whether each registrant continued to pose a danger to the community. The registrants argued that this one-size-fits-all practice denied them an individual assessment of whether they posed a future danger and denied them procedural due process.

Although the cases proceeded from different factual bases, and were premised on different constitutional grounds, the constitutional fate of registration and notification statutes rested with these Court decisions. In what can only be described as a one-two punch, the Court rejected both challenges. In *Smith*, the Court concluded that sex offender registration schemes are not criminal penalties, but instead are civil remedies that a state could employ to protect the safety and welfare of its citizens. Further, in *Connecticut Department of Public Safety*, the Court ruled that the use of a public website to disseminate personal information about all of its registrants—no matter the seriousness of their crimes or their potential risk of reoffense—was a legitimate tool that did not violate procedural due process. With these decisions from the Court in the same term, the message was clear: registration schemes are constitutionally permissible civil regulations despite the intrusive nature of the burdens they imposed.

Post-2003: The Era of Expansion in Sex Offender Registration Laws

Emboldened by the Court's decision that sex offender registration schemes are civil regulations, legislators seized upon the opportunity to expand the laws' reach and significance. The period post-*Smith* can best be described as a "race to the harshest," with each state serially amending their registration schemes to include more restrictive measures targeted at a larger group of people (Carpenter, 2010).

Emotional rhetoric serves as the legislative currency. Indeed, "the ensuing years [since SORA] have been marked by a dizzying array of increased registration and community notification requirements, the emergence of harshening residency restrictions, and the elimination of individuated risk assessment" (Carpenter and Beverlin, 2012, p.1078). Congress led the way. In 2006, it passed the Adam Walsh Child Protection and Safety Act ("AWA"). Included within the AWA was the Sexual Offender Registration and Notification Act (SORNA) which created new federally mandated guidelines for registration and notification laws, and penalties for the failure to comply.

SORNA's changes were striking. The new federal guidelines increased the number of offenses subject to registration, and they provided longer durational requirements for registration. With new parameters, state legislatures expanded the number of registerable offenses from an average of eight offenses in the 1990s to more than 40 offenses in some states. As part of that swell, SORNA requires individuals convicted of numerous low-level or misdemeanor offenses to now register as sex offenders. Additionally, registration reaches those who committed non-sexual crimes but where the victim is a child.

Durational registration requirements also increased from a minimum of 10 years to 15 years, and, in a few states such as California, offenders automatically faced registration for life for any registerable offense. Additionally, citizens have watched the goal posts move in their states as amendments repeatedly upgrade sex crime classifications to ones requiring lifetime registration. In Pennsylvania, for example, under changing classifications, more than 73% are now required to register for life.

In one of the most debated provisions, SORNA mandated registration for juvenile offenders under the juvenile court jurisdiction who were 14 years old and older. This change on its own was significant. But some states took it one step further. It only used SORNA provisions as guidelines, instead lowering the minimum age of registration from 14 years old to as young as nine years old.

SORNA also expanded the kind of personal information that would be collected from the registrants. The states followed suit. As states sought to craft rules surrounding dissemination of information, a question unfolded as to "the exact line at which the dignity and convenience of the individual must yield to the demands of the public welfare or of private justice" (Warren and Brandeis, 1890, p.214). In the case of sex offender registration, the subtext was clear: residents were entitled to great amounts of information about all sex offenders, without regard to their likelihood of reoffense. Changes made to Louisiana's registration scheme in the past decade typify the trend across the country to require more information. In 2001, Louisiana's sex offender statute required all registrants to provide the basics for registration, including address, place of employment, the crime for which the registrant was convicted, and any aliases the offender assumed. Today, Louisiana also requires of all registrants—no matter the level of dangerousness—palm prints, a DNA sample, and all landline and mobile telephone numbers (La. Rev. Stat. Ann. § 15 (2011)). Further, it endorsed residency restrictions and sanctioned the use of GPS tracking devices.

Most notably, and perhaps most troubling, SORNA shifted focus. It eliminated the requirement of individuated risk assessment in favor of conviction-based assessment. No longer would the need to register, or the severity of the burdens, be tied to individualized assessment of whether the offender posed a threat of future harm. Instead, registration and notification burdens would be tied to a predetermined classification of crimes irrespective of a particular registrant's dangerousness (42 U.S.C. §§ 16911(2)–(4), 16915(a), 16916). In practical terms, a registrant's danger would now be defined solely by the offense committed, not by an assessment of the offender's perceived future dangerousness.

The effect was palpable. Registry rolls swelled because of SORNA's increased number of registration-worthy offenses and retroactive applicability. Included on the registry were offenders who did not pose a significant danger, and if they had, it was often from decades earlier. This possible move was of great concern to Justice Ginsburg. In her dissent in *Smith v. Doe*, she cautioned against a system that focused exclusively on past crime as a "touchstone" because it "adds to the impression that the Act retributively targets past guilt." Justice Ginsburg was correct. Without individualized assessment, many non-dangerous people have been ensnared in a net cast far wider than originally anticipated.

The burdens of modern-day registration and notification schemes are devastating and crippling. Although the United States Supreme Court may have characterized registration and notification as civil remedies designed to protect a fearful public, the ever-expanding restrictions are significantly intrusive and leave the registrant with an overwhelming sense of isolation and shame. If registration schemes began in earnest in the 1990s because of the tragic deaths of three young children, harshening registration schemes began in earnest because of the Supreme Court's implicit permission to green-light the expansion.

THE NET WIDENS: CONSIDERING THE OTHER FACES OF REGISTRATION

Terminology affects our discussion of this issue. Registrants are legally characterized as "sexually violent predators," "sexual abusers," and "sexual predators" no matter their crimes. Despite their highly charged nature, these terms actually define a wide-ranging set of criminal behaviors, much of which is not predatory conduct.

And herein lies the problem of sex offender registries. Numerous adult and juvenile offenders who crowd the registry rolls are neither violent nor predatory. Of the 800,000 people currently on the sex offender registry rolls, only a small group of registrants fits the image of a dangerous stalking pedophile poised to rape and kill. Yet registries continue to expand despite the evidence that many offenders do not portend future dangerousness—either because they did not exhibit dangerous behavior when they committed the crime, or if they did, often the acts occurred decades earlier without proof that the offenders continue to be a sexual danger to their community.

Legislation that results from emotionally based incentives is fraught with dangers in drafting. This is especially true of sex offender registration laws, which trigger automatic registration in the hopes of corralling our fear of all sex offenders. Unfortunately, as a result, we have cast a net that captures equally the dangerous and the non-threatening. Painted in harsher terms by columnist Judith Levine, runaway sex offender registration laws result in "patent absurdities created by such laws—signs that legislators, in search of novel ways to torture so-called sex offenders, have abandoned consideration of efficacy or justice" (Levine, 2015).

This section introduces us to some non-dangerous registrants who have been swept up by over-broad and ill-defined sex offender registration laws.

Registrants who Commit Statutory Rape

Meet Zach Anderson. Zach was 19 years old when he traveled from Indiana to Michigan to have sexual relations with a girl he met online. That girl claimed to be 17 years old but in reality she was 13 years old. Zach was convicted of statutory rape, which is voluntary sexual intercourse with someone under a specified age who is conclusively incapable of giving consent because of age. States vary in setting the age of consent; generally, it ranges from 14 years of age to 18 years of age. In Michigan, where Zach and the girl had sexual intercourse, the age of consent is 16. Had she been 17, as Zach believed, there would have been no crime. But what of Zach's good-faith belief that she was 17? That belief is irrelevant for both conviction and registration. In most states, including Michigan, the prosecutor does not need to prove that the accused possessed a criminal *mens rea*. That is because the crime of statutory rape is a strict liability offense where the act of intercourse with the underage person is sufficient for conviction.

Not only is Zach's act sufficient for conviction without a culpable mental state, it is equally sufficient to require Zach to register as a sex offender. That is because in the vast majority of jurisdictions, conviction for statutory rape—whatever the underlying circumstances—is an automatically registerable offense. For many critics, automatic sex offender registration for statutory rape symbolizes the broken nature of a conviction-based assessment model that does not consider whether the offender poses an actual danger to the public. Certainly, this argument could be made for Zach, who possessed no criminal intent to have sexual intercourse with an underage girl, and who, the prosecutor had never alleged, was a threat to the public. Nevertheless, initially Zach was required to register as a sex offender for 25 years, even over the protestations of the girl and her family and Zach's community. Only with the support of the media might Zach's obligation to register be mitigated.

For Ricky Blackmun, his difficulties spiraled when he moved from Iowa to Oklahoma. Ricky was 16 years old when he was convicted as an adult of statutory rape with his then 13-year-old girlfriend. Although Ricky's crime was expunged in Iowa, his move to Oklahoma triggered registration. Not only did the move force Ricky to register in Oklahoma, he was labeled a tier III offender, considered the most dangerous classification in the state. This despite the fact that Ricky's record had been expunged in Iowa and he was never proven to be a danger to the community.

It is not only adults who must register when they engage in consensual relations with someone under age; juveniles must register as well. Indeed, registries are filled with underage offenders who had voluntary sexual relations with close-in-age underage partners. J.L. was 14 years old when he had consensual sexual relations with his 12-year-old girlfriend. Because of SORNA's guidelines, J.L. was deemed a "sexually violent predator" for having sex with someone under 13 years of age. J.L. was required to register for life.[1] And J.L. is not alone. Fifteen-year-old A.E. shared the same fate for engaging in voluntary sexual relations with his close-in-age girlfriend, and 15-year-old H.V. was deemed to be a "predatory offender" because he engaged in voluntary sexual intercourse with his 13-year-old girlfriend.[2] Even where the underage victim is above the age of 14, teens face the onerous burdens of registration. Maurice D., aged 17 years, engaged in consensual sexual intercourse with a 15-year-old girl. Logged in

1 People *ex rel.* J.L., 800 N.W.2d 720 (S.D. 2011).
2 *In re* A.E., 922 N.E.2d 1017 (Ohio Ct. App. 2009).

as "criminal sexual abuse" because of the girl's age, Maurice's act subjected him to registration as a sex offender.[3]

Equally difficult to justify is the State of Washington's blind adherence to the sex offender registration laws of another state. Here, Benjamin Batson was the collateral damage. Batson was convicted in Arizona of the statutory rape of a 17-year-old where the age of consent is 18 years of age. Batson's later move to the State of Washington presented a dilemma for Washington, where the age of consent is 16 years old. Batson found himself threatened with an obligation to register for an act that occurred more than 30 years previously and is lawful in Washington. Even the trial court that heard Batson's challenge to the duty to register mused about the irrationality of the state's position:

> I thought about this kind of practically, [if] Mr. Batson and I live on the same street. He happens to be from Arizona, he commits this offense in Arizona, moves to Washington, moves in next door, and I've engaged in the exact same conduct. We're next-door neighbors. Why should I be excluded from the class but he be included in it? What's the rational, reasonable, basis for doing that? (*State v. Batson*, 2015)

Child Registrants

When first adopted, sex offender registration laws were intended to apply only to adult sex offenders. But in a marked departure, the 2006 federal guidelines required that juvenile sex offenders adjudicated in juvenile court who were at least 14 years old must register as sex offenders. As was true of other SORNA provisions, a state's failure to mandate juvenile registration would result in the loss of federal funding.

To be sure, this change was controversial. Despite the threat of loss of federal funding for the failure to enact this provision of SORNA, states remain conflicted over whether to comply. A few states have flatly and publicly refused. They argue that the foundational policies of the juvenile justice system such as rehabilitation and confidentiality suffer when juvenile sex offenders must register for a term of years and face public scrutiny when their personal information is posted on the internet. The State of New York so responded:

3   *In re* Maurice D., 34 N.E.3d 590 (Ill. App. Ct. 2015).

New York has a long standing public policy of treating juvenile offenders differently from adult offenders so that juveniles have the best opportunity of rehabilitation and re-integration. The federal requirement that juveniles be placed on the Sex Offender Registry under SORNA is in direct conflict with that public policy. (Sugarman, 2011)

Employing automatic registration in the juvenile justice system is of great concern as well. It erodes the belief in rehabilitative measures if registration for a length of time is automatic and predetermined. In a letter to the U.S. Department of Justice, the General Counsel and Acting Chief of Staff of the Texas Governor wrote, "In dealing with juvenile sex offenders, Texas law more appropriately provides for judges to determine whether registration would be beneficial to the community and the juvenile offender in a particular case" (Boyd, 2011).

Some states have felt compelled to comply with SORNA's mandate but have limited registration to those who are at least 14 years old. But according to one published report, 24 states have no age minimum for child offenders; they require all child offenders—including those as young as nine years old—to register—sometimes, for life (Pittman and Nguyen, 2011).

Leah DuBuc is one such casualty. She was ten years old when, fully clothed, she simulated sex acts with her eight-year-old and five-year-old brothers. Because she committed the crime of criminal sexual conduct against a five-year-old, Leah was adjudicated as a sex offender in juvenile court. She was placed on the public adult registry when she was 12 years old, and required to continue registration for 25 years. In a blog that she wrote while in college—entitled "So, Who is Leah DuBuc Anyway?"—Leah described a journey filled with unrealized opportunities, lost housing, failed employment, loss of college internships, and bullying from her peers in college (DuBuc, 2007). Sadly, Leah's fate continues to be defined by that act as a ten-year-old. Despite earning a Master's degree in 2008, she remains largely unemployable. Leah left the country in the hope of starting a new life but returned because of family circumstances. And although her own state's laws have changed to remove juveniles under the age of 14 from the registry, vestiges of registration remain on the internet to haunt her (Stillman, 2016).

Other children as young as Leah have faced similar repercussions. Josh Gravens' fate was sealed at nine years old. After prolonged abuse by neighborhood boys, he acted out sexually with his six-year-old sister, which prompted the state to remove him from his home and require him to register as a sex offender. The repercussions of that act continue to haunt him today as Josh has struggled to maintain housing and employment.

When assessing a child's behavior, a system that fails to distinguish between the dangerous and the childish is doomed to produce irrational results. That could certainly be said of the following schoolyard pranks. In one, a humiliating battery was turned into a lifelong sentence for two 14-year-old boys who pulled down their own pants and sat on the faces of two restrained 12-year-old boys. In the other, a ten-year-old-girl pulled down the pants of a ten-year-old male classmate. In both situations, their acts were treated as sexual batteries rather than non-sexual offenses. For the 14-year-old boys, their schoolyard prank subjected them to automatic registration as sex offenders *for the rest of their lives*. A New Jersey sex crime defense attorney criticized the sentence, stating, "Punishment for bullying younger kids should be detention… Forcing them to register for Megan's law is first beyond the pale and second, cheapens the law" (Walmsley, 2011).

Slippery slopes are not merely the vision of alarmists. Even assuming there is merit to the sexual charges outlined above, the same cannot be said of the district attorney in Grant County, Wisconsin, who charged a six-year-old with a first degree felony for playing "butt doctor" with his five-year-old playmate. If this foolish charge were to prevail, the child would be forced to register as a sex offender when he turns 18. When pressed to explain the charge, the district attorney was reported to have said, "The legislature could have put an age restriction in the statute if it wanted to. The legislature did no such thing" (Sullum, 2011).

Registrants without a Sexual Motive

When registration laws were first introduced, courts supported the legislative will to protect minors from sexual predators. Today, however, courts no longer appear wedded to that justification. Due primarily to SORNA's lead, there has been an observable policy shift.

Today, courts regularly uphold legislation that requires registration for crimes involving juvenile victims *where no sexual component has been alleged*. Nineteen-year-old Ranier falls into this particular group. He robbed his 17-year-old female drug dealer, and because his victim was underage (and probably because she was female), Ranier was forced to register as a sex offender. This, even though all agreed that the robbery was not sexually motivated. In affirming automatic registration, the Georgia Supreme Court appeared unfazed by the apparent incongruity. It ruled that sex offender registration schemes were designed to protect all minors who were victims, irrespective of whether any sexual act was involved in the victimization (*Ranier v. State*, 2010). But dissenting Chief Justice Hunstein, concerned by the over-inclusiveness of such a pronouncement, stated that including crimes of this nature "serves merely to sweep within its purview those, such as [the appellant], who should not be characterized as 'sexual offenders'" (*Ranier v. State*, 2010).

Registrants Who Commit Non-Contact Sexual Offenses
Non-Sexually Exploitive Pornography

Child pornographers represent one of the fastest-growing groups of registrants. On the surface, this seems to be an obvious group the public would want to monitor. After all, child pornographers are among the most dangerous and abusive of sex offenders. Yet the relationship of sex offender registration laws to the crime of child pornography is a complex one. To the extent that one accepts the purpose and value of sex offender registration schemes, monitoring those who have been convicted of child pornography may make sense if it can be proven that offenders have physically and/or psychologically abused children and that they will continue to be a danger to children.

However, here is where complexities surface. Child pornography offenders can be broadly divided into two main categories: the creators and distributors, and the consumers. To target the consumers, the criminal definition of child pornography has evolved to include acts that arguably do not directly physically or psychologically harm children. Conviction of consumers of child pornography generally rest on two separate theories. First, as articulated in *New York v. Ferber* (1982), reputational damage to the exploited child occurs not only when the image is created, but each time the image is viewed by the consumer of pornography. Second, focusing on the consumer of child pornography has separate value from punishing the creator or distributor. The goal in punishing the consumer is to reduce the market for child pornography and ultimately chill the creation and distribution of it.

The reach of child pornography—punishing the maker, distributor, and possessor—calls into question whether all actors should be treated similarly for purposes of conviction and registration. In a lengthy and well-reasoned opinion justifying departure from the sentencing guidelines, the district court in *United States v. R.V.* (2016) rejected the contention that all offenders were equally culpable. Instead, the court differentiated among the actors, classifying them per their dangerousness and criminal *mens rea*. The court wrote, "Automatically equating non-production child pornography offenders—people who possess, acquire or distribute images of child sexual exploitation— with pedophiles or child molesters is misleading" (U.S. Dist. Ct. NY 2016).

Professor Carissa Byrne Hessick reaches a similar conclusion in "The limits of child pornography" (2014). She argues that, as an exception to First Amendment protections of private speech, the crime of child pornography should be narrowed to include only those acts that directly sexually exploit or abuse children in the creation of the image. Invoking the "principle of harm" as the touchstone for punishment of child pornography, she rejects the derivative and secondary "harm of circulation" that has become prevalent in prosecutions. Instead, Professor Hessick narrows the operating definition of child pornography to include depictions that are the result of (a) forcible sexual contact with another; (b) non-contact sexual activity that is the product of coercion; and (c) any sexual activity that is performed without consent.

Both the *R.V.* court and Professor Hessick have put forth rationales for limiting the reach of child pornography laws for the purposes of conviction and sentencing. It can be argued that the same limiting analysis should be applied to sex offender registration laws, which currently require automatic registration of all who are convicted of child pornography.

We already know that automatic registration is guaranteed to draw over-inclusive boundaries. Such is the case with child pornography convictions. Although Professor Hessick's article was not intended as an indictment of the collateral consequences of sex offender registration, her analysis is nonetheless helpful here. Requiring registration of all offenders, even those who have not engaged in the direct sexual abuse or exploitation of a minor, illustrates the pervasive failing that affects all sex offender registration laws: the lack of a sufficiently complex framework to differentiate the dangerous from the non-threatening. The *R.V.* court understood this proposition when it relied upon expert testimony that the recidivism rate was 3–5% for those whose sole offense was viewing child pornography (U.S. Dist. Ct. NY 2016).

Let's consider the following sexual activities through the lens of "the principle of harm" to see whether they are registration-worthy.

Sexting

Teenagers communicate differently today than a generation ago. And their preferred method of communication—a smartphone—makes them vulnerable to criminal prosecution for child pornography when they send or receive explicit photos over their phones or the internet. A 2012 study found that sexting behaviors are prevalent among adolescents and that "sexting occurred across sex, age, and race/ ethnicity. Specifically, more than 1-in-4 adolescents have sent a nude picture of themselves through electronic means, about half have been asked to send a nude picture, and about a third have asked for a nude picture to be sent to them" (Temple *et al.*, 2012).

Sexting fits within the prevailing definition of child pornography because it includes the photographing, videotaping, depicting on computer, filming, dissemination, or viewing of sexual acts or simulated sexual acts of a child under the age of 18. And because the crime of child pornography, however committed, automatically triggers sex offender registration, teenage sexters face significant burdens of registration. In "ripped from the headlines" stories across the country, high school students have been threatened with conviction for child pornography and registration as sex offenders for sending or receiving sexual images, often from someone or to someone in a consensual sexual relationship with them.

There are two ways to circumvent what many believe is an illogical fit: reclassify the act of consensual sexting as an activity that falls outside the bounds of child pornography (as Professor Hessick would argue), or eliminate automatic sex offender registration for this particular activity. Under Professor Hessick's definition, registration for this non-sexually exploitive activity does not serve the central aims of sex offender registration because the minor was not sexually abused or exploited in the creation of the image. At least one legislature would agree. Recognizing the inalterable damage that a conviction for child pornography brings, New Mexico passed a law in 2016 that exempts teenagers between 14 and 17 years of age from prosecution for child pornography where they willingly send explicit images of themselves to one another. In sponsoring the bill, State Senator George Muñoz stated, "Kids will be kids, and they're going to make mistakes. You can't punish them for the rest of their lifetime with a charge of child pornography... if they're consensually sending photos back and forth" (Levin, 2016).

Possession of Other Non-Sexually Exploited Pornographic Images

Beyond sexting, there are other images for which conviction and registration are mandated. Like sexted images, they raise similar concerns regarding their registration-worthiness. Professor Hessick notes two situations: computer-altered images that do not directly involve the exploitation of a child; and images of minors 16–18 years of age where the state permits consensual sexual activity in that age range. Like possession of sexted materials, these situations involve the creation or possession of depictions that appear to be the result of sexually abusive conduct, but often they are not.

In the case of the morphed computer image—a child's head superimposed on an adult's body in a sexual pose or position—no child has been directly harmed in the depiction. For the 17-year-old participating in consensual sexual activity that is filmed or recorded, it is the conflict between statutory rape laws and child pornography laws that create the tension. On the one hand, numerous states permit a 17-year-old to consent to sexual activity, although that age threshold does not apply to child pornography laws where the age is 18.

Both acts constitute child pornography. Yet, under the principle of harm, neither act involves sexual abuse or harm to a minor in the production of the image. Can it be said that the maker or viewer of these images poses a sufficient danger to the community to justify automatic registration as a sex offender?

Indecent Exposure

The crime of indecent exposure occupies an interesting, if not conflicted, position among crimes that warrant registration. On the one hand, some acts of indecent exposure are intended to cause alarm or fear of bodily harm on the part of the witness. But often the intent of the actor in committing the crime is more benign: to affront or surprise such as in an act of streaking, or to defy convention such as in an act of nude sunbathing where prohibited. This is what happened to Dean Edgar Wiesart, who pled guilty to indecent exposure because he and a girlfriend skinny-dipped in a Maryland hotel pool in 1979. A later conviction in the 1990s for possession of a controlled substance in South Carolina triggered a probation report revealing the previous conviction. Wiesart was notified that, under South Carolina law, he would have to register as a sex offender for life because of the previous incident. The absurdity of how this played out is best understood against a backdrop of automatic registration where the conviction serves as the sole driving force to determine registration. In 2008, Wiesart sought declaratory relief and was granted minimum relief when the court of appeals agreed that, under the statutory provisions as set out, Wiesart was entitled to a hearing to determine whether he was a sexual danger to the community. Odd, however, that despite the factual underpinnings of the indecent exposure conviction, the court expressly stated, "We do not pass judgment on the issue of whether the circumstances of this case warrant Wiesart's registration as a sex offender" (*Wiesart v. Stewart*, 2008).

Registrants Whose Crimes Occurred Decades Earlier

Because sex offender registration laws have been characterized as civil regulations, the Eighth Amendment's proscription against *ex post facto* principles does not apply. In practical terms, states are free to reach back in time to capture those whose offenses were committed prior to the enactment of registration laws or expanding amendments. Without an inquiry into whether these past offenders continue to pose a danger to the public, this automatic practice produces sweeping results that ensnares persons who are no longer dangerous. Certainly that was true for Michael McGuire. Twenty-five years after his conviction in Colorado for sexual assault against his former girlfriend, Mr. McGuire was forced to register as a sex offender for the first time at the age of 57 and in the state of Alabama—all precipitated by his move to Alabama to help care for his elderly mother. Until that time, and following his term in prison in the 1980s, Mr. McGuire led a full and productive life in Washington D.C. as a married man, a hairstylist, and jazz musician.

Unfortunately, and unbeknownst to Mr. McGuire, the move to Alabama would cost him his life as he knew it. Forced to register in Alabama for the rest of his life, Mr. McGuire has been brutalized by the "most comprehensive, debilitating sex-offender scheme in the land, one that includes not only most of the restrictive features used by various other jurisdictions, but also unique additional requirements and restrictions nonexistent elsewhere, at least in this form" (*McGuire v. Strange*, 2015). Barred from living in his family home because of residency restrictions, he has been declared officially homeless. And as a homeless man, he must register in person at both the City of Montgomery Police Department and the Montgomery County Sheriff's Department each week for the rest of his life. He must have at all times in his possession a driver's license or identification card bearing a designation that enables law enforcement officers to identify him as a sex offender. Most disturbing, the law identifies 115 ways for an offender to fail to comply with the host of restrictions, all which lead to lengthy prison sentences.

Why not move back to Washington D.C. one might ask? Sadly, Mr. McGuire's fate was sealed the moment Alabama forced him to register as a sex offender. That designation will follow him whether he moves back to Washington D.C., where he was never required to register, or relocates to another state for an attempt at a fresh start. This is the ugly underbelly of a conviction-based assessment model that never answers the real question at issue: whether Mr. McGuire poses a danger to the community in which he resides.

THE MYTH OF RECIDIVISM

It is easy to vilify all sex offenders. The images of the dangerous and violent pedophile are seared into our memories. This horror is real. But we must also be cautious in acting on these stories. A legislative agenda that is controlled by emotional rhetoric fosters inaccurate and embedded assumptions that are hard to remove. A review of the legislative history of sex offender registration legislation indicates the truth of this observation. Their genesis is infused with highly emotional language but devoid of scientific evidence for support. An indictment regarding the lack of scientific evidence comes from none other than the Department of Justice, which in 2015 wrote, "[T]here is little question that both public safety and the efficient use of public resources would be enhanced if sex offender registration laws were based on evidence of effectiveness rather than other factors" (Lobanov-Rostovsky, 2015).

As it turns out, more difficult than mounting legal challenges to these laws is countering successfully the emotion that shapes this particular debate. Comments by the legislative sponsor to Nebraska's proposed expanded sex offender laws tell the story. According to the appellate court reviewing the laws, the legislator "expressed 'rage' and 'revulsion' regarding persons who have 'these convictions'" and that "he did not 'buy' the idea of 'rehabilitation' or that 'people could change...[i]n [this] area'" (*Doe v. Nebraska*, 2010). The comments of U.S. Representative Ric Keller (R-FL) also illustrates the point: "The best way to protect children is to keep child predators locked up in the first place, because someone who has molested a child will do it again and again and again" (Petteruti and Walsh, 2008). New York Assemblyman Herbst vocalized it when he stated on the floor of the Assembly, "I don't know if, when [a sex offender is] released from prison, he will come back, but the statistics...have shown that *once a pedophile, always a pedophile*" (Petteruti and Walsh, 2008).

Not only is the discussion infused with emotion, but so too is the actual legislation. As noted previously, drafted laws affix statutory labels such as "sexually violent predators," "sexual abusers," and "sexual predators" to those who have committed sexual offenses— broad-brush terms used to encompass a wide-ranging set of criminal behaviors, many of which are not predatory conduct.

We have panicked when it comes to our dealing with convicted sex offenders. Historian Philip Jenkins' definition of "social panic" describes all too well this phenomenon of hastily crafted and serially amended registration and notification laws that ensnare equally the child rapist and the person who engages in consensual sexual intercourse with an underage person. The definition of a social panic, Jenkins writes, is one in which the "fear is wildly exaggerated and wrongly directed" (Jenkins, 1998, pp.6–7). The hallmarks of a social panic are (1) an official reaction that is not proportional to the actual threat; (2) leaders in the community who all speak of the threat in identical terms; and (3) media who are complicit in stoking the panic (Jenkins, 2009).

One factor in particular stands out. Courts and politicians all speak of the threat of sex offenders in identical terms. The position—indeed, the mantra actually—is that the rate of reoffense among sex offenders is "frightening and high" (*Smith v. Doe*, 2003). Unlike other criminals, the argument continues, sex offenders pose a significant continued danger to the public that justifies the intrusion and loss of individual rights that registrants endure.

But is this perception accurate? The answer is no; sex offenders do not recidivate at a rate that is "frightening and high." In fact, 20 years of studies actually support the opposite conclusion. Unfortunately, the emotion that cloaks the discussion has made it all but impermeable to analysis that contradicts the false narrative of high rates of reoffense. For example, the Department of Justice found that only 5.3% of sex offenders were rearrested for a new sex crime within three years after release from prison (Langan, Schmitt, and Durose, 2003). Similarly, the State of Connecticut, in a 2012 study, found that the recidivism rates of sex offenders after five years were 3.6% for rearrest and 2.7% for a new sex offense conviction (Office of Policy and Management, 2012). The Office of Policy and Management reported that the statistics were "much lower than what many in the public have been led to expect or believe. These low re-offense rates appear to contradict a conventional wisdom that sex offenders have very high sexual re-offense rates" (Office of Policy and Management, 2012, p.4). And Human Rights Watch reported in 2011 that the rate for adult sex offenders was only 13% (Pittman, 2013).

For child sex offenders, the statistics support a similar conclusion. Children who sexually offend are not more likely to reoffend than their non-sexually offending counterparts. On that point, Dr. David Burton wrote, "[Registration schemes] assume that past offenders will be future offenders. But when it comes to sexual offending, several decades of research prove otherwise" (Leon, Burton, and Alvare, 2011, pp. 144–5). Dr. Michael Caldwell's extensive research confirms this statement. His empirical studies, which span from the 1940s to 2014, show that child sex offenders recidivate at rates under 5% (Caldwell, 2014). So does Dr. Elizabeth Letourneau's study of the subject. Her results indicate that recidivism rates hover around 1% (Pittman and Nguyen, 2011).

So how did the false narrative of high recidivism rates seep into our jurisprudence? An excellent article entitled "'Frightening and high': The Supreme Court's crucial mistake about sex crime statistics" by Professor Ira Ellman and Ms. Tara Ellman (2015) suggests that the Supreme Court's assertion that sex offenders recidivate at a rate that is "frightening and high" can be traced back to the Court's erroneous reliance on a single report from the Department of Justice. Specifically, the authors argue that the report itself was based on a single pop-psychology magazine article with no supporting data to back up its assertion. Nevertheless, the material was used in *McKune v. Lile* (2002) to support the Court's claim "that recidivism rate of untreated offenders has been estimated to be as high as 80%." Its impact reverberated. *Smith*, which was decided the following term, adopted the *McKune* sentiment, and the phrase "frightening and high" was officially launched.

CHALLENGING THE CONSTITUTIONALITY OF SEX OFFENDER REGISTRATION LAWS

Sex offender registration laws have flourished largely unchecked. At a time where legislatures continually and serially amend registration schemes with impunity, the only recourse to righting the balance lies with the courts.

Making the Case for Punishment under the Eighth Amendment

Labels matter. Classifying a law as a civil regulation or criminal penalty has great legal significance. To withstand constitutional scrutiny, a civil regulation need only be rationally related to the civil purpose it is intended to serve. As noted previously, by contrast, a criminal penalty must meet the Eighth Amendment's prohibitions against cruel and unusual punishment and *ex post facto* principles. The problem is that sometimes it is difficult to tell whether a law is civil or criminal in nature. To aid in the determination, the Supreme Court crafted a two-step process in *Kennedy v. Mendoza-Martinez* (1962). It has come to be called the "intent-effects" test. The first step considers whether the legislature intended the statute to be a civil remedy or a criminal penalty. Assuming the legislature intended the regulation to be civil, the second step of the test asks whether, despite that legislative intent, the law is nonetheless so punitive that the regulation has lost its civil label and has been transformed into a criminal penalty.

As one can imagine, determining whether the "effect" of a piece of legislation is punitive despite its civil label requires careful analysis. On this, *Mendoza-Martinez* is equally instructive. It identifies seven factors to consider when deciding whether the legislation has been transformed into a criminal penalty despite legislative intent to draft a civil regulation:

> [1] Whether the sanction involves an affirmative disability or restraint, [2] whether it has historically been regarded as a punishment[,] [3] whether it comes into play only on a finding of *scienter*, [4] whether its operation will promote the traditional aims of punishment— retribution and deterrence, [5] whether the behavior to which it applies is already a crime, [6] whether an alternative purpose to which it may rationally be connected is assignable for it, and [7] whether it appears excessive in relation to the alternative purpose assigned. (1962, pp.168–169)

As applied to sex offender registration laws, courts have determined that states easily satisfy the first step of the *Mendoza-Martinez* test. Language found in registration statutes demonstrates that, on their face, these schemes reportedly serve non-punitive purposes to protect the community and assist law enforcement in conducting investigations and apprehending offenders. But, as *Mendoza-Martinez* is quick to caution, a purportedly civil regulation can be stripped of that classification if the effect of the legislation is nonetheless so punitive that it transforms a civil regulation into a criminal penalty.

At first blush, it would appear that the second step—the "effects" of the law—is equally well settled because of the Court's pronouncement in *Smith v. Doe* (2003) that the incidental burdens of registration did not turn the civil regulation into a criminal penalty. Comparing the burdens of registration with traditional notions of punishment, the Court concluded that registration statutes did not impose the hallmarks of imprisonment or banishment on registrants. The Court observed that offenders in Alaska were free to live where they wanted and to move unencumbered within the state. Further, in-person registration was infrequent, and the information posted on the internet regarding the petitioners' convictions was no greater than would have been gleaned from information noted in the public conviction.

Smith's minimization of the burdens of registration stands today. Most courts, on the strength of *Smith*'s reach, have rejected the notion that registration is punishment. There are a few exceptions. Several courts have relied on their own state constitutions to conclude that their state registration schemes have turned punitive under the *Mendoza-Martinez* test (*Doe v. Dep't of Pub. Safety*, 2013; *State v. Letalien*, 2009; *Wallace v. State*, 2009).

Extending that analysis under the federal constitution will require reimagining the conclusions of *Smith*. *Smith* was decided in 2003, and the Court's reasoning was based on its observations of Alaska's registration scheme from 1994. With a shifting landscape and decidedly harsher registration schemes in force, the *Smith* analysis invites reexamination of the "intent-effects" test to see if the ruling withstands modern scrutiny. Of the *Mendoza-Martinez* factors at play, two are especially ripe for reconsideration: (1) whether modern registration schemes incur an affirmative disability, and (2) whether registration schemes are now excessive in relation to the alternative purpose assigned.

Affirmative Disability or Restraint

At its core, the first *Mendoza-Martinez* factor of affirmative disability or restraint evokes images of imprisonment or loss of freedom of movement. Where the law does not impose a physical restraint, the Court has accepted that public shaming, akin to what occurred in colonial times, may serve as a substitute. As a consequence, and based on this narrow interpretation of affirmative disability or restraint, the Supreme Court has found that the denial of social security benefits, revocation of a driver's license, and debarment from the banking industry fall short of the first *Mendoza-Martinez* test despite the burdens that these governmental actions impose.

In line with this narrow interpretation, the *Smith* court concluded that burdens associated with registration and notification are punitive in nature. It dismissed the contention that registration burdens effectively create an affirmative disability, noting that the Alaskan law "imposes no physical restraint, and so does not resemble imprisonment, the paradigmatic affirmative disability or restraint" (*Smith v. Doe*, 2003, p.86). Further, the court found that registration "had not led to substantial occupational or housing disadvantages for former sex offenders that would not have otherwise occurred" (p.86).

However, *Smith* might conclude differently on the issue of an "affirmative disability or restraint" if modern-day sex offender registration schemes were put to the test. Serially amended restrictions severely limit the registrant's opportunity for employment and housing. Because of sweeping residency and presence restrictions, registrants are no longer free to move about their states as petitioners in Alaska were free to do. Indeed, given the aggressive and pervasive nature of residency restrictions today, the word that comes to mind is "banishment," a hallmark of colonial punishments. That is, in effect, what the California Supreme Court found in 2015 when it held that San Diego's all-encompassing residency restrictions were unconstitutional as applied to parolees. Parolees were effectively banished from 97% of San Diego County and, practically speaking, unable to rent in the remaining 3% of available housing. In arriving at its conclusion, the California court stated:

> [B]lanket enforcement of the mandatory residency restrictions of Jessica's Law, as applied to registered sex offenders on parole in San Diego County, cannot survive even the more deferential rational basis standard of constitutional review. Such enforcement has imposed harsh and severe restrictions and disabilities on the affected parolees' liberty and privacy rights, however limited, while producing conditions that hamper, rather than foster, efforts to monitor, supervise, and rehabilitate these persons. (Taylor, 2015, p.879)

Affirmative disability or restraint may derive from public shaming as well. Despite countless stories from registrants of isolation, ostracism, and humiliation, the *Smith* court rejected this characterization. Rather, the Court determined that the public dissemination of information on Megan's Law websites was no different from what could be found in the public domain from the conviction itself. The Court stated: "[T]he stigma of Alaska's Megan's Law results not from public display for ridicule and shaming but from the dissemination of accurate information about a criminal record, most of which is already public" (*Smith v. Doe*, 2003, p.98). The Pennsylvania Supreme Court in 2003 concurred when it stated in *Commonwealth v. Williams* (2003) that the "disclosure of factual information" about a person's history is not the same as shaming.

This is a correct assessment, perhaps, of 1994 community notification laws, but doubtfully accurate about today's laws.

The shame and ostracism that the registrant experiences under modern registration schemes far surpass the effects from information on a public criminal record. In addition to the widespread residency and presence restrictions that ostracize registrants, consider the following additions to sex offender registration laws since the first scheme was introduced. Today, in Alabama, for example, a registrant's driver's license is marked with the designation "sex offender," and several other states are pursuing similar actions. The designation is not only domestic; it is going international. Congress passed International Megan's Law, which contemplates that passports will include a permanent designation that the holder is a registered sex offender.

Excessive in Relation to Alternative Purpose Assigned

Ever-expanding sex offender registration laws suffer from excessiveness. Under *Mendoza-Martinez*, this factor focuses on whether the means chosen to implement the civil regulation is excessive in relationship to its assigned civil purpose. Like the first factor, this one has favored the states. The rational purpose for crafting registration laws has been to protect the public from dangerous sex offenders who are likely to reoffend. However, *Smith* was decided at a time when individual risk assessment was the norm and where registration burdens were more tailored. The court did not specifically address whether the state's purpose survives under the current conviction-based assessment model that requires automatic registration of all offenders without a demonstrated proof of the likelihood of reoffense.

Anchoring the state's argument is one dominant assumption: everyone convicted of sex offenses continues to pose a danger to the community. But that rationale ignores the effect of the current system in operation, which, by design and without individual risk assessment, ensnares the dangerous and non-threatening alike. It could be argued that serially expanding laws that are not tied to proof of dangerousness are excessive in relation to the alternate civil purpose assigned. Indeed, in her dissent in *Smith*, Justice Ginsburg cautioned against such a system for this very reason. The failure to provide for individualized assessment or offer the registrant the opportunity to demonstrate rehabilitation, she argued, was unconstitutional. She stated, "[M]eriting heaviest weight in my judgment, the Act makes no provision whatever for the possibility of rehabilitation: Offenders cannot shorten their registration or notification period, even on the clearest demonstration of rehabilitation or conclusive proof of physical incapacitation" (538 U.S., p.117). Her warning has come to pass. Some states have eliminated the waiver provision, and legislators in California, in 2016, introduced a bill that would eliminate removal from the registry.

Although one can appreciate the utility of a conviction-based assessment model, it comes at a cost. It must be balanced against the acknowledgment that automatic registration captures those who should not be characterized as sexual predators.

Arguing a Substantive Due Process Violation

Given the inherent unfairness of a system that paints all offenders with the same unforgiving brush, one might think that these laws are ripe for a successful due process challenge. Yet it has proven to be a foolhardy task to challenge sex offender registration laws under substantive due process. The landmark case of *Rochin v. California* (1952) cautioned that courts must subject due process claims "to the very narrow scrutiny which the Due Process Clause of the Fourteenth Amendment authorizes." To that end, the Court has held firm to the proposition that the right asserted must be "deeply rooted in this Nation's history and tradition" or "implicit in the concept of ordered liberty" (*Washington v. Glucksberg,* 1997).

In general, therefore, due process challenges rarely succeed unless they are tied to traditionally valued fundamental interests, which heighten the state's burden to prove a compelling need for the legislation and that the legislation is narrowly tailored to meet its goals. Without a fundamental right to anchor the challenge, the state's burden is significantly lessened. Great deference is afforded legislation as long as it is rationally related to a governmental interest. Indeed, as one scholar bemoaned, the rational basis test "was tantamount to declaring the legislation was constitutional" (Bice, 1980, p.4).

But this does not mean that the government has carte blanche. Despite the deference afforded, and taking a cue from *Rochin,* governmental actions must not offend "canons of decency and fairness...even toward those charged with the most heinous offenses" (*Rochin v. California,* 1952). To date, the courts have concluded that sex offender registration laws do not offend the canons of decency and fairness because burdens of registration only parallel the consequences that flow from a public conviction.

It can be argued, however, that modern sex offender registration burdens extend far beyond consequences that flow from conviction. Indeed:

> Registration burdens should not be viewed as isolated slices of prohibition; rather, they impact every aspect of life—where to live, where to work, where to travel, and with whom to associate. Indeed, there is no aspect of the sex offender's life untouched by the imprint of registration and notification. (Carpenter and Beverlin, 2012, p.1125)

Mounting a successful substantive due process challenge offers one way to counter such broad-based governmental persecution.

Arguing a Procedural Due Process Violation

One vulnerability of a conviction-based assessment model is that offenders are presumed dangerous to the community without an opportunity for them to be heard on whether that classification is accurate. This practice raises the question about whether offenders are deprived of procedural due process protections. After all, they face the loss of their liberty interest of reputation without a basic process in place to review the deprivation.

Unfortunately, such challenges have been unsuccessful in the courts. According to well-settled principles, the denial of the liberty interest of reputation alone is insufficient to trigger procedural due process protections. Rather, under a test articulated from the 1970s, called the "stigma *plus*" test, the loss of reputation from governmental action must also be accompanied by the denial or curtailment of an additional tangible benefit (*Paul v. Davis*, 1976).

One might imagine that registrants would easily be able to prove a curtailment of additional benefits because of the loss of housing and employment opportunities. Yet that is not the case. Indeed, sex offenders have had tremendous difficulty in the courts asserting a sufficient "plus" associated with the stigma attached to registration. The reason? As is true for other legal challenges mounted by registrants, the courts remain fixed by the view that any deprivation a registrant experiences flows directly and solely from a public statement of the conviction.

Given the law to date, the Pennsylvania Supreme Court's decision of *In re* J.B. in 2014 is groundbreaking. Invoking both substantive and procedural due process protections, the Court employed the fundamental right of reputation found in the Pennsylvania constitution to overturn mandatory lifetime registration for child offenders. In support of the result, the Court pulled back the curtain on sex offender registration schemes to expose the flawed, but universally held, presumption that child sex offenders reoffend at high rates. Although the decision may not be portable for its reliance on the loss of reputational value, its rejection of the wholly inaccurate assumption of high recidivism rates of offenders offers a legal justification to change the national narrative on sex offender registration laws.

CONCLUSION

Yes, it is true that the image of the violent pedophile haunts us. Yet the national response to the fear invoked by this image has produced sex offender registration laws that no longer serve their initial rational civil purpose. Capturing both the dangerous and non-threatening through over-broad and ill-defined legislation, registration schemes have left a segment of the population, undeserving of the opprobrium, devastated and oppressed.

Change is long overdue. It is time to consider meaningful reform that acknowledges the state's desire to protect the public, yet also reins in the emotional rhetoric that promotes the falsity of recidivism rates and the spiraling nature of the laws.

REFERENCES

42 U.S.C. § 14071.

538 U.S. at 117 (Ginsburg, J., dissenting).

Bice, S.H. (1980) "Rationality analysis in constitutional law." *Minnesota Law Review 65*, 1, 3–4.

Boyd, J.S. (2011, August 17) Letter to Linda M. Baldwin, Director of the SMART Office in the Dept. of Justice. Available at http://mobile.ncleg.net/documentsites/committees/JLOCJPS/2011-12%20Interim/October%2013,%202011%20Meeting/RD_SORNA_General_Information_2011-10-13.pdf (accessed January 26, 2017).

Caldwell, M. (2014) "Juvenile Sex Offenders." In F. Zimring and D. Tanenhaus (eds) *Choosing the Future for American Juvenile Justice*. New York, NY: New York University Press.

Carpenter, C. (2010) "Legislative epidemics: A cautionary tale of criminal laws that sweep the country." *58 Buffalo L. Rev. 1, 41 (2010)*

Carpenter, C. and Beverlin, A. (2012) "The evolution of unconstitutionality in sex offender registration laws." *63 Hastings Law Journal 1073, 1078 (2012)*

Commonwealth v. Williams, 832 A.2d 962, 975–76 (2003).

Connecticut Department of Public Safety v. Doe, 538 U.S. 84, 89 (2003).

Doe v. Dep't of Pub. Safety, 62 A.3d 123 (2013).

Doe v. Nebraska, 734 F. Supp. 2d 882, 898 (D. Neb. 2010).

DuBuc, L. (2007) "So, Who is Leah DuBuc Anyway?" Available at http://classes.kvcc.edu/ eng155/21410/ldubuc/all_about_me.htm (accessed January 24, 2017).

E.B. v. Verniero, 119 F.3d 1077, 1112 (3d Cir. 1997).

Ellman, I.M. and Ellman, T. (2015) "'Frightening and high': The Supreme Court's crucial mistake about sex crime statistics." *Constitutional Commentary*, Fall 2015. Available at http://nationalrsol. org/wp-content/uploads/2015/08/Frighteninghigh.pdf (accessed January 17, 2017).

Hessick, C.B. (2014) "The limits of child pornography." *Indiana Law Journal 89*, 4, 1437.

Indiana Code §§ 5-2-12-1–5-2-12-13.

In re J.B., 107 A.3d 1 (2014).

Jenkins, P. (1998) *Moral Panic: Changing Concepts of the Child Molester in Modern America*. New Haven, CT: Yale University Press.

Jenkins, P. (2009) "Failure to launch: Why do some social issues fail to detonate moral panics?" *British Journal of Criminology 49*, 1, 35–47.

Kennedy v. Mendoza-Martinez, 372 U.S. 144 (1962).

Langan, P.A., Schmitt, E.L., and Durose, M.R. (2003) *Recidivism of Sex Offenders Released from Prison in 1994*. Washington, DC: Bureau of Justice Statistics.

La. Rev. Stat. Ann. § 15:542(C)(1) (2011).

Leon, C., Burton, D.L., and Alvare, D. (2011) "Net-widening in Delaware: The overuse of registration and residential treatment for youth who commit sex offenses." *Widener Law Review 17*, 1, 127.

Levin, S. (2016) "New Mexico teens can now legally sext each other and exchange nude photos." *The Guardian*, February 26. Available at www.theguardian.com/us-news/2016/feb/26/new-mexico-legalizes-teen-sexting (accessed January 24, 2017).

Levine, J. (2015) 'The online-sex predator panic.' *The Boston Review*, December 8. Available at http:// bostonreview.net/us/judith-levine-luring-sexting-laws (accessed January 24, 2017).

Lobanov-Rostovsky, C. (2015) "Adult Sex Offender Management." U.S. Department of Justice, July 2015. Available at www.smart.gov/pdfs/AdultSexOffenderManagement.pdf (accessed January 24, 2017).

McGuire v. Strange, 83 F. Supp. 3d 1231, 1236 (MD Alabama 2015).

McKune v. Lile, 536 U.S. 24 (2002).

New York v. Ferber, 458 U.S. 747, 759–61 (1982).

Paul v. Davis, 424 U.S. 693 (1976).

Petteruti, A. and Walsh, N. (2008) "Registering Harm: How Sex Offenses Fail Youth and Communities." Justice Policy Institute, November 21. Available at www.justicepolicy.org/ images/upload/08-11_rpt_walshactregisteringharm_jj-ps.pdf (accessed January 24, 2017).

Pittman, N. (2013) "Raised on the Registry: The Irreparable Harm of Placing Children on Sex Offender Registries in the United States." Human Rights Watch. Available at www.hrw.org/ sites/default/files/reports/us0513_ForUpload_1.pdf (accessed January 24, 2017).

Pittman, N. and Nguyen, Q. (2011) "A Snapshot of Juvenile Sex Offender Registration and Notification Laws." Available at www.njjn.org/uploads/digital-library/SNAPSHOT_web10-28.pdf (accessed January 24, 2017).

Pub. L. No. 109-248, 120 Stat. 587 (2006) (codified as amended in scattered sections of 18 and 42 U.S.C. (2010)). (Adam Walsh Child Protection and Safety Act)

Ranier v. State, 690 S.E.2d 827 (Ga. 2010).

Rochin v. California, 342 U.S. 165, 168 (1952).

Smith v. Doe, 538 U.S. 84, 116 (2003).

State of Connecticut Office of Policy and Management (2012) "Recidivism among Sex Offenders in Connecticut." Available at www.ct.gov/bopp/lib/bopp/sex_offender_recidivism_2012_final. pdf (accessed January 24, 2017).

State v. Batson, 2015 WL 4251230 (Wash. App. Div. 1 2015).

State v. Letalien, 985 A.2d 4 (Me. 2009).

Stillman, S. (2016) "The List." *The New Yorker*, March 14. Available at www.newyorker.com/ magazine/2016/03/14/when-kids-are-accused-of-sex-crimes (accessed January 24, 2017).

Sugarman, R. (2011) Letter to Linda M. Baldwin, Director of the SMART Office in the Department of Justice, August 23, 2011. Available at http://mobile.ncleg.net/documentsites/committees/JLOCJPS/2011-12%20Interim/October%2013,%202011%20Meeting/RD_SORNA_General_Information_2011-10-13.pdf (accessed January 24, 2017).

Sullum, J. (2011) "Parents sue D.A. for charging their 6-year-old son with a felony for playing doctor with a 5-year-old playmate." *Reason*, November 23. Available at https://reason.com/blog/2011/11/23/parents-sue-da-for-charging-their-6-year (accessed January 24, 2017).

Taylor, 343 P.3d 867, 879 (2015).

Temple, J.R., Paul, J.A., van den Berg, P., Le, V.D., McElhany, A., and Temple, B.W. (2012) "Teen sexting and its association with sexual behaviors." *Archives of Pediatrics & Adolescent Medicine* 166, 9, 828–833.

United States v. R.V., F. Supp. 3d, 2016 WL 270257 (U.S. Dist. Ct. NY 2016).

Wallace v. State, 905 N.E.2d 371 (Ind. 2009).

Walmsley, K. (2011, July 27) "NJ case raises questions about Meghan's Laws." *ABC News*, July 27. Available at http://abcnews.go.com/US/nj-case-raises-questions-meghans-laws/story?id=14171897 (accessed January 24, 2017).

Warren, S.D. and Brandeis, L.D. (1890) "The right to privacy." *Harvard Law Review 4*, 214.

Washington v. Glucksberg, 521 U.S. 702, 703, 721 (1997).

Wiesart v. Stewart, 665 S.E.2d 187, n.7 (2008).

CHAPTER 12

Asperger's Syndrome and Downloading Child Pornography

Why Criminal Punishment is Unjust and Ineffective

John Douard and Pamela Schultz

INTRODUCTION

When we were asked to contribute a chapter to this book, both of us wondered what we could profitably write about criminal sexual conduct and the autistic spectrum disorder Asperger's syndrome (AS). We had said what we wanted to say in our book and journal articles about the disastrous moral panic that frames sex offenders as less-than-human monsters, and how laws are created that seem designed to externalize our anxieties about taboo sexual desires and conduct (Douard and Schultz, 2013). But, in fact, we had not considered the project presented in this book. When we think about sexual offenses and people with cognitive disabilities, we generally think about *victims* of sexual misconduct, and not about people with cognitive and affective disorders being accused, rightly or wrongly, of engaging in such behavior. That situation results in dissonance, because we are likely to be sympathetic to, for example, people on the autism spectrum, but react to sex offending with fear and loathing.

There are literary precedents for such dissonance: William Faulkner's Benjy and Harper Lee's Bo, for example, are characters about whom readers are supposed to be in two minds about their sexual interests. In our earlier work, we had been thinking about our criticism of sex offense laws as a defense of humane treatment for the indefensible. But people on the autism spectrum trigger our sympathy and, indeed, possibly our empathy. What happens when they get caught up in the legal universe of sex offense laws that are the direct response to irrational and immoral moral panic? These laws are intended to target offenders who have sufficient control over their sex-offending conduct that they are not even eligible for involuntary civil commitment unless special civil commitment statutes are implemented targeting such offenders. That question poses special problems that this chapter will address.

A review of the history of the autism concept and diagnosis, and the experiences of people with autism, reveals that they suffer from some of the psycho/social/sexual developmental problems exhibited by some people convicted of sex offenses. The most salient and significant of these problems is the difficulty that people with AS, and a fairly large class of sex offenders, have empathizing with others. Empathy is generally presumed to be the capability for responding with sensitivity and care to the suffering of others (Zahavi and Overgaard, 2012, p.3). Given that we tend to view the capacity to see through another person's eyes as one of the highest expressions of humanity, this observed lack of empathy was one of the reasons why, beginning in the 1930s, "a campaign was underway fought by intelligent, zealous, and influential Americans who believed that children [with the problems we now associate with autism] were a danger to society *and, worse, not fully human*" (Donvan and Zucker, 2016, p.48, emphasis added).

The tendency to stigmatize children with autism then—and to some extent even now—is grounded, we believe, on the fear that people who seem radically different from ourselves are dangerous. Although autism often causes "extremely disruptive antisocial behavior," persons on the spectrum may not have any other characteristics of difference. "It is this combination of pervasive disability and apparent physical normality that gives the stigma experienced by families with autistic children its unique quality" (Gray, 1993, p.114). Indeed, because it is not a disability that is obvious to the public, people afflicted with so-called "high-functioning" autism, including AS, may be "exposed to more incidents of stigmatizing reactions from others, without the obvious explanation of disablement that other conditions can call upon in public encounters" (Gray, 2002, p.743). As we show below, the disability central to the experiences of people with AS that is most significant in causing fear in others is their apparent lack of empathy.

Against that background, we ask the reader to imagine what it must be like to lack the type of neural functioning that enables us to recognize when our conduct may cause others to suffer, and to recognize when we are acting in ways that are prohibited by laws we do not understand. That is the sort of deficit with which people with AS must confront the complex network of laws prohibiting a wide range of sexual conduct. For people with AS to be classified as sex offenders, to be criminally liable for conduct they do not understand is morally wrong even if they know it is legally wrong, a double exclusion takes place from the culture of those who are regarded as "normal." They are stigmatized twice over. As attorney Mark Mahoney puts it:

> Their curiosity, unrestrained by social or legal taboos, of which they are unaware, leads them to view images of "underage" (i.e., younger than 18-years old) girls who are nearly their own age and years older than the level of their own social adaptation skills. This has resulted in criminal convictions, lengthy mandatory prison sentences, and a lifetime of reporting, ostracization, and residency restrictions as "sex offenders." (Mahoney, 2009, p.1)

Because possession and distribution of child pornography is a "strict liability" crime, not understanding that it is a crime is not a legal defense; only prosecutorial discretion can save them from this outcome. And prosecutorial imagination is severely circumscribed by pressures to get convictions (despite the Supreme Court's admonishment that their duty is to do justice and not just chalk up convictions).

In this chapter we will examine the legal, social, philosophical, and rhetorical problems that this subset of people charged with sex offenses must confront. We will argue that only a public health framework has the resources to respond creatively and appropriately to people with autism who are labeled sex offenders. After we examine briefly the relationship between a major problem for people with AS—their apparent difficulty empathizing with others—and our consequent tendency to treat them as less than fully human, we shall focus on one kind of legal problem that people with AS may have to confront: downloading child pornography. We shall conclude with suggestions for an appropriate and therapeutic response by the legal system to this problem, which the criminal justice system is simply not designed to address.

THE PROBLEM

The mother of autism activist and animal behavioral expert Temple Grandin described the problem that adults with autism must confront as their bodies mature and sexual desire becomes as paramount for them as it is for people who function within the species-typical range of capabilities:[1]

> Because of autism's skewed neurology, those with Autism Spectrum Disorder take in the world around them physical object by physical object—floor, ceiling, table, chair—with no sense of the whole picture, and no understanding that along with the chairs and tables there's a non-physical reality. As a result, they literally cannot see the forest for the trees, nor understand what we mean when we use the expression. This double lack inhibits their ability to grasp the idea behind a social exchange or to understand that the exchange is fluid and cannot be controlled precisely. Given these limitations, ASDs function best by memorizing each separate moment, much as you would memorize the spelling of a word. And they're good at this, very good... Though now equipped with a full-grown body and full-grown sexual drive, many ASD males are stuck emotionally at a prepubescent age. They look like grown men, but inside they're only 10 years old. (Cutler, 2013)

Like other autistic spectrum disorders, AS is a neuro-developmental disability characterized by deficits in several parallel neural processing systems expressed in a pattern of atypical behavior. It usually begins very early in life when the brain is still forming and has a high degree of plasticity (Baron-Cohen, 2011, pp.116–120). AS describes those people on the spectrum who are high-functioning and often quite verbal, who may pursue higher education, careers, and marriage, and who live semi- or fully independent lives. Most importantly for our purposes, however, people with AS have difficulties in cognitive and affective empathy, or the ability to successfully attribute cognitive and emotional states to others. Shortly we will examine that capacity in more detail. At this point, we emphasize that people with AS find it difficult, or even impossible, to engage in mundane social interactions and communication, and to adjust to change. Thus, people with AS

---

1   We will usually use the term "neurotypical," following the recent convention, to avoid using the highly contested term "normal" to refer to people who have standard, socially approved capabilities.

may engage in narrow, repetitive behaviors, and disturbances in their routines may result in public emotional meltdowns and cognitive discontinuities that are socially disruptive and even frightening, both to themselves and to those around them. Scholars generally agree that deficits in "social-emotional reciprocity characteristics can explain to some extent aggressive conduct, including criminal activities" (Sevlever, Roth, and Gillis, 2013, p.192). Prevalence of such conduct in criminal populations, and especially sexual offenses, is not well known at this point, but what statistics we have suggest that people with AS are less likely to commit crimes than people who are neurotypical (Mahoney, 2009, p.29). It is important to stress that the sex-offending behavior we are considering here—illegal downloading and viewing of images of children—does not involve aggression. But because people with ASD have limited intimate relationships, they have few sexual outlets (Sevlever *et al.*, 2013, p.194). As we will see, because their general intelligence is not affected, and they are, if anything, bound by rules that structure their experiences, individuals with AS may be hyper-moral. They may also, however, run afoul of the network of rules—including criminal laws—that have evolved to regulate the conduct of those of us who are neurotypical (Baron-Cohen, 1995). For example, the tendency of people with AS to engage in repetitive focused behavior may lead to focusing on downloading pornographic images as an expression of sexuality (Higgs and Carter, 2015, p.115).

Because they may have an emotional age that is younger than their physical development, some, though not all, adults with AS are far more comfortable interacting with prepubescent or pubescent children, and this can include sexual exploration. Relative to their neural wiring, this is normal. Moreover, the computer has become essential to the education, communicative capacities, and entertainment of adults with autism. As computer scientists and philosophers have shown, computers are extensions of our cognitive capacities, and this also applies to individuals with AS (Clark, 2008). We should not be surprised, then, when adults with AS are fascinated by and prone to downloading computer images of children engaged in sexual behavior. Because of their particular skill set, they often are exceptionally proficient computer operators, and the virtual world of the web is a predictable and comfortable setting for experimenting with images they can control.

Pornographic images are nearly unavoidable for people whose primary social interactions are computer-mediated virtual interactions.

As Mahoney points out, however, the distinction between ordinary pornography, which is not illegal to view or download, and child pornography is far less clear for somebody with AS than it is for neurotypical people (Mahoney, 2009, p.39). That viewing sexualized images of children may be harmful *to the children depicted* may also not be apparent to someone with AS, because, after all, they are literally just pictures. Moreover, we live in a culture that sexualizes children so thoroughly that some neurotypical men may well find images of very young-looking pubescent females at least mildly erotic. Some men with AS may find it difficult to delineate legally permissible images from illegal images.

However, there are no exceptions to child pornography laws for adults with AS, so they are treated by the courts, by the media, and by politicians as sex offenders. In short, lumped with neurotypical sex offenders, they are targets of the moral panic over sex offending that results in complex, costly, and utterly futile sex offender laws (Douard and Schultz, 2013). Rather than receiving the education/treatment to cope with their physical maturity responsibly, they are punished.

However, as we claim here and as this book is designed to show, no reasonable arguments exist for applying the punishment regimes to which we subject sex offenders, whether neurotypical or not. Most importantly, perhaps, is the stigma of being labeled sex offenders that follows adults with autism throughout their lives, a stigma that amplifies the stigma of the autism spectrum label itself. The source of the latter stigma has not, in our view, been adequately analyzed in terms of the distinguishing characteristic of personhood: that in our everyday lives we have points of view, and point of view is a necessary condition of empathy.

SUBJECTIVITY, DEHUMANIZATION, AND MONSTERS

In his classic paper on the ineliminable character of subjectivity titled "What is it like to be a bat?" Thomas Nagel (1974) contends that a conscious organism has a point of view. There is "something it is like" to be that organism, "something it is like *for the organism*... We may call this the subjective character of experience" (p.166). It is this characteristic of human conscious experience that enables most of us to connect to other persons in a way that people with AS are unable to. There is a double bind here: because people with AS have difficulty knowing what is like to be another person, we have difficulty knowing what it is like to experience the world as they do. Further, people with AS often fail to recognize that they are limited in just this way. After all, if a person lacks the ability to empathize, then they also lack the capacity to understand what it must be like to possess it. This is precisely why it is unjust to subject persons with AS to laws designed for people who "know what it is like" to be another person, and hence can knowingly victimize others. Neither punishment nor treatment alone will achieve a just outcome when persons with AS violate laws that presuppose a capacity they do not have, without considerable creative focus on helping them to acquire an ability most of us take for granted.

Subjectivity and Dehumanization

Nagel's example of a creature that we know has experiences, but whose experiences we simply cannot imagine, is the bat. The bat's experience is based on its sonar-centered sensory processes that are so far from our own experiences that we cannot know what it is like to be a bat. A similar point may be made about neurotypical persons' efforts to understand what it is like to experience the world as someone with AS. Moreover, the neural wiring of people with AS is such that they don't know what it is like to be other persons, and often do not recognize that they have this cognitive and affective failure. This crisis in subjectivity is well known, and constitutes one of the major sources of misunderstanding about the behavioral consequences of AS. Later we will explore the problem in somewhat more detail. For now, we simply will assume that most of us who are considered neurotypical do not know what it is like to have AS, and at least some people with autism have great difficulty knowing what it is like to have a point of view other than their own. We will argue that people with autism lack subjectivity, by which we mean simply a point of view. Another way of putting the point is that people with autism lack a "theory of mind" (ToM). Recently, the concept of empathy has been examined within the framework of the debate over theory of mind:

> On one side we find the *theory theory-of-mind* and on the other the *simulation theory of mind*. Theory-theorists typically argue that we attribute mental states to others on the basis of a theory of mind

that is either constructed in early infancy and subsequently revised and modified (Gopnik and Wellman 1995) or else is the result of maturation of innate mind-reading modules (Baron-Cohen 1995). Simulation theorists, on the other hand, deny that our understanding of others is primarily theoretical in nature and maintain that we use our own mind as a model when understanding the minds of others. Some claim that the simulation in question involves the exercise of conscious imagination and deliberative inference (Goldman 1995); some insist that the simulation although explicit is non-inferential in nature (Gordon 1986); and finally there are those who argue that the simulation rather than being explicit and conscious is implicit and subpersonal (Gallese 2003). (Zahavi and Overgaard, 2012, p.3)

In sum, a characteristic of having a point of view is that we are relatively successful mind-readers or, at the very least, are able to make inferences consciously or implicitly about another person's viewpoint. It is part of our ordinary social relationships that we can coordinate our conduct with that of others because we are able to attribute others' beliefs, desires, and emotions, and can take them into account in determining how to respond to their testimony and behavior. A problem that people with autism have, which is the result of their inability to grasp that others have a point of view, is what cognitive scientists call "mindblindness." The flip side of mindblindness is a deficit in the affective capacity to share the experiences of others. Both deficits have neural substrates that cognitive scientists are just beginning to understand.

Baron-Cohen (1995, 2011) has isolated a complex network of neural processes that, when functioning within a normal range, enable us to know what it is like to be another person, to experience another's pain, to respond to another's joys and sufferings, and to see the world from the other person's point of view. Those subjective experiences are also an essential capacity for learning to control our human environment, which is made up of potentially unpredictable persons like ourselves. These mind-reading skills are independent of general intelligence levels. We can control our human environments because we can imagine what it is like to be other people and can predict their behavior with some degree of facility (Baron-Cohen, 1995, p.4). People with AS, however, do not seem to have such facility and we often cannot predict *their* behavior (Baron-Cohen, 1995, pp.59–84).

Attribution of mental states "is our natural way of understanding the social environment" (Baron-Cohen, 1995, p.4).

There is an obvious irony here: people with AS seem to require behavioral routines to reduce stress, which should make their behavior *more* predictable than those who can respond to circumstances with greater spontaneity. But part of our conception of personhood with a full range of experiential capacities is precisely that our behavior, and especially our use of language, is intentional and responsive to the variety of circumstances in which we find ourselves.

That is not to say that people with AS do not have experiences, but that neurotypical people cannot experience the world as do people who process information in atypical ways. People with AS are like Nagel's bat; their senses and perceptions are moving to a rhythm that is difficult, if not impossible, for us to imagine because it is so different from our own. Baron-Cohen has distinguished people who lack the cognitive and affective capacities for empathy, but can develop other skills that enable the development of a moral conscience, from those who lack even those alternative routes to morally responsible conduct. He calls the latter "zero-negative" because they lack a moral conscience. He calls the former "zero-positive" because they need to construct rule-governed patterns of conduct to protect themselves from intense levels of stress and anxiety, and those rules often include moral rules (Baron-Cohen, 2011, pp.111–141). These repetitive or routine-based behaviors that people with autism exhibit should show that control is as important to them as it is for the rest of us, and hence prove that they are not so very different in the end. Yet until fairly recently, their lack of ToM and their routine, repetitive behaviors, in addition to myriad other manifestations of autism, have led us to view people with AS as abnormal, alien, and, in some circumstances, even frightening.

This situation is changing. Haskins and Silva have usefully differentiated between two non-exclusive AS deficit categories to frame the criminal activities that may be partially attributable to the disorder: (1) ToM deficits and (2) abnormally repetitive and narrow interests (Haskins and Silva, 2006, p.378). The problem, however, is that while psychological explanatory frameworks may demystify the behavior of people with AS, they do not enlighten us about the normative requirements of justice. Inclusion in the community of people who do not have a ToM, or cannot simulate others' experiences on the basis of their own, requires us to create structures that enable people with AS and neurotypical people to participate without us feeling as though the social order is always under threat of disruption. That has not always been the case. Until recently, we neurotypicals engaged in acts of symbolic purification to separate ourselves from people now placed on the autism spectrum, which included institutionalization, shifting blame from nature on to mother, keeping them out of public view, and so on. In fact, as noted above, early in the history of autism, the children who exhibited what we now would regard as autistic symptoms were treated as if they were less than human. They were placed outside the human community because we could not understand what it was like to be them. They appeared to lack that subjectivity we consider to be the essence of humanity. So while they did not look like monsters, they were treated as such. As John Donvan and Caren Zucker wrote about the parents of one of the first children to be recognized as having autistic symptoms:

> There is no way for us to know how much shame Mary and Beamon felt, but we know that during their youth, a campaign was under way, fought by intelligent, zealous, and influential Americans who believed that children like Donald were a danger to society and, worse, not fully human. (Donvan and Zucker, 2016, p.48)

In the 1960s, O. Ivar Lovaas, a psychologist who used cattle prods to "punish" children with autism into submission, explicitly used the monster metaphor to describe his "subjects": "They are little monsters. They have hair, a nose and a mouth—but they are not people in the psychological sense… It is a test for psychology" (cited in Donvan and Zucker, 2016, p.364). Leaving aside the impropriety of referring to any human being as a "monster," one might be forgiven for wondering who is the monster here, the "trainer" or the "subject."

Although our understanding of people with AS has increased in recent years, there is one area in which we lack a way to integrate that knowledge into a just framework for responding to socially disruptive, and illegal, behavior: sex offenses. Perhaps the most common sex offense that people with AS may commit is downloading child pornography. Because sex offenders, and especially child sex abusers, are framed as less-than-human monsters who lack the capacity to empathize with their victims, that frame is easily transferred to people who have difficulty with empathy but are, ironically, *hyper-moral* rather than immoral. However, as we shall see, the United States criminal justice system simply has no resources for responding appropriately to the downloading of child pornography by people with AS.

Framing Sex Offenders as Monsters

The stigma associated with autism spectrum disorders possesses similarities to the way in which we stigmatize people accused of sex offenses. People accused of sex offenses are regarded as particularly dangerous because they find it difficult to recognize the rights of others. In other words, sex offenders too are believed to lack empathy. More generally, the public responds to sex offenders the way the public once responded to children with autism: as people who are dangerous and threatening to the dominant social and moral order, and hence inhuman. Yet the very term "stigma" derives from the term "stigmata," a physical mark of difference or a visible sign of illness. Sex offenders, like people with autism, usually lack the obvious public marks of stigma we often associate with stigmatization. So to separate ourselves from them, we have employed the power of metaphor, and have framed the sex offender as a modern-day monster, basing our social, political, and legal interventions on the metaphor rather than on the facts.

Historically, we have applied the monster metaphor to those we deem too different from us to include in the category of human, which we view today not so much as a biological but a moral category. A brief overview of the monster metaphor in Western culture sheds light on its enduring social utility to distinguish "us" from "them." The monster has been viewed from the standpoint of physiological abnormality, sinfulness, or social anomie. The derivation of the term "monster" suggests violation of the natural and social order, since the Latin *monstrum* means both portent of evil and abnormal birth (Hanafi, 2000). In earlier centuries, "monstrous" births marked off the boundaries of the recognizably human, and at the same time connected the monstrous birth with sinfulness (Sharpe, 2010). Yet monstrous births were not always considered to be symbols of sin. Some writers, such as Augustine, viewed monstrous births as merely aberrations of nature. Prodigies, however, which were animals in human form, were another matter altogether. The prodigy was punishment for sin, the physical manifestation of God's displeasure over acts that

315

created moral disorder. By the 19th century, medicine had claimed authority to diagnose, treat, and measure deviance. A new concept of the "normal," grounded in 19th-century social statistics, created new categories of persons such as the mentally ill, disabled, and sexually deviant. According to Michel Foucault (2004), the monster became a legal concept used to highlight the differences between the normal and the abnormal, which was framed as a violation of societal and natural law.

Metaphor is fundamental to framing. Rhetorical theorist and philosopher Kenneth Burke described "frames of acceptance" as "the more or less organized systems of meaning by which a thinking man gauges the historical situation and adopts a role with relation to it" (1984a, p.5). These frames are situated within the collective culture; thus, we use frames to organize experience on both social and individual scales. Burke further elaborates upon this idea by claiming that frames determine what orientation or "general view of reality" (1984b, p.3) we have, which leads us to have a "sense of what properly goes with what" (p.74). Value judgments are inevitable in the process of framing because, as frames organize experience, they embody the morals, ethics, and overarching narratives of a society. The metaphor that "sex offenders are monsters" has framed understanding of child sexual abuse and exploitation throughout the 20th century and into the 21st (Douard and Schultz, 2013, pp.95–110).

If the inference is that sex offenders are born monsters with no control over their deviant impulses or are inhuman, amoral predators, then no wonder a popular belief is that offenders are unable to be rehabilitated, and are thus beyond redemption. It does not matter that no evidence exists to say that sex offenders inevitably recidivate, or that they are all irredeemably corrupt and ultimately evil. Fact and rationality are not as important as "commonplaces" when it comes to the rhetorical power of metaphor (Black, 1962). Commonplaces are associations between the tenor (subject) and vehicle (image that represents the subject) that make up a metaphor. These commonplaces are inferential assumptions that we make based on accepted, generally unquestioned, shared knowledges. The vehicle may influence the perception of a tenor to the extent that any other interpretation may be suppressed. Kenneth Burke described this process as using "terministic screens" that "direct the attention to one field rather than another" (1968, p.50). Hence, one could make the argument that metaphor is non-rational (Burke, 1984b, p.230). Because our commonly held metaphor of sex offenders as monstrous predators is non-rational, evidence to the contrary has been popularly ignored or dismissed.

Today, the impulse to consign sex offenders to that monstrous category has intensified because the line which separates what was traditionally conceived as "normal" sexual practices from the abnormal has become increasingly blurry. Due to the proliferation of mass and social media, child pornography online has become an increasing problem. It was difficult enough some years ago to fathom the presence of child sexual abuse and sexual abusers in some of America's households; now, thanks to the internet, the sexual exploitation of children has become readily available to anyone with access to a computer, tablet, or smartphone. When we could frame child sexual exploitation and abuse as a phenomenon perpetrated by people unlike ourselves, existing outside of polite society, spawned by monstrous desires, and perpetuated by monstrous individuals, we could feel at least secure in the belief that our carceral state would keep sex offenders off the street. The monster metaphor allowed us to assume that the perpetrators of sex offenses against children were driven by non-human, animal impulses over which they had little or no control. And believing in these rare and isolated monsters permitted us to distance ourselves from the crime and delude ourselves into assuming that it never happened in our backyards. Yet today we invite the internet into our homes, so the exploitation of innocents that we'd like to believe happens elsewhere enters into our homes as well. Child pornography is available, accessible, and difficult, if not impossible, to eliminate online. So to maintain the barrier between the normal and abnormal, we have focused our moral outrage on child pornography and have lumped online voyeurs into the same monstrous category as child molesters and rapists, whose inhuman qualities are unquestioned.

As our brief history shows, we have often used the monster metaphor as a means of categorizing anyone who physiologically, psychologically, and emotionally deviates from the status quo. Although, of course, sex offenders and people on the autism spectrum have many more dissimilarities than similarities, we have deprived each of their humanity. Because we have treated sex offenders as monstrous predators, abnormal and apart from us, our misunderstanding and dismissal has no doubt resulted in less effective policies, laws, and treatment modalities. The history of the movement to legitimize autism spectrum disorders shows that people with autism have also been isolated, alienated, and ignored. When we do not, cannot, or will not understand someone who seems to exist in a plane outside of our expectations of what human connection is and ought to be, someone who lacks the subjectivity required to empathize and relate to others, then we discount their essential humanness, and we may view them as unnatural, even monstrous. Certainly one of the reasons why advocates for those with autism have had to fight so persistently to be recognized as human and worthy of acceptance and understanding has been to gain more money, research, and adherents to their cause. If all people on the spectrum were to continue to be unfairly categorized as inhuman, incapable of interacting within "normal" society, and hence monstrous, then they would continue to be relegated to institutions and excluded from the human community.

However, now there are real treatments for autism or, more precisely, real educational models. These models may be expressions of symbolic purification, but they are more than that: they are strategies and structures designed to enable people with autism to communicate, to express what it is like to be them. One of the skills that people with autism must learn is how to avoid breaking the law. Criminal laws are justified both to punish those who may be blamed for committing crimes because they, in some sense, "could have done otherwise," and to prevent them from continuing to violate others' rights. But people with AS find it very difficult to avoid violating others' rights. They are not bad people—indeed, they may be more virtuous than most of us—but they have neuroprocessing deficits that cause mindblindness which may prevent them from developing social relations that rely crucially on empathy.

People with AS, like others on the spectrum, have difficulty developing social relationships with others, so it should not be surprising if they have difficulty developing romantic and sexual relationships. In particular, downloading and viewing pornography may well be the only relatively stress-free outlet for sexuality for someone with AS. While child pornography on the internet may trigger moral panic and disgust because such images victimize children twice over, the mindblindness of people with AS must be taken into account in devising optimal strategies for protecting society. They may understand they are downloading socially improper images, but they may not know they are violating a sense of trust and moral propriety.

Criminal punishment is simply an inappropriate response to the downloading of child pornography from the internet by people with AS. To see why this is so, we need to understand the new legal terrain in which this problem occurs.

The Legal Terrain: Laws and Monsters

The legal terrain we are approaching incorporates features of laws designed to remove sex offenders from society for as long as it takes to render them incapable of posing threats, especially to children; and the transformation—through stigmatization, moral panic, and scapegoating—of people who are different into monsters. That transformation involves identifying characteristics of personhood and denying that they can be attributed to a class of biological human beings. Persons have a theory of mind in terms of which they can recognize other persons as having cognitive and emotional abilities and experiences like themselves. People who can shamelessly trample on others' rights may fit a diagnosis of psychopathy. Psychopaths are most notable for being incapable of knowing what it is like to be a person whose rights have been violated. The lack of empathy is the lack of something we generally consider essential to personhood, if only because it is a mark of having a point of view.

The fundamental legal issue is whether somebody with AS, who lacks the capacity to grasp that other people have a point of view and therefore who may substantially lack empathy, is criminally culpable and therefore blameworthy if they are found to have downloaded child pornography. Somebody with autism can download images of children in sexual situations, and may even find such images sexually stimulating, but the concept of pornography involves images that require *construal* as improper representations of children. Because child pornography offenses are "strict liability" offenses, all that is required to convict is that the person knew or reasonably should have known that the images of children were pornographic. But if an adult who identifies with children cannot easily discern when images of children are inappropriate and perhaps even cruel, the problem cannot be resolved by the punitive resources of the carceral state. From a moral point of view and, we suggest, from a legal point of view, the important question is whether such downloading conduct of child pornography is, in fact, blameworthy. That problem of blameworthiness is linked to whether certain kinds of neurotypicality constitute *excuses*.

In the law, an excuse is a defense in civil and criminal law that mitigates an individual's blameworthiness for an illegal act. In criminal law, a person may be found guilty of committing an act, but may also be found to have a reason why they should not be held fully responsible for the act. As philosopher J.L. Austin noted in "A plea for excuses" (1957), "[when] I have broken your dish…maybe the best defense that I can find will be clumsiness." Unlike the insanity defense, which if successful can result in a defendant being found not guilty, a defendant with an excuse may be found guilty of committing the *act*, but that she should not be blamed for the act because she suffered from a mental or physical disorder that erases the mental state element of the crime. The excused act is not the act with which she was criminally charged. An excuse is not a justification, like self-defense, but it mitigates the conduct because the defendant had incomplete control over her conduct (Greenawalt, 1986, p.92).

The analysis of excuses in the law is well-trod territory in both case law and legal scholarship, particularly with respect to the role that mental illnesses may play in excusing otherwise criminal conduct. Cognitive and affective deficits generally, and the autistic spectrum disorders specifically, have not been carefully analyzed in terms of the possible role of such deficits as excuses. There are no unambiguous precedents to guide legal procedures in addressing the case where someone with AS downloads child pornography. We can, however, begin to examine the legal context of such conduct with the laws prohibiting viewing child pornography by people without such deficits.

In *New York v. Ferber* (1982), the United States Supreme Court held that the First Amendment did not forbid states from banning the sale of material depicting children engaged in sexual activity because the government has a compelling interest in preventing the sexual exploitation of children, and child pornography is intrinsically related to the sexual abuse of children. Moreover, such depictions have negligible artistic value.

The court said nothing about prohibiting the knowing possession of child pornography. However, federal law prohibits the production, distribution, reception, and possession of an image of child pornography using or affecting any means or facility of interstate or foreign commerce (18 U.S.C. § 2251; 18 U.S.C. § 2252; 18 U.S.C.

§ 2252A). State legislatures have enacted similar statutes. In *United States v. Stulock* (2002), the court held that a defendant must have done more than merely view the images. He must have performed an affirmative act of downloading or controlling them. Similarly, in *United States v. Kuchinski* (2006), the Ninth Circuit held that the trial court erred in increasing the defendant's sentence based on images the defendant had no knowledge were on the computer. Somewhat more clearly, the Georgia Appellate Court, in *Barton v. State* (2007), reversed a conviction when there was no evidence that the defendant took any affirmative action to save the images on his computer cache file or could have known, filed, or accessed those files; to be guilty of possession, the defendant would have had to either taken an affirmative step to save or download the images or know that the computer was saving the files. But some jurisdictions have focused on control of the images, apart from any affirmative step on the part of the defendants (*Com. v. Diodoro* 2007; *United States v. Romm*, 2006; *Ward v. State*, 2007). The Arizona Appellate Court acknowledged that there is disagreement among jurisdictions about what constitutes "knowing possession":

> The view that knowing possession requires an affirmative act on the part of the defendant to save the image or at least knowing that the computer is saving it seems consistent with the Arizona definition of knowingly possessing an item requiring a voluntary act on the part of the defendant giving him dominion and control over the items. In contrast, it could be contended that once a defendant knowingly receives such an image, the defendant has the ability to control it by downloading it, printing it or otherwise saving it. (*State v. Jensen*, 2008, p. 1051)

The court then found that the defendant had received the images as a result of an active search, even if he did not technically "possess" them. There is, therefore, a mental state element implicit in the concept of "knowing possession." The very act of possessing the images may be established by the act of taking a substantial step to download them. Presumably, at the current stage of technology, a computer that spontaneously downloaded child pornography would not be criminally liable.

Transmission, or distribution, of child pornographic images, with the ubiquity of peer-to-peer downloading and viruses that enable hacking into personal computers, constitutes a complicated area of law, but in some jurisdictions the State must prove that a defendant purposely transmitted child pornographic images for a conviction of transmission to stand (*Biller v. State*, 2013). Peer-to-peer or torrent internet sites permit you to download items from your computer without your knowledge and without your committing an affirmative act. The court in *Biller* noted that the definition of "transmit" in the pertinent Florida statute requires some act on the part of the defendant, more specifically "the act of sending or causing to be delivered any image" (p.1241). Merely having computer files available for download is insufficient to prove either the *mens rea* or the *actus reus* elements of distribution.

But a review of cases has produced little in the way of decisions regarding the question at issue here: whether somebody with the particular disabilities characteristic of AS can be found guilty of either the act or the required mental state of knowingly possessing and distributing child pornography. Much of the literature on this issue is concerned with the draconian sentences that people with autism are subject to if found guilty of violating child pornography statutes (Mahoney, 2009, pp.48–52). The sentences typically involve mandatory extended prison terms and mandatory minimum sentences that defendants must serve before being eligible for parole. In ordinary cases, it is at least arguable that such sentences are necessary to protect the public and to punish the offender, but when the defendant has neurological deficits of the magnitude typical of people with AS, the sentences not only seem unduly harsh but also serve no reasonable protective purpose. Although it is plainly true that a person with AS who is incarcerated will be unable to download child pornography, no treatment is possible in prison. More precisely, the rigorous educational regime required for people with autism to learn how to discern appropriate social responses is unavailable in prison, and when they are inevitably released they will not have the kind of control necessary to modulate their behavior in light of social and moral norms. Essentially, prison becomes a holding cell designed to allay public fears of child sex abuse.

Moreover, as forensic psychiatrist Richard Kleinmann testified in the New Jersey case *State v. Burr* (2007, p.1145), people with AS lack certain abilities that make most sex offenders successful in manipulating children: recognizing particularly vulnerable children; isolating children from caregivers; securing their trust; and, in general, the skills required to "groom" children. Their deficits, in other words, render people with AS *less* likely to commit contact sex offenses. So any ground people might have for fearing that adults who prey on children might use child pornography as a kind of precedent for committing contact offenses is simply not there for people with AS.

Criminal punishment is generally justified as either retribution for crimes committed or as deterrence to protect society. A third reason for punishment that is not often discussed is to symbolize the power of the State to maintain social order. Interpreting certain kinds of conduct as criminal marks a boundary between members of the civil community and those who have acted in ways that waive their membership. In the case of crimes that violate what a society takes as fundamental to human dignity, it is but a short step to regard those who commit such crimes as less than human. Those who seem to lack the capacity for empathy seem to lack the subjectivity at the heart of our recognition that others experience pain and suffering. One crucial implication of this focus on subjectivity—on the fact that conscious experience is what makes point of view possible and, further, makes control of one's environment possible—is that confrontation with human beings who do not appear to have a point of view threatens the social order. People with autism are persons, and are due the respect we owe persons. But many people with autism behave as if they do not have a point of view. Consequently, we cannot read their minds, and they cannot read ours. Therefore, coordinating our behavior with people whose minds we cannot read is, at best, a hit-or-miss proposition. As tolerant as we are, this sort of unpredictability can seem intolerable.

People with cognitive disabilities that severely disturb their capacity to have a point of view appear to threaten disorder if they are included in the human community because much of what we regard as rational conduct depends on us being able to relate via shared perceptions and experiences. Much of our understanding of our moral and legal responsibilities and rights flows from recognition of subjectivity. Our loathing of impurities extends to the notion that there is an ideal type of person, one who is like each of us in having a point of view about the world. It is precisely the unpredictability of people who are opaque in the way that people with autism are opaque that threatens the social order, and their disruptive and unpredictable behavior triggers fear and loathing. The repetitive stereotyped behavior and desire for routine seem out of place in the context of relatively spontaneous interactions that make up our day-to-day lives.

The least nuanced mechanism for sustaining social order in the face of such social disruptions is criminal law's regimen of punishments. People with AS who commit certain symbolically powerful crimes such as sex offenses that target children, including downloading pornography, become caught up in the web of laws that ignore their need for help rather than punishment. As Nick Durbin demonstrates in Chapter 10, someone with autism who violates the rules concerning child pornography is most likely an inappropriate target of criminal punishment. In the final section, we will argue that justice requires that they be diverted from the criminal justice system entirely and viewed as in need of treatment. The best models for such treatment, we will argue, have been developed in considerable detail, with an eye both on justice and on societal protection, by public health strategies.

PUBLIC HEALTH: A SITUATIONAL APPROACH TO SEX OFFENSES

Crime endangers the health of the republic. Elsewhere we have argued in detail that public health experts have designed models for responding rationally and justly to health problems that endanger the public (Douard and Schultz, 2013). The primary tools of public health are acquiring epidemiological knowledge, providing health-related information, and enabling the creation of a public health infrastructure that responds to public health threats within a framework of rights and liberties, to which all citizens are entitled in a democratic constitutional republic. Understood broadly enough, public health not only adopts a population-focused approach to diseases and illnesses but utilizes a situational approach to crime and crime prevention. Even if public health models are not the dominant way of approaching sex offending in general, they are indispensable as rational and just responses to the kind of sexual exploration by people with AS that can land them in legal trouble.

Criminologist Bill Hebenton distinguishes between "hot" and "cold" approaches to criminal conduct. Hot approaches focus on the character flaws of individual offenders, and devises ways to punish the wrongdoers. Hot approaches are deeply influenced by social factors such as moral panic over particular kinds of offenses (sex offenses, terrorism, early responses to autism), and lend themselves to a kind of moralizing discourse of exclusion. Hot policies are designed to remove offenders from society, not just to serve their criminal terms for the offenses they have committed but also to track or even institutionalize them to prevent recidivism. Cold approaches focus on situations. As Hebenton puts it:

> Situational analysis…suggests that situations affect crime in two main ways. First…studies emphasize the role of situations in motivating individuals to commit crime by imposing negative experiences. Second, theories of situational selection and victimization emphasize the role of situations in affecting the extent to which criminal motivations can be realized. (Hebenton, 2011, p.143)

In light of what we have discussed in this chapter, people with AS are particularly good targets of a cold approach. The difficulties they may have with respect to initiating, sustaining, and enjoying social relationships—especially sexual relationships—may well motivate them to engage in what they view as a private and anxiety-reducing use of the internet as a substitute for fraught relationships with people in their often limited social worlds. Moreover, the ease of internet use by people who tend to protect themselves from those social worlds is a significant reason for the downloading of child pornography. Not only is it unfair but it is also essentially beside the point to hold people with AS blameworthy for such conduct. This should motivate us to find alternative cold solutions.

Public health has a history of protecting the public by modifying situations in which we live together, from the extraordinary work on public hygiene in the 19th century to the strategies for reducing the incidence of HIV infection. We haven't the space to present anything like a complete public health model. But public health is a repository of strategies that can be used to divert people who commit sex offenses, and especially people whose culpability is reduced by virtue of their neurological deficits, from the criminal justice system to a civil public health regime. Up to a point, the diversionary mechanism of the drug court may serve as a stand-in for such policies. Drug courts divert drug addicts from prison to rigorous drug treatment programs, overseen by criminal courts but administered by drug treatment providers. While drug courts are limited by their being part of a criminal justice regime, and the participants in such programs may still have a criminal record, some states such as New Jersey must expunge the criminal record of successful drug treatment participants. Drug courts are a kind of public health approach to drug addiction, and they work by diverting drug offenders from one situation (prisons) to another situation (non-prison treatment programs).

A public health approach can, unlike prison or even civil commitment facilities, incorporate treatment modules that require people with AS to be *in* the social world. We have used the hybrid term "treatment/ education" because a major goal of treatment for individuals with AS who download child pornography is to "habilitate" rather than "rehabilitate" them. People with AS need education and training in a supportive environment (Griffiths and Federoff, 2009, p.366). This is one example of an approach to the issue of child pornography downloading by people with AS that reflects a cold approach.

Although drug courts might provide a first approximation of a public health alternative to imprisonment and blame, we advocate decoupling altogether the social response to sex offenses committed by people with AS from the criminal justice system. As we know from Nick Durbin's story, he urged the prosecutor to offer him treatment rather than criminal prosecution. The prosecutor declined to do so but allowed him to plead guilty to a non-contact sex offense, so Nick continues to have a criminal sex offense conviction on his record. Neither the prosecutor nor the experts involved in Nick's case thought he was a danger to society. If they had, they would not have recommended probation. There were no reasons to convict Nick of a criminal offense when he could have been ordered to undergo treatment, which in his case should be construed as a form of social education.

CONCLUSION

In this chapter, we have argued that people with AS who commit sex offenses should not be subjected to the practices of blaming individuals for the crimes they commit, and punishing them as retribution or deterrence. They should not be stigmatized as monsters or be subjected to moral panic. Rather, we must devise treatment and educational programs that focus on reducing the likelihood of recidivism. The situations in which people with AS find themselves, beginning in early childhood, often lead to the use of child pornography to substitute for problems they have developing normal social relationships. A picture is not a person, and a full repertoire of mind-reading capabilities is not necessary. We need not excuse the conduct to frame it as a public health problem that requires attention to situations rather than further isolating, alienating, and stigmatizing the individuals involved.

REFERENCES

Austin, J.L. (1957) "A plea for excuses." *Proceedings of the Aristotelian Society 57*, 1–30. Available at www.ditext.com/austin/plea.html (accessed March 3, 2017).

Baron-Cohen, S. (1995) *Mind Blindness: An Essay on Autism and Theory of Mind*. Cambridge, MA: MIT Press.

Baron-Cohen, S. (2011) *The Science of Evil*. New York, NY: Basic Books.

Barton v. State, 648 S.E.2d 660, 663 (Ga. App. 2007).

Biller v. State, 109 So. 3d 1240 (Fla. 5th DCA 2013).

Black, M. (1962) *Models and Metaphor*. Ithaca, NY: Cornell University Press.

Burke, K. (1968) *Language as Symbolic Action*. Berkeley, CA: University of California Press.

Burke, K. (1984a) *Attitudes toward History*. Berkeley, CA: University of California Press.

Burke, K. (1984b) *Permanence and Change*. Berkeley, CA: University of California Press.

Clark, A. (2008) *Supersizing the Mind: Embodiment, Action, and Cognitive Extension*. New York, NY: Oxford University Press.

Com. v. Diodoro, 932 A.2d 172, 174–75 n.5, PP11–12 (Pa. Super. 2007).

Cutler, E. (2013) "Autism and child pornography: A toxic combination." Available at www.thedailybeast.com/articles/2013/08/05/autism-and-child-pornography-a-toxic-combination.html (accessed January 24, 2017).

Donvan, J. and Zucker, C. (2016) *In a Different Key: The Story of Autism*. New York, NY: Crown.

Douard, J. and Schultz, P.D. (2013) *Monstrous Crimes and the Failure of Forensic Psychiatry*. Dordrecht: Springer.

Foucault, M. (2004) *Abnormal: Lectures at the Collège de France, 1974–1975* (G. Burchell, trans.). New York, NY: Picador.

Gallese, V. (2003) "The manifold nature of interpersonal relations: The quest for a common mechanism." *Philosophical Transactions of the Royal Society of London, Series B, Biological Sciences 358*, 517–528.

Goldman, A.I. (1995) "Interpretation Psychologized." In M. Davies and T. Stone (eds) *Folk Psychology: The Theory of Mind*. Oxford: Blackwell.

Gopnik, A. and Wellman, H.M. (1995) "Why the Child's Theory of Mind Really is a Theory." In M. Davies and T. Stone (eds) *Folk Psychology: The Theory of Mind Debate*. Oxford: Blackwell.

Gordon, R. (1986) "Folk psychology as stimulation." *Mind & Language 1*, 158–171.

Gray, D.E. (1993) "Perceptions of stigma: The parents of autistic children.' *Sociology of Health & Illness 15*, 1, 102–120.

Gray, D.E. (2002) "'Everybody just freezes. Everybody is just embarrassed': Felt and enacted stigma among parents of children with high functioning autism.' *Sociology of Health & Illness 24*, 7, 734–749.

Greenawalt, K. (1986) "Distinguishing justifications from excuses." *Law and Contemporary Problems 49*, 3, 89–108.

Griffiths, D. and Federoff, J.P. (2009) "Persons with Intellectual Disabilities Who Sexually Offend." In F.M. Saleh, A.J. Grudzinksas, and J.M. Bradford (eds) *Sex Offenders: Identification, Risk Assessment, Treatment and Legal Issues*. New York, NY: Oxford University Press.

Hanafi, Z. (2000) *The Monster in the Machine: Magic, Medicine, and the Marvelous in the Time of the Scientific Revolution*. Durham, NC: Duke University Press.

Haskins, B. and Silva, J. (2006) "Asperger's disorder and criminal behavior: Forensic-psychiatric considerations." *Journal of the American Academy of Psychiatry and Law 34*, 3, 374–384.

Hebenton, B. (2011) "From offender to situation: The 'cold' approach to sexual violence prevention?" *International Journal of Law and Psychiatry 34*, 3, 141–148.

Higgs, T. and Carter, A.J. (2015) "Autism spectrum disorder and sexual offending: Responsivity in forensic interventions." *Aggression and Violent Behavior 22*, 112–119.

Mahoney, M. (2009) "Asperger's syndrome and criminal law: The special case of child pornography." Available at www.harringtonmahoney.com/content/Publications/Aspergers%20Syndrome%20and%20the%20Criminal%20Law%20v26.pdf (accessed January 12, 2017).

Nagel, T. (1974) 'What is it like to be a bat?' *The Philosophical Review 83*, 4, 435–450.

New York v. Ferber, 458 U.S. 747 (1982).

Sevlever, M., Roth, M.F., and Gillis, J.M. (2013) "Sexual abuse and offending in autism spectrum disorders." *Sexuality and Disability 31*, 189–200.

Sharpe, A. (2010) *Foucault's Monsters and the Challenge of Law*. London: Routledge.

State v. Burr, 921 A.2d 1135 (N.J. 2007).

State v. Jensen, 173 P.3d 1046 (Ariz. App. 2008).

United States v. Kuchinski, 469 F.3d 853, 861–63 (9th Cir. 2006).

United States v. Romm, 455 F.3d 990, 998 (9th Cir. 2006).

United States v. Stulock, 308 F.3d 922, 924–26 (8th Cir. 2002).

Ward v. State, 994 So.2d 293 (Ala. Crim. App. 2007).

Zahavi, D. and Overgaard, S. (2012) "Empathy without Isomorphism: A Phenomenological Account." In J. Decety (ed.) *Empathy: From Bench to Bedside*. Cambridge, MA: MIT Press.

Afterword

*Tony Attwood, Noted Psychologist, Author and
Lecturer on Autism Spectrum Disorders*

Over the last decade, I have experienced a significant increase in requests for advice from both parents and lawyers, regarding clients with an Autism Spectrum Disorder (ASD) accessing child pornography. There are many reasons why someone with an ASD might develop an interest in child pornography. Sometimes they are already enjoying legal, mainstream pornography, and, in a bid to 'complete the collection', begin to explore illegal child pornography, without consideration of the devastating consequences of being discovered, arrested and charged. Another reason may be their social isolation. The Internet unlocks an alternative world, providing an escape from an arduous, lonely reality and offering a wealth of experiences otherwise elusive to them in real life. Many young adults with an ASD can have considerable developmental delay in their emotional and social maturity, such that children may be as perceived almost as peers. However, while the young adult has the emotional maturity of a child, their sexual interests and responses are those of an adult. At the same time, they have probably had limited success in both friendships and romantic relationships, and inadequate education in sexuality.

One of the major considerations when a person with an ASD is accused of accessing child pornography is the degree to which they may or may not understand the broader implications of what they have done. For example, they may have considerable naivety regarding both the personal and legal consequences of their actions. In addition, due to impaired Theory of Mind, they may also have limited ability to understand the thoughts and feelings of the child depicted in the pornography; and ignorance of the perspectives and legal codes of society, due to their isolation and inadequate education in sexuality and sexual mores.

As we move towards the third decade of the 21st century, the criminal justice system is attempting to address the issue of the accused having a diagnosis of ASD. Appropriate sentencing options are being explored, and psychologists and psychiatrists are gaining clinical experience in this area. However, there is remarkably little research to provide the information and guidance needed by the courts and clinicians. We hope that situation will change in the coming years.

The good news is that, in terms of therapy and education for those on the autism spectrum, there are programs being developed to provide knowledge for individuals about the personal and community consequences of accessing child pornography. We have many more strategies to facilitate the development of social and emotional maturity; and there are therapeutic programs to help repair the traumas of childhood, and comprehensive education in sexuality, enabling those on the autism spectrum to develop healthy relationships. By accommodating the characteristics and experiences of people with an ASD, these programs will go a long way towards providing an effective solution to the problem of such people accessing child pornography.

Judicial Diversion in Child Pornography Cases

Throughout this book, there is reference made to diversion as a potential way to resolve a criminal case, the potential application of diversion in child pornography cases, the harshness of sentences in child pornography cases, and the questionable effectiveness of these harsh sentences as a deterrent to child molestation. This Appendix provides some initial information about these subjects as well as offering a brief history of child pornography laws and sex offender registry requirements.

I. DIVERSION
A. Diversion Generally

Diversion is an alternative to prosecution offered to certain criminal offenders as an opportunity to have charges against them dismissed. In the federal criminal system, diversion is defined in the United States Attorneys' Criminal Resource Manual ("USAM") at Title 9, Section 22.000. Diversion is an optional program, initiated by a United States Attorney, and voluntarily agreed upon by the criminal offender.[1] In exchange for entry into the program, the criminal offender (the "divertee") must agree to waive his rights to a speedy trial and presentment of his case within the statute of limitations.[2] As an initial matter, the divertee must have the advice of counsel before entering any such agreement.[3]

---

1   *Id.*; see also USAM § 9-712.
2   *Id.* at § (B)(1).
3   *Id.* at § (B)(2).

Typically, diversion occurs at the pretrial stage; however, it can occur at any point prior to trial.[4] Offenders are diverted from traditional criminal justice processing and supervised by the U.S. Probation Service.[5] Upon successful completion of the program, participants either will not be charged, or, if they have been charged, will have the charges against them dismissed; those who do not complete the program successfully are returned for prosecution.[6]

A pretrial diversion agreement requires an offender to acknowledge responsibility for his behavior, without necessarily admitting guilt.[7] After entering into the agreement, supervision is tailored to meet the needs of the specific divertee.[8] Some divertees' supervision may include employment and counseling, whereas other supervision can include education, job training, or psychiatric care.[9] In all cases, supervision is not to exceed 18 months, but can be reduced.[10]

In order to take advantage of a diversion program, certification requirements must be met, and the United States Attorney must comply with pretrial diversion guidelines.[11] As stated in Section 9-22.100 (Eligibility Criteria):

> The U.S. Attorney, in his/her discretion, may divert any individual against whom a prosecution case exists and who is not:
>
>> Accused of an offense which, under existing Department guidelines, should be diverted to the State for prosecution;
>>
>> A person with two or more prior felony convictions;
>>
>> A public official or former public official accused of an offense arising out of an alleged violation of a public trust; or
>>
>> Accused of an offense related to national security or foreign affairs.

---

4   USAM § 9-22.010; see also USAM § 9-712(A).
5   USAM § 9-22.010.
6   *Id.*
7   USAM § 9-712(F).
8   *Id.* at § (E).
9   *Id.*
10   *Id.* at § (F).
11   See USAM § 9-8.190 (citing USAM § 9-22.000 *et seq.* (Pretrial Diversion)).

Since its implementation at the federal level in the Pretrial Services Act of 1982, pretrial diversion has been declining in use.[12] In 1999, 2716 of the 80,154 activated cases in the federal criminal system used a pretrial diversion program.[13] Conversely, nine years later, in 2008, 1426 of the 98,244 activated cases used a pretrial diversion program.[14] More tellingly, one-quarter of the 2008 pretrial diversion cases arose in only three districts (the District of New Jersey, the Eastern District of Virginia, and the Eastern District of Missouri).[15]

Originally, pretrial diversion was a program implemented to help juvenile offenders. It was later adopted in the federal judiciary with the passage of the Pretrial Services Act of 1982.[16] Pretrial diversion "was meant to be an alternative to prosecution for low-level criminal offenders who had identifiable rehabilitative needs."[17] Essentially, the program seeks to prevent criminal offenders from reoffending.[18] Section 9-22.010 of the USAM states:

> The major objectives of pretrial diversion are: to prevent future criminal activity among certain offenders by diverting them from traditional processing into community supervision and services; to save prosecutorial and judicial resources for concentration on major cases; and to provide, where appropriate, a vehicle for restitution to communities and victims of crimes.

B. Diversion in Child Pornography Cases

Federal pretrial diversion is an available option in cases where the divertee is accused of a sexual offense. However, the use of pretrial diversion in these cases is disfavored. USAM § 9-75.410 states that "[p]re-trial diversion for crimes involving child pornography, child sexual abuse, the sexual exploitation of children and obscenity is generally not favored…however, it may be an appropriate and just disposition in certain cases." Notwithstanding § 9-75.410, the ultimate decision whether or not to use pretrial diversion is in the hands of United States Attorneys.

---

12 See Joseph M. Zlatic *et al.*, *Pretrial Diversion: The Overlooked Pretrial Services Evidence Based Practice*, 74 Federal Probation 1 (June 2010).

13 *Id.*

14 *Id.*

15 *Id.*

16 See *Id.*

17 *Id.*

18 See USAM § 9-22.010.

There are not many specific reported instances where a pretrial diversion program has been used, in lieu of prosecution, in cases involving the federal child pornography laws. One reason why this may be the case is that diversion agreements are not matters of public record. In one child pornography case in which pretrial diversion was used, an Ohio criminal defense attorney entered into a pretrial diversion agreement after an investigation ensued regarding the attorney's use of pornographic materials in connection with his representation of accused pornographers.[19] The attorney represented multiple persons charged with violations of federal child pornography laws and statutes.[20] In representing his clients, the attorney "downloaded and manipulated images from the internet of real and identifiable minors and created a series of visual depictions of [those] minors engaged in sexually explicit conduct."[21] In essence, the attorney was compiling the material as court exhibits in cases where he was representing an accused.[22] Rather than prosecuting the attorney, the prosecution allowed him to enter into a pretrial diversion agreement "which states that his conduct violated 18 U.S.C. § 2252A(a)(5)(B), and wherein he agreed to refrain from engaging in similar conduct for eighteen months."[23]

It is important to note that a decision of a United States Attorney not to offer pretrial diversion to an accused is not reviewable by a district court.[24] This makes sense given that the decision to offer diversion involves prosecutorial discretion whether to pursue formal charges.

It is strongly suggested that diversion be considered in some cases as the best option for a defendant on the autism spectrum who is charged with possession of child pornography. The suggestion would be pertinent to an ASD individual who has no prior criminal record and poses a very low or no risk of causing harm to a child. The suggestion is based on the detailed information provided in subsequent chapters that such an ASD person committed the unlawful act without any or at least diminished criminal responsibility related to the neurological deficits of autism.

---

19   See *Boland v. Holder*, No. 1:09 CV 1614, 2010 WL 3860996 (N.D. Ohio Sept. 30, 2010).
20   *Id.* at *1.
21   *Id.* (citing Pretrial Diversion Agreement).
22   *Id.* at *1.
23   *Id.* at *2 (citing Pretrial Diversion Agreement).
24   See *United States v. Richardson*, 856 F.2d 655 (4th Cir. 1988).

II. HISTORY OF CHILD PORNOGRAPHY LAWS
A. History and Procedure

The United States Code defines child pornography as

> any visual depiction, including any photograph, film, video, picture, or computer or computer-generated image or picture, whether made or produced by electronic, mechanical, or other means, of sexually explicit conduct, where—(A) the production of such visual depiction involves the use of a minor engaging in sexually explicit conduct; (B) such visual depiction is a digital image, computer image, or computer-generated image that is, or is indistinguishable from, that of a minor engaging in sexually explicit conduct; or (C) such visual depiction has been created, adapted, or modified to appear that an identifiable minor is engaging in sexually explicit conduct.[25]

Child pornography guidelines have existed since 1987 and have been substantively amended nine times as of 2009.[26] These guidelines were promulgated by the United States Sentencing Commission (the "Commission"), which was created by Congress to "'establish sentencing policies and practices for the Federal criminal justice system' that implement the Sentencing Reform Act of 1984 ("SRA"), including the purposes of sentencing enumerated at 18 U.S.C. § 3553 (a)(2)."[27]

Through the years, Congress has expressed its will to increase guideline sentences for child pornography offenders.[28] Before the sentencing guidelines were in place, Congress passed the Protection of Children Against Sexual Exploitation Act of 1977 ("1977 Act").[29] The 1977 Act "prohibited the use of children to produce child pornography and established a ten-year statutory maximum for first-time trafficking offenders and a 15-year statutory maximum and a two-year mandatory

---

25   18 U.S.C. § 2256(8).

26   United States Sentencing Commission (2009) *The History of the Child Pornography Guidelines*, pp.1–2. Available at www.ussc.gov/sites/default/files/pdf/research-and-publications/research-projects-and-surveys/sex-offenses/20091030_History_Child_Pornography_Guidelines.pdf (accessed January 26, 2017).

27   *Id.* at 1 (citing Sentencing Reform Act of 1984, Pub. L. No. 98-473, Chapter II, § 212(a), 98 Stat. 1837 (1984) ("SRA"); 18 U.S.C. § 3553(a)(2)).

28   *Id.* at 6.

29   Protection of Children Against Sexual Exploitation Act, Pub. L. No. 95-225, 92 Stat. 7 § 2 (1978) (codified at 18 U.S.C. §§ 2251–2253).

minimum for subsequent offenders."[30] In 1984 and 1986, Congress passed harsher laws for producing, distributing, or displaying child pornography.[31] Congress believed that harsher sentencing for these offenses would curtail the growing problem of child abuse.[32]

The Commission promulgated its first set of guidelines in 1987 and there were no guidelines for the simple possession of child pornography, which, at the time, was not a federal crime.[33] Consequently, the Commission examined the existing sentencing practices and promulgated guidelines on a level basis, with a base offense level of 13, and a high level of 20.[34] Specific offenses, such as downloading an image of a child less than 12 years of age, were an automatic increase in two levels.[35] An automatic five-level increase was implemented for the distribution of child pornography.[36]

Through the years, the Commission continued to make various changes. In 1990, the Commission compiled a report on the status of child pornography prosecutions in the federal criminal system.[37] That report looked to Congress's legislative history and reasoned that Congress found that:

> (1) both commercial and non-commercial distribution and receipt of child pornography contribute to the molestation and abuse of children; (2) child pornography had become a highly organized, multi-million dollar industry that operates on a nationwide scale, but federal law enforcement efforts should not be limited to large scale distributors of child pornography; (3) child pornography causes substantial harm to both the child victim and to society as a whole since abused children tend to grow up "in an adult life of drugs and prostitution [and] become child molesters themselves, thus continuing the vicious cycle."[38]

---

30 United States Sentencing Commission, *supra* note 43, at 9 (citing Protection of Children Against Sexual Exploitation Act, *supra* note 46).
31 Child Abuse Victims' Rights Act, Pub. L. No. 99-500, 100 Stat. 1783, Title I, § 101(b) (1986), amended by Pub. L. No. 99-591, 100 Stat. 3341-75, Title I, § 101(b) (1986).
32 *Id.* at § 702(2).
33 United States Sentencing Commission, *supra* note 43, at 10.
34 *Id.*
35 *Id.*
36 *Id.*
37 *Id.* at 13.
38 *Id.* (citing USSC, Revised Report of the Working Group on Child Pornography and Obscenity Offenses and Hate Crime, 7–14 (1990)).

Evidently, Congress was very concerned about child abuse and molestation, and felt that those who viewed child pornography supported these actions. From 1990 until today, the Commission has continued to promulgate new regulations and make changes to existing ones.[39]

Different legislation came in different years. In 1990, 1991, 1996, 2000, 2004, and 2009, many changes were made to the guidelines. Offenses regarding child pornography were added and some punishments were made more severe, increasing punishment for base offenses.[40] For example, in December 1995, Congress passed the Sex Crimes Against Children Prevention Act of 1995 ("SCACPA").[41] In SCACPA, Congress directed the Commission to "[i]ncrease the base offense level for [child pornography offenses] by at least 2 levels…[and] to increase the base offense level by at least 2 levels… if a computer was used to transmit the notice or advertisement to the intended recipient or to transport or ship the visual depiction."[42] Guideline 2G2.4 increased the base offense level of possession of child pornography and added a two-level enhancement if a computer was used.[43] The trend in each amendment has been adding crimes and making punishment for existing crimes more severe. In fact, over the past 14 years, the average federal sentences for child pornography rose by about 300%.[44] In 1994, the mean sentence for child pornography offenders was 36 months, whereas the mean in 2008 was 109 months.[45]

B. Harshness of Child Pornography Sentences

Congress has provided for serious punishment for child pornography offenses. Under the federal sentencing guidelines, child pornography offenses have a base-level sentencing range of 27 to 33 months in

---

39 See generally United States Sentencing Commission, *supra* note 43.

40 See *id.* at 16–26.

41 *Id.* at 26 (citing Sex Crimes Against Children Prevention Act of 1995, Pub. L. No. 104-71, 109 Stat. 774 (Dec. 23, 1995) (hereinafter "SCACPA")).

42 *Id.* (quoting SCACPA §§ 2, 3).

43 *Id.* at 27 (citing USSG App. C, amendment 537 (Nov. 1, 1996)).

44 Kristin Carlson (2010) "Strong medicine: Toward effective sentencing of child pornography offenders." *Michigan Law Review First Impressions 109*, 27. Available at http://repository.law.umich.edu/cgi/viewcontent.cgi?article=1023&context=mlr_fi (accessed January 26, 2017).

45 *Id.*

federal prison.[46] Indeed, this base-level sentencing range is for an offender who has no criminal history and no offender enhancements.[47] There are enhancements in the guidelines depending on whether the offender used a computer, the age of the child victim depicted, and number of images viewed. For example, "[a] person with no criminal history, who uses the Internet to download a two-minute video depicting pornographic images of a ten-year-old child through a file-sharing network, would have a Guideline range of 87–108 months in prison."[48]

Those who argue that increased sentences are appropriate misconstrue the distinction between possession of child pornography and child sexual abuse that involves physical contact.[49] Specifically, three main arguments arise from three blurred distinctions: (1) severe sentences are necessary because possession of child pornography is equivalent to or worse than actual child sexual abuse; (2) possessing and viewing child pornography increases the chances that an individual will commit child sexual abuse; and (3) "because possession of child pornography is highly correlated with a history of contact offenses, punishing possessors of child pornography can serve as a proxy for sexual abuse."[50] However, these arguments have not been reasonably supported by empirical evidence.

C. Effectiveness of Child Pornography Sentences

Some studies have suggested that these harsh child pornography sentences do not seek their purpose: deterrence of child molestation.[51] In fact, "[t]he relatively low detection rate of child exploitation offenses…contributes to the insufficiency of the current sentencing regime."[52] Moreover, some argue that incarceration will not deter criminal pedophiles because they will always tend to act on their

---

46   U.S. Sentencing Guidelines Manual § 2G2.2 (2008).

47   *Id.*

48   Loren Rigsby (2010) "A call for judicial scrutiny: How increased judicial discretion has led to disparity and unpredictability in federal sentencings for child pornography." *Seattle University Law Review 33*, 4, 1319 n.2.

49   Hessnick, *supra* note, at 864 (citing Mark Hanse (2009) "A reluctant rebellion." *ABA Journal*, June 2009, at 57).

50   *Id.* at 864.

51   See *id.* at 29.

52   *Id.*

strong sexual fantasies.[53] Instead of attempting to address the root of the problem—reducing the pedophile's sexual attraction toward children—child pornography laws arbitrarily punish.[54] Indeed, "random elements of the offense, such as whether or not a computer was used in the offense, may dramatically affect the sentencing range. Use of a computer typically increases an offender's sentencing range by about twenty-five percent."[55] In addition, sentences are also increased depending on the number of images the offender possessed—the more images possessed, the harsher the sentence.[56] This arbitrary line wrongfully suggests that the more images possessed, the more dangerous the offender.[57]

The argument that child pornography is just as bad as or worse than child sexual abuse is misguided. In fact, the Supreme Court has held "that the First Amendment interest of child pornography possessors can be overcome only because private possession of child pornography may create a market for the creation of such images."[58] Essentially, any harm that arises out of viewing child pornography is only derivative of the underlying child sexual abuse. Furthermore, there is no empirical evidence that shows that severely punishing possession of child pornography prevents child sexual abuse.[59]

Punishing possession of child pornography in the same manner as contact offenses incorrectly applies traditional proportionality considerations in sentencing. Possessing child pornography is not the same thing as sexually abusing a child, and sentencing in these two different types of cases should not be the same. In many instances, those who possess child pornography may end up serving a longer sentence than those who actually commit the sexual abuse.

Additionally, because the sentencing guidelines are not mandatory, sentences vary depending on whether the judge departs from the guidelines in a particular case. Indeed, "[c]hild pornography sentences have thus functioned as the equivalent of a lightning strike; the congressionally mandated harsh sentences strike some defendants

---

53 *Id.*
54 *Id.*
55 *Id.*
56 *Id.*
57 *Id.* at 29–30.
58 Hessnick, *supra* note, at 867 (internal citations omitted).
59 *Id.* at 873–880.

but miss many others."[60] A judge in one case may apply mitigating factors, while, in another, the judge may ignore the mitigating factors.[61] This is contrary to the reason that the guidelines were implemented in the first place—as a way to achieve fairness and proportionality in sentencing defendants convicted of similar crimes.[62]

III. SEX OFFENDER REGISTRY HISTORY

Congress in 1994, through the Jacob Wetterling Crimes Against Children and Sexually Violent Offender Registration Act (hereinafter the "Wetterling Act"),[63] which was passed as part of the Omnibus Crime Bill of 1994, tasked the Attorney General with the duty of promulgating guidelines for states to track sex offenders.[64] States that did not promulgate such guidelines faced losing 10% of federal funds allocated under the Omnibus Crime Control and Safe Streets Act of 1968.[65] The guidelines were to require "a person who is convicted of a criminal offense against a victim who is a minor or who is convicted of a sexually violent offense to register a current address with a designated State law enforcement agency" for a period of ten years "since the person was released from prison, placed on parole, supervised release, or probation."[66] The same registration requirement applied to "a person who is a sexually violent predator," defined as "a person who has been convicted of a sexually violent offense and who suffers from a mental abnormality or personality disorder that makes the person likely to engage in predatory sexually violent offenses."[67]

---

60 Rigsby, *supra* note 65, at 1319–1320.
61 Compare *United States v. Rausch*, 570 F. Supp. 2d 1295, 1308 (D. Colo. 2008) (finding that although the guideline sentencing range was 97–120 months in federal prison, the defendant's poor physical health was a mitigating factor, and the defendant was only sentenced to one day in prison with credit for time served) with *United States v. Toothman*, 543 F.3d 967 (8th Cir. 2008) (upholding the district court's sentence of 97 months in prison even though the defendant had severe health problems).
62 Rigsby, *supra* note 65, at 1321.
63 This act is named after Jacob Wetterling. Jacob was a passenger in his mother's vehicle when their "ride home was interrupted by an armed man wearing a nylon mask who ordered the boy's companions to flee." See www.pameganslaw.state.pa.us/History. aspx?dt= (accessed January 26, 2017). He has not been seen since. *Id.*
64 H.R. 3355, 103rd Cong. (1994) (enacted).
65 *Id.*
66 *Id.*
67 *Id.*

The Wetterling Act was subsequently amended through the Pam Lychner Sexual Offender Tracking and Identification Act of 1996 (hereinafter the "Pam Lychner Act").[68] The Pam Lychner Act provided a new requirement that persons who commit particularly serious crimes and recidivists be subject to lifetime registration as sex offenders.[69] States were given three years to comply with the new requirements, and a possible extension of two years for states that could show a good-faith effort at compliance.[70]

Also passed by Congress in 1996 was Megan's Law,[71] which required law enforcement agencies to release information about registered sex offenders to the public.[72] It is up to individual states to determine what information should be made available and how it is to be disseminated.[73] However, states were compelled to "release relevant information that is necessary to protect the public concerning a specific person required to register under this section, except that the identity of a victim of an offense that requires registration…shall not be released."[74]

Between 1996 and the present date, the Wetterling Act has been amended several times. See the Jacob Wetterling Improvements Act, Pub. L. No.105-119 (105th Cong.) (1997); Protection of Children from Sexual Predators Act, Pub. L. No.105-314 (105th Cong.) (1998); Campus Sex Crimes Prevention Act, Pub. L. No.106-386 (106th Cong.) (2000); Prosecutorial Remedies and Other Tools to end the Exploitation of Children Today (PROTECT) Act, Pub. L. No.108-21 (108th Cong.) (2003); and Adam Walsh Child Protection and Safety Act. Publ L. No.109-248 (109th Cong.) (2006).[75] Adam

---

68 Pub. L. No.104-236, S. 1675, 104th Cong. (1996) (enacted). This act gets its name from Pam Lychner, a former flight attendant who was brutally assaulted by a twice-convicted felon waiting for her at a vacant house. See www.pameganslaw.state.pa.us/History. aspx?dt= (accessed January 26, 2017). The attack was stopped when her husband arrived at the scene.

69 Id.

70 Id.

71 This law is named after Megan Kanka, a seven-year-old girl from New Jersey. Megan was invited by her neighbor to see his puppy. The neighbor was a twice-convicted pedophile. He raped and murdered Megan and dumped her body in a nearby park. See www. pameganslaw.state.pa.us/History.aspx?dt= (accessed January 26, 2017).

72 See Pub. L. No.104-145, 104th Cong. (1996) (enacted).

73 Id.

74 Id.

75 A summary of these acts can be found at http://ojp.gov/smart/legislation.htm (accessed January 26, 2017).

Walsh was the son of John Walsh, who hosted the television show *America's Most Wanted.* John Walsh was an advocate of this law named after his kidnapped son who was murdered by a man who had also killed a number of other people. The Adam Walsh law established a national system for the registration of sex offenders that was designed to provide the public with detailed information about the offenders.

The culmination of these laws in its current form is found at 42 United States Code, Section 16901 *et seq.* In the declaration of purpose of the statute, Congress listed 17 incidents in which persons—mostly children (including the specific children after whom the previous acts were named)—were sexually assaulted, most of whom were also murdered.[76]

Most recently, on May 20, 2014, the United States House of Representatives voted to pass International Megan's Law to Prevent Demand for Child Sex Trafficking (hereinafter "International Megan's Law").[77] International Megan's Law would require foreign governments to be notified when a sex offender is traveling to their country.

The harsh laws that currently are adopted in states and by the federal government that prosecute sex offenders for possession of child pornography and require registration as a sex offender are strongly criticized in the recently published book *Caught: The Prison State and the Lockdown of American Politics,* by Marie Gottschalk (Princeton University Press, 2015); see Chapter 9, pp. 196–214.

---

76   *Id.*
77   H.R. 4573, 113th Congress (2014).

Subject Index

Author Index